To dear Bernard & Pristina
with all our love —
Christmas 2010.

Michael & Christopher.

THE CHRONICLE
OF PILGRIMAGE TO THE
HOLY LAND

THE ADVENTURES · THE EVENTS
THE HOLY SITES

RMC Publishing

THE CHRONICLE
OF PILGRIMAGE TO THE
HOLY LAND

THE CHRONICLE
OF PILGRIMAGE TO THE
HOLY LAND

Project Editor: D. Salomon
Concept and Design: Y. Salomon

Text Editor: Deborah Camiel
Translation: Betsy Karpenkopf
Photography: Moshe Milner, Zev Radovan,
Erich Lessing, Garo M. Nalbandian,
Arturo Mari—Vatican, the Israel GPO
Aerial Photography: Moshe Milner; Albatross -
Photographer: Duby Tal, Pilot: Moni Haramati
Reproduction Photography: Yossi Dana
Historical Photographs: Bonfils,
American Colony

© Copyright by Alfa Communication Ltd.

Distribution:

RMC Publishing Ltd.

1 Hamasger Street, Suite 103,
Ra'anana 43652, ISRAEL
E-mail: Info@RMC-Publishing.com
Tel: +972 77 21 20067 Fax: +972 1539 7729678
www.thechroniclebook.com

ISBN: 965-7240-00-X

Computer Graphics: Y. Patilon
Color Separations: Graphor Ltd.
Pre-press: Shekef-Or

Printed in the Holy Land
2008 Edition

Inside Cover
Background: **Crosses carved by pilgrims in the walls of the Crypt of St. Helena over the centuries.**
Inset: **Emperor Constantine the Great** *(left)* **and King Richard the Lionhearted** *(right).*
Introductory Photographs
1 **A world map from 1585, by Heinrich Bünting. The world is represented as a cloverleaf, with Jerusalem at the center.**
2-3 **Pilgrims in the atrium of the Church of the Holy Sepulcher, by M. Milner.**
4-5 **A view of Jerusalem from the Mount of Olives, by L. Mayer.**
6-7 **The Palm Sunday procession reaches the Lions' Gate, by M. Milner.**

CONTENTS

A Journey of Faith 7

Chapter I 8
The Footsteps of Jesus

Chapter II 32
The Byzantine Period
324-634

Chapter III 60
The Early Arab Period
634-1099

Chapter IV 76
The Kingdom of Jerusalem
1099-1187

Chapter V 104
The Second Crusader Kingdom
1187-1270

Chapter VI 120
The Mameluke Conquest
1260-1516

Chapter VII 138
Under Ottoman Rule
1516-1798

Chapter VIII 160
Into the Nineteenth Century
1798-1831

Chapter IX 180
The Advent of the Modern Age
1831-1876

Chapter X 220
The Sunset of the Ottoman Empire
1876-1917

Chapter XI 238
Twentieth-Century Pilgrimage
From 1917 Onward

Bibliography 256

A JOURNEY OF FAITH

Since the death of Jesus, pilgrimage to the Holy Land has been a dream for believers from all over the world. In the early days only a few made the trip, but after Christianity became the Roman Empire's official religion in the fourth century and the holy places were identified and memorialized, the number of pilgrims began to grow.

Most pilgrims, moved by religious fervor, were indifferent to the innumerable obstacles in their path and the hardships awaiting them. They were willing even to risk their lives in order to walk in the footsteps of Jesus and visit the places where he had lived out his ministry—especially Jerusalem, site of the crucifixion and resurrection. Today, in the age of jet travel, when travelers speed from one end of the world to the other in a matter of hours, it is nearly impossible to grasp the enormity of effort involved until just a few decades ago in a voyage to the Holy Land.

Most pilgrims made their way by sea; the trip, which lasted for weeks, entailed the most intolerable of conditions. Travelers were crowded into the belly of the ship; they subsisted on a diet of rancid food and were exposed to disease, the elements, and pirate attacks. Even after reaching the long-awaited shore, their difficulties were not at an end. Wars and political instability had impoverished the country, and the pilgrims encountered a desolate, deserted landscape. The conditions of the roads made travel by carriage impossible; the preferred modes of transportation were by foot or with pack animals (donkeys and camels). Bandits roamed the countryside, presenting a constant threat; their ambushes could cost the pilgrims more than their property. Conditions in the local hostels were inadequate, and many preferred to camp out-of-doors rather than make use of the available accommodations. Monasteries offered lodging and the chance to replenish supplies, but they were also vulnerable to attack.

For most of this period the Holy Land was under Muslim rule. The Muslims detested the Christians and did all they could to discourage pilgrimage, exacting taxes and sometimes demanding ransoms collected under the threat of assault or murder. These persecutions, along with restrictions instituted by the authorities on travel to holy places—foremost among these being the ban on visits to the Church of the Holy Sepulcher—were among the motivations behind the Crusades. The safety of Christian pilgrims was one of the more important objectives taken on by the Crusaders, who established special orders responsible for the maintenance and protection of travelers.

Many pilgrims have left us written and illustrated records of their journeys. Approximately 1,500 such accounts were written prior to the nineteenth century. During the nineteenth century that number surpassed 5,000 as the stream of visitors to the Holy Land increased dramatically. This album, *The Chronicle of Pilgrimage to the Holy Land*, contains a selection of these works. They bring home the sense of adventure, wealth of experiences, and powerful emotions that accompanied the pilgrims along their way, even as they provide extraordinary and authentic descriptions of the holy places and the ceremonies and traditions associated with them over the ages.

One of the earliest and most complete descriptions of a journey to the Holy Land is that of an anonymous pilgrim from the sixth century known as the "Traveler of Placentia," named for the city of his origin. He roamed the Holy Land for two years, traveling from the River Dan in the north to the Sinai in the south and visiting almost every holy site in the country, a feat that accords him an important place in the story told here.

We have chosen to end this volume with a description of visits by two popes—Pope Paul VI, who visited the Holy Land in 1964, and Pope John Paul II, who visited the Holy Land in 2000. The visits by the popes dramatically illustrate how much, and at the same time how little, the act of pilgrimage has changed over the centuries. Though the routes and places are much the same, modern modes of travel made it possible for Pope Paul VI to see most of the holy places in less than two days.

This is not a history book. It is an adventure book that aims to provide the reader something of the wonderment and grandness of the pilgrim experience in the Holy Land over the last two thousand years—an experience that has had no small part in shaping the culture of the Christian world. The stories here are accompanied by nearly one thousand maps, illustrations, etchings, lithographs, other historic representations (most the work of pilgrims or their contemporaries), and photographs—some recent and others more than a century old—that provide documentation of all of the relevant places and events. The material is arranged in a unique format—that of a newspaper chronicling Christian history and legend in the Holy Land from the birth of Jesus to the present day.

CHAPTER I

THE FOOTSTEPS OF JESUS

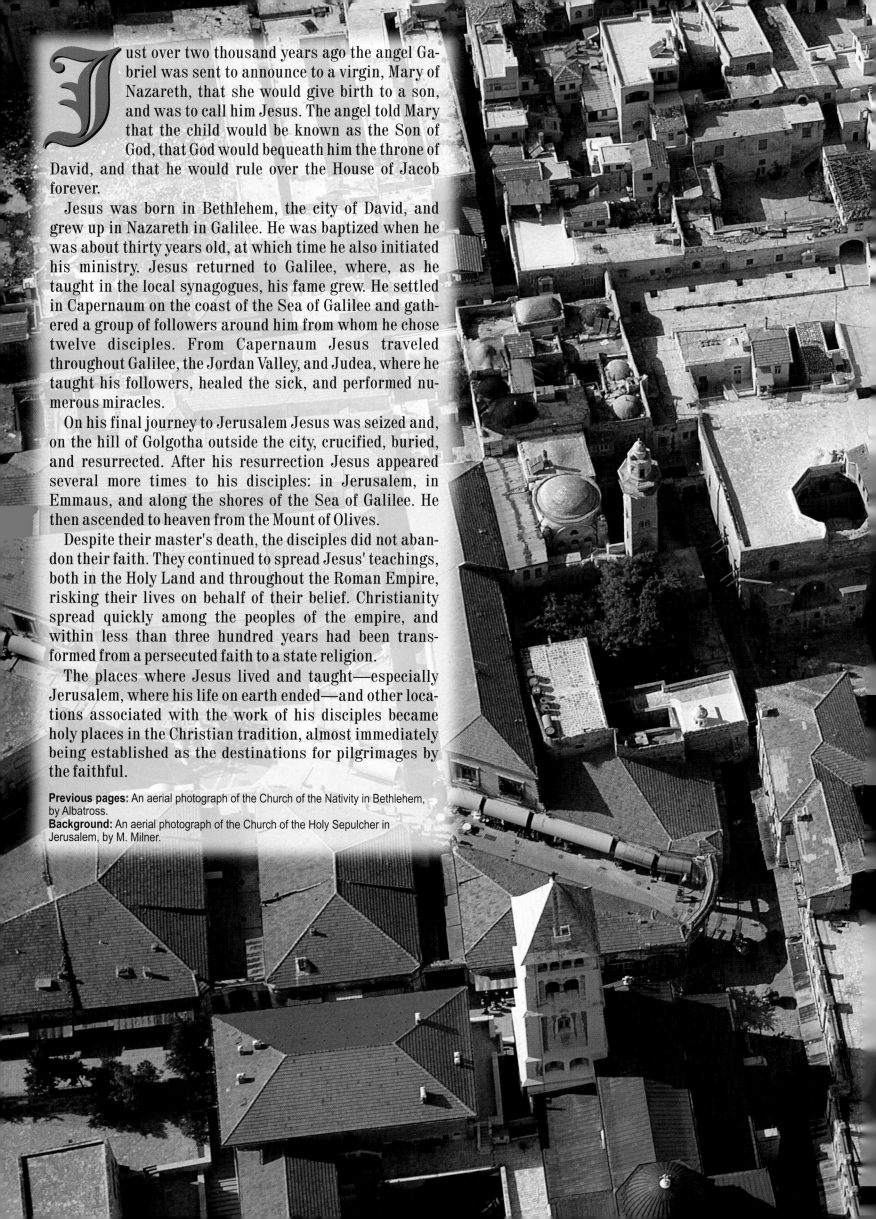

Just over two thousand years ago the angel Gabriel was sent to announce to a virgin, Mary of Nazareth, that she would give birth to a son, and was to call him Jesus. The angel told Mary that the child would be known as the Son of God, that God would bequeath him the throne of David, and that he would rule over the House of Jacob forever.

Jesus was born in Bethlehem, the city of David, and grew up in Nazareth in Galilee. He was baptized when he was about thirty years old, at which time he also initiated his ministry. Jesus returned to Galilee, where, as he taught in the local synagogues, his fame grew. He settled in Capernaum on the coast of the Sea of Galilee and gathered a group of followers around him from whom he chose twelve disciples. From Capernaum Jesus traveled throughout Galilee, the Jordan Valley, and Judea, where he taught his followers, healed the sick, and performed numerous miracles.

On his final journey to Jerusalem Jesus was seized and, on the hill of Golgotha outside the city, crucified, buried, and resurrected. After his resurrection Jesus appeared several more times to his disciples: in Jerusalem, in Emmaus, and along the shores of the Sea of Galilee. He then ascended to heaven from the Mount of Olives.

Despite their master's death, the disciples did not abandon their faith. They continued to spread Jesus' teachings, both in the Holy Land and throughout the Roman Empire, risking their lives on behalf of their belief. Christianity spread quickly among the peoples of the empire, and within less than three hundred years had been transformed from a persecuted faith to a state religion.

The places where Jesus lived and taught—especially Jerusalem, where his life on earth ended—and other locations associated with the work of his disciples became holy places in the Christian tradition, almost immediately being established as the destinations for pilgrimages by the faithful.

Previous pages: An aerial photograph of the Church of the Nativity in Bethlehem, by Albatross.
Background: An aerial photograph of the Church of the Holy Sepulcher in Jerusalem, by M. Milner.

Announces that She Will Give Birth to the Son of God

The angel Gabriel was sent by God to bring some news to a young virgin named Mary from the city of Nazareth: "Do not be afraid, Mary, you have found favor with God. You will be with child and give birth to a son, and you are to give him the name Jesus. He will be great and will be called the Son of the Most High. The Lord God will give him the throne of his father David, and he will reign over the house of Jacob forever; his kingdom will never end...

"The Holy Spirit will come upon you, and the power of the Most High will overshadow you. So the holy one to be born will be called the Son of God. Even Elizabeth your relative is going to have a child in her old age, and she who was said to be barren is in her sixth month. For nothing is impossible with God."

"I am the Lord's servant," Mary answered. "May it be to me as you have said."

Above: The crypt of the Basilica of the Annunciation.
Left: The Annunciation, by C. d'Arpino.

Mary Visits Elizabeth

Both Women Filled with the Holy Spirit

Obeying the words of the angel, Mary set out to visit her relative Elizabeth in Jerusalem. Arriving at Elizabeth's house, Mary greeted her. When Elizabeth heard Mary's greeting, the baby leaped in her womb, and Elizabeth was filled with the Holy Spirit. In a loud voice she exclaimed: "Blessed are you among women, and blessed is the child you will bear!"

And Mary said: "My soul glorifies the Lord and my spirit rejoices in God my Savior, for he has been mindful of the humble state of his servant. From now on all generations will call me blessed, for the Mighty One has done great things for me—holy is his name. His mercy extends to those who fear him, from generation to generation. He has performed mighty deeds with his arm; he has scattered those who are proud in their inmost thoughts. He has brought down rulers from their thrones but has lifted up the humble. He has filled the hungry with good things but has sent the rich away empty. He has helped his servant Israel, remembering to be merciful to Abraham and his descendants forever, even as he said to our fathers."

Miriam stayed with Elizabeth for about three months and then returned home.

The Visitation, by D. Ghirlandaio.

It's a Boy!

"His Name is John."

Much to the surprise and joy of all of Elizabeth's relatives and neighbors, who until then had shared her and Zechariah's sorrow that they did not have a child, a son was finally born to her.

When they came to circumcise the child, they were going to name him Zechariah after his father, but Elizabeth refused, saying, "No! He is to be called John."

Zechariah, who had been struck dumb upon being informed that a son would be born to him, concurred with his wife's decision, writing on a tablet: "His name is John." While those gathered at the circumcision ceremony, who knew that there was no one in Zechariah's family named John, tried to fathom the reason behind the choice, the power of speech suddenly returned to Zechariah, he too was filled with the Holy Spirit, and he began to praise God, saying: "Praise be to the Lord, the God of Israel, because he has come and has redeemed his people."

"Joseph, Do Not Be Afraid"

Angel Convinces Husband to Take Mary Home

The man Mary was pledged to marry was Joseph, a carpenter from the city of Nazareth. When Joseph, who was a righteous man, discovered that Mary was already pregnant, he decided to divorce her quietly, not wishing to expose her to public disgrace.

But then an angel appeared to him in a dream, saying, "Joseph son of David, do not be afraid to take Mary home as your wife, because what is conceived in her is from the Holy Spirit. She will give birth to a son, and you are to give him the name Jesus, because he will save his people from their sins."

When Joseph woke up, he did what the angel had commanded him and took Mary home as his wife.

Above: The Annunciation to Joseph. A detail from the ivory chair of Maximian from the mid-sixth century.
Left: The marriage of the Virgin, by Giotto.

JESUS BORN IN BETHLEHEM

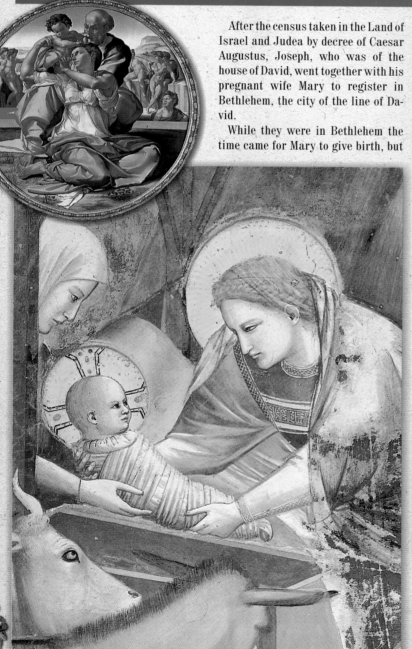

After the census taken in the Land of Israel and Judea by decree of Caesar Augustus, Joseph, who was of the house of David, went together with his pregnant wife Mary to register in Bethlehem, the city of the line of David.

While they were in Bethlehem the time came for Mary to give birth, but

Above: The Grotto of the Nativity.
Above left: The Holy Family, by Michelangelo.
Left: The Nativity, by Giotto.

Bethlehem was full of people who had come to register and Mary and Joseph could find no room at an inn. They finally found shelter in a grotto used as a stable, where Mary gave birth and placed her newborn son in the manger.

Tidings to the Shepherds

Several shepherds sleeping in a field near the city of Bethlehem were terror-stricken when an angel of the Lord appeared to them. The angel said: "Do not be afraid. I bring you good news of great joy that will be for all the people. Today in the town of David a Savior has been born to you; he is Christ the Lord. This will be a sign to you: You will find a baby wrapped in cloths and lying in a manger."

Suddenly a great company of the heavenly host appeared with the angel, praising God and saying, "Glory to God in the highest, and on earth peace to men on whom his favor rests."

The shepherds hastened off to the city of Bethlehem, where they found Mary, Joseph, and the baby wrapped in cloths in the manger, as they had been told.

Above: The annunciation to the shepherds, by the Limbourg brothers.
Right: The adoration of the shepherds, by P. de Champaigne.

Jesus Presented in the Temple

When the child was eight days old he was circumcised and named Jesus, the name the angel had given him before he had been conceived. When the time of their purification had been completed, Joseph and Mary went up to Jerusalem with the child to present him to the Lord in the Temple and to offer a sacrifice of "a pair of doves or two young pigeons."

In Jerusalem lived a righteous old man named Simeon, to whom it had been revealed by the Holy Spirit that he would not die before he had seen the Messiah. When Joseph and Mary

Top: Jesus' circumcision, by F. Barocci.
Above: The Presentation in the temple, by A. Lorenzetti.

brought the infant Jesus into the Temple, Simeon took him in his arms and blessed God, the child, and his parents.

There was also a prophetess there —Anna, the daughter of Phanuel. She was an eighty-four-year-old widow who never left the Temple and worshiped God day and night by fasting and praying. She also came up to give thanks to God, and she praised the child to all who were anticipating the redemption of Jerusalem.

Magi from the East Arrive in Jerusalem

Magi from the East who had seen the star announcing the birth of the king of the Jews arrived in Jerusalem in order to worship him.

The rumor of the birth of the Messiah had also reached the ears of King Herod, who ruled in the Land of Israel at that time and was disturbed at the omen. He hurriedly summoned to his palace all of the chief priests, who told him that the Messiah would be born in Bethlehem.

Herod called the Magi to him secretly in order to find out exactly when the star had appeared. Pretending that he too wished to worship the child, he asked them to go to Bethlehem and search for him.

The Magi set out in the direction of Bethlehem, the star guiding them until it stopped over the house where Jesus and his mother Mary were. The Magi entered, bowed down to the child, and presented him with gifts of gold, incense, and myrrh.

Having been warned in a dream not to return to Herod, the wise men returned to their country via an alternative route.

The three Magi. A sixth-century mosaic from St. Apollinare Nuovo in Ravenna.

Holy Family Flees to Egypt

The flight to Egypt. From a fifteenth-century manuscript.

An angel appeared to Joseph in a dream and commanded him to escape to Egypt with his wife and child because Herod was going to have the child found and killed. Hearkening to the heavenly messenger, Joseph and Mary took their young son and fled during the night to Egypt.

Jerusalem Whiz Kid

Precocious Youth of Twelve Astonishes His Teachers

The twelve-year old Jesus joined his parents, Joseph and Mary, when they traveled to Jerusalem for Passover, as was their annual custom. After the feast was over, Mary and Joseph departed for Nazareth, but Jesus remained behind in Jerusalem. His parents, thinking the boy was walking home somewhere among their company, only realized he was missing when they stopped for the night. They looked for him among their relatives and friends, but to no avail.

Panic-stricken, Mary and Joseph returned to Jerusalem, where three days later they found Jesus sitting in the Temple among the teachers, listening to them and asking them questions while everyone around him gaped in amazement at his intellect.

When Mary asked him why he had caused them so much worry, Jesus replied: "Why were you searching for me? Didn't you know I had to be in my Father's house?"

Finding the Savior, by W.H. Hunt.

Bethlehem Babies Executed

Herod, disappointed in his hope that the Magi would assist him in finding the baby who was to become the Messiah, plotted another course. In a desperate attempt to rid himself of the infant threatening his rule, he issued orders that all the children in Bethlehem two years of age and younger be executed. Herod's soldiers invaded the town, tore the innocent babes from their mothers' arms, and put them to death.

Stone Swallows Infant

Tradition has it that when Herod's soldiers went through Bethlehem murdering its infants, Elizabeth and her baby John fled their house in Ein Karem and hid behind a stone, which swallowed John up until the danger had passed. The stone is now in the present-day Church of the Visitation in Ein Karem.

Holy Family Returns to Holy Land

Above: Christ in the house of his parents, by J.E. Millais. **Below right:** The Holy Family, by W. Dobson.

After the death of Herod, an angel again appeared to Joseph in a dream and told him the time had come to return to his native land. Joseph, Mary, and their child Jesus returned to the Holy Land and settled in the town of Nazareth in Galilee.

John Baptizes Jesus in the Jordan

John the Baptist, the son of Zechariah and Elizabeth, went out preaching in the desert, saying, "Repent for the kingdom of heaven is near!"

Many of the residents of Jerusalem, Judea, and the whole region of the Jordan answered his cry and went to him in order to be baptized in the River Jordan and to confess their sins. To all of them John the Baptist announced that he was baptizing them with water but that after him would come one more powerful than he who would baptize them with the Holy Spirit and with fire. Among those coming to be baptized by John the Baptist was Jesus. At first John refused to baptize Jesus, claiming that it was not he who should be baptizing Jesus, but Jesus who should baptize him. He finally consented to Jesus' request, however, and when Jesus came up out of the water the heavens opened and the Spirit of God descended like a dove and lit on him as a voice from heaven said, "This is my Son, whom I love; with him I am well-pleased."

Above: The baptism of Christ, by P. Prugino and Pinturicchio.
Above right: The Monastery of St. John in the Desert. According to tradition, John the Baptist lived here in solitude until he began his activity.

Devil Tempts Jesus Three Times—and Fails

After his baptism Jesus was led by the Spirit into the desert, where he fasted for forty days. On the fortieth day the devil tried to tempt him with food, saying to him: "If you are the Son of God, tell these stones to become bread."

But Jesus answered him: "Man does not live on bread alone, but on every word that comes from the mouth of God."

Then the devil took him to Jerusalem and had him stand on the highest point of the Temple (the Pinnacle), challenging him, "If you are the Son of God, throw yourself down. For it is written: 'He will command his angels concerning you, and they will lift you up in their hands, so that you will not strike your foot against a stone.'"

Jesus answered him: "It is also written: 'Do not put the Lord your God to the test.'"

The devil, a tenacious character, tempted Jesus a third time. Taking

him to a very high mountain, he showed him all the kingdoms of the world, promising them to Jesus if he would only agree to worship him. But Jesus banished him with "Away from me, Satan! For it is written 'Worship the Lord your God, and serve him only.'"

Only then did the devil leave Jesus, and angels came and attended him.

The Mount of Temptation.

Strong Words in the Synagogue
Jesus Taken Forcefully to Nazareth Cliff

After withstanding all of the devil's temptations, Jesus returned to Galilee, where he taught in synagogues, becoming well-known throughout the entire region.

Finding himself one Sabbath in Nazareth, the city where he had been brought up, he went into the synagogue, as was his custom. When he stood up to read the Torah, he opened the book of the prophet Isaiah and read out of it to the congregation: "The Spirit of the Lord is on me, because he has anointed me to preach good news to the poor. He has sent me to proclaim freedom for the prisoners and recovery of sight for the blind, to release the oppressed, to proclaim the year of the Lord's favor." Then he rolled up the scroll and said: "Today this scripture is fulfilled in your hearing...Surely you will quote this proverb to me:

Jesus preaches in the synagogue of Nazareth, by J.J. Tissot.

'Physician heal yourself! Do here in your home town what we have heard that you did in Capernaum.'

"I tell you the truth," he continued, "no prophet is accepted in his home town. I assure you that there were many widows in Israel in Elijah's time, when the sky was shut for three and a half years and there was a severe famine throughout the land. Yet Elijah was not sent to any of them, but to a widow in Zarephath in the region of Sidon. And there were many in Israel with leprosy in the time of Elisha the prophet, yet not one of them was cleansed—only Naaman the Syrian."

The people in the synagogue were infuriated at Jesus' words, and they took hold of him and led him to the brow of the hill on which Nazareth was built in order to throw him down

The Mount of the Precipice.

the cliff, but Jesus walked right through the crowd and went on his way.

After being thrown out of Nazareth, Jesus went to live in Capernaum on the shore of the Sea of Galilee.

Men-Fishers: Jesus' First Two Disciples

One day Jesus was standing by the Lake of Gennesaret with the people crowding around him and listening to the word of God. He saw two boats left at the water's edge by fishermen who were washing their nets.

Jesus approached Simon Peter, one of the fishermen, and, sitting down in the boat, asked him to put out a little from shore, and he taught the people from the boat. When he had finished speaking, Jesus told Simon to move out into deep water and let down the nets for a catch. Simon said, "Master, we've worked hard all night and have not caught anything. But because you say so, I will let down the nets."

Above: The calling of the first apostles, by D. Ghirlandaio.
Left: Jesus commands Peter to let down his net. A sixth-century mosaic from the Basilica of St. Apollinare Nuovo in Ravenna.

When they pulled in the net they discovered that it was so full it had begun to break. Simon called to his partners for help and together they filled the two boats so full that they began to sink.

Then Jesus said to Simon Peter: "Don't be afraid; from now on you will catch men."

Then Simon Peter and his brother Andrew pulled their boat on to the shore, and so did their two friends, James and John, the sons of Zebedee, and, leaving everything behind, they followed Jesus.

A Miraculous Wedding in Cana

Jesus Turns Water into Wine

One Tuesday there was a wedding at Cana in Galilee. Mary, Jesus' mother, Jesus, and his disciples were among the guests.

In the middle of the wedding the wine ran out and Mary, concerned, turned to Jesus to rescue the event. Jesus tried at first to refuse her by claiming that his time to act had not yet arrived, but Mary, ignoring him, told the servants at the wedding to do whatever Jesus instructed.

Jesus told the servants to take six

The wedding at Cana, by G. David.

empty jars, fill them with water, and then draw some out and give it to the master of the banquet. When the master of the banquet tasted the wine, he called the bridegroom to him and praised him, saying, "Everyone brings out the choice wine first and then the cheaper wine after the guests have had too much to drink; but you have saved the best till now."

This was Jesus' first miracle, through which he revealed his glory to his disciples.

Jesus Travels Around Galilee

Moonstruck and Possessed Flock to Be Healed

After recruiting his first disciples, Jesus began to pass through the settlements of Galilee, teaching in synagogues, revealing the news of the coming kingdom of heaven, and healing the sick. His fame as a healer spread throughout Galilee and Syria, and soon people started to bring him all their sick, disabled, moonstruck, and possessed so that he could heal them. Masses of believers from throughout the Decapolis, Jerusalem, Judea, and Transjordan followed him all around Galilee.

In Capernaum, his new place of residence, Jesus would teach at the synagogue on the Sabbath. In the synagogue was a man possessed by a demon: on Sabbath, in the middle of the prayers, the demon began to cry, "What do you want with us, Jesus of Nazareth? Have you come to destroy us? I know who you are—the Holy One of God!"

"Be quiet!" Jesus admonished the evil spirit. "Come out of him!" And the demon threw the man down before them all and emerged without injuring him.

Another day as Jesus was traveling around Galilee a man with leprosy came toward him, bowed down before him, and begged him, "If you are willing, you can make me clean."

Taking pity on him, Jesus reached

People begin to bring Jesus all their sick, by J.J. Tissot.

out his hand and touched him, saying, "I am willing. Be clean!" The man was cured immediately.

In Bethsaida they brought a blind man to Jesus to be healed. Jesus took the man by the hand and led him out of the village. There he spit on the man's eyes and laid his hands on them until the man regained his sight.

Get Up and Go Home
Paralytic Leaves on His Own Two Feet

Jesus was by this time renowned as a healer of the sick. One day as he sat in the house of Peter's mother-in-law in Capernaum teaching the people, some men brought a paralytic before him to be healed.

The house was so crowded that the men could not find a way to bring the paralytic in the door, so they went up on the roof and lowered him into the house from above. Jesus, seeing their intense faith, blessed the paralytic, forgave his sins, and said to him: "I tell you, get up, take your mat and go home." The paralytic stood up in front of everyone and went home praising God.

The church above Peter's house at Capernaum.

12 Apostles Chosen from Among the Disciples of Jesus

Jesus sending off the apostles.

After a night of prayer on a mountain, Jesus gathered his disciples to him and chose twelve of them to be his apostles: Simon (who was also called Peter) and his brother Andrew, the brothers James and John, Philip, Bartholomew, Matthew, Thomas, James the son of Alphaeus, Simon (who was called "the Zealot"), Judas the son of James, and Judas Iscariot.

Jesus gave them the power to heal the sick and drive away demons, then sent them to spread the word of the kingdom of God in all the villages.

Demoniac's Wits Return: Pigs Jump to Their Deaths

On the eastern side of the Sea of Galilee, in the hills that border the Decapolis, lived a man possessed by an evil spirit. This unfortunate man shrieked and wounded himself with stones, but no one could help him, even when he was bound with ropes, because he would untie them and escape.

When the boat of Jesus and his disciples weighed anchor on the eastern shore of the lake and they disembarked, the man ran toward them from among the tombs. When Jesus saw him he said, "Come out of this man, you evil spirit!" And the spirit answered, "What do you want with me, Son of the Most High God? Swear to God that you won't torture me!"

"What is your name?" Jesus asked him.

Merchants Ousted from Temple

When it was time for Passover, Jesus and his disciples went up to Jerusalem. When Jesus entered the temple he found moneychangers and men selling cattle, sheep, and doves. Incensed by the desecration of the holy place, Jesus made a whip out of cords and drove the cattle from the temple. He overturned the moneychangers' tables and scattered their coins on the ground, then said to those who sold doves: "Get these out of here! How dare you turn my Father's house into a market!"

Jesus cleans the temple, by J.J. Tissot.

"My name is Legion," the evil spirit answered, "for we are many," and begged Jesus to send them into the pigs grazing nearby. Jesus agreed, and the demons left the man and entered the herd of pigs, which rushed down the steep bank of the mountain into the sea and were drowned.

Those tending the pigs ran off to the city and reported what had happened.

The church at Kursi on the border of the Decapolis.

Everyone rushed to the spot to find the demoniac sitting quietly and properly dressed—apparently in his right mind. Filled with fear after having heard the whole story from eyewitnesses, the inhabitants of the area pleaded with Jesus to leave their region.

"Talitha Koumi!"

John Asks Jesus, "Are You the One?"

When the young daughter of Jairus, head of the synagogue in Capernaum, was extremely ill, her father came to beg Jesus to heal her.

While Jairus was with Jesus, messengers came from his house to tell him his daughter had died. Jesus calmed him and said, "Don't be afraid; just believe."

The two went to Jairus' house with only Peter, John, and James, the brother of John. Once there, Jesus said to the mourners: "The child is not dead but asleep," but they laughed at him.

Jesus ushered the mourners out and went in to where the child was with only her father, her mother, and the three disciples. He took her by the hand and said to her, "Talitha koumi" ("Little girl, get up!"). Miraculously, the little girl arose, completely cured.

Another time, Jesus, his disciples, and the crowd of people that by now was always accompanying him went to the city of Na'in. When they approached its gates they saw that a dead person was being carried out of the city—the only son of a widow.

Jesus, whose heart went out to the widow when he saw her, said, "Don't cry." He went up and touched the coffin, saying, "Young man, I say to you, get up!" The widow's son sat up and began to talk.

News of the miracle spread throughout the country, reaching even John the Baptist, who sent two of his disciples to Jesus to ask him, "Are you the one who was to come or should we expect someone else?"

So Jesus replied, "Go back and report to John what you have seen and heard: the blind receive sight, the lame walk, those who have leprosy are cured, the deaf hear, the dead are raised, and the good news is preached to the poor. Blessed is the man who does not fall away on account of me."

The raising of Jairus' daughter, by J.J. Tissot.

John the Baptist Beheaded

Herodias Takes Revenge

King Herod had John the Baptist arrested after he had denounced the king's marriage to Herodias, wife of Herod's brother Philip. Herod was afraid to harm John because he knew him to be a righteous and holy man, but Herodias hated him and plotted to kill him. Her opportunity arrived at a banquet in honor of Herod's birthday. Salome, Herodias' daughter, danced before Herod and his guests, and Herod, pleased by Salome's dancing, promised to give her whatever she

Herod's feast, by Donatello.

desired, up to half his kingdom.

Salome hurried to ask her mother what to request, and was told: "The head of John the Baptist." The girl hurried back to Herod and said, "I want you to give me the head of John the Baptist on a platter right now."

The king was greatly distressed, but did not want to break the oath he had made before his highest officials and military commanders. He gave orders that John the Baptist be put to death and decapitated, and then presented his head on a platter to Salome, who gave it to her mother.

Upon hearing the news, John's disciples came, took his body, and laid it in a tomb.

The Beatitudes

"Blessed are the pure in heart, for they will see God."

When Jesus saw the crowds following him and his disciples, he went up on a mountainside and began to teach them: "Blessed are the poor in spirit, for theirs is the kingdom of heaven. Blessed are those who mourn, for they will be comforted. Blessed are the meek, for they will inherit the earth. Blessed are those who hunger and thirst for righteousness, for they will be filled. Blessed are the merciful, for they will be shown mercy. Blessed are the pure in heart, for they will see God. Blessed are the peacemakers, for they will be called sons of God. Blessed are those who are persecuted because of righteousness, for theirs is the kingdom of heaven. Blessed are you when people insult you, persecute you, and falsely say all kinds of evil against you because of me. Rejoice and be glad, because great is your reward in heaven, for in the same way they persecuted the prophets who were before you."

And he told them many other things, and the crowds were amazed at his teaching, because he taught like one who had authority and yet not like their teachers of the law.

The Mount of Beatitudes.

Multiplying Loaves and Fishes

When his disciples had returned to Jesus from their missions, he set out with them for a quiet place so they could get some rest, but crowds kept gathering around them to hear Jesus speak.

Jesus went out to them and began teaching them. As the day was waning, the disciples asked Jesus to send the crowds to the neighboring villages so that they could buy bread for themselves. But Jesus said to them, "You give them something to eat." When the disciples claimed they did not have that kind of money, Jesus asked: "How many loaves do you have?" "Five—and two fish," the disciples answered.

Jesus directed them to have all the people sit down in groups on the grass, fifty people per group. He took the five loaves and two fish, and looking up to heaven gave thanks, broke the loaves, and divided the fish.

To the surprise of the disciples, the five loaves of bread and the two fish were sufficient to feed the whole crowd—five thousand people—with twelve baskets of broken pieces of bread and fish to spare.

Above: The loaves and fishes. A Byzantine mosaic floor from the Church of the Loaves and Fishes at Tabgha.
Right: The multiplication of the loaves and fishes, from *Les Très Riches Heures du Duc de Berry*, by the Limbourg brothers.

Jesus Curses Galilean Cities
Korazin, Bethsaida, and Capernaum Doomed

Disappointed by the attitude of the inhabitants of the cities of Galilee, the region of his mission and the area in which he had performed most of his miracles, Jesus cursed them and prophesied their destruction: "Woe to you Korazin! Woe to you Bethsaida! If the miracles that were performed in performed in Sodom, it would have remained to this day. But I tell you that it will be more bearable for Sodom on the day of judgment than for you."

Capernaum was indeed almost totally leveled by an earthquake in the fifth century, and by the end of the seventh century had completely

The ruined synagogue at Korazin.

you had been performed in Tyre and Sidon, they would have repented long ago in sackcloth and ashes. But I tell you, it will be more bearable for Tyre and Sidon on the day of judgment than for you. And you Capernaum, will you be lifted up to the skies? No, you will go down to the depths. If the miracles that were performed in you had been ceased to exist. Korazin and Bethsaida were also eventually wiped out. The location of Korazin was only identified in the eighteenth century, while the site of Bethsaida was definitively determined only in recent years.

Jesus Predicts His Death
Gives Peter the Keys to the Kingdom of Heaven

When Jesus and his disciples reached the villages around Caesarea Philippi, Jesus warned them of his approaching death, explaining that "The Son of Man must suffer many things and be rejected by the elders, chief priests, and teachers of the law, and that he must be killed and after three days rise again."

At the same place, Jesus told Peter that he would have to instruct the people how to behave in Jesus' absence: "And I tell you that you are Peter, and on this rock I will build my church, and the gates of Hades will not overcome it. I will give you the keys to the kingdom of heaven; whatever you bind on earth will be bound in heaven, and whatever you loose on earth will be loosed in heaven."

St. Peter holding the keys. A bronze statue at the Church of St. Peter in Tiberias.

The Transfiguration

About a week after he predicted his own death, Jesus took Peter, James, and John up a mountain, where in front of the shocked disciples the appearance of his face changed and his clothes became as bright as a flash of lightning.

The disciples became drowsy, and when they awakened from their slumber they saw Moses and Elijah speaking with Jesus. When the two prophets left, Peter proposed that they erect three shelters on the spot—one for Jesus, one for Moses, and one for Elijah. While he was speaking, a cloud appeared and a voice from within it said, "This is my Son, whom I have chosen; listen to him."

Above: The apse of the Basillica of the Transfiguration.
Left: Mount Tabor, by Bonfils.

Sibling Rivalry

When Jesus arrived at the village of Bethany near Jerusalem, a woman named Martha opened her home to him. While Martha was busy serving the guests, her sister Mary sat at the feet of Jesus listening to what he said. Martha, annoyed at having to do all the work herself, asked Jesus to tell her sister to come help her, but Jesus answered her, "Martha, Martha, you are worried and upset about many things, but only one thing is needed. Mary has chosen what is better, and it will not be taken away from her."

How to Pray

The wall of vreses at the Eleona.

One time, as Jesus prepared to pray, one of his disciples turned to him and asked, "Lord, teach us to pray, just as John taught his disciples."

Jesus answered, "When you pray, say: 'Father, hallowed be your name, your kingdom come. Give us each day our daily bread. Forgive us our sins, for we also forgive everyone who sins against us. And lead us not into temptation.'"

Raising Lazarus

When Lazarus, friend of Jesus and brother of Mary and Martha of Bethany, fell ill, his sisters sent messengers to Jesus requesting him to come and heal his friend. Jesus delayed, however, and arrived on the outskirts of the village of Bethany four days after Lazarus was buried.

When Martha heard that Jesus had arrived in Bethany, she came out to him and said, "Lord, if you had been here, my brother would not have died."

Jesus commanded Martha to fetch her sister Mary, who was sitting in the house with those who had come to console her. When Mary arose and left the house, they went with her, supposing she was going to cry on her brother's grave.

When Jesus saw the sorrow of Mary and Martha and the weeping of the other mourners, he also wept, and went to the grave. At the tomb, he commanded the people to roll the gravestone away from the grave. Martha objected and said, "Lord, by this time there will be an odor, for he has been dead four days." Jesus replied to her that if she believed, she would see the glory of God.

Jesus prayed to God and then called out loudly to Lazarus. The dead man emerged from the grave wrapped in a shroud, his face covered by a cloth. Jesus told those assembled to remove the shroud, and let his friend go.

The raising of Lazarus, by L. di Tommè.

Crowds Hail Triumphal Entry of Jesus

Jesus' triumphal entry into Jerusalem, by Giotto.

"Hosanna in the Highest!"

When Jesus and his disciples approached Bethpage and Bethany at the Mount of Olives, Jesus dispatched two of his disciples, saying, "Go to the village ahead of you, and just as you enter it, you will find a colt tied there, which no one has ever ridden. Untie it and bring it here. If anyone asks you 'Why are you doing that?' tell him, 'The Lord needs it and will send it back here shortly.'"

Doing just as he had said, the two disciples brought the colt to Jesus. They threw their cloaks over the colt and Jesus rode it to Jerusalem. On their way, people mobbed the sides of the road, spreading cloaks or branches on it and crying, "Hosanna! Blessed is he who comes in the name of the Lord! Blessed is the coming kingdom of our father David! Hosanna in the highest!"

Jesus Washes His Disciples' Feet

During the Last Supper Jesus rose from the table, took off his clothing, and wrapped a towel around his waist. After that he poured water into a basin and began to wash his disciples' feet, drying them with the towel that was wrapped around him.

disciples' feet, Jesus said to them: "Now that I, your Lord and Teacher, have washed your feet, you should also wash one another's feet, as I have set you an example that you should do as I have done for you. I tell you the truth, no servant is greater than his

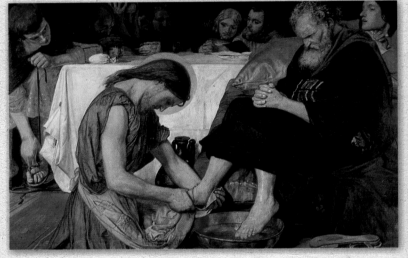

Jesus washing Peter's feet, by F.M. Brown.

Peter, astonished, said, "Lord, are you going to wash my feet?"

"You do not realize now what I am doing, but later you will understand," answered Jesus.

"No, you will never wash my feet," said Peter, continuing to resist.

"Unless I wash you," said Jesus, "You have no part with me."

After he had finished washing the

master, nor is a messenger greater than the one who sent him. Now that you know these things, you will be blessed if you do them." Later he added, "I give you a new commandment: Love one another. As I have loved you, so you must love one another."

The Last Supper

When the day of Passover came, Jesus commanded Peter and John to prepare the Passover meal. When they asked where he wanted them to do so, Jesus told them to go into the city, where they would see a man carrying a jar of water. He instructed them to follow him home and say to him, "The Teachers asks: Where is the guest room, where I may eat the Passover with my disciples?"

According to Jesus, the man would show them a large upper room, completely furnished, and there they would make preparations for the holiday.

When Jesus and his disciples sat down to the feast, Jesus told them that it was to be his last Passover meal before his suffering commenced, and that he would not eat again before

entering the kingdom of heaven.

Then he took the cup of wine, gave thanks, and said, "Take this and divide it among you."

He took the bread, gave thanks, gave it to the disciples and said, "This is my body given for you."

After the meal he blessed the cup of wine and said, "This cup is the new covenant in my blood, which is poured out for you."

At the conclusion of the meal Jesus said to his disciples that one of them would betray him, turning him in to the Romans. The disciples, upset, pleaded with him to disclose which of them it would be.

The Last Supper, by C. Rosselli.

Affliction in Gethsemane

Suffering Unto Death

At the end of the meal Jesus and his disciples went out, as was their daily custom, to the Mount of Olives. On the way, Jesus predicted to his disciples that they would all fall away that night. To Peter, who protested, he foretold that that very night, before the rooster crowed twice, he himself would thrice disown Jesus.

In the courtyard of Gethsemane

Above: Judas' betrayal, by Giotto.
Right: The Rock of Agony in the Church of All Nations in Gethsemane.

Jesus parted from his disciples, saying "Sit here while I pray," and took with him only Peter, John, and James.

Saying to them, "Stay here and keep watch," he went a little further away, fell to the ground, and prayed to his Father that he might take from him the cup of suffering. An angel appeared to him and strengthened him. Jesus, in anguish, continued to pray, his sweat falling like drops of blood to the ground.

JESUS ARRESTED

"The hour has come; the Son of Man is betrayed into the hands of sinners."

At a late hour on Passover eve, Jesus was caught by a mob armed with swords and clubs, sent by the chief priests and elders of the people. The crowd was led by Judas Iscariot, who had betrayed his teacher for thirty silver shekels. A sign between the betrayer and the mob had been determined—the man whom Judas Iscariot kissed would be the man they were after.

Jesus, who knew in advance of their arrival and was prepared for it, woke Peter, James, and John, who were accompanying him, and said to them: "The hour has come; the Son of man is betrayed into the hands of sinners."

When they went out into the crowd,

Jesus is arrested, by B. da Siena.

Holy Grail Mystery

Where is the Holy Grail from which Jesus drank at the Last Supper? According to legend, the grail was transferred to Rome by Peter or Mark and used by the popes until 258 AD. In that year, Emperor Valerian demanded that the church transfer all of its treasures to him. In order to rescue the valuable grail from the emperor, it was smuggled to Spain and today is kept in the Chapel of the Holy Grail in the cathedral of Valencia. According to testimony from the Byzantine period, the grail used to be displayed in the Church of the Holy Sepulcher. One traveler who visited Jerusalem in the sixth century recorded that he saw the grail in the Church of the Holy Sepulcher and that it was made of granite. Conversely, another pilgrim, who visited the spot in the seventh century, testified that the grail was made of silver.

Another version has it that the grail was made of green glass and was removed from Jerusalem to the Cathedral of San Lorenzo in Genoa by Italian soldiers who served in the army of Baldwin I during the First Crusade.

The British have their own tradition, according to which the Holy Grail was brought by Joseph Arimathea, Jesus' wealthy relative, to Britain, where it has remained ever since, housed in Canterbury Cathedral.

A sixth-century mosaic from the Basilica of St. Vitale in Ravenna.

Judas Iscariot approached them, welcomed Jesus, and kissed him—the mob's cue to seize him. Peter, in an effort to protect Jesus, drew his sword and cut off the ear of a servant of the high priest, but Jesus commanded him to desist, and healed the man's ear. Afterwards he turned to the crowd and asked: "Have you come out as against a robber, with swords and clubs? When I was with you day after day in the temple, you did not lay hands on me. But this is your hour, and the power of darkness."

Abandoned by his disciples, Jesus was led by his captors to the palace of the high priest, where the scribes and elders assembled. The high priest turned to Jesus and asked him: "Are you the Christ, the Son of the Blessed?" And Jesus replied, "I am."

At dawn Jesus was arrested and turned over to Pilate, the Roman governor of Jerusalem.

JESUS

First thing in the morning, Jesus was led from the house of Caiaphas the high priest to the palace of Pontius Pilate, the Roman governor, to whom he was turned over for trial.

Pilate asked him,: "Are you the king of the Jews?" and Jesus replied, "Yes, it is as you say." The priests spoke against him, but Jesus was silent and did not respond to their words.

Pilate's wife sent her husband a message asking him to let Jesus go because he was a righteous man.

on him, and struck him on the head with a staff. Afterwards they took off the scarlet robe, put his own clothes back on him, and led him away to crucify him.

As they were leaving the courthouse they met a man named Simon of Cyrene, whom they forced to carry Jesus' cross to Golgotha. A great many people followed the procession, including women who mourned and wailed for the prisoner. But Jesus turned and said to them, "Daughters

Pilate, who released one of the Jewish accused each Passover in honor of the feast, turned to the priests and the people, proposing to release either Jesus or the murderer Barabbas. The priests persuaded the people to demand the liberation of Barabbas and the crucifixion of Jesus.

When Pilate heard them he washed his hands and said, "I am innocent of this man's blood." Then he gave the order to release Barabbas and to hand Jesus over to the soldiers.

The soldiers stripped Jesus of his clothing, dressed him in a scarlet robe, set a crown of thorns on his head, and put a staff in his right hand. They knelt in front of him and mocked him—"Hail, king of the Jews!"—spit

Top: Jesus carrying the cross, by E. le Sueur.
Above: Jesus before Pilate, by the Master of Schotten.

of Jerusalem, do not weep for me; weep for yourselves and for your children."

When they reached Golgotha they nailed Jesus to the cross and hung above his head a sign reading "This is Jesus, the king of the Jews." The soldiers divided the clothes they had taken off him amongst themselves and cast lots for his undergarments.

The crowd, the soldiers, and one of the two robbers who were crucified on either side of him mocked Jesus. Hurling insults at him, they taunted, "Aren't you the Christ? Save yourself

Clockwise from upper left: "Ecce homo" ("This is the man"), by L. Cigoli; the carrying of the cross, by S. Martini; the silver disc signifying where the cross was placed; Station VII—Jesus falls for the second time; Station II—Jesus takes up the cross; the flagellation of Jesus at the pillar, by Caravaggio.

CRUCIFIED

over all the land and lasted until the ninth hour. At about the ninth hour Jesus cried out in a loud voice, "*Eloi, Eloi, lama sabachthani?*" (My God, my God, why have you forsaken me?). And one of those standing beneath him put a sponge dipped in vinegar on a stick and offered it to Jesus to drink. Then Jesus cried out and gave up his spirit. At the moment of his death, the curtain of the temple was torn in two from top to bottom and the earth shook and the rocks split and the tombs broke open and the bodies of many holy people who had died were raised to life.

Above: Christ bearing the cross, by M. Palmezzano.
Below: Christ being nailed to the cross, by Fra Angelico.

and us!" The second criminal rebuked the first, asking, "Don't you fear God, since you are under the same sentence? We are punished justly for we are getting what our deeds deserve. But this man has done nothing wrong." Then he turned to Jesus and said, "Remember me when you come into your kingdom." Jesus answered, "I tell you the truth, today you will be with me in paradise."

At the sixth hour a darkness came

CHRIST BURIED

Clockwise from upper left: Pietá, by Michelangelo; the Calvary; the Stone of the Anointing; the Chapel of the Holy Tomb; the descent from the cross, by the Master of St. Bartholomew.

As evening drew near, the soldiers came to break the legs of the crucified in order to hasten their death. When they saw that Jesus was already dead, they did not break his legs, but one of them pierced his side with a spear, bringing a sudden flow of blood and water.

When night fell, Joseph of Arimathea, who was a secret disciple of Jesus, asked Pilate to let him take Jesus off of the cross and bury his body. He and Nicodemus, who had brought with him about seventy-five pounds of myrrh and aloes (scented oils), rubbed the body with them, wrapped it in shrouds, and buried it in a new tomb in the garden near the place of crucifixion.

Jesus Resurrected!

After the Sabbath, at dawn on the first day of the week, Mary Magdalene and the other Mary went to look at the tomb. While they were there, a great noise was heard and an angel of the Lord came down from heaven, rolled back the stone from the grave, and sat on it. His appearance was like lightning and his clothes were white as snow. The guards were so afraid of him that they shook and became like dead men.

The angel calmed the frightened women and said: "Do not be afraid, for I know that you are looking for Jesus who was crucified. He is not here; he is risen just as he said."

Mary Magdalene immediately ran to

Above: Jesus reveals himself to Mary Magdalene, by J.J. Tissot.
Left: The resurrection of Christ, by J.C. Loth.

Peter and John to tell them that Jesus was not in his tomb. Hurrying to the place, the two saw the empty grave and the discarded shrouds lying inside it with their own eyes.

After they left, Mary Magdalene remained crying outside of the tomb, when suddenly Jesus appeared from behind her. She did not recognize him at first, and thought he was the gardener, but when he called to her she knew him and put out her hands to him. Jesus said "Do not hold on to me, for I have not yet returned to the Father. Go instead to my brothers and tell them, 'I am returning to my Father and your Father, to my God and your God.'"

Jesus Appears to His Disciples

On the evening of the first day of the week, all of the disciples except Thomas were gathered in a locked house. Suddenly Jesus stood among them; he blessed them and showed them his hands and his side.

When they later told Thomas of Jesus' reappearance, he refused to believe it, saying, "Unless I

The incredulity of St. Thomas, by Guercino.

see the nail marks in his hands and put my finger where the nails were, and put my hand into his side, I will not believe it."

Eight days later, when the disciples had gathered again, Jesus appeared among them once more, turned to doubting Thomas and said, "Put your finger here; see my hands. Reach out your hand and put it into my side. Stop doubting and believe."

Encounter at Emmaus

On the third day of the week, two of Jesus' followers were traveling to the village of Emmaus near Jerusalem. As they talked about the events of the past few days, Jesus joined them, but they did not recognize him. They told the "stranger" about Jesus' deeds, about his being handed over to the Romans and crucified, and about the disappearance of his body from the tomb.

When they reached Emmaus, the two unsuspecting men invited Jesus to join them for supper, and he agreed. Once at the table with them, he took bread, gave thanks, broke it, and began to give it to them: suddenly they recognized him, but only to have him disappear from sight again.

The supper at Emmaus, by Rembrandt.

The Primacy of Peter: "Tend My Sheep"

Jesus appeared one more time to his disciples—at Tabgha near the Sea of Galilee.

The disciples had gone out to fish, but had caught nothing. When morning came, they returned to shore and saw Jesus standing on the beach, though they did not recognize him.

Jesus turned to them and said: "Friends, haven't you any fish?"

"No," they replied.

"Throw your net on the right side of the boat and you will find some," Jesus said.

The disciples did as he had said, and the net was so full of fish that they could not haul it in.

"It is the Lord," John called to Peter, and Peter jumped into the water and swam to shore. The other disciples followed in the boat to the beach and found there burning coals with fish on them and some bread. Jesus gave the disciples food and sat with them. At the end of the meal, Jesus asked Peter: "Simon son of John, do you truly love me more than these?"

"Yes, Lord, you know that I love you."

"Tend my sheep."

Left: Jesus reveals himself at the Sea of Galilee, by J.J. Tissot.
Right: The Mensa Christi at Tabgha.

Jesus Ascends into Heaven

Christ in his glory, by A. Carracci.

On the fortieth day after his death, Jesus was revealed to his disciples in Jerusalem. He shared a meal with them, spoke of the kingdom of God, and commanded them to wait in Jerusalem until they were baptized with the Holy Spirit, which was soon to occur.

They then went with Jesus to the Mount of Olives, where they asked him, "Lord, are you going to restore the kingdom to Israel at this time?"

"It is not for you to know the times or dates the Father has set by his own authority," Jesus replied, "but you will receive power when the Holy Spirit comes on you; and you will be my witnesses in Jerusalem and in all Judea and Samaria, and to the ends of the earth." After he finished speaking, Jesus rose into the sky carried on a cloud, as the disciples watched. Suddenly, two angels appeared next to the disciples. "Men of Galilee, why do you stand here looking into the sky? This same Jesus who has been taken from you into heaven will come back in the same way you have seen him go into heaven."

Speaking in Tongues
The Holy Spirit Touches the Disciples

When seven weeks had passed after the Passover feast, all of the disciples gathered in the attic. Suddenly, a loud noise like the sound of a violent wind was heard, and what seemed to be tongues of fire came down from heaven and came to rest on each of them. All of the disciples were filled with the Holy Spirit and they began to speak in other tongues.

When they heard the noise, a large crowd of people who dwelt in Jerusalem—people from all nations—gathered, and the disciples began to speak to each of them in his or her own language, telling them of the greatness of God.

Above: The Cenacle. **Below:** The Holy Spirit descends, by G. Muziano.

Disciples Incarcerated in City Prison

From the day the Holy Spirit infused them, the disciples began to perform signs and wonders, healing many of the sick. Such acts earned them the esteem of the people, and many joined their ranks. The high priest and his associates were consumed with jealousy, and the former issued an order for the arrest of the disciples. They were accordingly sent to jail, where the city guard watched over them.

That night an angel appeared at the jail, took the disciples out of prison and commanded them: "Go stand in the temple courts and tell the people the full message of this new life."

At daybreak the empty jail cell was discovered and its former inmates found in the temple courts teaching the people. The high priest and his associates apprehended them and brought them before the Sanhedrin, shrieking, "We gave you strict orders not to teach in this name, yet you have filled Jerusalem with your teaching and are determined to make us guilty of this man's blood."

The apostles answered, "We must obey God rather than men!" Though some among the Sanhedrin demanded the disciples' execution, it was finally decided to flog them and order them not to speak in the name of Jesus. The disciples bore their punishment with light hearts, happy to be considered worthy of suffering for proclaiming the name of Jesus, and never stopped teaching his word throughout the city.

The prison cells in the Church of Saint Peter in Gallicantu (the House of Caiaphas.)

James Dies, Peter Arrested

Herod, having made up his mind to strike back at the Christians, gave orders to execute James the Elder, brother of John, and cut off his head.

angel appeared above him and tapped him on the leg to wake him. When Peter arose, the chains dropped from his hands. (When the empress

Peter ran to Mark's house, where his friends were lodging, to tell them what had happened.

The next morning, when Peter's disappearance was discovered, Herod, livid with rage, had the guards executed.

The execution of St. James the Elder, by L. Monaco.

(The Armenians believe the burial place of Saint James' head is in the Armenian Church of Saint James, where the spot is marked by a circle on the floor).

When Herod saw that the deed did not occasion any protests, he gave orders to arrest Peter, planning to place him on trial immediately after Passover. In order to ensure that the prisoner did not escape, four companies of soldiers were set to guard him.

The night before the trial Peter slept in chains between two guards, with additional guards watching the portal of his cell. In the dark of night, an

The deliverance of Saint Peter from prison, by Raphael.

Eudocia returned to Rome from Jerusalem at the end of the fifth century, she brought the chains with her as a gift for her daughter Eudoxia, wife of Emperor Valentine II. She built the Eudoxiana Basilica—today San Pietro in Vincoli, in which the chains are still displayed—in their honor.)

The angel carried Peter over the military guard, who noticed nothing, and through the iron gates of the prison. When they reached the end of the street the angel disappeared and

Stephen Stoned to Death

False Witnesses Make the First Martyr

Stephen, one of the seven deacons chosen to take care of the community of Christians in Jerusalem, was a righteous man who performed many signs and wonders among the people. His deeds aroused enemies for himself in one of the synagogues in the city, and they incited people to say that they heard Stephen speak words of blasphemy against Moses and God. As a result of the accusation, Stephen was brought to trial before the Sanhedrin. False witnesses gave testimony that he spoke endlessly against the temple and the law—deeds whose punishment was execution.

Stephen was sentenced to death by stoning. Taken by force outside of the city, he was stoned with rocks as he cried, "Lord Jesus, receive my spirit." Before he sank into the sleep of death, the martyr managed to call out one last time to God—"Lord, do not hold this sin against them." Righteous people removed Stephen's corpse from the place he was stoned, buried him, and eulogized him.

The stoning of St. Stephen, by G. Vasari.

Mary Falls Asleep and Ascends to Heaven

Thomas Has His Doubts

After the death of Jesus, his mother Mary lived on Mount Zion in the house where the disciples and the first Christians gathered. It would later be the site of the Hagia Zion Church, "mother of all churches."

When it came time for Mary to leave this world, she fell asleep at home surrounded by all of Jesus' disciples except Thomas. After she fell asleep, Jesus came down and took her soul to heaven. The apostles laid the body in a casket and buried it in Gethsemane in the Jehoshaphat Valley. After the burial, Jesus descended again and took Mary's body to heaven as well.

Clockwise from upper left: The Virgin on her deathbed in the crypt of the Church of the Dormition; the Tomb of the Virgin; the crypt in the Church of the Tomb of the Virgin Mary; the Madonna drops her belt, by F. Granacci.

Three days later, tradition says, Thomas arrived in Jerusalem and asked to bow down before Mary. When they told him that Mary had risen to heaven, he refused to believe it and requested that they open the grave for him. When they opened Mary's casket they found it full of lilies and roses, a wonderful scent arising from it. Thomas cast his eyes to the heavens and saw Mary there surrounded by a halo; she uncinched her belt and it fell into the hands of doubting Thomas. The "Traveler from Placentia," who visited Jerusalem in the sixth century, saw the belt displayed in the Church of the Holy Sepulcher.

At the end of the fourth century an ornate church was erected over Mary's burial grotto. The upper church was destroyed and restored several times over the years, but the crypt has been preserved in its original condition.

James the Younger Stoned to Death

James the Younger, the brother of Jesus, who served as a bishop of the Christian sect in Jerusalem, was sentenced to death by the court of the Sadducees despite the opposition of the Pharisees, who thought the decision was a miscarriage of justice.

James was taken up to the Pinnacle, where they demanded that he speak to those gathered below, dissuading them from believing in Jesus. When he refused, he was cast down and stoned.

In the fifth century, a church was built on the place where the house of James had stood, and his bones brought for burial under its altar. The church—today the Armenian Church of Saint James—was dedicated to James the Elder, whose head is also buried there.

James the Younger was considered the first bishop of Jerusalem, and in the Byzantine period they still displayed his chair at the Hagia Zion Church. Today the ornate chair standing in the Armenian cathedral is known as "the chair of St. James" and serves the Armenian patriarch (the successor of James the bishop, according to Armenian tradition) on the saint's name day.

The chair of St. James in the Armenian cathedral.

CHAPTER II

THE BYZANTINE PERIOD

324-634

During the period of Byzantine rule, the Holy Land witnessed one of the largest cultural revolutions of its history—the triumph of Christianity and its rise to political power. The process of the establishment of Christianity in the Holy Land was lengthy: having commenced during the lifetime of Jesus and his Apostles, it continued with the foundation of early Christian communities that were involved in a constant struggle against the monarchy and the pagan, Jewish, and Samaritan inhabitants of the

effected the elevation of Christianity to the primary position in the triad, and the new religion, with its novel socioreligious values, vastly altered the face of Roman society.

In the land of Jesus' birth and death, the spread of Christianity and its accumulation of power were more rapid than in other provinces. In 325 AD, the year in which the first ecumenical Council of Nicaea convened, Christianity became the empire's official religion. In 326 (or 323) the empress Helena, mother of Constantine, traveled to the Holy Land, and the finding of the True Cross as well as the original construction of churches in Ein Karem, Sinai, and the Mount of Olives are attributed to her. Helena's visit augmented the imperial court's sense of obligation towards the Holy Land.

From the early days of Christianity until the fourth and fifth centuries, Christians gathered to worship in build-

Holy Land. A new age dawned in the year 324 AD with the victory of Constantine, the first Christian Roman emperor. With the Holy Land firmly in his hands, a new period of Christian control began that was to continue uninterrupted until the Arab conquest in the seventh century.

Byzantine culture was a fusion of three basic influences: Roman culture, Hellenistic culture, and Christianity. While the first two embodied elements of continuity and tradition, the third represented a revolutionary innovation. Constantine's grasp of the imperial reigns of power

ings that resembled private homes. This type of community edifice, which was called a *domus ecclesiae*, was comprised of a large room (*agape*) for worship, ritual, and communion, and service and storage rooms. There was often also a special baptismal chamber (*baptysterium*) and a room for those who were not yet baptized (*catechumeni*) and were thus forbidden to behold the ceremony of the *eucharistia*, which would subsequently be known as "mass" in the West. A church of this design was discovered under the octagonal church at Capernaum at the site presently regarded as Peter's house. The structure served the Judeo-Christian community of Capernaum until the fourth century, at which time a spacious building measuring approximately 21 by 21 meters was erected on top of these rooms. The building continued to be used as a church until the mid-fifth century, when it was replaced by the octagonal church.

The first four churches in the Holy Land—the Church of the Holy Sepulcher, the Church of the Mount of Olives (the Eleona), the Church of the Nativity in Bethlehem, and the church in Mamre near Hebron—were all constructed under the initiative and with the funding of Emperor Constantine and his mother Helena. Constantine's building projects in Jerusalem quickened the development of the city, so that in the course of the fourth century Jerusalem was transformed into an important pilgrimage center. The short rule of Emperor Julian the Apostate (361-363) imposed a two-year hiatus in the Christianization

of Jerusalem and the Holy Land, but upon his death Christianity once again deepened its roots. Many churches were built, with vast amounts of money invested in their construction. Thousands of pilgrims flocked to the holy places, filling the churches and prompting local clerics and monks to pressure their communities and the state towards further development. Churches were erected in even the smallest of villages, while mid-sized towns often contained several.

Fourteen churches graced the town of Madaba in Transjordan, and in Jerusalem the number of churches and chapels reached several dozen. In the fifth century, the development of Jerusalem benefited from the interest of Empress Eudocia, wife of Emperor Theodosius II. In her lifetime, many public religious buildings were constructed in the holy city and its walls rebuilt. The city reached the pinnacle of its growth in the sixth century, particularly during the rule of Emperor Justinian (527-565), who was renowned for his building projects throughout the empire, including the Holy Land.

In the year 614 the Persians conquered Jerusalem and ruled it for fifteen years until their expulsion by the emperor Heraclius, who restored Byzantine rule to the Holy Land for eight additional years until its conquest by the Muslims in 638.

In the course of the Byzantine period the population of the Holy Land experienced significant growth, which bore implications for the economic and social activity of the region. The increase in population required new stores, markets, inns, and guesthouses, as well as a consonant rise in the number of religious and civic institutions—churches, academies, and social venues. While Christians were already making pilgrimages to the Holy Land in the first centuries of the first millennium, no descriptions of these journeys have survived. Beginning in the fourth century, after the Christianization of the Roman Empire, pilgrimage became a mass phenomenon. From this period are preserved several descriptions of journeys to holy sites, such as those of the pilgrim Egeria and the Traveler from Placentia. Notably, pilgrimage in the Byzantine period was easier and more convenient than in later ages. Sea travel was usually safe, paved roads connected the furthest reaches of the empire, and travel by coach was still possible. (Coaches disappeared from the Holy Land after the Arab conquest in the seventh century, when the roads became unsafe, to return only in the second half of the nineteenth century.) The authorities undertook the establishment of special hostels for pilgrims, enabling them to avoid the regular state hostels, which were considered corrupt. Many pilgrims even settled in Jerusalem and Bethlehem.

CONSTANTINE BUILDS CHURCH OF HOLY SEPULCHER

Emperor Erects Magnificent Edifice on Site of Jesus' Crucifixion and Burial

Emperor Constantine on horseback.

In 326, shortly after his victory over the last of his rivals, Emperor Constantine ordered that the site of Jesus' crucifixion, burial, and resurrection be located. The spot on which the Roman temple of Aphrodite and the civic basilica of Aelia Capitolina stood was shortly identified as the place in question. Immediately after the determination, the emperor commissioned the construction of a magnificent church to mark the focal point for pilgrims from throughout the empire. Today information regarding the shape of the church he built is based on historical sources, especially the description of Eusebius, the bishop of Caesarea, in his book *Vita Constantini.*

In the first stage of construction, the natural hill of Golgotha was leveled so that the site of the crucifixion and the adjacent empty grave would stand out from their surroundings as rock-hewn monuments.

The church complex is comprised of several sections. Entrance to the church was from the east; from the Cardo Maximus, the main street of Aelia Capitolina, steps ascended to the anterior atrium, a trapezoidal courtyard with dimensions of 3 by 22 and 28 meters. Three openings led from the atrium to the basilica, or Martyrium, which was divided by four rows of columns into a nave and four aisles (reconstructions have theorized that the dimensions of the basilica were 36 by 42, with a height of 22 meters. According to modern scholarship, part of the foundations of the Roman basilica were reused for the Christian edifice. The basilica's apse, whose remains were discovered be-

neath the floor of the present-day Catholicon, curved west in the direction of the Holy Garden, an expansive colonnaded courtyard. In the Holy Garden's southeast corner rose the rock of Golgotha, upon which a cross was later affixed. The Chapel of Golgotha was erected here abutting the rock. Beyond the internal atrium

to the west rose the main part of the church, housing the burial grotto, called Anastasis ("resurrection from the dead"). The rock-carved tomb had stood at first in an open courtyard approximately fifteen square meters in size, but in the mid-fourth century a rotunda whose diameter reached thirty-five meters was built around the tomb (the ancient rotunda's lower portions still comprise the base of

today's rotunda to a height of about eleven meters). An internal circle of columns and pilasters supported the dome of the rotunda, which rose to a height of double that of the rotunda's walls. The Church of the Holy Sepulcher was appended by a number of rooms and chapels, altogether creating an architectural complex whose length exceeded 130 meters and whose average width exceeded 60 meters.

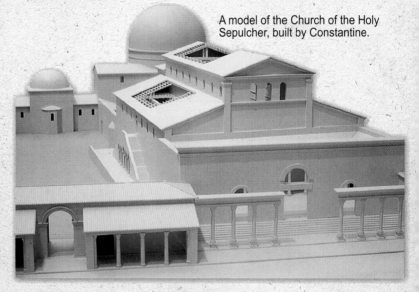

A model of the Church of the Holy Sepulcher, built by Constantine.

The Churches on the Mount of Olives

Until the days of Constantine, the Mount of Olives was one of the focal points of the Christian community of Aelia Capitolina. The mountain enjoyed a special status since it was there, in a grotto, that Jesus taught his disciples in the hours before his death. It was also there that he appeared before them after he rose from the dead, and from there he rose to heaven. The first Christians identified the place of Jesus' ascension as being near to the grotto and, indeed, in the description of Eusebius (c. 260-340), bishop of Caesarea and author of the book *Onomasticon*, the two sites are mentioned together. A certain amount of confusion arose from the description, however, since it seemed to say that it was Helena who built a church on the spot of the ascension, while a later source asserts that the church commemorating the ascension was built adjacent to the Eleona Church in the latter part of the fourth century by a Roman noblewoman named Poemenia.

About the church over the grotto where Jesus taught there is no doubt, at least, that it was built by Helena. It was known by the name of Eleona (from the Greek word *elaion*, meaning "Mount of Olives"). An ornate church that faced west over the city, it was designed on three levels con-

nected to each other by staircases in order to solve the problem of the mountain's steep incline. The entrance was on the lower level, the atrium on the middle level, and the basilica on the uppermost level.

Eleona Convent on the Mount of Olives.

True Cross Revealed to Empress Helena

Tradition attributes the discovery of the True Cross to the Empress Helena (mother of Emperor Constantine) to whom the exact location of the cross was revealed in a dream. When Helena arrived at the spot, a grotto near the site of the crucifixion, she found three crosses. The sign reading "Jesus Christ King of the Jews" was found off to the side, where it could provide no help in identifying the True Cross. In order to divine which of the three was the True Cross, the bishop of Jerusalem and Helena took them to a Roman noblewoman who was mortally ill. When they showed her the first cross, she was shaken by such terrible convulsions that they feared for her life. Her condition worsened when they showed her the second cross, but when they finally brought out the third she became better and rose from her sickbed. The tradition goes on to relate that Helena divided the cross in two and sent one half to her son, Constantine. She had a silver frame made for the second half in which it was kept in a special chapel built for it in the Church of the Holy Sepulcher.

The Emperor Constantine. A mosaic in Hagia Sophia, Istanbul.

Constantine and his mother Helena. An eleventh-century wall painting at the Hosios Loukas Monastery, Greece.

The vision of St. Helena, by P. Veronese.

Helena Tours Ein Karem

326

Builds Two Churches: One for the Children, One for the Baptist

The Emperor Hadrian. A sculpture found in Beit She'an.

When the empress Helena arrived in Ein Karem, birthplace of John the Baptist, she came upon a temple to Aphrodite erected by Emperor Hadrian. Within was a statue of the goddess, a copy of a statue by the famous third

century Greek sculptor Pericles. Helena ordered the temple razed and the statues of Aphrodite and Adonis (standing next to it) shattered, and then built a church dedicated to the children massacred by Herod in the temple's stead. On a hill opposite she commissioned a church dedicated to Elizabeth, mother of John the Baptist. Both structures were destroyed during the Persian conquest and later reconstructed in the Crusader period.

The remains of the first church were discovered accidentally in 1939 when a British artillery regiment set its heavy guns in the courtyard of the Church of Saint John the Baptist in Ein Karem. The floor suddenly collapsed, revealing a splendid Byzantine mosaic floor and a broken statue of Aphrodite underneath.

Ein Karem, by C.W. Wilson.

351

Cross of Light in Jerusalem's Skies

During Pentecost festivities on May 7, 351, a cross of light appeared in the skies over Jerusalem, spreading from Golgotha to the Mount of Olives for hours. The sighting was reported by Bishop Cyril of Jerusalem in a letter sent to Emperor Constantine II. Orthodox churches celebrate the event to this day in an annual ceremony on May 20 (May 7 according to the Julian calendar) in the Church of the Holy Sepulcher.

Egeria in the Holy Land

In 1884, in the library of one of the monasteries in Arezzo, Italy, a Latin document describing a pilgrimage to the Holy Land came to light. Both the beginning and end of the text were missing, as were two pages from the middle. The composition was a letter written by a woman at the end of the ancient period, but the name of the author and other identifying details seemed to be hopelessly lost. In the twentieth century, comparisons with other manuscripts and various citations in different historical documents helped to identify the writer as the nun Egeria, who was, apparently, a wealthy woman of Spanish origin who traveled to the Holy Land in the late fourth century. During her journey, Egeria visited Egypt and Sinai, toured the holy places in the Holy Land and Syria, and even settled in Jerusalem for several years, apparently between 381 and 384. One of the most interesting parts of Egeria's letter is a section describing the Jerusalem Liturgy and the liturgical cycle of the Christian year. Egeria recounts in great detail the religious ceremonies performed in Jerusalem, the prayers and processions, and the experience of participating in them.

The Great Week

A Day Planner

The Sunday that opened the Great Week before Easter was packed with celebrations that began at the Anastasis and near the cross. On Sunday morning people gathered at the Martyrium. Egeria explains the name of the church, which was built at Golgotha behind the cross, as referring to the place where Jesus was tortured.

Before the mass, the archdeacon announced that on that day everyone was to meet at the Eleona Church at the seventh hour (one o'clock in the afternoon). He also informed the crowd that for the whole week believers would meet daily at the Martyrium at the ninth hour. After the mass, the bishop was led with hymns to the Anastasis, where the customary Sunday ceremony was held, after which everyone quickly returned to their homes to eat so as to arrive on time at the Eleona. At the seventh hour the devout climbed the Mount of Olives to the church. When the bishop took his seat they recited the appropriate hymns and read verses.

At the ninth hour (three o'clock in the afternoon) they climbed, again singing hymns, to the Imbomon (bema), the place from which the Lord ascended to heaven, and sat there. The people, notes Egeria, always sat in the presence of the bishop, around whom only deacons were permitted to stand. Here, too, hymns appropriate for the time and place were chanted, while between hymns the people read verses and prayed. When the eleventh hour struck (five o'clock in the afternoon) they read from the Gospel how the children received the Lord with palm branches and fronds, saying, "Blessed is he who comes in the name of the Lord!" The bishop and all of the people then rose and walked down the Mount of Olives, the believers responding to the bishop, "Blessed is he who come in the name of the Lord!" All of the children—even those too young to walk who were held in their parents' arms—carried branches, some of palm and some of olive. They led the bishop from the top of the mountain to the city and through the whole city to the Anastasis, just as the Lord had been led. When they reached the Anastasis it was already evening, but

> ### All of the children—even those too young to walk who were held in their parents' arms—carried branches.

despite the late hour the evening prayer was nonetheless held and then prayers and the dismissal were said next to the cross.

The following day, Monday, all of the services customarily held at the Anastasis were performed from the first cockcrow until morning, and at the third and the sixth hours the same things were done as on all the days of Lent. At the ninth hour everyone gathered at the Martyrium, and there, until the first hour of the night, they recited hymns, read verses, and conducted prayer services. Later they held evening prayers, so that it was already night when the dismissal was held at the Martyrium. After the mass the bishop was led with hymns to the Anastasis. Upon entering the Anastasis the people said one psalm, prayed, and held the dismissal.

Tuesday was like Monday, except that at night, after the dismissal at the Anastasis, the people proceeded to the Eleona, where the bishop entered the grotto in which the Lord taught his disciples and read the words of the Lord written in the Gospel of Matthew, at the place where it says: "Watch out that no one deceives you." It was very late when he finished; the people prayed and held the dismissal.

Wednesday proceeded as had Monday and Tuesday except that after the night mass (Lucernare) at the Martyrium the bishop was led with hymns to the Anastasis, where he entered the cave and stood behind the grille. A presbyter stood before the grille, and he took the evangel and read from the part where Judas Iscariot went to the Jews to determine what they would give him if he turned the Lord over to them. And when the verses were read, Egeria writes, the sighs and moans of the listeners filled the room, and all were moved to tears. A prayer service was held and blessings made, followed by the dismissal.

On Thursday, from daybreak, all that was customarily done at the Anastasis was done by morning,

The garden at Gethsemane.

again by the third hour (nine o'clock in the morning) and again by the sixth hour (twelve noon). At the eighth hour the people gathered according to custom in the Martyrium, earlier than on the other days because the dismissal was held earlier, at approximately the tenth hour. Before the dismissal the archdeacon announced that at the first hour of night everyone was to gather at the Eleona Church.

After the dismissal they approached from Behind the Cross, said one hymn, held a prayer service, and the bishop conducted the Eucharist ceremony with everyone taking part. Sacrifices were never offered Behind the Cross except for on this one day. Afterwards the people went to the Anastasis, prayed, made blessings, and held the dismissal. They hurried home to eat, since immediately after the meal everyone would go to the Eleona and there, until approximately the fifth hour of the night, would chant hymns and recite verses, interspersing them with prayers and even readings from the Gospel about when the Lord spoke to his disciples while sitting in the grotto that is now in the Eleona Church.

From there, at about the sixth hour of the night (midnight), the people ascended, singing hymns, to the Imbomon, where they again recited verses and suitable hymns. At daybreak they made their way, singing hymns all the while, from the Imbomon to the place where the Lord prayed; as is written in the Gospels: "He withdrew about a stone's throw beyond them." According to Egeria, on that spot stood an elegant church. The bishop entered with all of the people,

A Byzantine-period oil lamp.

and they recited the prayers and sung the hymn for that day, and then read from the Gospels where Jesus said to his disciples: "Watch and pray so that you will not fall into temptation."

After another prayer service, everyone, including all of the children, proceeded on foot to Gethsemane with the bishop, singing hymns. Because everyone in the crowd was tired from the vigils and the daily fasting, the group moved slowly, singing hymns, all the way to Gethsemane. More than two hundred church candles were prepared to illuminate their way. When they arrived at Gethsemane, the prayer service was followed by a hymn and a reading from the part of the

Gospels in which the Lord was turned over to the Romans. Egeria relates that the sighing and crying of the assembled was so loud that the sound of it surely reached the city. They then made their way on foot to the city, singing hymns and arriving at the gate at dawn. From there the faithful once again set out through the city, for

Jerusalem from the road leading to Bethany, by D. Roberts.

on this day especially, no one—not rich or poor, young or old—retired from the vigil until morning. And so they led the bishop from Gethsemane up to the city gate, and from there through the entire city up to the cross. Day was beginning to break as they reached the cross. There they read from the Gospels once more how the Lord was brought before Pilate, and all the things that Pilate said to the Lord or to the Jews. Afterwards, the bishop turned to the people and encouraged them, saying that they had labored all night and that they must still labor that day. And then he sent them to their homes to rest until the second hour of the day, when they

would have to return to Golgotha for the Veneration of the Cross. At the sixth hour they would gather in the courtyard Before the Cross and devote themselves to reading verses and prayers until nighttime. After the dismissal Behind the Cross before sunrise, all of the devout immediately went to the Church of Zion to pray by the pillar next to which the Lord was flogged.

After leaving the Church of Zion, the people rested briefly in their homes before returning to Golgotha. The bishop's throne was placed Behind the Cross. Before it stood a cloth-covered table on which was placed a silver and gold box containing a piece of the holy cross. The deacons, who stood around the table, opened the box, and the wood of the cross and the sign with the words "Jesus Christ King of the Jews" were laid on the table. The bishop held the ends of the holy piece of wood in his hands, and the deacons watched while each of the faithful leaned over the table and kissed the holy cross. Egeria

claims that one of the faithful had once taken a bite out of the holy wood, stealing a piece of it, so that now the deacons supervised the ritual, watchful that no such thing should ever happen again. The people passed by, one by one, each one leaning over and touching the cross and the sign, first with their forehead and then with their eyes; they kissed the cross and moved

on, no one touching it with their hands. Afterwards, the deacon took the ring of Solomon and the horn with which kings were anointed in his hands and the believers filed past, kissing both. From approximately the second until the sixth hour the people advanced, entering one way and exiting the other. At the sixth hour they gathered Before the Cross, in a large courtyard that stood between the cross and the Anastasis. So many of the devout assembled that the doors could no longer be opened. The bishop's throne was placed Before the Cross, and from the sixth until the ninth hour verses were recited: every mention of suffering in the Book of Psalms and of the apostles—both from the letters of the apostles and from the Book of Acts. They read from the Book of Prophets where it says

that the Lord must suffer and from the Gospels where suffering is mentioned. The recitation of verses and the singing of hymns continued from the sixth hour until the ninth hour in order that, Egeria notes, the people would realize that all that the prophets had prophesied concerning the suffering of the Lord had indeed come to pass, both according to the Evangelists and the writings of the apostles. For those three hours the people learned that nothing happened that was not foretold, and nothing was said that was not completely fulfilled. Verses from psalms were interspersed among the verses of prayers, and the prayers were suited to the day. Egeria recounts that on that day and during those three hours there was no one who could help but cry in light of the great suffering of the Lord.

Towards the ninth hour the people read from part of the Gospel of John, in which Jesus was resurrected. This was followed by a prayer and dismissal. Immediately after the dismissal the people gathered in the Martyrium and observed the customary practices for that week. After the dismissal they went to the Anastasis

The grotto at Gethsemane.

and read from the Gospel about Joseph asking Pilate for the body of the Lord and laying him in a new grave. A vigil was not announced at the Anastasis, since the people were tired, but it was customary to hold a vigil there. Any one who so desired or was able to do so held a vigil —usually the clergy, the strong, and the young. They recited hymns throughout the night until morning, some from the evening and others from midnight, depending on their strength.

On Saturday at midnight everyone performed the customary ceremonies until the sixth hour, but from the ninth hour the regular Saturday rituals were halted while preparations were made for the Easter vigil at the Martyrium.

Easter in Jerusalem

Egeria Reports on the Ceremonies

A gold ring shaped in the likeness of the Anastasis, found in a sixth-century building in Jerusalem.

Before the Easter vigil, children who had already been baptized were led together with the bishop to the Anastasis. When the bishop passed the grille of the Anastasis one hymn was chanted. Then the bishop held a prayer service for the children and entered with them into the large church, where he held the customary vigil with the entire congregation. After the dismissal in the large church, the believers entered the Anastasis and again read from the Gospel about the resurrection. A prayer service was held and the bishop again performed the Eucharist. Everything was done in haste so that the congregation would not be delayed too long.

The ceremonies during the eight

A baptismal basin from the Byzantine-period at the Church of St. James in Jerusalem.

days of Easter proceeded as they did everywhere during Easter. The grandeur and the schedule throughout the eight days of Easter in the large church, the Anastasis, at the cross, and at Eleona, as well as in Bethlehem and at the Lazarium, were as during

the Epiphany. On Sunday, Monday, and Tuesday the ceremony of the Eucharist was held at the Martyrium and after the dismissal the congregation walked from the Martyrium to the Anastasis singing hymns. On Wednesday they gathered at the Eleona, on Thursday at the Anastasis, on Friday at the Church of Zion, on Saturday Before the Cross, and on Sunday, the eighth day, again at the large church—the Martyrium. During those eight days of Easter, after the meals, the bishop, the clergy, all of the children who had already been baptized, and those from among the people who wished to do so, climbed up to the Eleona to chant hymns and hold prayer services both in the Eleona Church and at the Imbomon. Towards evening they descended to the Anastasis singing hymns. Thus they did each of the eight days. But on Easter Sunday, after the dismissal at the Anastasis, the people led the bishop singing hymns to the Church of Zion. When they arrived they sang the appropriate hymns, held a prayer service, and read from the part of the Gospel about that day when, at the very place the Church of Zion stood, the Lord came in to a closed room to see his disciples. They read that one of the disciples, Thomas, was not there,

A mosaic floor from the Basilica of the Nativity, built by Constantine in 332.

and that when he returned and the other apostles told him they had seen the Lord, he told them, "Unless I see...I will not believe it." After reading this, at about the second hour of the night, a prayer service was again held and then everyone returned home.

On the eighth day of Easter Sunday, immediately after the sixth hour, the entire congregation ascended with the bishop to the Eleona. At first they sat in the church, chanting hymns and holding a prayer service appropriate for the time and place, then again ascended from there singing hymns to the Imbomon, where they did similar things. When the time came, all the people led the bishop singing hymns to the Anastasis and entered the

Anastasis at the customary time of the evening prayer, Lucernare. After Lucernare was said at the Anastasis and next to the cross, the people led the bishop with hymns to the Church of Zion. Upon their arrival, hymns were recited and the Gospel read again from the section where on the eighth day of Passover the Lord entered the place where his disciples were and rebuked Thomas, who had not believed. They then read the entire chapter. A prayer service was held and after the faithful were blessed in the customary manner, each one returned home as on the first day of Easter.

Above: The aedicule of the Holy Tomb, by D. Roberts.

A Byzantine-period oil lamp.

Epiphany

The Epiphany was celebrated in Jerusalem on January 6. The pages describing the ceremonies on the eve of the holiday are missing from Egeria's letter, but from other sources we know that the festivities of the evening began with a ceremony in the Grotto of the Shepherds in Bethlehem and continued in the Grotto of the Nativity and the Church of the Nativity. The believers and the bishop of Jerusalem then returned to the holy city, reciting Psalm 118:26 on the way.

Here Egeria takes up the story. Immediately upon the procession's pre-dawn arrival, the bishop entered the Anastasis, where the lamps were already lit, together with all of the faithful. A psalm was recited, a prayer service held, and the bishop blessed the assembly. Afterwards he and the believers returned to their homes,

Above: The tomb of Lazarus in Bethany, by L. Mayer.
Below: A drawing of a pilgrim ship from the fourth century found in the oldest part of the Church of the Holy Sepulcher.

curtains with gold hems, and all of its gold ritual utensils and precious gems were displayed along with innumerable candles, lanterns, lamps, and other ritual objects.

On the first day, the ceremony was held in the large church in Golgotha. After the service in the church, during which a sermon was given, verses read, and hymns sung, the believers walked, singing more hymns, to the Anastasis, where the dismissal took place at about the sixth hour. And so it went for three days.

The fourth day was celebrated at Eleona, the church on the Mount of Olives that struck Egeria as lovely. On the fifth day the locale moved to the Lazarium (the Church of Lazarus), situated about fifteen hundred steps outside of Jerusalem. On the sixth day services were held at the Church of Zion, on the seventh day at the Anastasis, and on the eighth day at a spot near the cross.

The Epiphany was thus commemorated in Jerusalem for eight days as the festivities moved between the holy sites. In Bethlehem too the Epiphany was celebrated for an entire eight days. On the eve of the holiday, after the devout had returned with the bishop to Jerusalem, all of the clergy and monks in charge of the church in Bethlehem continued reciting psalms and hymns.

The fortieth day of the Epiphany was also celebrated with great pomp, this time at the Anastasis. Sermons were delivered, and the crowd heard the evangel relating how on the fortieth day Joseph and Mary brought Jesus to the Temple, where Simeon and the prophetess Anna, daughter of Phanuel, saw and spoke about the Lord. The Sacraments and mass followed.

though the monks remained to recite hymns until daybreak. At the second hour, everyone gathered in the large church at Golgotha. On that day, the church at Golgotha, the Anastasis Church, the Chapel of the Cross, and the Church of the Nativity in Bethlehem were ornamented with elaborate decorations. The church in Jerusalem was decorated with silk screens and

The Festival of the Encaenia

The Church of the Holy Sepulcher was consecrated by Constantine on September 14, 335, in an event accompanied by great festivities. The date corresponded to the day of the finding of the cross, and was afterwards celebrated yearly with solemn magnificence. Egeria's letter provides an account of the first three days of the annual ceremonies. She relates that the days during which the church at Golgotha, which is called the Martyrium, and the church at Anastasis were dedicated to God were called the Encaenia, and that the festival of the Encaenia was celebrated for eight days. For many days beforehand, monks, apotactites, and pilgrims from all the provinces streamed into Jerusalem. Egeria estimates that more than forty or fifty bishops also assembled in Jerusalem together with many of their clergymen. During the festivities, all of the churches were decorated as if for Easter or the Epiphany, and people gathered daily in the various holy places. On Sunday and Monday the believers went to the Martyrium, and on Tuesday they convened at the Eleona Church, on the site of the grotto where the Lord taught his disciples on the Mount of Olives.

Constantine and his mother Helena at the foot of the cross. Central part of a sixth- to tenth-century tryptich.

Saint Jerome Arrives in Holy Land

Biblical Translator Settles in Bethlehem

Among those arriving in the Holy Land from Rome in the fourth century was Eusebius Hieronymus (Saint Jerome), one of the Latin church fathers (342-420). Hieronymus, a native of Dalmatia, was a monk who lived as a hermit in the Syrian Desert and studied Hebrew with Jewish teachers in Syria and the Holy Land. He was the secretary of Pope Damasus I (382-384), and in Rome directed a group of contemplative nuns who attempted to live a life similar to that of the monks in Egypt. Under the influence of Pope Damasus, Hieronymus inserted corrections into the Latin version of the New Testament.

After the pope's death in 384, Hieronymus and his students de-parted Rome for Bethlehem, which they reached in 386. On the way they traveled through Syria and Egypt seeking to learn, as many others had before them, about the monastic lifestyle.

Hieronymus settled in Bethlehem, where he founded a monastery and translated the Old Testament from Hebrew into Latin. His translation became known from the thirteenth century onward as the Vulgate, a Latin word meaning "popular." Hieronymus died and was buried in Bethlehem, though his bones were later moved from the crypt in the Church of the Nativity to the Basilica of Santa Maria Maggiore in Rome.

Saint Jerome, by B. Cavarozzi.

Four Holy Nuns

Widows Join Jerome

In the second half of the fourth century, four nuns journeyed from Europe to the Holy Land, where they founded and led convents. All four were canonized after their deaths. Saint Paula (347-404), a wealthy Roman matron from an aristocratic family, studied with Hieronymus in Rome. After being widowed at the age of thirty-three, she dedicated her life to study, and when Hieronymus departed for the Holy Land in 385, she and her daughter, Eustochium (370-419), accompanied him. In Bethlehem Paula built four

Saint Paula, by the master of the Staus Madonna.

Saint Eustochium, by the master of the Staus Madonna.

monasteries, a hostel for pilgrims, and a school where Hieronymus taught children Greek and Latin. After her death in 404 she was entombed in the crypt of the Church of the Nativity.

Paula's daughter perpetuated her mother's work, leading the nuns, learning Greek and Hebrew, and assisting Hieronymus in his work of translating the Old Testament. Saint Eustochium died a swift death in 419 a short time after a mob plundered and set fire to her convent.

Saint Melania the Elder (342-410) was another wealthy Roman matron from a noble family who was widowed young—in her case, at the age of twenty-two—and led a monastic life ever after. In 372 she left Rome, visited Egypt, and arrived in the Holy Land, where she established a double monastery on the Mount of Olives: a convent with separate wings for monks. She returned to Rome in 399. She fled the Visigoth invasion to Malta, and then returned to Jerusalem, where she died. Saint Melania's granddaughter, Saint Melania the Younger (383-439), was a devout and ascetic woman who, after the deaths of her two children, sold her property and dedicated the revenues to the poor, to the church, and for the emancipation of slaves. During the invasion of the Visigoths she fled, together with her husband, to Africa, where she established two convents. In 417 Melania the Younger and her husband reached the Holy Land and joined Hieronymus' group in Bethlehem. One year after the death of her husband in 432, she moved to Jerusalem, founded a convent for nuns on the Mount of Olives, and dedicated her life to prayer and good works. She died in Jerusalem on December 31, 439.

All of these convents were closed after the deaths of their benefactresses.

Hagia Zion on Mount Zion

Hagia Zion was considered "the mother of all churches." It was built on the site where, according to tradition, the Last Supper was held and Jesus was revealed to his disciples after his death. It is known that the Christians already maintained a small church on the site at the beginning of the second century. Another church was built there in 347, and in 390 a large basilica was erected. This last church was called Hagia Zion. Adjacent to it was built a small chapel dedicated to the Last Supper. An Armenian traveler who visited the site in the seventh century related that the ceiling of the chapel was painted with scenes of the holy supper of the Redeemer. Displayed in the church was Jesus' pillar of the flagellation and crown of thorns, as well as the lamp that served him when he taught his disciples. Also preserved in the church was the stone about which it was said "the stone the builders rejected has become the capstone," and the stone with which Saint Stephen was martyred. Hagia Zion became even more important after the bones of Saint Stephen, discovered in the village of Jimal, were transferred there. In the seventh century it started to be identified as the place where Mary, mother of Jesus, fell into eternal sleep, and a chapel dedicated to her was established in the church's north-west corner. Hagia Zion was razed during the Persian invasion in 614, restored twenty years later, and again demolished at the end of the tenth century.

Hagia Zion, a detail from the Madaba Map.

Theodosius Builds Church of the Tomb of the Virgin

At the end of the fourth century, the burial place of Mary, mother of Jesus, from which she also ascended to heaven, was determined to be in the Jehoshaphat Valley, in accordance with a tradition mentioned in the Apocrypha from the period. The Church of the Tomb of the Virgin was apparently built at the end of the fourth century by Theodosius I. It was designed in the shape of a cross with Mary's tomb in the center. In the sixth century, an octagonal upper portion was added to the church and the lower portion became a crypt. The upper church was destroyed in the Early Arab Period, but the lower level has been preserved to this day.

Above: The Church of the Tomb of the Virgin, by E. Pierotti.
Left: The crypt in the Church of the Tomb of the Virgin, built by Theodosius.

415
Stephen's Bones Discovered

The location of the bones of Saint Stephen, the first Christian martyr, was revealed in a dream to a clergyman from Jerusalem in 415. The bones were uncovered not far from Jerusalem, in the village of Jimal, in a crypt later identified by the Christians as that of Paul's teacher, Gamliel the Elder. The bones were brought to Hagia Zion on Mount Zion, where they were preserved until 439, at which time they were transferred to the newly built basilica of Saint Stephen north of Damascus Gate.

The remains of the Basilica of Saint Stephen at the monastery of Saint Etienne in Jerusalem.

444
Empress Eudocia Builds Jerusalem
Empress directs building projects, including church dedicated to St. Stephen

Empress Eudocia, wife of Emperor Theodosius II, visited Jerusalem in 438 and again several years later in 444, at which time she settled there in a type of self-imposed exile after arguing with her husband. Eudocia built an ornate church where Stephen, the first Christian martyr, was stoned and buried. The edifice was constructed in 439 and consecrated on May 15 of that year in the presence of Cyril, the bishop of Alexandria, who was invited by the empress to honor the ceremony with his attendance. The remains of the saint were finally transferred to their permanent resting places, though the building of the entire church was completed only a year later. The magnificent church was reconsecrated in 460. (Some claim that two different churches dedicated to Saint Stephen were built on the Mount of Olives: the first was consecrated in 439, and the saint's bones were transferred there from Hagia Zion. When the second, more elaborate church was built in 460, the saint's bones were moved once again.)

During his stay in the holy city, Cyril was also invited to preside over the burial ceremony of the remains of martyrs from Persia and Armenia in a small shrine donated by the empress to the convent established by Melania the Younger. Melania herself had purchased a few relics of Stephen to put in the chapel in her convent, and Eudocia did the same, later taking the relics to Constantinople. Eudocia continued her building work in Jerusalem after she settled permanently in the holy city, and was probably re-

Empress Eudocia.

sponsible for constructing the basilica at the Pool of Siloam mentioned by the Traveler from Placentia at the end of the sixth century. The empress' most impressive building project was the reconstruction of the wall surrounding the southern end of the city to include both Mount Zion and the Pool of Siloam.

Population Booms! Hol

The significant growth in the number and size of cities in the Holy Land was the direct result of the growth in the country's population. The findings of the excavations at Scythopolis (present-day Beit She'an), for example, demonstrate that during the Byzantine period the city expanded markedly towards the south. Evidence of a population increase can be found in Jerusalem as well—especially in the vicinity of today's Jewish Quarter and south of the Temple Mount. Similar data has also been found indicating significant increases in the population density of Caesarea and Gerasa (present-day Jerash), cities that had previously been sparsely populated. The large cities of the Negev—Shivta, Rehovot in the Negev, and apparently also Halutza, the biggest of them all—developed during this period from small, ancient settlements into large-scale cities with ornate civic buildings and large, impressive churches.

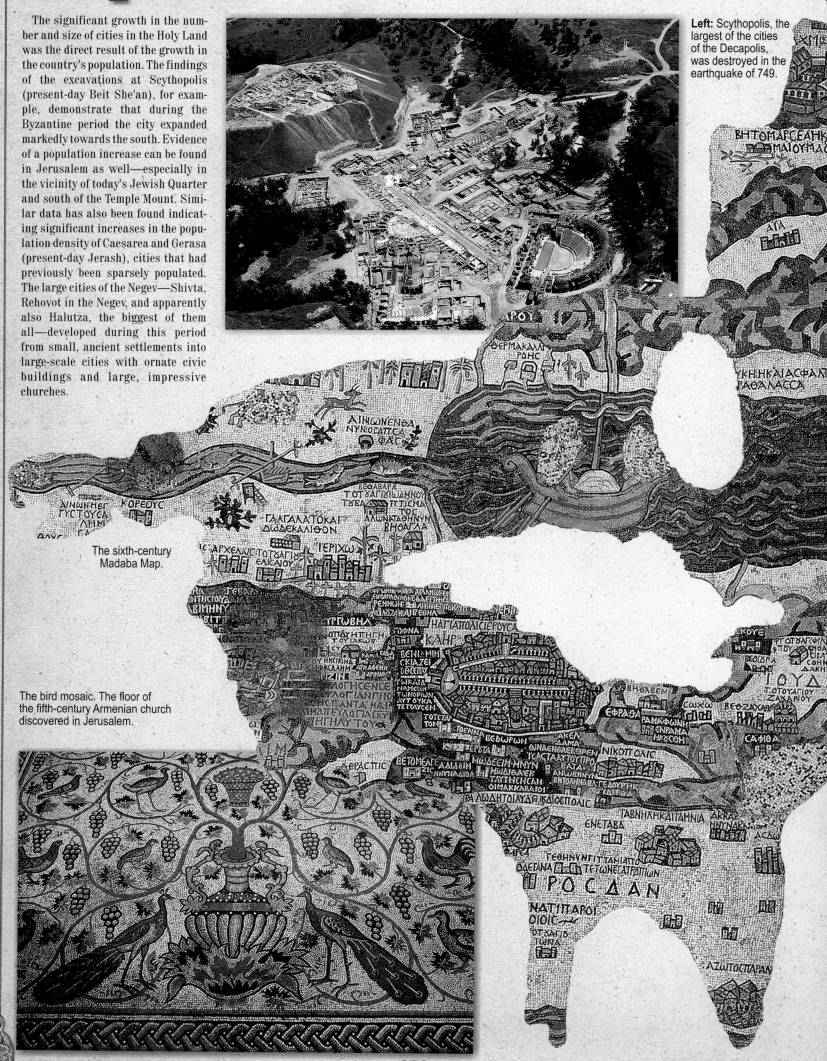

Left: Scythopolis, the largest of the cities of the Decapolis, was destroyed in the earthquake of 749.

The sixth-century Madaba Map.

The bird mosaic. The floor of the fifth-century Armenian church discovered in Jerusalem.

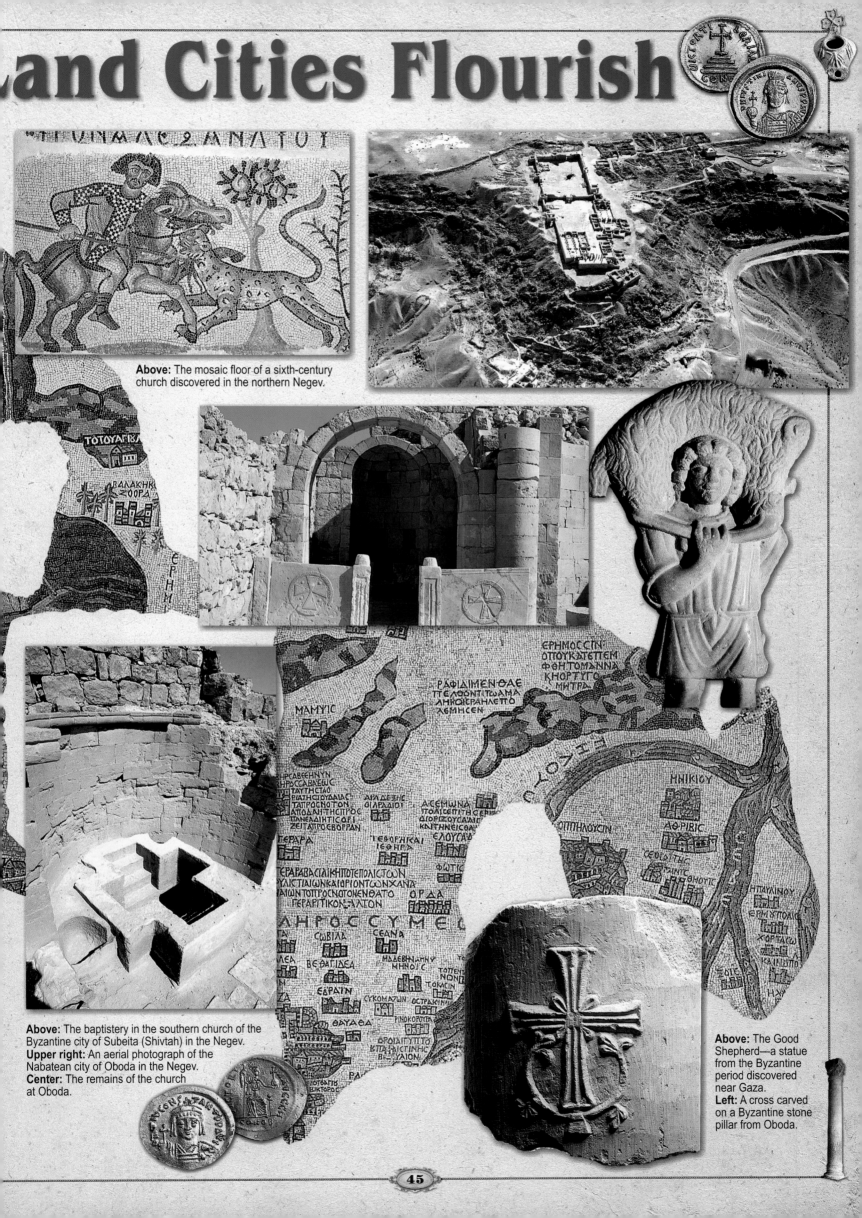

and Cities Flourish

Above: The mosaic floor of a sixth-century church discovered in the northern Negev.

Above: The baptistery in the southern church of the Byzantine city of Subeita (Shivtah) in the Negev.
Upper right: An aerial photograph of the Nabatean city of Oboda in the Negev.
Center: The remains of the church at Oboda.

Above: The Good Shepherd—a statue from the Byzantine period discovered near Gaza.
Left: A cross carved on a Byzantine stone pillar from Oboda.

Monasticism in the Holy Land
The Contemplative Life

Saint Catherine's Monastery in Sinai.

Christian monasticism reached the Holy Land at the end of the third century CE, became established during the fourth century, and reached its peak in the fifth and sixth centuries. The monastic movement in the Holy Land acquired many admirers and had a significant effect on life there during the Byzantine period. The leaders of the monks intervened in central issues that influenced the fate of the Holy Land for generations—especially matters concerning religious disputes. Although the number of monks was not large in comparison to the population in general, and it is doubtful whether it was ever greater than several tens of thousands, they nonetheless had considerable impact on the social and religious life of the Byzantine Holy Land, as well as on the physical map of the country.

Remains of monasteries are scattered throughout the Holy Land, some within cities and settled areas—generally adjacent to a holy site or as part of the central church complex—and some in outlying rural areas. Most famous were the monasteries established in the wilderness, especially the Judean Desert (then called "Jerusalem's Desert") and the Sinai desert, near the traditional

Mount Sinai. Many of the monasteries were severely hurt during the Persian invasion of the Holy Land (614 CE) and declined even further during the Muslim period, but quite a few others survived. Some Greek monasteries that have existed almost continuously since the Byzantine period are still functioning today.

From the point of view of their internal organization, the monasteries can

be divided into two principal types: the laura, the contemplative monastery; and the *coenobium*, the cooperative monastery. The latter revolved around monks who lived in complete communality and with scrupulous obedience as an organized community under the authority of an abbot.

During the fourth decade of the ▶

Above: The carved stone stairs leading to the summit of Mount Sinai, by D. Roberts.
Left: The church at Saint Catherine's, built in the sixth century.

fourth century, the monk Chariton developed a lifestyle that combined contemplation with the coenobitic life. This type of lifestyle was dubbed "laura," meaning "path" in Greek. The laura was so called after the paths that ran between the monks' cells and symbolized the corridor leading from this world to the next. Established in isolated places, lauras provided the setting for a reclusive monastic life. A

of apprenticeship preceding the almost total seclusion of the laura.

Remains of dozens of Byzantine monasteries have been discovered in the Holy Land. Some are the ruins of a simple group of buildings or a few natural caves improved slightly by carving out the rock. More often, the remains are those of a richer complex including a church, dining room, bakery and kitchen, administrative

Above: The monastery at Kursi was the largest monastery in the Holy Land during the Byzantine period.
Left: The Quarantel Monastery, founded by Chariton.

buildings, and cisterns. If the monastery was built near a pilgrimage site, it would also have had a hostel for pilgrims. Among the monasteries of this type are the three desert monasteries that exist to this day (after renovations and rebuilding): the Mar Saba Monastery, the Monastery of George the Chozibite at Wadi Kelt, and the Quarantel Monastery founded by the monk Chariton on a cliff overlooking Jericho.

A hermit saint, by G. Muziano.

Saint Euthymius 405

Holy Land Hermit

One of the founders and key figures of monasticism in the Holy Land was Euthymius the Great, an Armenian bishop from Melitene (present-day Malatya in eastern Turkey) born in 377. His parents, who prayed for a child, had vowed to dedicate any offspring to the service of God, and, in 395, at the age of eighteen, Euthymius was ordained into the priesthood and, despite his youth, put in charge of supervising all of the monks in the district.

In 405, after ten years of service, Euthymius made his home in a hermit's cave and learned how to make rope, a craft considered to be inferior in the external world but fairly popular among monks. Later he went into seclusion in various places in the Judean Desert. In 411 Euthymius founded a laura whose remains still exist in Wadi Mukallik, a canyon descending from Jerusalem to the Dead Sea. That same year he settled in a cave in the Judean Desert. In 428 Euthymius founded a large laura similar to that of Chariton in the same

area. Its remains can be seen today within the ruins of Khan el-Akhmar, some three kilometers south of Ma'aleh Adumim.

Euthymius, a member of the second generation of Judean Desert monks, penned a rule that encompassed all the various aspects of monastic life and organized the daily life of a monk in a schedule that included physical labor. According to his system, which was later given official sanction by Saint Sabas, a monk who wished to be in seclusion was required to first live a coenobitic life for a time.

Many miracles were attributed to Euthymius. It is said that a group of four hundred Armenian pilgrims once arrived in the Holy Land, and on their way to the River Jordan wanted to visit a laura of one of their countrymen. The monk in charge of the larder lost his composure upon seeing the masses of pilgrims he had to feed, and Euthymius reenacted the miracle of the loaves, feeding the entire group.

Euthymius was famous for his asceticism, and he had many admirers. Pilgrims often visited him, seeking spiritual guidance. Among them

Ornamentation on the base of a column from saint Martyrius Monastery.

was Eudocia, the wife of Emperor Theodosius II, who lived in Jerusalem for the last eighteen years of her life, and traveled to the desert to see and consult with Euthymius.

Saint Euthymius died in 473 at the age of ninety-six. His feast day is January 20. Five years after his death, Martyrius, the bishop of Jerusalem, and Euthymius' pupils transformed the laura into a coenobium. The new monastery and church were consecrated in 482 and Euthymius' bones transferred there.

monk's cell was a building, hut, or cave. The cells themselves were sometimes narrow and uncomfortable, but could also be spacious and comfortable residential complexes. The laura monks, who were also led by an abbot, remained alone in their cells six days a week and assembled in the monastery for a common meal on Saturday evening and joint prayer on Sunday. At these gatherings they would collect the produce for market and receive food supplies and raw materials for work. Some monks did not leave the laura for months or even years, living in total seclusion in the heart of the desert. In general, life in a laura was considered the highest form of monastic service, and many monks viewed the coenobium as a necessary period

Saint Gerasimus Establishes New Laura

SAIN

One of Saint Euthymius' students and friends was Saint Gerasimus, a native of Asia Minor. In 455 Gerasimus founded a laura about five kilometers north of the Dead Sea and one kilometer south of Ein Hogla. Within the laura he established a coenobitic monastery for training candidates for a life of seclusion. A monk named John Moschus, who lived in the late sixth century and beginning of the seventh century, wrote a history of monks and monasteries. He relates in his book *The Spiritual Meadow* that Saint Gerasimus pulled a thorn from the paw of a lion who then befriended him and performed errands for his monks. When Gerasimus died in 475 (two years after Euthymius), the lion, who was inconsolable, lay down on his friend's new grave and died. It is in reference to this story that Saint Gerasimus is represented in art as a lion.

Gerasimus' monastery was destroyed and rebuilt several times. It was most recently renovated at the end of the nineteenth century and today is called Deir Hajla—a name reminiscent of the name Beit Hogla, a

settlement on the edge of the territory of the tribe of Judah *(Joshua 15:6)* that appears in the Madaba Map.

The inner courtyard at Deir Hajla Monastery.

Saint Sabas, who was born in Cappadocia, in 439, came to the Holy Land at the age of eighteen. Staying at first in a monastery in Jerusalem, he proceeded from there to Euthymius' laura in the Judean Desert. Since he was young, Euthymius entrusted him to Saint Theoctistus, who mentored him for seventeen years.

Sabas lived as a hermit for several years in various secluded sites in the Holy Land. It is said that a lion guarded him in the desert. After pupils gathered around him, he founded a laura in his place of seclusion on the southern slope of the Kidron gorge in 483. Due to the personal example provided by Sabas, the laura—which came to be known as the Great Laura—flourished, and the number of monks in it grew to one hundred and fifty. In 492, when his friend and countryman Theodosius was elected monastic superior of all coenobitic monks, the patriarch of Jerusalem granted Sabas supervision over all lauritic monks in the Holy Land. Sabas founded four lauras, among

Wadi Kelt's Monastery of Saint George

An ancient decoration at the Monastery of Saint George.

the caves along its cliffs in which hermit monks have lived in isolation intermittently from that time until the present. Today the monastery is known as the Monastery of Saint George after a Cypriot monk named George the Chozibite who lived in the sixth century. The monastery was renovated between 1878 and 1901, and the bell tower was built in 1952.

Left: The Monastery of Saint George.
Below: Balconies to monks' cells at the Monastery of Saint George.

The Monastery of Saint George was established in the Judean Desert in the 480s by John of Thebes, later called John the Chozibite after Choziba, the site in Wadi Kelt on which the monastery was located, approximately five kilometers west of Jericho. Even today visitors to the wadi can see

ABAS FOUNDS THE GREAT LAURA

them the New Laura in Tekoa (507), which emerged out of a rebellion by the monks, and six cooperative monasteries. Sabas also founded four hostels: two in Jerusalem—one opposite the Citadel (on the property of the present-day Anglican Christ Church and the mosque behind it)—and two in Jericho.

Sabas died on December 5, 532, at the age of ninety-three. In 1256 his bones were transferred from his monastery to Venice, but were returned on December 11, 1965, after Pope Paul VI's visit to the Holy Land.

The monastery of Saint Sabas in the Kidron gorge is the only monastery in the Judean Desert that has existed continuously from ancient times until today. Today it is called Mar Saba, *mar* meaning "Christian saint" in Arabic. The Mar Saba Monastery was renovated with funds provided by the Russian government in 1840. After having been robbed and damaged five years previously in the peasant and Bedouin rebellion against the rule of Mohammad Ali and his son Ibrahim

Pasha (1834-1835), and then shaken by an earthquake in 1837, it was refurbished as a fortified village surrounded by a wall. Today the monastery, inhabited by Greek Orthodox monks, is coenobitic. Since entrance to it is forbidden to women, a "Women's Tower" was erected outside of its walls, apparently by the empress Eudocia (though tradition attributes it to Saint Sabas' mother). The monastery's library, which was housed in the tower and contained a number of rare manuscripts, was transferred in the 1970s to the Greek Orthodox patriarchate in Jerusalem.

Clockwise from upper left: The church in Mar Saba, by D. Roberts; aerial photograph of Mar Saba Monastery, "The Women's Tower" at upper left; Mar Saba Monastery in 1631, by E. Roger; Saint Sabas in his coffin; the Skull Room at Mar Saba.

Theodosius the Cenobiarch

One of the greatest of the monks in the third generation of the Judean Desert monks was Theodosius the Cenobiarch. Theodosius, who was born in Cappadocia in 423, came to the Holy Land in 450 and remained for a period at a monastery in Jerusalem. In 455 he entered a monastery situated on the road to Bethlehem, but an effort to appoint him abbot prompted his departure, and he finally found lodging in the cave east of Bethlehem where, according to tradition, the three Magi stayed on the first night of their flight from Herod. A small group of monks—Greeks, Armenians, Georgians, and others—gathered around Theodosius and dedicated themselves to caring for the sick, elderly, and mentally ill. The group grew in size until 476, when Theodosius finally founded a large coenobitic monastery numbering four hundred monks. It

The Monastery of Saint Theodosius.

contained a large church for Greek speakers and three prayer houses for those who spoke other languages. In 492 the patriarch of Jerusalem appointed Theodosius monastic superior of all coenobitic monasteries in the Holy Land. Hence his Greek sobriquet, "Cenobiarch."

Theodosius died on January 11, 529 at the age of one hundred and five. Today the monastery he established is called the Monastery of Saint Theodosius. It has been rebuilt several times. Within the confines of the monastery is the cave in which Theodosius secluded himself and in which he is buried along with his mother, sister, and Sophia, the mother of Saint Sabas. The bones of the monk and historian John Moschus were also transferred here after he died in Rome. The monastery is located seven kilometers east of Bethlehem on the road to Abu Dis.

The Bishop Who Refused to Be Ordained 497
Modest Monk Hides Out

The monk John Hesychast (454-559) was born into a distinguished Armenian family, and at the age of twenty-eight was ordained as a bishop in Armenia. Ten years later he retired from the bishopric to become a hermit in the Judean Desert. In 491 he settled in the Kidron gorge near Saba's laura and pursued a contemplative life. As befitted his status as an apprentice contemplative, he was given maintenance duties at the laura that he

Left: Inside Mar Saba Monastery.
Right: Monks' cells at Mar Saba, by C.W. Wilson.

obediently fulfilled, carrying water from the valley, cooking for the builders, and frequently retiring alone to the desert. Near the end of 497, Sabas declared John ready to be ordained, and took him to Jerusalem. Before the patriarch ordained him as a priest, John asked him to hear his confession in private. Only then did the monk disclose that he was already a bishop. The patriarch, keeping John's secret, told Sabas only that what John had disclosed to him made it impossible to ordain him. Only later did the monks of Mar Saba Monastery learn that the holy contemplative was a bishop.

Emperor Justinian—the Great Builder

In 1884, during preparatory excavations for the building of a new Greek Orthodox church, an ancient mosaic map was uncovered in the city of Madaba in Jordan. Large portions of the map were damaged in the process of the discovery, but the section depicting Jerusalem survived unharmed. From it we learn a great deal about the sights in Jerusalem in the second half of the sixth century, at the end of the life of Emperor Justinian (527-565). The Madaba Map clearly shows the main streets of Jerusalem: the Cardo Maximus, leading from Damascus Gate in the northern wall to the Nea Gate in the internal wall of the Nea Church, and the street almost parallel to it, the Cardo Vallensis. The southern portion of the Cardo Maximus was built in the days of Justinian, and connected the Nea

The enormous vaults that supported the Nea Church.

In the cellar of the Nea Church was found a Greek inscription noting that the church was built through the generosity of Emperor Justinian.

Church—"Nea" meaning "new" in Greek—with the Church of the Holy Sepulcher. The splendid street was wide and lined by rows of columns on either side; the religious processions of the city passed along it. Construction of the Nea Church, whose full name was the New Church of Saint ▶

Mary, Mother of God, was also completed during the reign of Justinian. Details of the magnificent church are known mainly from the biography of Saint Sabas written by his student Cyril of Scythopolis and the writings of Procopius of Caesarea on public buildings constructed during the time

Remains of the capitals of the Nea Church.

Remains of the Cardo Maximus.

of Justinian. From Procopius' precise description we know that the Nea Church stood on the side of a mountain. The hilly terrain did not allow the church to be built along its planned dimensions, so the architects widened the plot by means of a large

terrace supported by huge piers. The exact location of the Nea Church was unknown until the discovery of its ruins during the modern excavations in Jerusalem's Jewish Quarter. The network of giant vaults on which the church was built is especially impressive. An inscription on the southern wall of the fourth vault confirms the

identity of the entire structure as the Nea, though a question remains as to its date. The inscription apparently relates to the completion of the construction of the underground vaults in 535, while the entire structure was consecrated, according to testimony of Cyril of Scythopolis, some eight years later, in 543.

Church of the Nativity Rebuilt

Justinian Does It Again!

The Church of the Nativity in Bethlehem was one of the first three churches built by Constantine in the Holy Land. Constructed as an ornate basilica, it enjoyed the benefit of generous governmental funding. The goal of the builders was twofold: to

The Basilica of the Nativity built by Emperor Justinian.

Emperor Justinian holding the Hagia Sophia. A mosaic in the Hagia Sophia.

A detail from a Byzantine mosaic floor in the Basilica of the Nativity.

commemorate the birthplace of Jesus and build a church for gatherings and worship. Accordingly, the structure was designed in two distinct but connected sections. Over the grotto in which Jesus was born was built an octagonal structure from which the basilica extended westward. The basilica itself, whose length and width were almost equal, was divided into a nave and four aisles by four rows of columns. A wide portal with three steps led from its nave to the octagonal structure above the grotto. Elaborate mosaics and marble covered the floor and walls of the basil-

ica. This original church was demolished, under unclear circumstances, in the period of the emperor Justinian—perhaps during the Samaritan rebellion (524) that resulted in the destruction of a great many churches.

After a time, the Church of the Nativity was rebuilt. The previous octagonal edifice over the grotto was reconstructed in the triapsidal shape of the structure that stands on the spot today. The columns of the nave were replaced and a narthex added, causing the atrium to be moved west. The walls of the new church, as well as its grotto and facade, were overlaid with

marble and gilded mosaics, and a marble floor was placed over the previous floor. Two new entrances to the grotto were added. The western facade of the Church of the Nativity was enhanced with an elaborate mosaic depicting the birth of Jesus and the adoration of the Magi. According to legend, this mosaic, in which the Magi could be seen approaching from the east, saved the church from the Persians who invaded the Holy Land in the seventh century. The Persians, not wanting to desecrate the images of their holy forefathers, refrained from damaging the church.

A Byzantine baptismal basin in the Church of the Nativity in Bethlehem.

The Traveler from Placentia

One of the most interesting pilgrimage histories that survives from the Byzantine period is that of an anonymous pilgrim usually called the "Traveler from Placentia" (present-day Piacenza, in Italy). The Traveler from Placentia toured the entire Holy Land. Beginning his journey in Constantinople, he made his way through Lebanon to the Holy Land, where he visited Galilee and the Sea of Galilee, the Jordan Valley, Samaria, Jerusalem, Bethlehem and Jericho, and the cities of the Negev. He continued to Egypt and then returned to Jerusalem, where he fell ill and was miraculously cured. Afterwards, he departed the holy city for Jaffa, Caesarea, Galilee, Syria, and Mesopotamia, whence he returned to his homeland. The journey took three years and its story was set down in writing only after the writer's return to Placentia, which may account for some inaccuracies in the travelogue. From the text, it seems that the Traveler made his way in the company of others, some of whom were from his hometown (one of them, mentioned by name, died during the journey).

The spring at Cana, by D. Roberts.

Traveler Retraces Jesus' Steps

The Traveler from Placentia and his party arrived from Lebanon at the Samaritan camp at the foot of Mount Carmel one mile from Shikmona. A half-mile above the camp was the monastery of Saint Elisha. The Traveler reports the existence on Mount Carmel of a small round stone that made a sound when moved, though it was solid. It was a stone with certain powers, he wrote, as any woman or animal who touched it would never

Above: The Synagogue Church in Nazareth.
Left: The Tabor, by Raboisson, 1887.

miscarry. From the coast, the Traveler turned inland to Sepphoris on the border of Galilee, where he admired the jug and the bread of Saint Mary and saw the bench on which she was sitting when the angel appeared to her. From Sepphoris he traveled three miles to the village of Cana, where Jesus attended the wedding and performed the miracle of the water and the wine. The Traveler sat on the same seat that Jesus had, even carving the names of his parents on it. He also saw two of the water jugs, one of which he filled with wine and carried to the altar. After bathing in the spring at Cana in order to be blessed, he went on to Nazareth, where, he wrote, many miraculous events occurred. He relates that in the synagogue he saw the book where the Lord wrote the letters of the alphabet. In ▶

the same synagogue was a beam on which, according to tradition, Jesus had sat with the other children. The Traveler writes that while Christians were able to both move and pick up the beam, Jews were totally unable to make it budge. He reports that the home of Saint Mary was a basilica, and that the Nazarene women surpassed all Hebrew women in the Holy Land in their beauty, which they inherited from Mary, who was related to them. He notes that despite the fact that little love was lost between the Jews and the Christians, all of these women were nonetheless full of love, and that, to his eyes, the entire district resembled paradise. Though the grains and fruit resembled those in Egypt, the wine, oil, and fruit were superior to their Egyptian counterparts. The millet, according to the Traveler, grew higher than a man.

From Nazareth the Traveler continued to Mount Tabor, which rose high in the middle of a fertile plain. The circumference of the mountain was six miles, the ascent leading to it was three miles, and its summit covered an area of one mile. Three basilicas stood on the mountain at the place where Peter said to the Lord, "I will put up three shelters."

Nazarene women next to the Fountain of the Virgin, by D. Roberts.

The Tiberias Sea and the Jordan

Above: The church over the house of Peter at Capernaum.
Right: The River Dan.

In the city of Tiberias, recounts the Traveler from Placentia, were hot, saltwater baths, though the seawater was fresh. At Capernaum he saw Peter's house, over which a basilica had been built. From Capernaum he passed by camps, villages, and cities to arrive at two springs, the Jor and the Dan. The two rivers that issued from them converged to form the River Jordan, which then entered the Sea of Galilee and passed through it, flowing out of it once again on its southern shore.

Upon his return to the Sea of Galilee, the Traveler went to the place where the Jordan exited it. He crossed the river there and went to a city called Gader, where there was a hostel for the enjoyment of the public and hot springs called Termas Helias. The springs were frequented by lepers, who came there to be cured. In front of

the water source was a large tub. When it filled up, the doors were closed and the patients sent inside with lamps and incense to sit in the tub for the night. The Traveler writes that a patient who was going to recover would have a vision in a dream. When that happened, the baths were closed for seven days, at the end of which the patient was cured. At Gader, one of the Traveler's party, John of Placentia, died.

From Gader along the Jordan

Ruins of the ancient bathing pools in Gader.

The Traveler followed the River Jordan to Scythopolis (present-day Beit She'an), going on from there through Samaria and Judea on his way to Sebastia, where the prophet Elisha was buried. From Sebastia he descended to the fields, cities, and villages of the Samaritans. The Samaritans, he relates, so despised the Christians and the Jews that they burned any traces of them left in the streets. Christians were forbidden to touch anything before paying for it, and the coins they used for payment were first thrown into water, since the Samaritans were unwilling to take anything from Christian hands.

Some confusion obscures the next section of the Traveler's account, because he writes (improbably) that he next reached the place where Jesus fed five thousand people with five loaves of bread, which he describes as a wide plain with olive trees. Afterwards he continued on to the site of

Jesus' baptism. There, he notes, were located the heights of Hermon (Mount Mizar) of the Book of Psalms. The Traveler recalls how a cloud rose from the springs at the foot of the mountain during the first hour, and when the sun set it passed over Jerusalem, the basilica in Zion, the basilica of the tomb of the Lord, and the basilica of St. Mary and St. Sophia at the Praetorium, where the Lord was judged. Dew fell like rain over the holy sites, and the Traveler recounts that the doctors gathered it and used it to prepare all of the meals in the hostels, since it was believed to cure many ills wherever it fell, according to Psalm 133:3—"It is as if the dew of Hermon were falling on Mount Zion."

The Traveler relates that on that side of the Jordan, two miles from the river in the valley where Elijah hid when the raven brought him bread and meat, is the spring where Saint John performed baptisms. Many hermits ▶

(cont.) From Gader along the Jordan

dwelt around the valley. Nearby was the city of Livias, where two and a half of the tribes of Israel stayed before crossing the Jordan. People drank from a freshwater spring there for purification and the healing of many diseases. Not far away was the Dead Sea, into which the Jordan flowed near Sodom and Gomorrah and at

straw nor wood floated on the Dead Sea, nor could human beings swim in its waters. No life survived in its waters, and anything thrown in would sink to the bottom.

The Traveler spent the Epiphany near the Jordan, and he recounts a number of miracles that occurred at the place of Jesus' baptism that night.

Above: The ancient avenue of columns at Sebastia in Samaria.
Left: A Samaritan Torah scroll.

whose shores sulfur and clay accumulated. In July, August, and September lepers often soaked in the sea for entire days. In the evenings they would bathe in the baths of Moses, and sometimes, the Traveler adds, "God willing," one of them was cured. The Traveler was amazed that neither

A column surrounded by a grille was erected on the site, and at the place where the water returned to its riverbed, a cross was set up in the water. Marble stairs led down into the river from both sides. On the eve of the Epiphany, a large crowd of people held vigils. Morning prayers were said at

the fourth or fifth cockcrow. When morning prayers were over, the priest descended to the river accompanied by the deacons.

When the priest began to bless the water, the Traveler claims, the Jordan immediately receded and its water stood until the baptism was finished. Shipowners from Alexandria had people there with jugs full of scented oil, and while the water was being blessed before the baptism, they poured them out into the water and then filled them up again with the scented riverwater, which they then used as a blessing before sailing. When the baptism was over, the people went down to the river to receive a blessing wearing linen clothes or

wrapped in fabric that would later serve them as shrouds. When the proceedings ended, the waters returned to their place.

On that bank of the Jordan was a cave with cells for seven virgins, who were sent there as children. Whenever one died, the Traveler relates, she was buried in her cell and a new cell dug for the next girl sent to the cave so that the number of virgins was always seven. Outside the cave were people who took care of them. According to tradition, the handkerchief that covered the Lord's face was kept here. Across the Jordan, not far from the baptismal site, stood the Monastery of Saint John the Baptist, which contained two hostels.

Jericho

Jericho was situated six miles from the River Jordan. It looked like the Garden of Eden to the Traveler, though its walls lay in ruins. The Traveler reports that the house of Rahab still stood in the town, though in his day it served as a hostel. The room where Rahab left the spies was dedicated to prayer to Saint Mary.

According to the Traveler, the large stones carried by the Israelites from the Jordan were to be found behind the altar of a basilica not far from the city of Jericho. In front of the basilica was a field that Jesus himself had sown. No one maintained the field any longer, the Traveler reported in amazement, but it continued to thrive untended. It was harvested in February and part of the crop used for the Easter communion ceremony. After the harvest it was plowed and harvested again, then plowed once more and left alone.

A spring whose water had been

turned into freshwater by the prophet Elisha provided for the needs of all of Jericho. The Traveler reports that grape arbors grew around it, as did date trees whose fruit (which the Traveler took back home with him) weighed one pound each. He also saw a lemon tree with branches two feet long and two fingers thick producing fruit weighing forty pounds. Boxes full of the spot's grapes were sold on the Mount of Olives on Ascension Day, and on Pentecost grape juice was made from them and jugs of it offered to pilgrims.

When the Traveler and his group left Jericho, coming opposite Jerusalem not far from the city, they saw the tree Zacchaeus climbed in order to see Jesus. The tree, enclosed in a prayer room, had grown out through the roof, but was dried up. When they left Jericho's gate and traveled west, they arrived at the ruins of Sodom and Gomorrah. The Traveler recalls that a dark cloud and the scent of sulfur

Jericho, by Bonfils.

wafted over this part of the country. He adds that whoever said that Lot's wife was getting smaller because of

the animals who lick the salt were lying: she stood in much the same condition as ever.

The Mount of Olives and the Jehoshaphat Valley

On the Mount of Olives, the Traveler visited Bethany near the tomb of Lazarus and passed many monasteries, of both men and women. On the summit, at the place from which the Lord ascended to heaven, he saw many wonders and the cell in which Saint Pelagia hid and was buried. The Mount of Olives, he notes, was the site of the graves of Jacob, Cleopas, and many saints. From the mountain he descended to the valley of Gethsemane and the place where Jesus was handed over to the Romans. So that they might be blessed, the Traveler

Gethsemane *(below)* and the Tomb of Lazarus at Bethany *(right)*, by Bonfils.

and his companions sat in the three seats where Jesus had once sat. In the same valley they saw the basilica named for Saint Mary (the Church of the Tomb of the Virgin), which people say was her home and from which her body ascended to heaven. This same valley was also called the Jehoshaphat Valley.

From Gethsemane they ascended the many steps to the gate of Jerusalem. To its left was a grove of olive trees containing the fig tree on which Judas hanged himself. His rope was still there, surrounded by stones. The city gate abutted the ornate gate that was once the gate of the Temple; its threshold and floor still survived. As he entered Jerusalem, the Traveler knelt and kissed the holy ground.

Left: The Tomb of the Virgin, by L. Mayer.

Above: The stairs ascending from Gethsemane to the city gate.
Right: The Jehoshaphat Valley, by L. Mayer.

The Holy Sepulcher

In Jerusalem the Traveler admired the tomb of Jesus. He writes that it was carved of natural stone—the same stone on which the Lord's body had been laid—and that a copper lamp burned day and night at its head. Earth had been laid outside of the tomb and those entering were able to obtain a blessing from it. The stone that covered the tomb, which stands in front of the opening to the tomb, was the same color as the stone of the tomb, since it was hewn out of the rock of Golgotha. It was decorated with gold and precious gems and looked like a millstone. The tomb's ornamentation was unfathomable: bracelets, necklaces, rings, tiaras, twisted belts, sashes, imperial crowns of gold and precious stones, and an empress' jewels hung from iron chains. The tomb was designed as a kind of silver canopy, and an altar stood before it.

It was eighty steps from the tomb to Golgotha, where one could ascend the steps that Jesus climbed to the Crucifixion. The Traveler adds that one could see the place Jesus was crucified, where the stain of blood was still visible on the rock. To the side of Golgotha was the altar of Abraham, where the patriarch almost sacrificed his son and where Melchizedek also performed sacrifices. Next to the altar, the Traveler writes, was an alcove where running water could be heard: if one throws a piece of fruit or something that can float into it, the article will afterwards reappear at the Pool of Siloam.

The Traveler estimates the distance between Siloam and Golgotha to be one mile. From Golgotha to the cross,

both inside Constantine's basilica along with the tomb, were fifty steps. In the basilica was a cubicle containing the wood of the cross and the sign the Romans hung above Jesus' head: "Jesus Christ King of the Jews." The cross, he notes, was made of walnut wood. When it was removed from the cubicle to the chapel for worship, a star would appear in the sky and move over to the spot where the cross was placed. According to the Traveler,

when the cross was being worshipped, the star stood precisely overhead. Oil for blessing was brought in small flasks. The moment the wood of the cross touched the opening of a small flask, the oil bubbled and shot out, and if the vial wasn't closed, all of the oil immediately spilled out. As the cross was returned to its place, the star also moved back to its place, and by the time the cross was secured in the cubicle, the star

Worshipers inside the tomb, by L. Mayer.

had vanished.

In the tomb were also the sponge and the stick read about in the Gospel, the onyx goblet with which Jesus made a blessing at the Last Supper, Mary's belt and scarf, and many other miraculous artifacts: a figure of the blessed Mary rose on high. The seven marble seats of the elders were also kept there.

The Basilica of Hagia Zion

In the basilica of the Hagia Zion were objects that caused much amazement on the part of the Traveler and his company, including the stone that the builders rejected. When Jesus Christ entered the church, which was then the house of Saint James, he found the stone and he set it as a capstone. When one lifted it, the Traveler writes, and put one's ear to the same corner, a noise like the chattering of a crowd of people could be heard.

In that same church was the pillar where the Lord was flagellated, and on it was a mark where, when Jesus embraced it, his chest had stuck to the marble and his hands and fingers had touched it. The Traveler says that people who took the dimensions of these marks and carried them around their neck were healed of all illness. On the same column was the horn where the kings, including David, were anointed. The crown of thorns, the spear with which Jesus was stabbed in his side, and many of the stones with which Stephen was stoned were also kept in the basilica. The Traveler writes of a small pillar that held the cross on which Peter was crucified in Rome and the goblet with which the Apostles conducted mass after the resurrection, among other miraculous things. The Traveler relates that in a convent of nuns at Hagia Zion he saw a man's skull attributed to Theodota the holy martyr enclosed in a gold box decorated with precious stones. He notes that many drank out of it for good luck.

Jerusalem's Churches

From Hagia Zion the Traveler went to the basilica of Saint Mary (the Nea Church, built by Justinian), where he found a large community of monks, hostels for men and women pilgrims, countless dining tables, and more than three thousand beds for the sick.

The Traveler from Placentia prayed at the Praetorium, where the Lord was judged and where a basilica to Saint Sophia had been built. In the basilica he saw the seat on which Pilate sat when he judged the Lord, as well as the square stone in the middle of the Praetorium that the accused would stand on so that the people could see and hear him. The Lord had stood on the square stone to be judged ▶

The stairs descending to the Siloam (the Gihon), by the Comte de Forbin.

by Pilate. Jesus' fine foot, small and delicate, his normal average height, handsome face, curly hair, pleasant hand, and long fingers, could all be seen in a picture drawn while he was still alive and carved in the Praetorium. The Traveler reports that a great many miracles issued from the stone on which Jesus had stood. Believers took dimensions from his footprints, connected them to various diseases, and were cured. The stone was decorated with gold and silver.

The Traveler and his party then went on to an arch where the ancient city gate once was, and descended a great number of stairs from there to the Siloam. Above the Siloam was a vaulted basilica, and where the Siloam bubbled up beneath it were two man-made marble seats divided by a lattice. Men bathed in one and women in the other, in order to be blessed. Many miracles were known to have occurred, and even lepers purified, in the waters of the Siloam. People were always found bathing in a large man-made pool on the spot.

The Siloam spring was enclosed, the Traveler explains, by the walls that Empress Eudocia had added to the city. She had also built the basilica and the tomb of Saint Stephen, next to which was her own tomb.

Next to the Siloam was the field that

Above: Bethesda Pool, by H.B. Tristram.
Left: Haceldama—the Field of Blood.

was purchased for the price of the Lord: It was called Haceldama—Field of Blood—and all strangers were buried there. Among the graves were the cells of servants of God, people of many virtues. Fruit trees and grapevines covered most of the field.

In the city was a swimming pool with five halls (the Pool of Bethesda). The basilica of Saint Mary, in which many miracles were said to have occurred, was in one of them. The pool had become a cesspool and everything in the city was washed there. In one dark corner was found the iron chain with which the wretched Judas strangled himself.

On the Road to Bethlehem

On the road leading to Bethlehem, three miles from both Jerusalem and Bethlehem at the edge of Rama, the Traveler reached the tomb of the matriarch Rachel. In the middle of the road was a rock from which water flowed, seemingly without movement. The Traveler reports that, although water was taken from the rock, the same amount—about four liters—always remained. He hails the freshness of the water as indescribable and recounts the legend according to which Saint Mary, on her flight to Egypt, sat in that spot and was thirsty, so that the water spouted forth. The Traveler visited the church at the site.

Bethlehem was the most wonderful place, writes the Traveler, with many servants of God. He visited the grotto where Jesus was born and saw the

Above: Rachel's Tomb, by L. Mayer

Right: Hebron, by C.W. Wilson.

Below: The Grotto of the Nativity in Bethlehem, by L. Mayer.

mon. Also in the vicinity was the grave of the children murdered by Herod. They had all been interred in one tomb, and when it was opened their bones could be seen.

Before Bethlehem was a monastery surrounded by a wall, with many monks within. Twenty-four miles from Bethlehem were the oaks of Mamre where, according to tradition, Abraham, Isaac, Jacob, Sarah, and even the bones of Joseph were buried. On the spot was a basilica with rows of columns around an uncovered courtyard, which a grille divided in half. Christians entered on one side

manger decorated with gold and silver. The opening to the grotto, in which lamps burned night and day, was narrow. The visitors saw the cave that Hieronymus had dug out of the stone for his own burial. Half a mile from Bethlehem, the Traveler writes, were the graves of David and Solo-

and Jews on the other, and incense was burned everywhere. On the day after the birth of the Lord, the burials of Jacob and David were celebrated there with great devotion by countless Jews from all over the country, who burned much incense and offered gifts to the servants there.

Into the Desert

From Jerusalem the Traveler descended on the road leading to Gaza and Ashkelon, on the way passing the well that Abraham and Jacob dug in Beersheba. In Ashkelon he saw the Well of Peace—a wide well in the shape of a theater into which one descended by means of steps. The three martyred Egyptian brothers were buried there. The Traveler then made his way to Gaza, which he describes as a wonderful city of honest people, all excelling in their generosity and love of strangers. Two miles outside of Gaza the Traveler's party came upon the grave of the church father Hilarion.

The travelers then went on to the city of Halutza, at the edge of the

companion searched for her in the desert for two days, and upon his return was very sad, though he refused to reveal whether or not he had found her. Upon his return, he had none of the dresses, dates, lupine, nor baskets of roasted chickpeas that he had taken with him on his outing.

From Halutza the Traveler turned towards the desert. At the twentieth mile, he writes, stood a fortress with the hostel of Saint George, where travelers could find shelter and hermits, a living. The Traveler occasionally saw people with camels, but they fled from him. They were from Ethiopia, and he describes them as having cut nostrils, cut ears, small overshoes, and rings on their big toes.

water from the rock, and went on from there to the Horev, the mountain of God. On his way to Mount Sinai he met a large crowd of monks and hermits carrying crosses and singing psalms. They greeted the Traveler and his party by bowing down to the ground, and the Traveler and his companions

Ashkelon. A detail from a mosaic floor at Umm Rasas.

spring was enclosed within a monastery surrounded by fortified walls. Three abbots, well-versed in Latin, Greek, Syriac, Egyptian, and Bessas, lived there, as did many translators. This, the Traveler writes, was the refuge to which the monks withdrew from the world. The Traveler and his group climbed three miles up the mountain to the cave where Elijah hid when he fled from Jezebel. In front of it was a spring that irrigated the mountain. From there they climbed another three miles to the mountain's summit, where they found a small prayer site, about six feet on either side. No one dared spend the night there, but the monks climbed up to worship as soon as dawn broke. The Traveler notes that many visitors to the place shave their beards and hair and scatter it at the site out of devotion, and even he did so, shaving his beard. Between Sinai and Horev was a valley where, the Traveler records, dew called manna fell from the sky at fixed times, setting and becoming like

Women. A detail from a mosaic floor in a sixth-century church in the northern Negev.

desert leading to Sinai. The bishop there told them a story of a local aristocratic girl named Maria whose groom had died on their wedding night. That same week she sent her family away and divided up her property among the poor and the monasteries. On the seventh day after her marriage, her groom's clothing was taken, never again to be found. It was rumored that Maria was in the desert across the Jordan, walking among the reeds near the Dead Sea. In that region, the Traveler relates, a convent of fifteen or seventeen girls had been founded, and the Christians maintained them. They had one donkey and were training a lion cub that was huge and terrifying to look upon. When the Traveler's caravan approached the cells, all of the animals in it urinated at the sound of its roar, some of them even collapsing from fright. Supposedly, the Traveler reports, the donkey drove the lion to pasture.

A devout Christian who accompanied the Traveler offered the nuns one hundred *solidi*, but they refused to accept it. He sent to Jerusalem for vegetables, thirty dresses, and lamp oil, and had them all brought to the women's cells. They told him of the miraculous deeds of Maria, who had gone into the desert. The Traveler's

When asked about the rings, they answered that Trajan, the Roman emperor assigned them the rings as a marker. From there the Traveler and his companions walked through the desert for five or six days, and the

The Chapel of Saint Elias on the summit of Mount Sinai.

rubber kernels. The monks collected the manna in jugs, and their many filled jugs were kept in the monastery. They distributed little flasks of the kernels as a blessing.

From Mount Sinai the group traveled to Eilat, from which one could set sail for India in spice ships, though the Traveler preferred to go to Egypt. On his way he passed the city of Faran, where Moses fought Amalek. A city with strong walls encircling it, the Traveler later recalled it as being a wasteland, except for the presence of water and dates. Eight hundred soldiers whose task was to protect the monasteries and monks of the city lived in Faran with their families. Faran was in the land of Midian, and its inhabitants were considered to be descendants of the family of Jethro, Moses' father-in-law.

Lion. A detail from a Byzantine mosaic floor at Nirim in the Negev.

camels carried water for them. When the water in the skin pouches became bitter, he writes, they put sand in it and it became sweet again.

On the eighteenth day the Traveler reached the place where Moses drew

did the same. The monks led them to the valley between Horev and Sinai. At the foot of the mountain was the spring where, according to tradition, Moses saw the miracle of the burning bush and watered the sheep. The

Persians Conquer Holy Land and Jerusalem

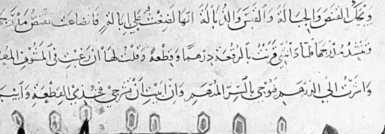

The beginning of the seventh century witnessed one of the climaxes of the long and bitter struggle between the Eastern Roman Empire (Byzantium) and Sassanian Persia. After a period of relative peace during the fifth century, the conflict erupted in full force in the second half of the sixth century, during the days of Emperor Justinian. The war exhausted both powers. Renewal of the treaty between them in 561 brought only a temporary peace, since its conditions were harsh and humiliating for Byzantium. The Byzantine emperor Maurice (582-602) took advantage of the inheritance wars in Persia to extort terms of peace from Chosroes II (590-628), a competitor for the Persian throne whom he supported—which the Persians could not long sustain. Chosroes finally exploited the assassination of Emperor Maurice in 602 as an excuse for violating the peace treaty. Casting himself as avenging the death of Maurice, he invaded Byzantium's borders. Persia's wars against Byzantium were wars of looting and marauding more than of conquest. Their central objective was to fill the empty coffers of the Sassanian kingdom with booty from Byzantine cities that capitulated only in battle and with ransom payments from those that willingly surrendered. The defensive disposition of the Byzantine Empire collapsed easily, exhausted from the lengthy wars it had been fighting simultaneously on a number of fronts, and the empire relinquished large expanses of territory to the Persians. The conquest of Jerusalem occupies a central position in this chapter of history, not only in Christian sources but in Persian records as well. The treasures of the holy city had beckoned to the Persian kings for a long time. After Jerusalem fell—in the wake of a twenty-day siege—its inhabitants were slaughtered in a brutal massacre. Accounts from the period record enormous numbers of victims that range from six thousand to sixty thousand.

Soldiers of the Persian sultan. From a thirteenth-century Persian manuscript.

True Cross Falls into Persian Captivity

The Persians easily discovered the True Cross, which had been hidden by the Christians. Razing the Church of the Holy Sepulcher, they removed the True Cross, took the bishop of Jerusalem captive, and transferred them both to Chosroes in Persia together with the treasures of the city. The Persian victors also dispatched a large number of exiles, most of them superb craftsmen and artisans whose trades would be useful to the Sassanians.

A detail from a mosaic in the sixth-century Archiepiscopal Chapel in Ravena.

Emperor Heraclius Returns the True Cross to Jerusalem 629

The emperor Heraclius crushed the Persians in 628, and in 629 concluded a peace treaty with them according to which the Persians returned all of the territories conquered from Byzantium, liberated Christian prisoners of war, and returned the True Cross to the emperor. In 629 or 630 the emperor brought the cross back to Jerusalem in a victory procession. The day of the cross' return to Jerusalem was declared a holiday, the Feast of the Exaltation of the Holy Cross, and is celebrated to this day on September 14, the date of the finding of the cross.

Left: The Golden Gate. According to tradition, when Emperor Heraclius returned to Jerusalem with the cross, he intended to take it in a triumphal entry through the Golden Gate. When he approached the city the gate was suddenly blocked up and a voice came out of the heavens: Jesus entered this gate with humility and you too must enter it with humility. Only when the emperor dismounted his horse was the gate open before him.

Emperor Hercalius returns the cross, by M. de Matteo Lambertini.

CHAPTER III

THE EARLY ARAB PERIOD

634-1099

This era in the Holy Land was marked by frequent governmental change. The period opened with the Muslim conquest of the Holy Land and Jerusalem from the Byzantine Christian rulers, and concluded with the Christian recovery of the same territory from the Muslims.

After the death of Muhammad in 632, Abu Bakr took political and religious control of the Muslim Arabs. The title he was granted—caliph (Muhammad's surrogate)—would be used from this time on by those standing at the head of the Muslim nation. Abu Bakr succeeded in preserving the power consolidated by Muhammad by preventing the apostasy of the Arab tribes, who had seemingly converted to Islam during the period of Muhammad, but attempted to liberate themselves from the chains of Islam immediately after his death.

Abu Bakr invaded the Holy Land in March of 634 in order to wrest it from the Byzantines. The first force invaded Eilat in an offensive aimed at the coastal area, while the second force penetrated from Transjordan. The latter was halted at its first clash with the Byzantine army, but the force that attacked from the south overpowered the Christians on the outskirts of the city of Gaza. Abu Bakr asked for assistance from Khaled Ibn al-Walid, who was at the time on the banks of the Euphrates engaged in a war with the Persians. Khaled marched to the northern borders of the Holy Land, penetrated it via Galilee, and joined the Muslim force already within the country.

The decisive battle between the Muslims and the Byzantines was fought at the end of July 634. Subsequent to their victory there, the Muslims conquered most of the cities in the Holy Land.

Abu Bakr did not live to complete the task of conquest, and upon his death in August 634, Omar Ibn al-Khattab, who was to be the founder of the Muslim empire, rose to power. Ibn al-Khattab conquered the Persian empire, the western reaches of the Byzantine Empire, and completed the occupation of the Holy Land. In 638 he also won Jerusalem.

After the assassination of Ibn al-Khattab in 644, the caliphs Uthman Ibn Affan (644-656) and Ali Ibn Abu Talib (656-661) rose to the throne. In Muslim historiography, the first four caliphs symbolize the unity of Islam, and are thus called "Al-Rashdun" ("The Upright"). Before his death in 639, Caliph Omar Ibn al-Khattab had appointed Mu'awiyya Ibn Abu Sufyan, a member of one of the distinguished families in Mecca that had persecuted Muhammad at the beginning of his career, governor of Syria. Mu'awiyya conducted a lengthy struggle with the caliph Ali Ibn Abu Talib, and in 660, half a year before the latter's death, he declared himself the fifth caliph and founded the Umayyad Dynasty, which ruled the Arab empire until 750. Since the Mu'awiyya caliphate was not accepted by many Islamic circles, especially among the Prophet's family in the city of Medina, from which the "upright" caliphs operated, Mu'awiyya moved the capital of the Muslim empire to Damascus. Mu'awiyya visited the Holy Land often, and his coronations took place in Jerusalem. His heirs also accorded Jerusalem much importance and continued to visit the country.

The Umayyad caliphs expended much effort towards fortifying the cities and ensuring the safety of the roads in the Holy Land. Their building projects on the Temple Mount, especially the Dome of the Rock and Al-Aqsa Mosque, contributed to Jerusalem's transformation into Islam's third most important city.

Historians estimate that only after the conquest of Jerusalem did the Arab rulers understand its enormous religious significance. Their esteem for the sacred city is evidenced by the fact that a short while after its conquest, several of the Prophet Muhammad's acquaintances from Medina settled there, including the brother and nephew of Hasan Ibn Ta'abet, Muhammad's court poet.

During the entire period of Umayyad rule, the caliphate was forced to deal with rebels who refused to recognize its right to rule the Muslim world. The rebellion led by the house of Abbas in 750 brought about the fall of the Umayyad Dynasty.

The Abbasid caliphs ruled in the Holy Land from 750 to 878 and 905 to 935. With its rise to power the Abbasid Dynasty claimed leadership of the Sunni movement, and like the Umayyads was forced to deal with rebellious Shiites, who claimed that only relatives of the Prophet had the authority to lead Islam.

The establishment of the house of Abbas was a blow to Jerusalem's status, as the second Abbasid caliph, El-Mansur (754-775), transferred the empire's capital to Baghdad in 762. The Holy Land's loss in stature was expressed by decreasing investment in development and fortification of the country. Jerusalem's religious significance was undermined, and the rulers' interest in it lessened.

The Abbasids collaborated with the Franks during the days of Charlemagne, and within the framework of this alliance the Franks took care to strengthen the status of European Christians in Jerusalem. In the course of the same period, Roman activity in Jerusalem was also augmented. Even though the final split between the Byzantine Church and the pope occurred only in 1054, competition existed between the Church in Byzantium and the followers of the pope previously. After the division, Roman activity in Jerusalem increased.

As the power of Arab elements in the Abbasid caliphate lessened, non-Arab elements came to the fore. Persians and Turks gained control of the army and of central positions in the caliphate; many of them ruled various districts of the empire. These local rulers often took advantage of the weakness of the central caliphate to throw off the yoke of the Abbasid rule, declaring the independence of their fiefdoms. One of these governors was the Turk Ahmad Ibn Tulun, who established a dynasty that ruled in Egypt from 868 until 905. In 878, Ibn Tulun also gained control over Syria and the Holy Land.

The severance of the Holy Land from the Abbasid caliphate contributed to its economic development and a rise in its strategic importance. The Holy Land became a battleground between the various forces penetrating it from the north and the government in Egypt, while the regional Bedouin tribes who took advantage of the conflict became the true masters of the land. The rule of the Tulunids in Egypt ended in 905, and Egypt and the Holy Land returned to the hands of the Abbasid caliphate for thirty years, though its hold on the Holy Land during this period was tenuous.

In 935, the Turk Muhammad Ibn Toaj took control of Egypt, founding a dynasty that was to rule in Egypt until 969 and in the Holy Land until 970. Throughout the entire period of his rule, Toaj's regime fought invaders who entered the Holy Land from the north—especially Bedouin tribes, Karmathians (Shiite Muslims), and Byzantines— exploiting the governmental impotence that resulted from factionalism among the Muslims.

In 969, the Fatimids, one of the Shiite sects that undermined Abbasid rule, conquered Egypt. One year later, while the Byzantines attacked the Holy Land from the north, the Fatimids conquered it from the south. During the period of Fatimid rule in Cairo, the countries under their control prospered, but the dynasty was never able to establish a stable government in the Holy Land, as a wide coalition of Arab tribes, Karmathians, and Byzantine Christians consistently opposed its rule. In 975, the Byzantine emperor, aided by an anti-Fatimid coalition, attempted to conquer the Holy Land. It appears that the Christian leadership in Jerusalem was in contact with the Byzantine invaders.

During Fatimid Caliph Tahir Ali's rule, Jerusa-lem's wall was renovated and the costs extracted from the inhabitants of the city, whose economic situation was desperate in the wake of the many wars the city had undergone. The Christians appealed to Constantine IX, the emperor of Byzantium, who agreed to fund the portion of the wall encompassing the Christian Quarter. The northern portion of the city, in which most of the Christians resided, was apparently encircled by another wall at the time. The work of renovating the wall was completed in 1063.

Among the non-Arab forces that grew gradually stronger in the Middle East were the Turkish Seljuk tribes. In 1071, Atsaz Ibn Ouk, a Turkish dignitary dispatched to the Holy Land as a Fatimid emissary to fight the rebel Arab tribes, betrayed his superiors. Ramla fell to him that year, and he occupied Jerusalem in mid-1073 after a two-year siege. In 1077, the residents of Jerusalem rebelled against the Seljuks and Atsaz once again besieged the city. The rebels surrendered in return for Atsaz's promise not to harm Jerusalem's inhabitants. Upon his entry into the city, the Seljuk leader massacred three thousand people.

On August 26, 1098, the eve of the Crusader occupation, the Fatimids succeeded in regaining control of Jerusalem, but their rule did not last much longer. The efforts being made in Europe to rescue the holy places from the Muslim infidels soon bore fruit, and Crusaders carrying flags bearing the cross soon arrived to occupy the Holy Land.

Previous pages: The Dome of the Rock, by M. Milner.
Inset: The Dome of the Chain.
Background: The underground pools in Ramla, built at the end of the ninth century, by M. Milner.

Jerusalem Surrenders to Caliph Omar

Caliph Promises Christians Freedom of Worship. Patriarch Dies of Broken Heart.

In February of 638, after a siege of almost two years, the patriarch Sophronius, leader of the Christian community in Jerusalem, agreed to transfer the city to the hands of the Arab army. Despite the desperate situation of the populace and the meager state of ammunition and supplies in the city, the elderly patriarch made the capitulation conditional upon the arrival of the Arab ruler, Caliph Omar, in Jerusalem to vouch for the security of its Christian inhabitants and their freedom of worship.

Caliph Omar, who was in Transjordan at the time, agreed to the patriarch's provisos, but imposed one of his own: Christian inhabitants who wished to remain in Jerusalem would pay a permanent tax to the Muslim authorities. The surrender of the city was accepted by Khaled Ibn Ta'abet el-Fahami, commander of the besieging Arab army. The caliph himself arrived in the holy city only a few days later, riding on a camel and wearing a camelhair cloak. According to legend, he went on foot from the entrance of Jerusalem to the place where the ancient Jewish Holy Temple had once stood. Sophronius escorted him to the Church of the Holy Sepulcher, where the caliph prayed on the steps before the doors of the church.

Omar gave orders to clear the Temple Mount of the large amounts of refuse that had accumulated there since the destruction of Herod's Temple in 70 AD and to build a mosque south of the site on which the Temple had stood.

The mosque was a modest structure, as is apparent from the description of it by the French bishop Arculf who visited Jerusalem some thirty years later. According to his testimony, the mosque was a square building of rough wooden planks and beams erected on top of ruins and able to accommodate about three thousand people.

Jerusalem's relinquishment into Muslim hands was a harsh blow for the Christians, who found their loss of control over the holy city unbearable. On March 11, approximately one month after the city's fall, the patriarch Sophronius died, apparently of a broken heart, and for the next sixty years none other was appointed in his stead.

Left: The new Mosque of Omar, built next to the Church of the Holy Sepulcher in the thirteenth century.

Right: Caliph Omar supervises construction on the Temple Mount.

Below: Sophronius' capitulation of Jerusalem, written in Arabic for the conquering Caliph Omar.

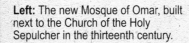

Arabs Destroy Holy Monasteries

During his Christmas Eve sermon at the Church of the Holy Sepulcher in 634, Sophronius, the elderly patriarch of Jerusalem, complained of the violence of the Arab battalions that prevented people from traveling from Jerusalem to Bethlehem to celebrate the holiday.

The Saracens (an epithet applied to Eastern peoples which originated in the corruption of the Arabic word *sharq,* meaning "east"), he said, pass through countries where they are forbidden, looting the cities, ruining the fields, setting fire to the villages, and destroying the holy monasteries.

After Caliph Omar prayed on the steps of the Church of the Holy Sepulcher in the wake of his conquest, part of the church was turned into a mosque. An Arabic inscription carved in a stone *(above)* from the church commemorates the event.

Building New Churches Forbidden

Jews or Christians who adhered to their respective faiths after the surrender of Jerusalem to the Muslims were defined as *dhimmi* under Muslim law, and had restrictions placed upon them that were intended to ensure their subordination to Muslim believers. The restrictions were codified as a group of twelve regulations that came to be known as the Terms of Omar.

The Terms of Omar prohibited *dhimmi* from building houses of worship that were higher than the Muslim mosques or competed with them in grandeur. Effectively, the construction of new churches and monasteries was forbidden. In addition, *dhimmi* were not permitted to hold public religious services and were obliged to wear special clothes.

Other rules forbade riding horses (a privilege reserved for Muslims only) and compelled *dhimmis* to entertain in their homes for three days any Muslim who so desired.

A Muslim horseman.

Drastic Reduction in Number of Pilgrims to Holy Land

Roads to Sea Blocked after Caesarea's Fall. Emigrants Flee Economic Crisis.

The number of Christian pilgrims to the Holy Land plummeted as a result of the Arab occupation. Caesarea, the last Byzantine fortress and port in the Holy Land, was conquered in 640, and the arrival of Christian pilgrims by sea almost entirely arrested. From the few surviving reports of the period, it appears that from the beginning of Arab occupation in 634 to the stabilization of Arab dominion under the dynasty of the Umayyad caliphate in Damascus in 661, complete chaos reigned in the Holy Land. The Arab tribes emerging from the Arabian Peninsula were unaccustomed to Western forms of government, and every power-broker legislated as he wished in the area under his control, often compelling pilgrims to pay baksheesh for any "special arrangements." Every pilgrimage to the Holy Land involved procuring permission from the authorities, who viewed any non-Muslim as an enemy whose movements had to be monitored. The monk Bernard the Wise, who visited the Holy Land at this time, records in his

memoirs that the Muslim captain of his ship forced him to pay for going ashore simply because he was an "enemy." The Muslims also levied

taxes and duties on whatever merchandise the pilgrims brought with them.

The sharp decrease in the movement

of pilgrims and trade with the West caused a serious economic crisis in the Holy Land. As a result, many Christian inhabitants emigrated.

The ancient port of Caesarea.

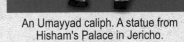

Umayyad Caliph Mu'awiyya Crowned in Jerusalem

Relations between Church and Arab Government Improve. Pilgrims Return.

The inauguration of Caliph Mu'awiyya, founder of the Umayyad Dynasty, took place in Jerusalem in 660. Christian sources report that on the day of his inauguration the new caliph visited the Church of the Holy Sepulcher and the Tomb of the Virgin Mary in Gethsemane.

During the era of the Umayyad rulers, relations between the church and the Arab government improved. Caliph Mu'awiyya even allowed an emissary from Rome to supervise the property and lives of the Christians residing in Jerusalem. At the same time, the Muslim governors of Jerusalem influenced the appointment of the Christian patriarchs in the city, seeing to it that their cronies were installed even if they lacked the requisite skills for the position. Thus, for example, El-Mansur of Damascus, who had promoted the Muslim occupation of Jerusalem and was hated by local Christians, was the first patriarch appointed in the city. Later, a Christian carpenter who worked in the caliph's court was granted the position.

The Umayyad caliphs dedicated

much effort to fortifying the cities and securing the roads of the Holy Land. Port cities that had been incapacitated in the wake of raids by Arab battalions also gradually began to function again. Trade with the West picked up. Pilgrimages to Jerusalem and the holy places were renewed.

An Umayyad caliph. A statue from Hisham's Palace in Jericho.

A mosaic from Hisham's Palace in Jericho, from the eighth century.

A decorated window at Hisham's Palace.

Veronica's Handkerchief Discovered in Jerusalem

Above: Jericho in the Madaba Map.
Left: Two angels hold Veronica's handkerchief, by Claude Vignon.

Had it not been for the storm, we would not be in possession of Arculf's memories, and we hear nothing more of him from the time he left Scotland and sailed for Gaul.

Arculf provided a detailed description of Jerusalem and its holy places including a sketch of the Church of the Holy Sepulcher that constitutes the first of its kind. He counted eighty-four towers and six gates (only three of which were important: the first facing west, the second north, and the third east) in the city wall. He also visited Jericho—where he recounted that he saw the house of Rahab the harlot, intact except for its roof—Hebron, Nablus, the Dead Sea, Nazareth, Tiberias, Galilee, Damascus, and Egypt.

The story of Arculf in the Holy Land was later excerpted by the Anglican church historian Bede, whose widely distributed abbreviated version greatly encouraged the movement of pilgrims from the British Isles to the Holy Land.

According to a report by Bishop Arculf of Gaul, who made a pilgrimage to the Holy Land around the year 680, the handkerchief with which Jesus wiped his face when he was brought to the cross was later found. According to the bishop, the handkerchief had been taken from Jesus' grave after his resurrection and hidden.

At the conclusion of his visit to the Holy Land, the bishop set sail for Gaul, but a storm that blew up on the way carried his ship to the shores of the island of Iona off of western Scotland. The abbot of the monastery on the island took notes on Arculf's descriptions, and his records were preserved in various manuscripts.

Above: Tiberias, by H.F. Lynch. **Below:** Nablus, by P. Lortet.

Heavens Clean Jerusalem's Streets

Every year on September 12, a fair was held in Jerusalem during which much buying and selling transpired. Crowds of diverse people from various countries thronged to the city to stay for several days in its hostels, bringing with them beasts of burden—camels, horses, donkeys, and oxen—that choked and befouled the holy city's alleys. The stench caused much distress to city residents, who were embarrassed to walk about during the fair.

On the evening after the conclusion of the fair, the Gallic Bishop Arculf reported, an amazing event transpired: a driving rain commenced, and the streets were washed clean of all the excrement and filth. This was possible, said Arculf, because God established Jerusalem on a steep slope running northeast from the Mount Zion ridge. The rainwater did not collect in the street; it flowed toward the lowlands. The flood that pelted the city finally coursed through the gates east of the Kidron River and the Jehoshaphat Valley, carrying the vast amounts of refuse with it. The moment the streets were clean, the rain ceased.

A map of Jerusalem by Bishop Arculf.

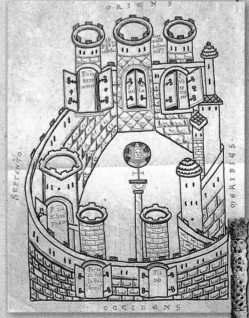

691

Jerusalem Becomes Muslim Holy City

Umayyad Caliphs Copy Byzantines and Establish Grand Religious Structures

The caliphs of the Umayyad Dynasty, imitating the Byzantine rulers of Jerusalem who preceded them, erected resplendent structures to commemorate sacred events. During their reign, the Dome of the Rock and Al-Aqsa Mosque were built, and a series of elaborate palaces and administrative edifices were constructed south of the Temple Mount.

The tremendous power and wealth of the Umayyad caliphs allowed them to engage the services of the best artisans throughout the Arab empire, including Byzantine architects who had formerly specialized in building churches.

The Dome of the Rock was built during the rule of Caliph Abed al-Malik on the site of Solomon's Temple. According to an inscription on the building, the structure was inaugurated in February of 691. It is not a mosque, but an ornate shrine intended primarily to impress believers. According to the account of the Arab geographer Al-Mukaddasi, a native of Jerusalem, as well as other records, the elaborate structure, whose external walls were adorned with mosaics and semiprecious stones, competed with the most richly-decorated of Jerusalem's churches. Researchers believe that the Dome of the Rock was designed as an octagon covered with a dome so that believers could encircle it as they do the Kaaba in Mecca.

Caliph Abed al-Malik also built Al-Aqsa Mosque ("The Far Mosque")— some say on the remains of an ancient Byzantine church—on the Temple Mount to commemorate the place from which Muhammad ascended to seventh heaven.

According to Bishop Arculf, Jews and Christians were responsible for supplying oil for illuminating the mosques of Jerusalem.

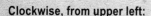

Clockwise, from upper left:
Muhammad's ascension to seventh heaven; the *mihrab* (a niche indicating the direction of Mecca) in Al-Aqsa Mosque; the interior of the cupola of the Dome of the Rock; the main hall of the Dome of the Rock; a stained glass window in the Dome of the Rock; one of the carved wooden panels that covered Al-Aqsa's interior in the seventh century.

Ramla—Holy Land Capital

Jerusalem Transformed from Capital City to Country Town

Ramla, by D. Roberts.

The decision by Caliph Suleiman, son of Abed al-Malik, to establish a new seat of Arab government and capital of the Holy Land sealed the fate of Jerusalem as a peripheral city for most of the period of Arab rule in the region.

Ramla, the new capital, situated in the central Holy Land at the crossroads between Jaffa in the west and Jerusalem in the east, Beersheba in the south and Damascus in the north, was established in 716. It quickly displaced Jerusalem: a contemporaneous Arab historian wrote bitterly that Jerusalem, the city of King David and King Solomon, had become one of the outlying towns of Ramla. In the tenth century Ramla was the largest city in the Holy Land, and was considered, with its minarets and white houses, to be one of the loveliest cities in the region. But in 1033 and again in 1068 the town was struck by severe earthquakes. The city crumbled, thousands of houses tumbled down, and many people were killed or injured. Whatever the earthquakes did not manage to demolish, the Bedouin tribes who later invaded Ramla and disrupted the trade routes to it did. The Bedouin attacks on the city especially hurt its non-Muslim inhabitants, who were forced to flee to fortified cities or other countries.

Saint Willibald Saved from Search

Smuggles Holy Jerusalem Balsam to Tyre

One of the reasons for the dearth of written testimony by Christian pilgrims from the Early Arab Period was the suspicion with which the Arabs regarded every Christian traveler and the resulting baggage searches they carried out, during the course of which anything written or any special item being taken out of the country was confiscated.

Bishop Willibald from Germany, who departed Europe in 721 for an extended journey to the Holy Land, recorded how he outwitted the Muslims' strict supervision: during his visit to Jerusalem, he purchased a bottle of medicinal balsam, hid it inside a hollow stick, put oil on top of it, and sealed the shaft at the top.

When the bishop and his party reached Tyre, they were stopped by the inhabitants and a careful search was made of their belongings. Had a forbidden object been discovered, the members of the party would have been sentenced to death. In fact, the searchers did detect the hollow staff, but when they opened it and found only the regular oil and not the hidden medicinal resin, they allowed the bishop and his companions to continue on their way.

Bishop Willibald visited Jerusalem four times during his trip to the East. He traveled widely in the Holy Land and in his memoirs was the first to

Saint Willibald was the first to describe the Mar Saba Monastery.

describe the Mar Saba Monastery. At the time, there were still wild carnivores in the Holy Land, and Willibald himself, as he relates, encountered a lion.

Saint Willibald asking for Mary's blessing. A mosaic in the Church of the Dormition.

Revolt in Jerusalem: Abassid Dynasty Comes to Power

745

City Inhabitants Revolt against Caliph. Strengthened Opposition Puts New Caliph in Power.

In 745, Jerusalem's Muslim inhabitants revolted against Caliph Marwan II, whose retaliatory measures were cruel. Marwan demolished the walls of the city and his soldiers punished its residents severely.

The destruction was completed by Bedouin tribes from the Arabian Peninsula who raided the area, looting everything in their path. What the Bedouins did not wreck, the famine, epidemics, and earthquakes that followed in their wake did.

The weakness of the central government was exploited by the strong and discontented opposition of the Muwali—Muslims of non-Arab descent (Persians, Egyptians, Turks, and others)—who were passed over when bribes were distributed. They succeeded in subduing the exhausted Umayyad army and installing a new caliph, a descendant of Abbasid, the uncle of the prophet Muhammad.

Jerusalem. A mosaic from the eighth century at Umm Rasas in Jordan.

747

Earthquake Rocks Bethlehem
Church of the Nativity Saved

An earthquake that flattened Bethlehem in 747 caused almost no damage to the Church of the Nativity, according to the diary of a Spanish priest who visited the city in 750. The priest relates that although almost all of the houses in the city were leveled, the Church of the Nativity remained standing: even its mosaic floor, the most beautiful the priest had ever seen, was unharmed.

Many edifices in Jerusalem, including the Al-Aqsa Mosque and the Dome of the Rock, were wrecked in the same earthquake.

The priest's fragmentary diary is one of the few testimonies left by pilgrims of the period.

780

Pilgrim's Guide Published

One of the more prominent pilgrimage authors of the Early Arab Period was the monk Epiphanius, who wrote a pilgrim's guide during the second half of the eighth century. On the subject of Jerusalem, the guide mentions David's Tower, the Church of the Holy Sepulcher, the Sheeps' Pool (Bethesda), the Holy of Holies on the Temple Mount, the Foundation Stone, and Al-Kas (the basin for ritual ablutions).

The guide also details new sites, such as Saint George's Tomb in Lydda, which was to be found in a large church along with the remains of the wheel on which the saint was tortured. Epiphanius was the first Christian to mention the city of Ramla by name.

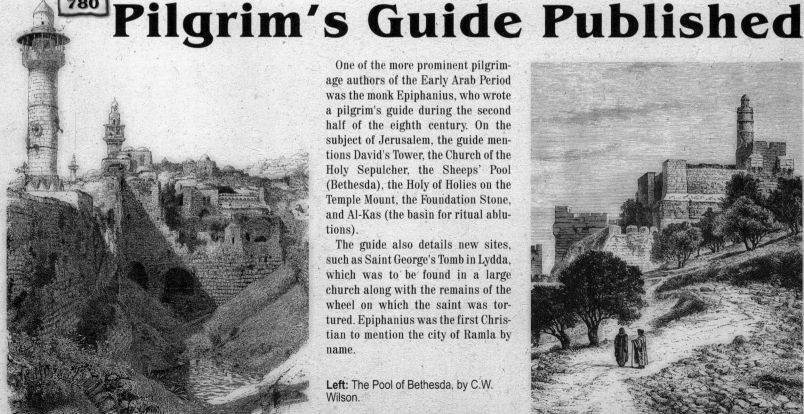

Left: The Pool of Bethesda, by C.W. Wilson.

Right: The route from Jerusalem to Bethlehem, by F. de Saulcy.

Charlemagne and Caliph Harun al-Rashid Sign Agreement

Movement of Pilgrims to Holy Land Increases. Christian Construction in Jerusalem Renewed.

The hardships involved in making pilgrimages to Jerusalem and the Christian holy places, as well as the great suffering of Christian pilgrims during their visits to the Holy Land, brought about the direct intervention of the Frankist king Charlemagne, the most important European ruler of the period.

In 797, Charlemagne dispatched a three-member delegation to Caliph Harun al-Rashid in Baghdad. The agreement that was signed as a result of the visit enabled a renewal of Christian construction in Jerusalem and increased the movement of pilgrims from Europe to the Holy Land. The accord between the two major players of the West and East caused an almost immediate transformation in the Muslim authorities' attitude towards Christian pilgrims. By the beginning of the ninth century, the Jerusalem patriarch Theodosius wrote to a friend in Constantinople that Christians were allowed to build churches and live according to their faith without being subject to oppression. The monk Bernard the Wise from the Mont Saint Michel abbey in the English Channel, who visited the Holy Land around 870, was astonished at the peace and security of the roads.

The measure of security was such that even women began joining the pilgrims. In the second half of the century nuns were reportedly serving in the Church of the Holy Sepulcher. In 880, the two saints Salome and Judith, formerly reclusive nuns in Bavaria, joined the women serving in a holy capacity in Jerusalem.

In addition to the proposed agreement with Caliph Harun al-Rashid, Charlemagne sent a letter to the patriarch of Jerusalem offering to lend his protection to the Church of the Holy Sepulcher. In response, the patriarch sent the emperor the key to the Church of the Holy Sepulcher and the flag of the city of Jerusalem. The two tokens reached Charlemagne on Christmas in the year 800, the day he was anointed emperor of Rome by Pope Leon III.

Bernard the Wise, who stayed at a hostel that was built in Jerusalem at the initiative and funding of the emperor, was especially impressed by Charlemagne's building drive in the city. In his notes he mentions several other buildings erected by Charlemagne, including monasteries for men and women, a library, a market, and a farm in the Jehoshaphat Valley intended to support these institutions.

In a bookkeeping account of the emperor's works that was published after his death is a long list of Christian buildings in Jerusalem and the people who inhabited them, as well as the costs of maintaining the churches and paying salaries to clerks. The expenses were high, and Charlemagne's son, Emperor Louis, was forced to levy a tax of one dinar per annum on all citizens of his kingdom in order to fund the maintenance of the sacred places in the Holy Land.

Historians believe that Charlemagne's ninth-century initiative to renew the wave of pilgrimage to Jerusalem and the interest he showed in the city, together with rising religious fervor in Europe, formed the basis for the later awakening of the Crusades.

Charlemagne. A bronze statue from the ninth century.

The coronation of Charlemagne by Pope Leo III.

Bedouin Attack Monasteries

Hermits Disappeared from Judean Deserts

Frequent changes of government and the transfer of the capital from Damascus to Baghdad did not improve the economic situation of the Muslim empire. The fact that the center of the government was now far to the east allowed Bedouin tribes to increase their attacks and their authority in parts of the Holy Land, Syria, and Transjordan. They accordingly stepped up their plundering raids on unprotected settlements and monasteries, in many instances murdering the inhabitants. In 796, Bedouin sacked the Mar Saba Monastery, burnt it down, and massacred all of its inhabitants. The Bedouin raids of the period eventually resulted in the disappearance of hermit monks from the Negev and Judean Deserts.

Thirty Holy Places in Jerusalem

A Christian source from the beginning of the ninth century counted approximately thirty places holy to Christians in Jerusalem, most of them on the Mount of Olives and some in the Kidron Valley and along Jerusalem's main street. At the time, most of the religious institutions were under the authority of the Greek Orthodox Church; only a minority had been established by other Christian sects.

The Jacobite Church maintained the church at the Mary Magdalene Monastery that was destroyed in 807 and rebuilt only in 1029. The center for

The Crypt of the Finding of the Cross.

Georgian monks was at a monastery in the Valley of the Cross, though they had another monastery on Mount Zion. Pilgrims who arrived in Jerusalem congregated around the Church of the Holy Sepulcher and usually enjoyed the same freedom of worship as local Christians. Every September 14, the festival of the Church of the Holy Sepulcher, called in Arabic "Id al-Zalib" (Holiday of the Cross), was celebrated. According to tradition, it was the anniversary of the day Emperor Constantine and his mother found the cross in Jerusalem.

The Monastery of the Cross in the Valley of the Cross.

Church Encourages Sinners to Make Holy Land Pilgrimages

A pilgrim with a stave.

Difficult living conditions in Europe at the end of the eighth century and the beginning of the ninth resulted in a significant rise in crime. The church and the authorities fought the phenomenon by sentencing criminals to exile and excommunication.

In the ninth century, however, the church began to encourage sinners to make pilgrimages to the holy places in order to pray and request forgiveness for their sins. Later, the church formally instituted a pilgrimage to the Holy Land as part of a route to repentance for sinners *(poenitentia)*.

The stream of pilgrims to the Holy Land subsequently grew, but the quality of the participants dropped—apparently one of the reasons for the scarcity of travel books and descriptions of journeys from the period. The few records that have been preserved were written by priests and bishops, almost the only people among the pilgrims capable of documenting their experiences.

Thanks to contacts between Emperor Charlemagne and Caliph Harun al-Rashid, special hostels for pilgrims to the Holy Land were built during this period. Additional hostels were constructed in the eleventh century by merchants from Amalfi in Italy.

Riots in Jerusalem

Patriarch Murdered at Church of Holy Sepulcher

In the tenth century, Muslim fanaticism spread to Jerusalem. In the opinion of the greatest of the Arab historians, Ibn Khaldun (1332-1406), the cause was the sacking of Mecca, the capital of Islam, by the Karmathians—a fanatical Shiite sect—in 930. The Karmathians broke the Black Stone and transferred it to their capital, the city of Al-Hasa. Afterwards, some Muslim pilgrims traveled to Jerusalem instead of Mecca.

The rise in importance of Jerusalem as a holy city for Muslims increased Muslim fanaticism in the city and brought about a significant increase in the number of attacks on Christian believers and their houses of worship. Thus, for example, the Muslims occupied the church adjacent to the Church of the Holy Sepulcher and turned it into a mosque.

On Palm Sunday in 937, a frenzied Muslim crowd attacked Christian celebrants at the Church of the Holy Sepulcher, and after looting the church, set it ablaze. The structure was renovated, but in 966, after attempts by the Muslim governor of Jerusalem to extort money from the Christian patriarch failed, the governor's men attacked the Church of the Holy Sepulcher and other churches in the city, looting their contents and torching them. Patriarch John VII, trying to defend the Church of the Holy Sepulcher with his body, was murdered by the angry mob, and his corpse burned.

Ruins in Jerusalem's Old City, by F. de Saulcy.

Increasing Numbers of Pilgrims from European Nobility

Fatimid Attempts to Secure Roads Bring Rise in Movement of Pilgrims

The Fatimid government, in contrast to its predecessors in the region, viewed pilgrims and tourists as an important source of income and tried to facilitate their travel. Thus, for example, the Fatimids permitted Christian pilgrims to visit holy places located in villages and towns that had become Muslim, like Cana and Nazareth. In a few instances they even allowed the Christians to restore the houses of worship that had once stood at these sites.

The efforts by the Fatimid authorities in the second half of the tenth century to secure the roads in the Holy Land and encourage visits of Christian pilgrims in Jerusalem and at holy places in the country brought an almost immediate rise in the number of pilgrims. Among them were many members of the aristocracy, like the counts of Anhalt and Verdun. Noblemen from Vienna and other places in Europe made the trip as well. The improvement in the safety of the roads also gave rise to a renewal of women pilgrims from the European aristoc-

racy. One of them was Judith, the duchess of Bavaria and the sister-in-law of Emperor Otto I, whose extended visit in Jerusalem took place in 970. She was preceded by Countess Hilda,

who died on the way to Jerusalem in 969. The many visits of senior clergy to the Holy Land also indicate the

relative equanimity with which pilgrimage was regarded. Saint Conrad, the bishop of Constance, came to Jerusalem three times. Saint John, the bishop of Parma, made six pilgrim-

ages to the holy city. Both left behind reports of their travels in the Holy Land.

Nazareth, by H.B. Tristram.

Byzantine Attempt to Liberate Holy Places Fails

Joint Attack by Byzantine Army and Muslim Tribes Curbed by Egyptian Fatimid Army

The Byzantine attack on Holy Land ports, which commenced as a result of an agreement signed between Byzantium and the Muslim tribes in 974, was in effect a continuation of an attack of the previous decade.

In view of the disintegration of Abbasid rule in Baghdad and the corresponding weakening of local government in the Arab empire, the Byzantine leadership assumed it could occupy the region anew, thus liberating the holy places from Arab rule. Its army succeeded in vanquishing Aleppo, Antioch, and Northern Syria.

Almost simultaneously, Egyptian forces attempted to gain control over the region from the south. At the time, Egypt was ruled by the Shiite Fatimid Dynasty that controlled North Africa and was related to the Prophet's family through his daughter Fatimah. The Fatimids, who had already declared themselves the legal caliphs, now took advantage of the impotence of the Abbasids to conquer Mecca and Medina, Syria, and the Holy Land. In

Christian horsemen attack a fortified city.

the inevitable clash between the Byzantine Christian forces from the north and the Fatimid Muslim forces from the south, the latter emerged victorious. The Christian forces withdrew, leaving the Holy Land in the hands of the Muslims for more than a century.

Holy Land Agriculture Ruined

During the Early Arab Period, the Holy Land deteriorated from an agricultural land into a wasteland. The degeneration had two main causes: the Arab *dhimmi* laws and the great invasions of the Bedouin tribes that arrived from the Arabian Peninsula either in the wake of the Arab army or as part of it.

The Arab rulers did not nationalize lands; they levied a permanent tax on them. The arrangement appeared ideal to the Arab authorities: their dependents would continue to work the land and the taxes they paid would maintain its actual lords.

But while the tax rate was fixed, crops changed from year to year. In years of drought or years in which the

crops did not thrive, the number of Christian farmers who could not meet the tax payments and were forced to abandon their lands swelled.

The Bedouin tribes who were granted rights to settle large portions of the Holy Land also forced local farmers out, looted their property, and evicted them from their villages. Only in 1029 did the Egyptian Fatimid army succeed in overcoming the Bedouin tribes and expelling them from the Holy Land. By then, after four centuries of Arab rule, most of the villages had been deserted and entire agriculturally rich regions had become wastelands.

An Arab fellah working in the fields.

CALIPH AL-HAKIM DESTROYS CHURCH OF HOLY SEPULCHER

Damage to Church Horrifies Christian World. Caliph Demands Christian Conversion to Islam.

In September 1009, the Fatimid caliph Al-Hakim (996-1021) gave orders to raze the Church of the Holy Sepulcher. According to Muslim sources, he did so because of the church's ostentation and high status as a pilgrimage center. The damage to the holy place horrified the Christian world.

Al-Hakim did not content himself with destroying churches and synagogues throughout the kingdom; he enlarged his program to the persecution of Christians and Jews, forcing them to become Muslims or leave the country.

Where he failed, the powerful earthquake of 1016 succeeded, leveling cities and holy places in the Holy Land. In 1020, a year before his death, the caliph reversed his edicts with the same precipitousness with which he had formerly announced them, and gave permission for the Christians in the Holy Land to renew the construction of their houses of worship.

Caliph al-Hakim orders the destruction of the Church of the Holy Sepulcher. From a fourteenth-century Persian manuscript.

Package Deal: Church of Holy Sepulcher in Exchange for Mosque

In 1027, a cease-fire agreement was signed between the Byzantines and Caliph al-Tahar. It contained bilateral permission to reopen both the Great Mosque in Constantinople and the Church of the Holy Sepulcher in Jerusalem. At the time, however, the Christians in Jerusalem were in such dire financial straits that only two decades later, in 1048, were they able to complete the restoration of the church.

Pilgrims Organize in Large Groups

Convoys and Armed Escorts Reduce Robbers' Success Rate

The 1029 victory of the Fatimid army over the Arab tribes, and the latters' expulsion back to the Arabian Peninsula, improved the level of safety on the roads, but moving securely through the Holy Land was still a dubious proposition.

A solution to the shaky security situation was provided by the pilgrims themselves, who began to organize themselves into large groups. At the beginning of the eleventh century, the count of Normandy set out at the head of a group of seven hundred pilgrims. When they arrived in the Holy Land, the pilgrims hired Fatimid soldiers to escort them throughout their journey.

In 1054, three thousand pilgrims led by the bishop of Cambria in France set out for the Holy Land. In 1066, the wave of Christian pilgrims reached a new high when a convoy of twelve thousand pilgrims arrived in Jerusalem from southern Germany and Holland. Pilgrimages en masse, usually escorted by guards from a local army, while greatly reducing the success rate of looting attacks, did not succeed in subduing them completely. In 1065 a convoy of seven thousand pilgrims departed Germany, only to be attacked by Bedouin near Ramla. Intervention on the part of the local emir and his army extricated the convoy, which suffered huge losses, though it nevertheless continued on its way.

The mosques of Constantinople.

Seljuks Conquer Jerusalem

In 1073, the Seljuks captured Fatimid Jerusalem and destroyed the city's environs.

The Seljuks were tyrannical, malevolent occupiers, and the city's inhabitants revolted at the first opportunity.

The rebellion was crushed with an iron fist in 1076. Even the few inhabitants who managed to escape to the Al-Aqsa Mosque were executed: only those citizens who hid in the Dome of the Rock were saved.

CHAPTER IV

THE KINGDOM OF JERUSALEM

1099-1187

he principalities established by the Crusaders after the First Crusade were collectively called "The Kingdom of Jerusalem" (Regnum Hierosolymitanum). In the narrow sense, the name referred to the southernmost of the four Crusader principalities (Edessa, Antioch, Tripoli, and Jerusalem) that spread from the Gulf of Alexandrata in the north to Eilat in the south. The Jerusalem principality, which was also called "The Kingdom of David" and even "Israel," was founded by what was left of the First Crusade's army after its three year journey from the moment it departed Europe until after the wars it fought in Syria and eastern Asia.

In May 1099, the Crusader army appeared on the coastal road leading from Lebanon to the Holy Land. It made its way via Caesarea to Ramla, and from there ascended to Jerusalem, the conquest of which was the declared objective of the Crusader movement.

The Crusaders' initial thrust after their conquest of the capital was directed at the country's interior. Bethlehem, whose residents were Eastern Christians, had surrendered even before Jerusalem was taken. Jericho and Nablus likewise capitulated to the Crusaders while Tancred took over Beit She'an and Tiberias without a battle, transforming the latter into the capital of a new principality—of Galilee.

The last serious attempt by the Egyptians to engage the Crusaders in armed conflict ended in the defeat of Egypt at the Battle of Ashkelon (August 1099) and gave the Crusaders time to vanquish the coastal cities. Jaffa, abandoned by its Muslim residents, served as a principle port for the Crusaders, who were dependent during this early period on their supply of troops, horses, weapons, and provisions from abroad.

The conquest of the other coastal cities—in which the Crusader regiments were aided by the fleets of the Italian cities of Venice, Genoa, and Pisa—continued from 1100 to 1110. Haifa, whose fortress was small but nevertheless significant, due to its shipyard, was conquered first, in 1100. Afterwards, Arsuf (1101), Caesarea (1101), Acre (1104)—whose superior port was protected by strong walls—Beirut (1110), and Sidon (1110) were all subdued. Only two of the coastal cities remained in Muslim hands: Tyre, which was ultimately won by the Crusaders in 1124, and Ashkelon, which was wrested from Egypt only in 1153.

The conquest of the ports facilitated the renewal of military and commercial ties with Europe and aided in cementing the relationship between the Crusader nation in the Holy Land and the northern principalities of Tripoli and Antioch. In addition, the victories prevented Egypt, whose naval force was still far more powerful than that of the Crusaders, from using the coastal cities as bridgeheads for invading the Crusader realm.

The further advance of the Crusaders was directed northwards to Terre de Suete, eastwards from the Sea of Galilee to the Golan, the Hauran, and up to Damascus, and southwards from Moab and Edom down to Eilat. The 1129 conquest of Banyas—subsequently lost by the Crusaders in 1132 but retaken by them in 1140—secured their control of the main road for military movement and the transfer of goods from Damascus to the port of Tyre.

The expansion of the Crusaders into southern Transjordan began as early as 1100. They gained control of Eilat in 1113 and in 1142 fortified Le Crac, solidifying their hold on this territory and establishing their supervision of the land link between Syria and Egypt as well as the pilgrim route (Darb el-Haj) from the Muslim north to Mecca and Medina in Arabia.

This broad extension of Crusader power in the south, in tandem with the expansion of the barony of Tripoli and the principalities of Antioch and Edessa in the north, awakened opposition in the Muslim world. In 1113 at the Seljuk center in Mosul a movement emerged that was intended to unify the Muslim principalities of Iraq and Syria in a joint operation against the Crusaders. It reached its peak during the days of the Muslim ruler Zanghi, who in 1127 succeeded in gaining control of the entire Iraqi-Syrian territory with the exception of Damascus, which preserved its independence and even became an ally of the Crusaders. The first fruit of the Muslim reunification was the 1114 fall of the principality of Edessa to Zanghi and the resulting exposure of the northeastern border of the Crusader kingdom.

The Second Crusade (1146-1149), led by the kings of Europe, did not bring much benefit to the Crusaders. They were unable to regain Edessa, and their foiled attack on Damascus in 1148 proved to be a political error that aided Nur a-Din, Zanghi's successor, in entering the city in 1154, whereupon he formed a unified Muslim bloc in the north.

This uniform front, in preventing the Crusaders from expanding eastward, directed them towards Egypt, where internal wars were then weakening the country's power of resistance. Among other considerations turning the Crusader troops westward was the danger of Egypt's unification with the Nur a-Din kingdom. The Crusaders invaded Egypt several times until their final determined march on the land of the Nile compelled the Egyptians to appeal for help to Nur a-Din; with his assistance, the Egyptians managed to expel the Crusaders from their territory.

In 1170, Saladin, the son of Ayub, ascended the throne in Egypt and steered its foreign policy towards unification with Syria and Iraq, finally conquering Aleppo in 1183. Though at first he made only hesitant attempts to penetrate the Crusader frontier, in 1177 these forays developed into a concerted strategic campaign. Saladin invaded Daron and Gaza, conquered Ramla, lay siege to Lydda, and advanced on Arsuf. Only at the Battle of Montgisart was he at last defeated by Baldwin III. His attempts to impose a naval blockade on the Crusaders from 1179 to 1182, which were accompanied by attacks on Galilee, Beit She'an, and Beirut, came to an end in 1182 with a new Crusader victory at the Battle of Forbelet.

In 1183 an adventurous attempt was made by Reynald de Chatillon to conquer Eilat, gain control of the Red Sea, and reach Mecca and Medina. That same year, Saladin conquered Beit She'an, laid siege to Le Crac, and destroyed Nablus, Samaria, and Jezreel. His engagements with the Crusaders culminated in the Battle of Karnei Hattin in July of 1187 and the terrible defeat of the Crusader army, which had set out from Sepphoris to the aid of the besieged city of Tiberias. In the wake of the catastrophe at Karnei Hattin, all of the Crusader cities and fortresses in the Holy Land—including the capital of Jerusalem—surrendered to Saladin.

❧

Because of Jerusalem's special status, its principality was the most important in the Crusader realm and only its ruler was known by the title of "king"; rulers of other Crusader lands made due with the title of "comte"—as in Tripoli—or "prince," as in Antioch and Edessa. Because of its stature, as well as the religious and political interests it shared with the northern Crusader holdings, the Kingdom of Jerusalem was forced from time to time to enter into the tangled problems of these nations.

The Kingdom of Jerusalem was a feudal state that adopted the eleventh-century governmental system of France. Godfrey of Bouillon made do with the title of "Protector of the Holy Sepulcher," but his successors were crowned as kings.

The primary institution of the kingdom was the High Court (Haute Cour)—a council of the direct vassals of the king that was joined from the mid-twelfth century onward by the sub-vassals of the kingdom. The powers of this body were undefined, and it changed from an entity dedicated to advising and assisting the strong rulers of the first part of the twelfth century to an equal of the kings by the end of that period. In the thirteenth century it assumed total control of the kingdom.

The High Court was the locus of most of the authority of the Crusader government in the Holy Land. It operated as a court in conflicts between the direct vassals of the king and was in charge of legislation, administration, and finance. It dictated matters of state, empowered peace treaties, and declared war.

As were other medieval nations, the Kingdom of Jerusalem was divided into feuds belonging to the vassals of the kingdom. The special status of the Crusader rulers meant that even the large principalities of Edessa, Antioch, and Tripoli, which were autonomous states in every other regard, were considered vassal states of the kings of Jerusalem.

Within the kingdom itself, the Holy Land was divided into four large baronies: the barony of Jaffa-Ashkelon; the barony of Galilee, whose capital was Tiberias; the seigniory of Sidon-Caesarea and Beit She'an; and the seigniory of Montreal-Hebron. To the four major baronies should be added those of Joscelin de Courtenay, which included large territories in Western Galilee and a significant number of smaller seigniories. A separate status was reserved for the ecclesiastical seigniories: Lydda and Nazareth. The baronies were organized like minor kingdoms, and at their head was a "court" composed of the baron's vassals.

Cities played an important role in the Crusader realm—a phenomenon found in the Christian world at the time only in Byzantium and Italy. While the cities in the Crusader kingdom did not quite achieve communal independence, they did enjoy a certain autonomy. They had a Cour des Bourgeois, which performed judicial, administrative, and policing functions and was headed by a nobleman who was called a "vicomte." These courts, of which there were thirty-seven at one point, wielded authority over the non-aristocratic Frankish population and were present in every Frankish settlement. Municipal military authority was in the hands of a special governor—the Castellanus Chatelain.

The development of trade brought about the creation of what came to be known as "Harbor Courts" (Cour de la Chaine), handling only disputes that arose as a result of naval transactions. They were directed by naval experts.

The colonies of traders from the cities of Italy, France, and Spain (Amalfi, Genoa, Pisa, Venice, Marseilles, and Barcelona) who settled in the Crusader ports were called communes. Due to the assistance these European cities had provided the Crusaders throughout the conquest of the Holy Land, the communes were granted a long list of privileges—most of them commercial and a few of them administrative. The communes enjoyed an autonomy that was expressed by their ownership of special quarters in the port cities. These quarters generally contained a market, commercial enterprises belonging to the commune, a church, a bakery, and a bathhouse, all of which endowed the quarter with the character of an independent domain within a city. In the Holy Land, the major centers of the communes were in Acre and Tyre.

The majority of the population in the Holy Land during this period was not Franks, but Muslims, Eastern Christians, Jews, and Samaritans, and the Crusaders allowed the local sects a good deal of autonomy. When such populations resided in a city, they usually did so freely, despite having to pay special taxes. The Crusader kingdom's relative weakness from a numerical point of view mandated the utilization of all its forces for defense purposes. The Frankish population was comprised of about one hundred and twenty thousand people. Out of these, the state was able to muster an army of six hundred cavalry and about five thousand infantry troops—huge numbers relative to the standards of the time. Together with the forces of the military orders and the regiments from the principalities of Antioch and Tripoli, the Crusader force is estimated to have consisted of about 2,000 cavalry and about 18,000 infantry.

The principle force of the Crusader army was the heavily armed cavalry. Each cavalier was equipped with an iron helmet, armor, a shield, two swords (long and short), and a spear. Alongside the cavaliers, each of whom required at least three horses and the support of two batmen, the Crusaders established a light cavalry force similar to that of the Muslims. This corps was composed mostly of natives of the Holy Land—Armenians, Maronites, Syrians, and even Muslims—who were called "Turcopliers" (Turks). Similar to it was a light cavalry force of Mounted Sergeants.

The main weapon of the light cavalry was a small bow whose efficiency the Crusaders had learned from the Turks. The infantry was mainly an archery corps with crossbowmen and spearmen.

The Crusader strongholds were superior in both size and quantity to all fortifications built in the Holy Land before and after them. The permanent state of war in which the Crusaders existed and the severe shortage of the soldiers whose mission was to maintain it spurred the Christian rulers to erect an extensive network of fortifications intended to defend the borders of the state and points of strategic importance like river crossings, junctions, hills, and plains.

The military orders, which were later to play an important political role in Europe, were founded in the Holy Land during this period, and it was in them that the Crusader ideal was most completely realized. Common to all of these orders was the notion of the perfect Christian: warrior and monk combined. As the Kingdom of Jerusalem fell into decline, almost the entire burden of defending its weakened borders fell on these orders, which accordingly entrenched themselves in all of the outlying strongholds of the realm.

Agriculture was the mainstay of the Crusader Kingdom, though it remained the occupation of locals only. Content to simply collect produce from the holdings of the peasants, the Crusaders relinquished direct cultivation of their lands to the native population. The populace that worked in agriculture was mostly Muslim, but in certain territories—the vicinity of Jerusalem, Bethlehem, Mount Tabor, and Nazareth—the Syrian Christian agricultural population survived as well. It is worth noting the attempts of the Crusaders to develop agricultural roots in the Holy Land by creating villages populated by Europeans. The charters the Frankish settlers of these spots received assured their personal freedom and granted them about 175 acres per family. They enjoyed the privileges of legal autonomy, low taxes, and a portion of the booty taken from Muslims. Such villages (sometimes consisting of five hundred or more people) were larger than the other agricultural settlements in the country, were built around fortresses that served as shelter in times of trouble, and occasionally grew into walled towns. In general, however, the Crusader population refused to leave the cities, and in the thirteenth century such rural experiments were not renewed.

Trade in the Holy Land peaked during the Crusader period as the country became one of the important crossroads of international commerce. Trade routes between the Far East, India, Madagascar, Africa, and Europe traversed its length and breadth. The main middlemen in the movement of merchandise were the Italian communes, which concentrated a significant portion of products from the East in the ports of the Holy Land, then transferred them to Italy and from there to France, Germany, and England. The Crusader cities, the meeting points for Muslim and Armenian Christian merchants on the one hand and European merchants on the other, were ideal as the setting for the midway trade between the East and the West.

Pope Calls for Crusade to Liberate Jerusalem

Knights Asked to End Feuding and Save Holy Sepulcher. Excitement Abounds.

On November 27, 1095, the last day of the Council of Clermont, Pope Urban II appealed to the noblemen of Europe and their knights to embark on a crusade to save the Holy Tomb in Jerusalem from the Muslim heretics. From the minutes of the council as recorded by Guibert de Nogent, who left us with a historical account of the times, the church was not only concerned with the liberation of the holy places, but wished to bring an end to the wars between noblemen that had weakened the Christian world. In the absence of strong central governments in Europe, the armies of the various noblemen were engaged in local feuds, leaving the Continent easy prey to invaders from the East.

The pope implored the noblemen to desist from their territorial battles, which he claimed were rooted in avarice and conceit. He proposed that they dedicate themselves instead to a war that would ensure them glory in this world and the next. The pope's call to liberate Jerusalem from the infidels ignited all of Europe with a religious fervor that surprised even church leaders. The noblemen, for their part, were tempted by the pope with promises of new estates and war booty. To the masses of believers who would join the crusade, the papal authority promised pardon for their sins in the next world and great wealth in this one.

Pope Urban II preaches at the Clermont Council of 1095. From a fifteenth-century French manuscript.

Four European Centers Established in Anticipation of Crusade

Godfrey of Bouillon leading his men. From William of Tyre's thirteenth-century book.

Following Pope Urban II's call to liberate the Holy Sepulcher in Jerusalem from the nonbelievers, the commanders of the proposed crusade established four European centers from which the expeditions would proceed. Each center was responsible for organizing and equipping its own army. Two centers were established in France: the first, commanded by Duke Robert of Normandy, mustered the Normans and the Anglo-Normans in northern France; the second, under the command of Raymond of Saint-Gilles, the baron of Provence, was organized in southern France. The third camp, commanded by Duke Godfrey of Bouillon, gathered together those joining the ranks from the Netherlands and Germany. A fourth camp, based in Italy and under the command of Bohemund and Tancred, assembled mainly Norman participants from Sicily and southern Italy.

Adhemar of Puy, the papal representative, was appointed commander in chief and assigned responsibility for the organization of the entire campaign. The camps were to convene in Constantinople in anticipation of their passage to the East.

Crusader knights leave their homes and depart for the crusade. From a fifteenth-century French manuscript.

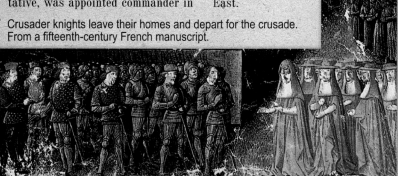

1096 Thousands of Pilgrims Massacred

Seljuks Ambush Faithful As They Cross Bosporus

Pope Urban II's call to liberate the Holy Land excited both the spirit and the faith of many common people. Groups of faithful began to move east across Europe on what was later called the Peasants' Crusade. Peter the Hermit, a religious leader whose great rhetorical skills attracted a significant following among the peasants and common folk, led one of the largest of these groups. These believers, putting their faith in God, embarked on their journeys without any preparations, relying almost exclusively on divine protection. Despite the many dangers, many even took along their wives and children. Their ignorance about the nature of the journey was so great that at every stop they asked the local population if they had reached Jerusalem yet. Since they had neglected to make sufficient preparations, their supplies were depleted while they were still in Bohemia, and they began to confiscate food and supplies from the local inhabitants. The harm they caused, especially in Hungary and the Balkans, provoked increasing hostility. Eventually, fighting broke out and many of the pilgrims were killed.

Peter the Hermit's party arrived at the Bosporus, which then separated the Byzantine and Seljuk forces, at the beginning of October, 1096. Believ-

Peter the Hermit at the head of the Peasants' Crusade. A medieval manuscript.

ing that the heavens were watching over them, they crossed the straits, and were immediately ambushed by the Seljuk army awaiting them. According to one of the accounts, the well-trained Seljuk soldiers attacked with drawn swords, killing peasants, clerks, priests, monks, women, and children. Among the few who succeeded in escaping the slaughter was Peter the Hermit.

The cruel massacre shocked Europe and provoked a call to avenge the blood of the slain, adding the sentiment of revenge to the religious fervor that already gripped the Continent. Many knights and warriors who had not previously joined the Crusader camp did so as a result of the heartless slaughter. Others, however, understood the incident as a punishment sent from heaven for the looting and wanton destruction that had preceded it.

Crusaders Enter Holy Land

The Crusaders entered the Holy Land from the north after marching almost without stopping to the port city of Tripoli in northern Lebanon. There, residents of the city barricaded themselves behind the city walls while the Crusaders, spurred on by the fervor of the masses of pilgrims, did not pause to conquer the city, but continued their journey south. They also circumvented the other fortified coastal cities, the majority of which were under control of the Egyptian Fatimids.

Approximately mid-way between Caesarea and Jaffa, the Crusader army turned east towards Ramla. They arrived there on June 3, 1099 to find the city empty of inhabitants. The residents of neighboring Lydda had also left their homes, but only after burning down the Monastery of Saint George. The Crusaders rested three days in Ramla, left behind a garrison, and moved on to Jerusalem.

On June 7, 1099, at the conclusion of a 3,000-mile journey, the Crusaders stood northwest of Jerusalem at the tomb of the prophet Samuel and gazed at the holy, fortified city. Overcome with emotion, the Crusaders kneeled and offered a prayer of thanksgiving. The mountain was afterwards known as Montjoie (Mount of Joy) in remembrance of the elation of the Crusaders at that moment.

Above: Crusader knights, by G. Doré.
Left: Crusaders on their way to the Holy Land. From William of Tyre's thirteenth-century book.

At the Gates of Jerusalem

Crusaders bow in a prayer of thanksgiving at the sight of Jerusalem from Montjoie, by G. Doré *(below)*; and the tomb of the prophet Samuel on the summit of Montjoie *(left)*.

Lydda: First Latin Bishopric in Holy Land

The remains of the Church of Saint George, by C.W. Wilson.

The first Latin bishopric in the Holy Land was established in Lydda, the birthplace of Saint George. According to tradition, Saint George is buried there in the crypt of the Church of Saint George.

The establishment of the Lydda bishopric was announced during the Crusaders' stay in Lydda and Ramla on their way to Jerusalem. Later, the two cities were declared an ecclesiastical seigniorage—property of the church, that is—though in 1119 the king of Jerusalem reduced the area of the estate and redefined Ramla and its environs as a separate seigniorage, belonging to one of his noblemen.

CRUSADERS CONQUEF

Eyewitness Raymond of Aguilers reports from th describe the shocking scenes, you wouldn't belie by Excitement. Enormous Stream of Donatio

Crusaders before the walls of Jerusalem, during the first foiled attack. From a medieval manuscript.

On Friday, July 15, 1099, a little more than a month after the siege on Jerusalem had begun, the Crusader army breached the city's walls and occupied it, its defenders incurring heavy losses. According to estimates, the number of dead climbed to between twenty and thirty thousand people.

Despite the relative brevity of the siege, the Crusaders suffered grave losses as well. The city walls were too high to be surmounted without siege towers, but their construction required wood, and the hills around Jerusalem were bare. The Crusader commanders, having failed to solve

Crusaders breach the wall of Jerusalem, by G. Doré. The siege towers were built from ships dismantled at the port of Jaffa, by H. Wölffli (left).

the problem, nevertheless surrendered to pressure of the masses of excited and impatient pilgrims, who had been agitated by Peter the Hermit: on June 13, an order was given for the soldiers to storm Jerusalem's walls.

"God is omnipotent. If he wishes, he will conquer the city walls even if he has only one ladder," the hermit promised the restless masses and the Crusader leaders. But lacking the proper equipment for overcoming the wall and ramming the gates, the attackers were easily repulsed by the Fatimid Egyptian forces that had dominion over the city.

The scarcity of wood for siege tow-

Godfrey of Bouillon, and Tancred, attempted to breach the wall by means of a second siege tower near Herod's Gate. Both attacks were repelled.

The following day at daybreak, a second offensive commenced. This time, Godfrey of Bouillon's soldiers

Right: Peter the Hermit encourages the Crusader warriors.

Below: Saint George exhorts the Crusader warriors during the breakthrough to Jerusalem, by G. Doré.

ers was finally remedied in the form of a Genovese fleet of ships anchored in the port of Jaffa at the time. The ships' masts and other fittings were dismantled and brought to Jerusalem. Over the next three weeks, two large siege towers were erected. On July fourteenth, the Crusaders drew one siege tower close to the city wall in the vicinity of Mount Zion and a unit of knights commanded by Raymond of Saint-Gilles attempted to storm its way onto the wall. Another force, commanded by Robert of Normandy,

succeeded in attaching the siege tower to the city wall and penetrating the fortifications. The defenders inside, thrown into a panic, retreated from their positions before the oncoming Crusaders. Meanwhile, a second force commanded by Tancred advanced towards the Temple Mount, and a third outfit commanded by Raymond of Saint-Gilles invaded the city from the direction of Mount Zion and made its way towards Jerusalem's Citadel. "This was not the cruelest battle in which I have ever partici-

JERUSALEM

attlefield: "If I were to e." Christian World Gripped estores Holy Places.

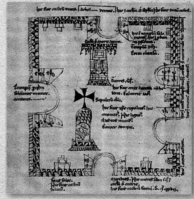

Above: A scene from the massacre in Jerusalem, by G. Doré.
Left: A twelfth-century manuscript Illustration of the Crusaders at Jerusalem's gates.
Below: The Crusaders, like other conquerors before them, looted Jerusalem. Antiochus loots Jerusalem, a fifteenth-century French manuscript.

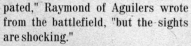

A map of the 1099 occupation of Jerusalem depicting the array of Crusader forces around the city walls.

pated," Raymond of Aguilers wrote from the battlefield, "but the sights are shocking."

The last of the city's defenders soon ensconced themselves in the Citadel, the obvious impregnability of which finally convinced the Crusader commanders to permit them to leave the city in safety.

The news of the occupation of Jerusalem was received with unprecedented excitement in Europe. An enormous stream of donations began to arrive in Jerusalem and the occupied areas, dispatched to expedite the immediate restoration of the Church of the Holy Sepulcher and the holy places in Nazareth, many of which had been destroyed or turned into mosques over the years. A huge wave of pilgrims from all over Europe began to make its way to the shores of the Holy Land.

The day of the liberation of Jerusalem was declared a formal holiday and celebrated with a grand procession that set out from the Church of the

Holy Sepulcher in the early hours of the morning for the Templum Domini (on the Temple Mount), the patriarch marching at its head. Prayers were held in the square in front of the Templum Domini, after which the cortege proceeded outside the city's eastern wall to honor the graves of those who fell in the campaign to occupy the city. After crossing Jehoshaphat Street (today the Street of the Lions, near the Lions' Gate), the procession went on to the northeastern corner of the wall, where a large cross marked the spot at which Godfrey of Bouillon's knights had breached it. Once there, the patriarch gave a sermon and prayers were said.

True Cross Discovered in Jerusalem

In August 1099, about one month after their conquest of Jerusalem, the Crusaders discovered a small piece of the True Cross secreted in a cache in the city.

According to a report from Fulcher of Chartres, who participated in the First Crusade and then settled in Jerusalem, the cross, hidden in times past by clergymen, was discovered by a Syrian believer who received the information from his father. The holy cross, which was covered in silver and gold, was carried in a festive procession to the Holy Sepulcher, those escorting it singing songs of thanksgiving to God for preserving the precious artifact.

According to Ansellus, a priest who served in the Church of the Holy Sepulcher in 1120, after Saint Helena found the true cross she gave orders to cut it in two; one part she left in Jerusalem and the other half she took to her son Constantine in Constantinople.

The Jerusalem cross was later captured by Khosrow, the king of Persia, and then restored to Jerusalem by the Emperor Heraclius. After the latter's death, local Muslims wanted to torch the cross. The Christians of Jerusalem decided to divide the cross into many pieces and send them to communities of believers throughout the world, so that even if the Muslims succeeded in burning one piece, the other pieces would survive.

According to Ansellus, in Constantinople there were three crosses in addition to the emperor's cross, two crosses in Cyprus, one in Crete, three in Antioch, one in Edessa, one in Alexandria, one in Damascus, one in Ashkelon, four in Jerusalem (with the Syrians, with the Greeks at Mar Saba, with the monks in the Jehoshaphat Valley, and with the Latins), one was held by the Georgian patriarch, and the king of Georgia guarded one.

Ansellus succeeded in purchasing the King of Georgia's cross from his widow, who had settled in Jerusalem, and he sent it to the Church of Notre Dame in Paris, where he had served before being dispatched to the Holy Land.

A fragment of the True Cross located in the Church of the Holy Sepulcher.

An Epistle to the Pope

A letter from the leaders of the First Crusade to the pope, written in September 1099, records the capture of Jerusalem and the victory at Ashkelon.

A letter from Daimbert, archbishop of Pisa, papal legate, Godfrey of Bouillon advocate of the Holy Sepulcher, and Raymond of Toulouse, and all the army in the land of Israel, to the pope and all the Christian faithful.

Since the army was suffering greatly in this siege from lack of water, a council was held, and the bishops and leaders preached the necessity of walking round the city with bare feet. The Lord was pleased with this act of humility, for on the eighth day after we performed it he handed over to us the city, together with his enemies. This was on 15 July 1099.

If you want to know what was done to the enemies we found in the city, know this: that in the portico of Solomon and in his Temple, our men rode in the blood of the Saracens up to the knees of their horses. Then we made arrangements as to who should hold the city. The others desired to return out of love of home and piety towards their parents. But then the news came that al-Afdal, vizier of Cairo, had come to Ashkelon with a multitude of pagans, to take captive the Franks who were in Jerusalem, and to capture Antioch: so he claimed but the Lord had decided otherwise.

When we had found out for certain that al-Afdal's army was at Ashkelon, we set out to meet them, leaving our baggage and our sick with a garrison in Jerusalem. When the two armies caught sight of each other, we knelt and called on God our helper.

In our army there were not more than five thousand cavalry and fifteen thousand infantry, while the enemy could have had a hundred thousand horse and four hundred thousand foot. Then God's doing was marvelous in the eyes of his servants, since, before we entered the conflict, by our charge alone we drove this multitude to flight and tore away all their weapons, so that even if they wanted to fight back they lacked the equipment in which they trusted. More than one hundred thousand Saracens fell there by the sword, but their fear was such that at the gate of the city of Ashkelon around two thousand were suffocated in the crush. Countless more died in the sea; thorn-bushes caught many. The world itself clearly fought for us, and had not the spoils of the camp detained many of our people, there would have been very few enemy left.

On the day before the battle the army captured many thousands of camels and cattle and sheep. And when at the princes' command the people let them go, because they were going to fight, wonderful to relate, the camels formed many and multiple squadrons, and the cattle and sheep likewise. Moreover these animals marched in company with us, so that when we halted they halted, when we advanced they advanced, when we charged they charged. Also clouds protected us from the heat of the sun and cooled us down.

This battle took place on 29 July 1099 at Ashkelon against al-Afdal. A hundred thousand Egyptian horse and forty thousand foot were conquered by a small army of Christians. Thanks be to God. Here the letter ends.

Mosque Becomes Palace for Jerusalem Kings

The first palace of the Crusader kings was the building of the ornate Al-Aqsa Mosque, which the Crusaders called Solomon's Temple. The first three kings of the Kingdom of Jerusalem, Godfrey, Baldwin I, and Baldwin II, lived in the palace.

Tancred of Apulia Conquers Galilee with 80 Knights

At the head of a regiment of eighty knights, the Norman prince Tancred of Apulia swiftly succeeded in conquering Nablus, Beit She'an, Tiberias, and Mount Tabor. Finding himself in a favorable position, Tancred then led his small army to the Golan Heights and Transjordan, forcing the Muslim rulers of Damascus to negotiate an agreement introducing joint control of the territory south of Damascus.

Tancred's ambitions were consonant with his status, which was higher than that of the majority of the other noble Crusaders. Most of the other participants were minor nobility or knights, and were satisfied with conquering estates for themselves. Tancred sought to establish for himself an independent principality whose capital would be Tiberias, whose port would be in Haifa, and which would include the Sea of Galilee and the entire Galilee northwards up to the outskirts of Damascus. Tancred also intended to advance on Acre, but the unexpected death of Godfrey de Bouillon, king of Jerusalem, resulted in a slight change of

plans; Tancred now sought to reposition himself so as to better compete for the inheritance. Instead of Acre, he turned to Haifa, which was less fortified, and vanquished it. Nevertheless, he lost the contest for Jerusalem to Baldwin I, Godfrey's brother. His plans to invade Galilee were also interrupted when, the prince of Antioch languishing in Seljuk captivity, the people of the principality invited Tancred to rule over them. He accepted their invitation and was crowned prince of Antioch.

A capital from the Crusader Church of the Annunciation in Nazareth, rebuilt during the reign of Tancred of Apulia.

Godfrey of Bouillon, Protector of the Holy Sepulcher

Godfrey of Bouillon's seal.

After conquering Jerusalem, Godfrey of Bouillon was appointed ruler of the liberated city, and took upon himself the title "Protector of the Holy Sepulcher." One year afterwards, he died of fever and was buried in the

Church of the Holy Sepulcher. The grave disappeared in the great fire of 1808, after which much of the church was destroyed.

According to legend, shortly before

request and opened the box while standing on the wall of Bouillon Castle. Inside the box were seeds that scattered in the wind around the courtyard of the citadel, disappearing into the cracks of the stones. Since then, every June, the month in which the Crusaders first arrived in Jerusalem, pink flowers bloom in the courtyard of Bouillon Castle, their wonderful scent filling the air with the aroma of holy Jerusalem.

A Crusader king in Jerusalem. A fourteenth-century French manuscript illustration.

Above: Godfrey's tomb in the Church of the Holy Sepulcher.
Right: Godfrey's sword, spurs, and cross, kept today in the Church of the Holy Sepulcher.

his death Godfrey summoned one of his most loyal knights and presented him with a small box, extracting from him a promise to take it to Godfrey's home in Bouillon, and only there to open it.

The knight fulfilled Godfrey's last

First Order of Knights Established in Jerusalem

Hospitalers to Care for Sick and Needy While Fighting the Good Fight

Above left: Godfrey of Bouillon's seal.
Above: Hospitaler knights in their fortress on Rhodes.

The entrance portal of Santa Maria Latina, the Hospitaler church in Jerusalem, by E. Pierotti.

In 1100, a group of knights from the Crusader force that conquered Jerusalem announced their intention to dedicate their lives to caring for the sick and needy. The announcement, which came a short time after the conquest of Jerusalem, was a response to the great suffering that the Crusaders had witnessed on their long march to the city. Members of the group established the Order of Hospitalers, named for Saint John the Baptist, and proceeded to tend the unfortunate from among their fellow Crusaders.

The Knights of the Order of Hospitalers wore black robes with a white, eight-pointed cross (a Maltese cross) on the upper left-hand side. Their activities earned them the esteem of the Crusader royal house, which gave them buildings in the Muristan area of Jerusalem for their activities. The pilgrim John of Würzburg, who arrived in the city several years after the order began its activity, relates that next to a lovely church dedicated to John the Baptist was a hospital in whose rooms were too many patients to count. He estimates that it accommodated at least two thousand patients, and that from among them more than fifty died every day, only to be replaced by new ones.

The Knights of Saint John provided a service previously unavailable outside of church institutions: hospitals and hostels for pilgrims. Their efforts were applauded by both the secular authorities and the church, and in 1113 the pope approved the order's code.

As the successes of the well-organized and effective Hospitaler Order mounted, it received many gifts of property from the kings of Jerusalem, on which the knights erected churches, hostels, and hospitals. The order's headquarters in the Muristan Quarter of Jerusalem survive to this day. Baldwin II, the king of Jerusalem, assigned Ein Karem, birthplace of their patron John the Baptist, to the order of knights. There the Hospitalers established two new churches: one, erected over the ruins of a Byzantine church dedicated to Elizabeth, was dedicated to John the Baptist; the second, built on the ruins of a Byzantine church dedicated to Zachary, was dedicated to the visitation of Mary with Elizabeth and is therefore called the Church of the Visitation.

The welcome work of the Order of Hospitalers earned them celebrity among the pilgrims and, subsequently, throughout Europe, securing for them many donations of property and money from abroad as well. In the thirteenth century, according to the records of the order, the Hospitalers already owned close to nineteen thousand country estates in Europe.

Because of the increasing dangers to life and limb on the roads of the kingdom, the Knights of St. John eventually began to provide escort and security services to the pilgrims as well. From the diary of one pilgrim we learn that the Saracens ambushed the Christians, hiding in mountain crevices, caves, and among the rocks in wait for those who lagged behind their convoys. According to the order's archival sources, in the middle of the twelfth century over three hundred sword-bearing knights were escorting pilgrims on the roads.

Not only the security needs of the pilgrims caused the Knights of Saint John to widen their expertise to the military field. The weakening of the empire and the resulting transfer of security services to the orders forced them to shoulder more and more general security assignments. Thus, for example, when Mount Tabor became the northern border of the Crusader realm in the middle of the thirteenth century, the Hospitalers took upon themselves the responsibility of defending it. According to their records, fifty-six Crusader fortresses within the Kingdom of Jerusalem and Syria were under their command.

Arsuf: City Conquered Despite Collapse of Attack Tower

Genovese Fleet Helps in Siege: Receives One Third of City and Its Fields

Arsuf was a small, fortified port city—one of the most ancient in the Holy Land. After the fall of Jerusalem and Ashkelon, it surrendered to Godfrey of Bouillon, who agreed to accept its capitulation in return for the payment of a heavy tax and the right to appoint his own governor. After a short time, however, the city refused to pay the tax and the Crusader governor was severely tortured and returned, bleeding, to the Crusader camp. The Crusaders placed a siege on the city, but the lack of a naval force rendered it ineffective. Only in the winter of 1099 did a large fleet arrive from Pisa to help construct the naval blockade of Arsuf that finally brought about the city's second surrender. A peace accord was subsequently reached with Godfrey of Bouillon.

In 1101, the Genovese fleet arrived in the Holy Land, providing the Crusaders with the naval force necessary to conquer the coastal cities. The Genovese agreed to place the fleet at the disposal of the Crusaders in return for trading rights and free anchorage at Holy Land ports.

The siege of Arsuf, though ultimately successful, began with a disaster. The tall attack tower erected by the Crusaders collapsed, casting the hundred soldiers on it to their deaths. Those who fell into the city—and into the hands of the Muslims—were crucified and hung on the walls. The enraged Crusaders stormed the walls with ladders, taking control of them after a three-day battle. Following extensive negotiations, the Muslim residents of the city were permitted to leave the city, though without their property. Genoa received one third of the city's territory and fields in return for its help.

A crucified knight on the wall of Arsuf, by G. Doré.

Crusader Fortresses Built in Holy Land

The Holy Land had never witnessed a building campaign as intensive as that of the Crusader period. Remains of Crusader structures from the twelfth and thirteenth centuries are more numerous than remains from any other period. Though they built many religious institutions, the Cru-saders lived into fortresses. In rural areas, country houses were built around a fortress in which the inhabitants gathered during times of danger.

The fortresses and fortified cities were the foundation of the Crusader's defense doctrine, and they established a defense capability greater than that of the Muslim enemy, who, despite a numerical advantage, was unable to sustain a siege for more than a few weeks.

The actual construction of Crusader fortresses combined European build-ing techniques with those learned in

Above: The remains of the Belvoir Crusader fortress.
Left: An aerial photograph of Belvoir.

the Byzantine and Muslim East. The fortresses and citadels were designed not according to a uniform standard, but individually, in conformance with existing conditions. Built to last, the fortresses were usually large, and always made of stone.

One of the greatest achievements of Crusader architecture in the Holy Land was undoubtedly the Belvoir fortress built during the second half of the twelfth century. Belvoir was de-fended by an external wall that encom-passed an internal wall surrounding a wide courtyard, residential buildings, and stores. The sturdy fortress, which was surrounded by a dry moat ten to twelve meters deep, was close to impregnable. Designed to withstand the conditions of even an extended siege, it was one of the last fortresses in the Holy Land to be evacuated by the Crusaders.

saders invested most of their efforts in strongholds.

The scope of the construction was dictated by the dimensions of the Crusader kingdom, which covered an area approximately six hundred by forty-five miles. The Crusader force, which defended this territory on a permanent basis against recurring attacks by Muslim regiments and protected the many pilgrims who moved between the port cities and holy places in the country, numbered sev-eral hundred mounted knights and several thousand more foot soldiers and horsemen, most of whom were recruited from among the pilgrims themselves.

The stone ramparts that the Cru-saders erected effectively replaced men in various defense tasks. For-tresses were situated at strategic points along main roads and around cities. They were constructed at tacti-cally advantageous observation points in sensitive outlying areas and at weak points throughout the kingdom. Crusader engineers and architects also transformed all of the cities, monasteries, churches, and other structures in which the

1102 Storm in Jaffa
More Than 1,000 Drown. Ships Shattered.

When the Crusaders approached Jaffa in 1099, its Muslim inhabitants leveled the city and its port before abandoning it. The Crusaders reno-vated Jaffa and its harbor, which served as the principle anchorage of the Crusader kingdom during the latter's early years. Only after the conquest of Acre and Tyre did the port of Jaffa decline in impor-tance.

In 1101 the Muslims tried to recon-quer Jaffa in order to block the Cru-saders' marine supply route, but the attempt failed. In April of that year, thirty-two ships from the Genovese fleet dropped anchor in the Jaffa harbor and were received with great ceremony by King Baldwin I. A treaty signed between them, written in gold

Jaffa's port, by C.W. Wilson.

and later kept at the Church of the Holy Sepulcher, granted the Genovese an entire quarter in Jaffa.

On October 13, 1102, a ferocious storm struck the port of Jaffa, result-ing in the deaths of more than one thousand people and the loss of many ships. The pilgrim Saewulf, who had arrived at the port the previous eve-ning, relates that when his ship weighed anchor in the harbor he was told to make haste to the beach since a storm was about to break out. The following morning, as he was leaving church, he heard the crashing of waves and the cries of people. Upon reaching the beach, he saw a terrible storm raging, with waves the height of mountains. Countless bodies were floating in the sea and being tossed onto the beach. Ships collided and shattered into splinters. Out of the thirty large vessels that had been anchored in the port of Jaffa that day, only seven were saved.

King Baldwin I Conquers Acre

In 1103, King Baldwin I attempted to invade Acre, but failed and retreated. In the spring of 1104, he approached Acre again, this time aided by a fleet from the Italian city of Genoa. The king signed an agreement with the Genovese according to which they would receive one third of the booty, an entire quarter of the city, income from the taxes on the port, a church in the city, and one third of the land surrounding the city.

The siege on Acre lasted twenty days, at the conclusion of which the Fatimid governor of the city, the emir Tahar, fled. Negotiations followed, and Baldwin accepted the city's surrender, allowing anyone who so desired to leave with their property. On May 26, the city surrendered but the troops from Genoa did not honor their agreement, and fell upon inhabitants attempting to leave the city. According to sources, they killed approximately four thousand people. Though Baldwin was enraged with the Italians, he harmed neither them nor their rights regarding the city's conquest.

Above: Acre functioned as the second capital of the first Kingdom of Jerusalem. **Above right:** A coin of King Baldwin I.

Acre's Status in the Twelfth Century

After its conquest, Acre became the most important port of the Crusader kingdom. Imports and exports passed through it, as did the majority of pilgrims on their way to or from the Holy Land. Acre's port also served as the principle port of Muslim Damascus. Despite the frequent wars between the Christians and Muslims, trade continued in the city almost undisturbed, carried out mainly by Muslim merchants who were generally treated with tolerance, since their activities benefitted the city's Christian inhabitants. The treasury of the kingdom also siphoned off its share of the duties levied on goods that arrived or departed through Acre's markets and harbor.

At a time when Christians throughout the Crusader kingdom were fighting for their very existence against the Muslim enemy, in Acre a life of luxury and tranquillity—based in part on trade with the same Muslim enemy—was led. Acre occupied a vital and distinguished place in the Crusader kingdom; it was one of the cities owned directly by the king, and often served as an alternative capital to Jerusalem. The high court of the kingdom convened in either Jerusalem or Acre. Not merely a legal institution, the high court also served as a council of the elders of the nation, dealing with matters of foreign and domestic policy. Noblemen who were members of the high court lived in Acre so that they could participate in its meetings.

The king's palace in Acre was more splendid than his palace in Jerusalem. Acre was wealthier than Jerusalem: in the event of war, Acre was required to place eighty knights at the disposal of the king, whereas Jerusalem was required to provide only sixty-one. Since the outfitting and funding of these knights was the responsibility of local noblemen according to the extent of their property, we may assume that the number of noblemen in Acre (or the amount of their assets in the city) was larger than in Jerusalem. The number of merchants and wealthy residents was greater in Acre than in Jerusalem, as was the total number of inhabitants.

In contrast to the instability of life that prevailed in the Crusader kingdom due to the ongoing wars, the sudden and frequent deaths of its

A map of Acre from the mid-twelfth century on which the principle buildings and markets of the city are marked. On the upper left, the palace of the Crusader kings; on the lower right, the Hospitaler palace; the Templar palace is located on the left in the quarter surrounded by an additional wall.

rulers and noblemen, and the enmity between Christians and Muslims, life in Acre appears to have been problem-free: wealth, luxury, security, freedom from worry about the future, and cooperation between Europeans and native inhabitants, Christians and Muslims, was the order of the day.

The luxurious lifestyle of the Europeans in Acre amazed and impressed other Westerners. At the time, life in Western Europe was marked by hardship. Clothing was made of wool and rarely laundered. Opportunities to bathe were few. The largest castles in Europe were crudely and simply furnished, while carpets were almost nonexistent. Even the food in Europe was monotonous, especially during the long winter months.

Life in the Frankish East was startlingly different. Every nobleman and wealthy merchant furnished his city house in expensive grandeur: carpets and tapestries, elegantly inlaid and decorated tables, carved trunks, white bed linens, clean tablecloths, eating utensils of gold and silver, and often even porcelain imported from the Far East.

Dress was equally ornate. When a knight was not wearing armor, he sported a silk robe and usually a turban on his head. Women adopted the Eastern custom of wearing a long dress with a short jacket on top, decorated with rich lace made from gold thread and often studded with diamonds. In the winter they wore furs, as did their husbands. Whenever Western women went out onto the street they were veiled, according to Muslim custom, though they covered themselves not out of modesty but in order to protect their made-up complexions.

This lifestyle, naturally, was that of the noblemen and wealthy merchants. The lives of the commoners, slaves, and servants were much harder. In the city itself there was overcrowding. Dirt and sewage flowed in the streets, causing the outbreak of epidemics that killed many of the pilgrims.

King Sigurd of Norway Arrives in Holy Land

Sigurd I, the king of Norway, arrived in the Holy Land in 1110 at the head of a delegation of sixty ships, which anchored in Acre after a journey via England, Spain, and Sicily. The tour represented the first royal visit by a European king to the Kingdom of Jerusalem, and the young Norwegian king was received by King Baldwin with great pomp and ceremony. After visiting the holy places in Jerusalem, Sigurd was invited to participate in the conquest of Tyre. He and his men courteously joined their host for the seasonal blockade of the Muslim coastal city, performing excellently in battles that finally brought about its conquest.

Sidon, by D. Roberts.

1111 Genovese, Pisan, and Venetian Fleets Conquer Coastal Cities

Europeans by Sea, Crusaders by Land

Assaulting the fortified cities along the Mediterranean coast gradually became the major summer occupation of the Crusader army. The standard set by Baldwin I, who was crowned king of Jerusalem in 1100 after Godfrey's death, was permanent and repetitive: every summer, the naval fleets of Genoa and Pisa blockaded the city of choice by sea while the Crusader army, led by the king, attacked from the beach.

The European ships arrived every year between Easter and autumn in order to participate in the siege of a different city. Since during the winter the eastern coast of the Mediterranean was stormy and perilous, the siege season was planned to avoid those particular months.

In return for their assistance in the sieges, the principalities of Genoa and Pisa, owners of the fleets, received special rights to trade and settle in the conquered cities. The success of the system soon convinced the powerful Venetian fleet—which until then had controlled the trade with the eastern Muslim countries and had feared that aiding the Crusaders would anger its clients—to join the arrangement.

Crusaders break into the Caesarea mosque, by G. Doré.

By 1111, all of the coastal cities from Beirut in the north to the Sinai Peninsula in the south, aside from Tyre and Ashkelon, were in Crusader hands. Tyre was conquered in 1124. Ashkelon managed to withstand the repeated attacks of the Crusaders until 1153.

The Handsome Hero from the North

Fulcher of Chartres went on crusade in October 1096, in the entourage of Stephan, the count of Blois. His *Historia Hierosolymitana* describes the various men and their leaders, events that occurred on the journey, and how Baldwin persuaded Sigurd I to join in the successful siege of Sidon.

"Meanwhile a group of Norwegians, whom God had urged to come from the western sea, put in at Jaffa to make the journey to Jerusalem. Their fleet consisted of fifty-five ships. Their leader, King Sigurd, was a young man of outstanding beauty. When King Baldwin returned to Jerusalem, he was delighted at their arrival and spoke in a very friendly fashion to them, advising and begging them, for the love of God, to remain for a while in the Holy Land and help him to further and augment the Christian cause.

"They received his plea kindly, and answered that they had come to Jerusalem for no other purpose, but that wherever the king wanted to go with his army, they would gladly go at the same time by sea, as long as he would provide them with the necessary victuals. This was agreed and acted upon.

"At first they arranged to go to Ashkelon, but then a better counsel prevailed, and they went to besiege Sidon. King Baldwin moved his army from Acre, while the Norwegians went by ship from Jaffa. At that time the fleet of the emir of Egypt was lying hidden the port of Tyre; from there the Saracens often attacked in the manner of pirates those Christians new to the land, and they were strengthening the defenses of the coastal cities which the Egyptian caliphs still possessed. But when they heard rumors about the Norwegians, they did not dare to leave the port to Tyre or to meet them.

"When the crusaders arrived at Sidon, King Baldwin besieged it from the land and the Norwegians from the sea. Then he constructed siege-engines and terrified the enemy within, to the extent that those who were mercenaries requested the king to allow them to leave the city unharmed and, if he wished, to keep the farmers in the city to till the land for his own profit. Their request was granted. The mercenaries left without being paid, and the country-people remained in peace, in accordance with the arrangement."

Pilgrims Invited to Participate in Battles
Caught in Attacks, Pilgrims Become Fighters

Many of the pilgrims who came to the Holy Land during the Crusader period found themselves involved in clashes with Muslims. Actually, Western pilgrims were part of the security and economic infrastructure of the Holy Land. Caught up in battles against marauders or Muslim army units, many of them aided their escorts in fighting off the attackers.

The pilgrim Conrad of Monferrat relates how he arrived in Tyre on his way to visit the sacred sites of the Holy Land only to find himself participating in the defense of the city from an offensive by Saladin's army a short time after the Crusader defeat at Karnei Hattin. Tyre was the only coastal city that did not surrender to Saladin, and it later served as a bridgehead for the landing of a Crusader force during the Third Crusade.

The pilgrims' attitude towards the Crusaders was usually one of admiration, and the various knightly orders, of course, were also the objects of great appreciation. Such warm sentiments were not shared by all of the pilgrims, however; in his memoirs, the Russian abbot who accompanied Baldwin I's military crusade to Galilee during his visit to the Holy Land in 1106 expressed irritation about the fact that when he wanted to visit Mount Tabor and Nazareth, which were not on the route of the military crusade, he and his entourage were allocated only seven escorts. "When the objectives of the Crusader and the pilgrim part, their paths also part," the Russian monk noted.

Templum Domini—Temple of the Lord

The Crusaders identified the Dome of the Rock with the Holy Temple and called it Templum Domini—the Temple of the Lord. One of the most significant sites in Crusader Jerusalem, the Templum Domini was second in importance only to the Church of the Holy Sepulcher.

In 1115, renovations were initiated in the shrine to ready it for use as a church—a reconstruction project that was to last for twenty years. The walls of the edifice were decorated with Christian pictures and inscriptions, and a gold cross was affixed to its dome.

The Foundation Stone in the Templum Domini was covered with marble and an altar dedicated to St. Nicholas built on it. An iron grille meant to deter those who would have liked to take pieces of the holy rock

Crusader lamps and the grille surrounding the rock at the Templum Domini, by C.W. Wilson.

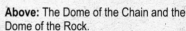

Above: The Dome of the Chain and the Dome of the Rock.
Left: The Oriental ornamentation on the Dome of the Chain.
Below: A Crusader baptismal basin near the Dome of the Ascension.

Augustinians Acquire Church of Holy Sepulcher

When the Crusaders invaded Jerusalem they expelled the local clergy from the Church of the Holy Sepulcher and appointed new priests. In 1114 the church was transferred to the Augustinian canons, who built a residence for themselves on the roof of the Chapel of Saint Helena in the eastern portion of the church. Together with the church the Augustinians also received church-held real estate that included large territories in Jerusalem and its environs.

The remains of the Augustinian halls.

home with them was also erected around it. The grotto beneath the rock was used as a crypt and identified as the place where Jesus sent away the adulterous woman and where the angel announced the birth of John the Baptist to Zachary. The inauguration of the Templum Domini took place in 1136 at a grand ceremony in the presence of a papal emissary.

A baptistery was built next to the Templum Domini, though in 1200 it was transformed into the Muslim structure known today as the Dome of the Ascension. The Dome of the Chain, east of the Dome of the Rock, was turned into a church dedicated to James, Jesus's brother, who was thrown from a corner of the Temple Mount (the Pinnacle) and buried, according to tradition, in Zachary's tomb in the Kidron Valley.

The Dome of the Ascension.

Jerusalem: City of Churches and Monasteries

The wave of construction that engulfed the country in the period of the first Kingdom of Jerusalem, which lasted from 1099 to 1187, less than ninety years, competed in its dimensions with that of the Byzantine period, which had lasted almost three centuries. A great many of the Crusader churches and monasteries were built on the remains of Byzantine churches that had been destroyed in the Arab Period, but many buildings

Above: A Crusader capital in the Chapel of the Ascension on the Mount of Olives.
Right: The facade of the Crusader Church of the Tomb of the Virgin Mary, by Bonfils.

were constructed on new sites as well.

The Al-Aqsa Mosque on the eastern side of the Temple Mount was renamed Templum Solomonis (Solomon's Temple) and turned into a royal Crusader palace. From 1118 on it served as the center of the newly-founded Order of the Knights Templars—the Knights of the Temple.

The greatest building efforts were invested in the reconstruction of the Church of the Holy Sepulcher. The resulting structure, completed in 1149, incorporated the Byzantine church buildings on the site, or what remained of them. The new edifice included Golgotha, the Church of Saint Helena, and the small chapels connected with the story of the last hours of Jesus as they are described in the New Testament.

Dozens of churches were built during the Crusader period in the Patriarch Quarter surrounding the Church of the Holy Sepulcher, especially in the Muristan area to the south of the courtyard of the Church of the Holy Sepulcher. The most well known was the Church of Saint Mary la Latine, which included an ornate hostel. The entire precinct, which has been well preserved, is today combined with the later German Church of the Redeemer. Not far from there is the Church of Saint Mary la Grande, whose column capitals are among the most beautiful from the Crusader period ever found in the Holy Land. The nearby Church of Saint Anne, built in the twelfth century in the Romanesque style, is one of the most impressive of the period.

Many churches and monasteries were erected on holy sites outside the walls of Jerusalem, including the Saint Mary of Mount Zion Monastery and the Monastery of the Tomb of the Virgin Mary in the Jehoshaphat Valley (where many high-ranking Crusaders were buried).

A large concentration of churches and monasteries accumulated on the Mount of Olives—the Monastery of the Ascension on the top of the mountain, Gethsemane Church at its foot, and the convent at Bethany, built by Melisande in 1144 for her sister Yvette. The convent has a large church and a fortified tower intended to protect the nuns within from Muslim attacks.

The remains of the convent built by Melisande in the village of Bethany, by C.W. Wilson.

The largest and most ornate church built in the Holy Land by the Crusaders, second only to the Church of the Holy Sepulcher in magnificence, was the Church of Saint John the Baptist east of the city wall. The Gothic-Romanesque-style church incorporated in its new design the remains of structures from the Byzantine period that had been destroyed by the Persians in 614 and in the earthquake that shook the city in 747. The church, which stands on the site where according to tradition the head of John the Baptist was buried, was transformed into a mosque by Saladin after his conquest of Jerusalem, though Christian pilgrims continued to visit it.

Jerusalem, Acre, and Tyre Home to the Crusaders
Choice Real Estate in the Hands of Italian Communes

Most of the population of the Kingdom of Jerusalem was concentrated in three cities: Jerusalem, Acre, and Tyre. According to Crusader accounts from the mid-twelfth century, the population of Acre, the largest city in the kingdom, was an estimated sixty thousand people and the population of the second biggest city, Tyre, about fifty thousand. Jerusalem, the capital of the kingdom, was third in size, with only twenty-five thousand inhabitants. Aside from the three major cities, there were an additional twenty municipal concentrations in the kingdom, the population of each of which was about five thousand souls.

The concentration of the civilian population in the main cities was primarily a result of security concerns: in those days, the Crusader fortifications were virtually impregnable.

The fortified cities were protected first by an outer wall and then by a

fortress that stood at the heart of the city and served as a base for the local garrison.

The fortifications of the citadel were usually stronger than those of the city itself; it was meant to face the enemy independently, holding out long after the city had already fallen. The wall of the citadel was usually double the height of the city wall. In Acre, for example, the city wall was 16 meters high while the citadel's wall rose to a height of 34 meters. At the city gates double doors were installed that turned on hinges set in the wall and locked by means of an enormous beam affixed in brackets on the doorposts of the wall. Turrets rose on either side of the gate.

Additionally, the cities were stocked with provisions that would ensure their citizens' ability to withstand a siege of many years, despite the fact that sieges in the East usually did not

last more than a few weeks—at the most, several months.

The majority of the urban population was middle class, and lived generally in neighborhoods demarcated according to country of origin. Nevertheless, the best property, especially in the coastal towns, was owned by the Italian communes, which had acquired it in return for services rendered to the Crusader armies by the fleets of the Italian republics and principalities.

Aside from the fortified cities, the Crusader realm included dozens of villages settled by European Christians. For security reasons, most of them were larger than the native villages, and consisted of about five hundred people. They were fortified, provided with a watchtower, and usually situated near a larger citadel, to which their inhabitants could repair in case of an emergency.

All Roads Lead to Jerusalem

After the conquest of the Holy Land by the Crusaders and its liberation from the Muslims, hoards of pilgrims began to stream into it. They usually followed the shortest route inland from the coastal city at which they disembarked—usually Acre or Jaffa—to Jerusalem. But even this abbreviated route, which was determined mainly due to its relative safety, was not entirely secure even when Crusader power was at its peak. Bands of Muslim marauders ambushed pilgrims on the roads and the danger was considerable. Many of the devout also died along the way from the hardships of the journey, the heat, thirst or some combination of the three. Their bodies were often left lying along the roadside, as digging graves in the hard and rocky soil was virtually impossible.

Jerusalem itself was a lively burgeoning city. During this period, its "holy geography" was being shaped. Dozens of sacred sites—most of them determined according to traditions preserved from the Byzantine period but many according to later traditions as well—were identified anew and renovated. The process of rediscovery was accompanied by the establishment of dozens of churches in Jerusalem and its environs. Renovation of the Church of the Holy Sepulcher represented the apex of this Christian building campaign.

Many of the pilgrims who came to Jerusalem continued, after a visit to the Church of the Holy Sepulcher and the holy places in and around Jerusalem, to Jericho, Mount Quarantel, and the baptismal site on the River Jordan—a route that became known as the "path to the kingdom of God." On Easter of 1172, the pilgrim Theodorich estimated the number of pilgrims moving along the route at about sixty thousand.

The Jerusalem-Jericho route was the most difficult and dangerous of the pilgrim routes in the Holy Land. The hazardous and bumpy road, the oppressive heat, and the bands of Bedouin brigands made passage on it extremely perilous.

In order to better defend the pilgrims from the plunderers, the Templars established fortresses along the way. The most important of them was along Ma'aleh Adumim (the Red Ascent). This fortress, like others in the Kingdom of Jerusalem, fell after the Battle of Karnei Hattin into the hands of the Muslims, who called it "Al-Hamra" (The Red).

Not all of the Crusaders were content with playing it relatively safe on the short route from Jaffa to Jerusalem, or the pilgrimage to the baptismal site on the Jordan. To pilgrims who disembarked in the Holy Land at the port of Jaffa, an alternative route including the holy sites in the north of the country was also available. The route led first from Acre to Sepphoris; after seeing the grave of Saint Nicholas, the pilgrims continued on to Nazareth, where they visited the Church of the Annunciation, Joseph's workshop, Mary's Well, and the Mount of the Precipice. At Mount Tabor the pilgrims were shown the location of the Transfiguration and the Sermon on the Mount was read to them.

The northern route then led the pilgrims to the village of Cana, where they were shown the wine jars from the New Testament wedding, and to the village of Na'in, where the miracle of the resurrection of the widow's son occurred. From there they went on to Tiberias and to Beit Saida, north of the Sea of Galilee. The pilgrims visited the house of Peter's mother-in-law at Capernaum and the site where the miracle of the loaves and fishes was said to have occurred. From there they could continue on to Jerusalem along the route Jesus and his disciples took on their last journey together; a trip that entailed much hardship and many logistical and security problems. As the problems besetting the Crusader kingdom mounted, so the number of the tours along this route lessened until the thirteenth century, when they disappeared entirely.

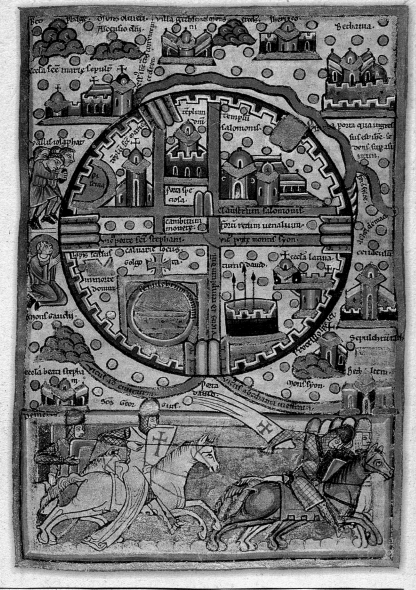

The Hague map of Jerusalem, circa 1170.

1118 King of Jerusalem Ensconced in Citadel

The courtyard of the Citadel (David's Tower).

In 1118, the royal palace, home to the Crusader kings in Jerusalem, was transferred from the Temple Mount to the Citadel by order of Baldwin II, the third king of the Crusader kingdom. The move was motivated by security considerations. The abandoning of Jerusalem by many Crusaders, especially for the coastal cities of Acre and Tyre as well as for Antioch, the largest city in Crusader territory, had essentially emptied Jerusalem of its inhabitants. Those responsible for the safety of the king feared that the diminished numbers would make it difficult for them to defend the palace on the Temple Mount, which was quite exposed and far from the main military force of the city. The Citadel, on the other hand, where the garrison was located, was designed to endure an extended siege and had plenty of water and wheat, as one Abbott Daniel, who visited Jerusalem several years earlier, testified.

Order of Knights Templars to Protect Pilgrims
King Baldwin II Provides Patronage and Palace

The first military order of knights was established in Jerusalem in 1118. Its founder, the knight Hugue de Payns, said at the order's inauguration that its objective was to provide protection for pilgrims making their way from the coastal cities to Jerusalem and the other holy places in the Crusader kingdom.

The king of Jerusalem, Baldwin II, who saw the new order as important, hastened to extend his patronage to it. Later that same year, once the Crusader kings had transferred their place of residence from the Templum Solomonis (the present-day Al-Aqsa Mosque) to the Citadel (the present-day Tower of David), Baldwin granted the former palace on the Temple Mount to the knights of the new order. Adopting the name of their new home, they were ever after called the Knights Templars.

The Templars renovated the Templum Solomonis to suit its new role. They built halls, cellars, and stables in the subterranean network of the Temple Mount; the stables, known today as Solomon's Stables, had room for two thousand horses or fifteen hundred camels according to the report of the German priest John of

Würzburg in the travel book he penned after his visit to Jerusalem in 1165. The Templars refurbished the structure's upper section and rebuilt the arches of its facade (still visible at the front of the Al-Aqsa Mosque).

Within a short time, the Order of the Knights Templars expanded into countries in Europe and around the Mediterranean. The image of the knight fighting in the name of the church and protecting the defenseless from the murderous attacks of the heretics who preyed upon their souls was further glorified by stories of the knights' heroism recounted by pilgrims who returned home after journeying to the Holy Land. The attraction was enormous, and many young knights looking for adventure joined the order, which accordingly fashioned for itself a mysterious image, a

Above: Templar knights, by G. Doré.
Above right: The Templar seal.

rigorous training regime, and special ceremonial rites.

The reputation the Templars earned for themselves in Europe also enabled them to develop a thriving economic sideline: international banking. They offered pilgrims their services in transferring money safely from their

countries of origin to the Holy Land. With the assistance of savvy financiers, the Templars soon controlled a thriving banking network, which encompassed all of Western Europe by the thirteen century. In many instances the order lent money to noblemen residing in the Crusader kingdom. Often, when borrowers found themselves unable to repay a loan, a portion of their property was transferred to the order as reimbursement.

The Templars, like the more veteran order of the Hospitalers, also received many gifts of property from kings and princes in exchange for their services. Thus, for example, Richard the Lionhearted gave the Templar Order the island of Cyprus, which he had conquered on his way to the Third Crusade. (The order later relinquished the island, which they found impossible to manage due to a lack of manpower.)

Later, the Templars and the Hospitalers constituted the kernel of permanent military power on which the defense of the Kingdom of Jerusalem rested. The two fortresses held by the Templars were the fortress at Atlit—Chateau des Pelerins (the Pilgrims' Fortress)—and the fortress in Safed.

German Knights Establish Teutonic Order

The Roots of the Prussian Empire

A third order—the Teutonic Knights—was founded in the Holy Land by Germans at the end of the 1120s. Initially intended to care for patients and pilgrims from Germany, its establishment was the result of the quarrels and enmity between the German and French Crusaders and pilgrims, and it accepted into its ranks only knights of German extraction.

The priest John of Würzburg, who visited Jerusalem in 1165, sheds some light on the discrimination suffered by the Germans in the Crusader kingdom. Among other things, he complains that Godfrey of Bouillon was not recognized as the conqueror of Jerusalem because of his German descent, and that the French took the glory due him for themselves. Elsewhere he tells of a German knight, one of the heroes of the battle of Jerusalem, who was buried in the Church of the Holy Sepulcher. According to the priest, the French had erased the original German inscrip-

The remains of the Church of Saint Mary, part of the complex of the Order of Teutonic Knights in Jerusalem.

tion on the tomb and inscribed a French text in its place in order to

obscure the brave knight's German identity. In protest, John angrily carved a German response on the grave: Not the French, but more daring warriors, the Germans, saved this city from the rule of heretics.

The Teutonic Order did not win great popularity among the Kingdom of Jerusalem's governmental circles, whose clear partiality for the French was due to the great weight of French participation in the Crusades. Land deeds from the Crusader period provide telling testimony to the preference; almost all of the sixty villages owned by the German order were bought in full by cash, as opposed to being received as gifts from the kingdom or the local noblemen, as was common in the cases of the Hospitalers and Templars.

On the other hand, the Teutonic Order enjoyed the support of the pope, who often intervened on its behalf, of Kaiser Heinrich VI, and of Friedrich II, who served for fifteen years as king of Jerusalem. The latter even helped the Teutonic Knights obtain for them-

The Remains of the Beaufort.

selves a prize that other orders never achieved: their own kingdom. Led by Hermann of Salza, under the patronage of Friedrich II and with the assistance of Conrad, king of Swabia in northern Poland, the Teutonic Knights overcame the northern region along the Baltic Sea and founded what was later to become the Prussian state.

The Teutonic Order's main fortress, where its activity first began, was the Beaufort, an impressive stronghold that served as a center of government in the outlying region north of Galilee (present-day southern Lebanon).

Though it was not as large as the other two orders, the role of the Teutonic Order was important in the defense of the Crusader kingdom, and its knights were known for their iron discipline and excellent military capabilities.

Crusaders Renovate Church of the Nativity

In 1110, the Church of the Nativity was elevated to the rank of cathedral, and throughout the remainder of the century the Crusaders thoroughly renovated the church. The work was contracted out to local artisans led by an English supervisor. Additional buildings were erected adjacent to the church, including another church, a monastery, and a belfry that survives to this day.

The walls and columns of the basilica were adorned with rich paintings and mosaics in the Eastern style.

Top: Jesus' triumphant entrance into Jerusalem. A Crusader mosaic in the Basilica of the Nativity.

Bottom: The remains of the Crusader mosaics on the walls of the basilica.

Left and right: Some of the columns of the basilica, which are embellished with paintings of saints, survive to this day.

1140

The Knights of Saint Lazarus and the Lepers

Aside from the three major Crusader orders of knights—the Hospitaler, the Templar, and the Teutonic—during the twelfth century, other, smaller orders arose, the most prominent of which was the Order of Saint Lazarus, whose mission it was to care for the victims of leprosy.

Members of the order were knights who had become infected during the crusade with the horrible disease of leprosy; in those days, still incurable. The order began its activity by setting up an institution for the treatment of lepers near Jerusalem's northern wall. Later the knights built homes and churches for lepers in Tiberias, Ashkelon, Caesarea, and Acre, where the quarter in which they lived was adorned by Saint Lazarus' Tower.

In the mid-twelfth century, the Order of Saint Lazarus also became, out of necessity, a military order, and its members took part in Crusader battles.

Almost no historical material about most of the other minor orders has survived, aside from their names—the Order of the Sword, the Order of the Holy Spirit, the Order of San Lorenzo of the Knights, the English Order of Thomas of Canterbury, or the Spanish Order of Saint James—and the roles they were assigned in the defense of the city of Acre.

Crusader-Muslim Collaboration

Banias, which had been a thriving city during the Arab Period, was transferred to the Ismail sect in 1126. Three years later, members of the sect were massacred in Damascus. The Ismails, who feared they could not continue to defend Banias, proposed to the Crusaders that they take it over in exchange for providing protection to the sect. Baldwin II accepted the proposal and the Crusaders turned Banias into a base for raids against Damascus.

In 1132, a cease-fire was declared between the opposing sides, but the governor of Damascus soon violated it, conquering Banias. In 1138, Banias rebelled against Damascus and opened its gates to Zanghi, governor of Mosul and an enemy of Damascus. Damascus proposed to the Crusaders that they join forces against Zanghi; the Crusaders agreed on the condition that Banias be returned to them.

The Muslim-Christian siege commenced in May of 1140 and the city fell after one month. Banias and its environs became a holiday and hunting spot for the Crusaders and aristocracy of Damascus. The peace lasted for nearly ten years, and was violated only when the Second Crusade attempted to conquer Damascus.

In 1157, half of Banias was transferred to the Hospitalers, who soon became discouraged with the city and abandoned it. In 1164 Banias fell to the Muslims for the last time, never to revert to Crusader hands.

Second Crusade at Gates of Holy Land

In the spring of 1148, after many misadventures, the various camps involved in the Second Crusade began to appear on the western horizons of Syria and the Holy Land. The forces of Louis VII, the French king, weighed anchor at the port of Antioch in March of that year; one month later Conrad III arrived with his German knights. At the same time, an additional French force, commanded by Alphonse Jourdain, son of Raymond de Saint-Gilles, the hero of the First Crusade, also landed in the Holy Land. This vital reinforcement, despite the terrible losses it incurred on its journey to the Holy Land, nevertheless appeared to wield immense power, and aroused great hopes in the Crusader kingdom: this time, surely, the Crusaders' hopes would be fulfilled.

The primary objective of the Second Crusade was to reconquer Edessa, using Antioch as a base of operations. But relations between Louis VII and Raymond of Poitiers, the prince of Antioch, suddenly cooled (possibly because of the development of inordinately warm relations between Elea-

Louis VII fighting the Saracens.

nor of Aquitaine, Louis VII's beautiful wife, and the prince). Louis VII left Antioch and set off on a campaign to Jerusalem.

In June 1148, the Crusader council of state convened in Acre and mapped out a strategy for the conquest of Damascus. The offensive subsequently failed,

and the Crusaders were forced to beat a hasty retreat westward. In short, the Second Crusade, in which Europe had invested such great effort and high hopes, was a complete debacle, and in September 1149 Conrad III departed Acre on his way back to Germany. Half a year later, during Easter of the year 1150, Louis VII returned by sea to France.

Rumors from the Queen's Bedroom

Rumors and hearsay leaking out of the castle of Raymond of Antioch referred to his inappropriately intimate relationship with his beautiful niece and ward Eleanor of Aquitane, the wife of Louis VII. The cuckolded king departed Antioch in all possible haste. The romantic triangle ended in divorce.

The following view of events was penned by William, archbishop of Tyre, who wrote the most important account of the kingdom of Jerusalem between the death of Fulcher of Chartres circa 1127 and his own death, which was probably early in 1185. In this case, his information was obtained second-hand, as he was studying in France at the time of the events:

"When Prince Raymond of Antioch heard that Louis VII, the king of France, whose arrival he had been awaiting with the utmost eagerness for many days, had reached his land, he summoned the nobles and the principal people of the whole region and, with this chosen train, went out to meet the king. He brought Louis in state into the city of Antioch, showing him every respect, with all the clergy and the entire people coming out to meet him...

"Queen Eleanor, who was a foolish woman, sided with him, and he planned to take her from the king, either by violence or by secret designs. As I said, she was a highly imprudent woman. In defiance of her royal dignity, and neglectful of the laws of marriage, she was unfaithful to her husband's bed.

"When the king discovered this, he forestalled the prince's attempts: on the advice of his nobles he brought forward the time of his departure and left Antioch in secret with his people. He, who had been received with such honor on his arrival, left ignominiously."

King Louis VII and Eleanor of Aquitaine before departing on the crusade.

A kings' council at Acre prior to the siege of Damascus. From William of Tyre's book.

Won the Princess and the Principality—Twice!

Reynald of Chatillon, a handsome French knight, arrived in Antioch together with the army of Louis VII, king of France, and remained there when the latter returned to his country at the end of the Second Crusade. After the death of Raymond, prince of Antioch, in a battle opposite the ruler of Damascus in 1149, Reynald began to court his widow Constance, having fallen captive to her charms. The widow wanted to marry the knight of her dreams, but she needed the consent of King Baldwin III, who was participating in the Crusader siege of the city of Ashkelon at the time.

Reynald did not hesitate; he parted from his friends and joined Baldwin's army near Ashkelon. After having proved himself in battle, he won the king's approval to marry Constance

the merry widow. Reynald was crowned prince of Antioch and led his army from victory to victory until the day he and several of his men fell into an ambush set for them by the Muslims and were taken captive.

During the sixteen years Reynald spent in prison he learned both Arabic and Turkish. Finally liberated, he learned to his disappointment that during his years of absence he had been widowed and that his wife's son from her previous marriage had occupied his throne.

But Reynald got lucky, and the seignior of Transjordan died, leaving behind him a daughter—an only child, Eschive de Milly. Reynald, whose good looks and charm had remained undiminished throughout his years in captivity, did not find it

difficult to win the heart of the young heiress (not to mention the dowry that accompanied her), and he became the lord of the seigniory of Transjordan. His command of both the languages and the customs of his Muslim neighbors enabled Reynald to form friendly relationships with the Bedouin tribes of the region, and after he built himself a fleet of ships, his army and those of his Bedouin allies attacked the cities of the region from Mecca and Medina to Jedda and Cairo, enriching his treasury and glorifying his name.

Reynald's daring raids made him especially hated by Saladin, who finally got his revenge at the Battle of Karnei Hattin, where he killed Reynald with his own hands after the noble knight refused to convert to Islam.

A portrait of Saladin from a fifteenth-century Italian manuscript.

Crusaders Rebuild Church of Holy Sepulcher
Twenty Years to Consolidate Holy Sites

On July 15, 1149, fifty years after their occupation of Jerusalem, the Crusaders reconsecrated the Church of the Holy Sepulcher; the building and renovation work had lasted more than twenty years. At the time of their takeover of Jerusalem, the Crusaders had thought the existing church, partially ruined, too small, and they added a tall edifice that consolidated all of the holy sites under one roof. The construction was hampered by a couple of serious obstacles: existing with lovely mosaics; the construction of an ornate basilica in place of the courtyard of the Holy Garden (today's Catholicon); the restoration of the Chapel of the Hill of Golgotha and its sites; the renovation of the Crypt of the Finding of the Cross, the Stone of the Anointing, and the smaller chapels, especially those in the eastern corridor of the church; the fashioning of a new southern facade; and the building of a campanile.

The nave of the Catholicon is divided

buildings on the site that could almost not be altered because of their sanctity and the poor state of the construction, which necessitated expensive and time-consuming renovations that relied upon daring and original solutions to architectural problems.

Among the work the Crusaders carried out in the Church of the Holy Sepulcher were various projects: the embellishment of the rotunda's dome into a central hall and four aisles that end on the east in an ambulatory and three chapels. The dome at the juncture of the central hall and the transept is the largest and one of the most impressive built by the Crusaders in the Holy Land. The basilica has been almost perfectly preserved to this day.

Clockwise from upper left: A Crusader mosaic on the wall of Calvary; a detail from marble carvings that decorated the facade of the church; the facade of the Church of the Holy Sepulcher, by E. Pierotti; a profile of the Church of the Holy Sepulcher as it looked during the Crusader period, by the Vicomte de Vogüé, 1860; the Holy Tomb, by D. Dapper.

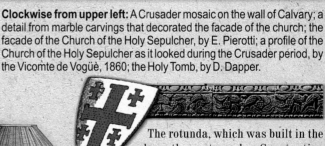

The rotunda, which was built in the eleventh century by Constantine Monomachus, also underwent a few changes. On each side of the great arch that connected it to the choir were placed a pair of columns. The keystone of the arch was adorned with a figure of Jesus the youth. The right-hand side of the arch was decorated with the image of Mary, and the left-hand side, with the angel Gabriel. The figure of Jesus was attended by verses from the Gospels in Latin and Greek.

The back of the arch was enriched with a scene of Jesus' ascent to heaven. The windows of the dome were decorated with the figures of the Apostles; next to each one was a Latin inscription noting his name. In the center of the group of Apostles was Saint Helena in royal robes and her name in Greek and Latin.

The southern part of the rotunda is decorated with the figures of the prophets. Each carries a scroll of verses from his sayings in his hands, and Constantine stands in the center bearing a globe and a cross. The prophets and the emperor look toward Jesus, who was painted on the triumphal arch separating the rotunda and the Catholicon.

The aedicule of the tomb, which had been exposed to the elements, was in need of urgent repairs at the advent of the Crusader reign, and it was accordingly covered with marble on the outside and mosaics on the inside. A rectangular chapel entered through one of three openings led to the Chapel of the Holy Tomb. In its center was a small altar made of a fragment of the stone slab that had once sealed Jesus' tomb. The ceiling of the part of the chapel leading to the inner chapel was overlaid with a mosaic depicting the scene of the burial and the visit of the women.

The Chapel of the Holy Tomb was small, as it is today. The low opening leading to it forced visitors to crawl inside. Above the tomb, five oil lamps burned night and day. By the eve of the Crusader conquest, only a small portion of the original rock of the sepulcher remained—the patriarch of Jerusalem had severed and hidden part of the rock from which the tomb of Jesus was made, as well as the remains of the True Cross. Although according to legend the rock was found and returned to the spot, not much was left of the original tomb. In 1170 the tomb was covered in gold in accordance with the request of the Byzantine Emperor Manuel Comnenus.

The chapel itself was round. On the outside it was encircled by ten col-

umns bearing attractive arches, from which lamps hung. The upper portion of the chapel of the sepulcher was encircled by a bronze grille, and a chimney through which the smoke from the lamps flowed was installed in it. The chimney was covered by an attractive dome supported by twelve double columns and covered in gold. Above it, a silver life-size statue of Jesus stood until 1172, when it was replaced by a cross topped by a gilded dove. To the west of the aedicule was a chapel that was intended for local residents. It was referred to as the *kabbet* (head) because of its position at the head of the tomb.

Golgotha, which until this period had been located in a separate building, was now integrated into the new church and enlarged. Eighteen steps led to Golgotha on the north, but the main vestibule was from the atrium in the south. From the right of the church's facade was a staircase leading to a small portico supporting a dome and decorated with pictures and mosaics; here sat the guards of the chapel of Golgotha before an engraved door leading from the portico to the chapel. (Today the door is blocked and both the shape and character of the portico has changed. The spaces between its columns are blocked, and it has been turned into a chapel dedicated to the suffering Mary.)

The chapel of Golgotha, which according to ancient sources was particularly splendid, was divided into two naves and covered by four vaults supported by massive beams. Mosaics covered the chapel from its ceiling to its foundations. The floor was inlaid with tiles in a variety of colors and shapes. Under the chapel of Golgotha was the Chapel of Adam, which served as the crypt of Golgotha.

South of the church, double wooden gates covered with bronze were built. Above the lintels were wonderfully-carved marble panels and a gable enhanced with colorful mosaics that have not survived. One panel portrays the Madonna and Child. In another, Jesus' resurrection and his apparition before Mary Magdalene is de-

Details of the marble carvings that decorated the church's facade.

picted. The eastern gate, closed today, was apparently blocked at the end of the twelfth century by Saladin, since there was no need for it, as only a few pilgrims made it to the church after the expulsion of the Crusaders by the Muslims.

Pilgrims often expressed their astonishment at paving of the atrium, which was apparently renewed at the same time as the church's facade. During the Middle Ages, there were apparently three chapels to the east of the atrium: the Catholic chapel of the three Marys, a chapel in the possession of the Armenians, and an additional chapel, whose function is today obscure. On the south the courtyard was enclosed by a portico formed by six columns bearing arches reminiscent in shape of those that rise above the stairs ascending the Temple Mount. The arches were apparently destroyed in the thirteenth century, and only the bases of the columns are visible today.

After the conquest of Jerusalem by the Crusaders, entrance to the Church of the Holy Sepulcher was possible from the west as well. This portal, which was installed in the upper galleries in exact alignment with the east-west axis of the rotunda, was in use in the twelfth century, though it is blocked up today. Though pilgrims arriving from the direction of Jaffa Gate often used this entrance, it was not possible to descend from here directly into the church; in order to reach the floor of the rotunda one had to use the stairs near the gates on the south.

On their tour of the church, pilgrims would visit the chapel dedicated by the Catholics to the holy cross. Part of the True Cross lay there inside a special box, ever ready to be carried into the battlefield by the patriarch or soldiers specially appointed to the task.

Continuing their tour eastward,

pilgrims would arrive at the Prison of Jesus, twenty steps away from the Chapel of the Cross, and then stroll along the corridor curving from the vestibule to the chapels lining the ambulatory. Thirty steps led down to the Chapel of Saint Helena, where the site of the finding of the cross, hammer, nails, and crown of thorns was pointed out in an adjacent grotto down a short flight of steps.

As was customary in Crusader churches in Europe, the Church of the Holy Sepulcher also had a campanile, which unfortunately obscured some of the decorations of the church's facade. The tower's base was the chapel of Saint John the Baptist, which abutted the rotunda. Its first floor, which has survived the ravages of time, has four arches bolstering the upper floors and a window in the shape of a

The portico that led from the atrium to Golgotha.

flower on its eastern wall. Above the first floor was a second story with double windows. The third story had a blocked-up arch with a single window in its center; above it was a series of graduated battlements. The tower was surmounted by an octagonal dome with a cross atop it.

In 1187 Saladin shattered the bells of the tower and crushed its cross. Almost four centuries later, in 1545, the tower began to crumble and an earthquake finally collapsed the dome, which, as it fell, destroyed the dome of the chapel at its feet. The partially destroyed tower, exposed to the elements, managed to survive until 1719, when the danger it posed to the dome of the rotunda led to the dismantling of its two and a half upper floors.

Jerusalem: Queen Melisande Entrenched in Citadel

Son Baldwin III Can't Wait to Rule

Foulque d'Anjou, heir to Baldwin II and husband of his daughter Melisande, came to power in 1131. Upon his death in 1143, the government remained in the hands of his wife, who played the role of regent for her son, Baldwin III, who had just turned thirteen.

In 1152, when Baldwin turned twenty-one, he did not consent to the renewed coronation of his mother. During Easter of that year he was crowned king, but Queen Melisande refused to relinquish control, and she rallied around her a group of noblemen from Jerusalem and drew the church to her side with gifts and acts of char-ity. Baldwin's faction was composed of a group of barons and military men whose loyalty to him had developed during the war campaigns they had lived through together.

The country wavered for a time on the verge of a civil war, but an agreement was finally reached that temporarily divided the kingdom of Jerusalem. The young king received Tyre, Acre, and the coastal areas, while his mother continued to rule Jerusalem and Nablus. Melisande also controlled the Sharon region, which was officially in the hands of her younger son, the count of Jaffa.

But Baldwin was unwilling to abide by the agreement indefinitely, and before long demanded that his mother return Jerusalem to him. When she refused, he mustered his troops, conquered Nablus, and advanced on Jerusalem. Melisande had believed that the inhabitants of the holy city would stand by her, but they turned out to be supporters of the king's legitimacy as ruler, and they opened the city gates to him.

The queen fled to the Citadel and dug in there. Baldwin laid siege to the stronghold, and when his siege machines began to destroy the fortifica-

Above: Baldwin III demands that his mother relinquish the throne. From a thirteenth-century manuscript from Acre. **Left:** Baldwin III's seal.

tions of the Citadel the queen agreed to open negotiations, at the end of which she surrendered Jerusalem and was granted continued control of Nablus.

Women Join Crusades

The Church Objects

The wave of excitement that crashed onto Europe, sweeping the Continent's men into the Crusades, was actually sustained primarily by women. Young women promised their hearts to their knights and wooers if they left on a campaign to liberate Jerusalem. Women encouraged their husbands to leave for a journey that would bring them honor in this life and salvation in the next. They composed songs of praise and promised devotion to heroes who departed for the Holy Land.

Women help defend the Crusader cities. A thirteenth-century manuscript from Acre.

Many women joined their husbands or brothers on the journey, and various travelogues describe their role in preparing food for the warriors, transporting ammunition, and caring for the wounded. One journal describes at length a woman doctor who saved many wounded and ill people from death. Elsewhere, a woman warrior "whose arrows caused many losses to the Muslim soldiers" is mentioned. Among the women who participated in the Crusades was Queen Eleanor of Aquitaine, who joined her husband King Louis VII of France on the Second Crusade in 1149.

Other women on crusade included Queen Eleanor of Castile, wife of King Edward I of England, who set out in 1271, and Edward's daughter Joan, who was accompanied in 1290 by her husband Gilbert of Clare, the earl of Gloucester. Forty-nine women were among the 453 passengers aboard the ship *The Saint Victor*, which set sail in 1250. Some were escorted by their husbands, but many came to the Holy Land on their own.

Saint Hildegund was brought to Jerusalem by her father at the age of twelve, disguised as a boy. When she returned to Europe, she persisted in her deception and eventually became a Cistercian monk at a men's monastery. The fact that she was a woman was discovered only upon her death in 1188.

There were also women like Euphrosyne, the princess of Polotsk and the abbess of the convent there, who came to Jerusalem so that she might be buried there. She died a short time after arriving in the holy city on May 23, 1173, and was buried at the

Quite a few women joined their husbands on the crusade. A fourteenth-century Italian manuscript.

Monastery of Saint Theodosius in the Judean Desert. After Jerusalem fell to Saladin in 1187, her body was removed to Kiev for reburial.

Ten years later, Margaret from Beverley in Yorkshire arrived in Jerusalem. While participating in the defense of the city against Saladin's troops, she was wounded and captured by the Muslims. Held as a prisoner of war for many months, she was even sentenced to hard labor. After being released she returned to Jerusalem, and subsequently retired to a monastery in France.

Despite the religious fervor that women contributed to the Crusades, the church did not approve of their participation. It viewed pilgrimage, first and foremost, as a journey to purify the soul and seek forgiveness and pardon. Sexual relations en route, even between husband and wife, were explicitly forbidden by the edicts of the church in order to ensure a pure arrival at the city of God.

Crusaders Import Italian Brides

A great many Crusaders could not manage to find wives from among the daughters of the Franks and Europeans in the Holy Land. In order to prevent these young men from casting their eyes further afield and becoming involved with local Muslim women, a special importation of young women from southern Italy, especially from the district of Apulia, was arranged. These young women and their children were called "Pullani" (possibly after their place of origin), a term that gradually came to mean "bastard."

Among the common folk were many that married Syrian and Arab women who were willing to convert to Christianity.

Coronation of Crusader Kings

Religious Ceremony or Nobleman's Banquet?

During the days of the first Kingdom of Jerusalem, the coronation ceremony of the king was a combination of a religious rite and a European-style aristocratic banquet. The first to be crowned in the Church of the Holy Sepulcher was Godfrey of Bouillon, who received the title of Protector of the Holy Sepulcher. Baldwin I, who succeeded him, refused to have the ceremony take place in Jerusalem because he did not want to assume a gold crown adorned with precious stones at the site where Jesus, the king of kings, was humiliated unto death and crowned with thorns. He insisted that his coronation be held instead at the Church of the Nativity in Bethlehem, where that of his successor, Baldwin II, would also take place.

The kings who followed Baldwin II were crowned at the Church of the Holy Sepulcher in a ceremony con-ducted by the patriarch. After the coronation, in which the heads of the church and the noblemen of the kingdom participated, a festive procession left the church in the direction of the Temple Mount.

Its first stop there was the Templum Domini, located in the edifice known today as the Dome of the Rock. Inside the church the king would remove his crown and lay it on the altar, which was dedicated to the Presentation of Jesus in the Temple. Finally the procession would arrive at the Templum Solomonis (Al-Aqsa Mosque) where a festive banquet was held for city notables and guests of the king from throughout the kingdom and from other Crusader principalities and baronies beyond its borders.

The coronation of a king. The opening letter of a medieval French manuscript.

The Tombs of the Crusader Kings

On July 16, 1149, the day after the consecration of the Church of the Holy Sepulcher, a memorial service was held for soldiers who had fallen in the conquest of Jerusalem. The festivities surrounding the consecration continued for an entire year and ended on July 18, 1150, at a jubilee ceremony in memory of the death of Godfrey of Bouillon.

Baldwin I on his deathbed, by G. Doré.

The brave king was buried at the foot of Golgotha. His tomb, as well as that of his brother and successor, Baldwin I, was situated in a square courtyard enclosed by a low wall that formed a sort of corridor to the Chapel of Adam (called Golgotha during the Crusader period). According to Wilhelm of Tyre, Godfrey of Bouillon was buried underneath Calvary, and ever after the spot was reserved for the succeeding kings.

King Baldwin II was moved on his deathbed to the residence of the Latin patriarchs in order to return his soul to his maker as close as possible to the tomb of Jesus. He died on August 21, 1131 and was buried next to the two previous kings. At the time, the courtyard was still open to the sky.

When King Foulque d'Anjou, who was married to Melisande, Baldwin II's daughter, died in Acre in 1144, his body was brought to Jerusalem and buried among his fellow kings. His and Baldwin II's tombs were in the entrance to the room adjacent to the

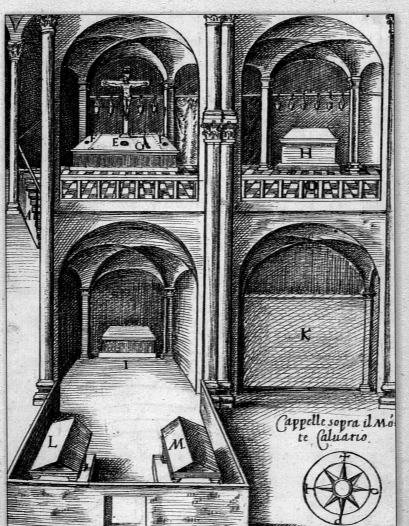

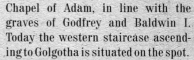

Golgotha and tombs of the Crusader kings, by V. Pavi.

Chapel of Adam, in line with the graves of Godfrey and Baldwin I. Today the western staircase ascending to Golgotha is situated on the spot.

Baldwin III, Foulque's son, who died in Beirut in 1162, was the first king to be buried along the choir hall (in the entrance corridor). Theodorich, who visited the site in 1172, notes that his tomb was splendidly decorated in white marble. Further on was the tomb of King Amalric I, the brother of Baldwin III. Baldwin IV was buried in 1186 south of his father Amalric, and a short while later his young nephew Baldwin V was laid to rest beside him.

Baldwin IV's tomb is the closest to the sepulcher of Jesus. In the eighteenth century a still-legible inscription on his tombstone read that in the grave was buried the seventh king, the boy Baldwin, in whose veins flowed the blood of kings.

On the tomb of Baldwin V, which was drawn in detail by Elzear Horn in 1724, was a portrait of Jesus in the Byzantine style, which possibly saved the tomb from the eventual destruction that was the fate of the others. The tomb was decorated with mother of pearl and a pattern of interwoven columns reminiscent of a decoration in one of the niches in the Dome of the Rock.

The graves of the Crusader kings, often vandalized, were finally completely demolished in 1808 during renovations of the church carried out by the Greek Orthodox.

Church of Saint Anne

The Church of Saint Anne was built over the remains of a Crusader church and convent on the spot where according to tradition Anne and Joachim lived and Mary the mother of Jesus was born.

Until the arrival of the Crusaders, the place was maintained by four nuns. In 1104, King Baldwin I evicted his Armenian wife, forcing her to retreat to the ancient convent. In 1130 the daughter of Baldwin II dwelt in the convent for a short time; later, Theodora, the widow of Baldwin III, also resided there.

At about the same time, the present-day church and adjacent convent were built on the site. The walls of the church were adorned with pictures depicting scenes from the lives of Joachim, Anne, and Mary. The kings of Jerusalem enriched the convent with gifts and donations, endowing it with, among other things, the income from the three markets in central Jerusalem. The church, renowned for its beauty, was often described by pilgrims in their writings.

After he conquered Jerusalem, Saladin turned the Church of Saint Anne into a Muslim theological school called Salahiya, after himself. In the mid-nineteenth century the edifice was returned to the French, who renovated it and turned it back into a church.

The Church of Saint Anne, by E. Pierotti.

675 Knights on a Good Day

According to the account of John of Ibelin, the seignior of Jaffa, in 1170 the Crusader army in the Kingdom of Jerusalem numbered around 675 knights. In terms of the Middle Ages, the force was large. Not even in the most famous battles in European history of the period did more warriors participate, and during some of the major Crusader military campaigns—such as the invasion of Egypt headed by Amalric I, which depended upon slightly more than three hundred knights for its success—seemingly small numbers of knights overcame whole cities.

John of Ibelin records not only the amount

from municipal properties (essentially protection money). The average income of a knight was between 450 and 500 besants (the coin of the realm) per annum, about what he would receive from a village, if he had one. Not much was left from a knight's pay, however, since his expenses were high. He was required to pay out of his own pocket for the maintenance of his assistants, equipment, and horses—expenses that amounted to about 30 besants per month.

On the other hand, the knights also enjoyed a great many privileges. In court, their evidence was sufficient to establish the guilt of a man

Knights pursuing Arabs. From a fifteenth-century French manuscript.

Heinrich II, the duke of Austria, on his way to the crusade. From the dukes of Babengers family tree.

of knights in the Crusader army but their responsibilities and privileges as well. The knights, obliged to fight in the army of the kingdom, received feudal grants in return for their services. They were usually in the employ of a feudal lord who was himself under an obligation to draft and provide for a certain number of recruits in accordance with his status, the amount of property he owned, and the number of knights connected to his feudal holding.

Knights received payment either directly from their lords or as income

of lower status accused of harming them, and like the noblemen, they had been granted immunity from arrest.

Next to the knights—a type of medieval armored corps—was the cavalry, whose troops did not enjoy the status of the knights. John of Ibelin's record listed 5,025 such mounted sergeants; the quota for the kingdom's army was usually supplied by the church and the Crusader cities. They served together with the infantry, most of whom were recruited from among the Crusaders and became salaried soldiers.

Agricultural Production Recovers

The Crusader period saw an impressive recovery in the realm of agricultural production. After four hundred years of Arab control, during which local agriculture was systematically destroyed by Bedouin tribes from the Arabian Peninsula, the rural population started to show signs of recuperation. Twelve hundred villages of at least twenty houses each dotted the countryside. In every settlement, a *ra'is* or village head was responsible for collecting taxes for the nobleman or knight who owned the village. The three major crops in such hamlets were wheat, grapes, and olives, and for part of the period cotton cultivation and the manufacture of textile products was also undertaken.

Aqua Bella, a Crusader manor house.

Pilgrimage Pays Off: Principle Source of Income to Kingdom of Jerusalem

Sailing Fee Goes to Kingdom's Treasury

The stream of pilgrims arriving mainly from European nations was the principle source of income for the Crusader Kingdom of Jerusalem. An extensive industry of souvenir manufacture, food services, lodging, transportation, and guides thrived around the pilgrims. In addition, the state coffers were entitled to one third of the sailing fees paid by pilgrims to the shipping companies that transported them to the Holy Land. The treasury of the kingdom was also the sole heir to the property of any pilgrim who died in the Holy Land without leaving a will.

The Kingdom of Jerusalem's only serious branch of export was that of holy souvenirs—relics—which were thought to atone for sins. Especially famous was the relic industry run by the monks of Ein Karem. Business records of the period note that among the souvenirs in demand were slivers from the rock that hid Elizabeth, John's mother, from Herod's soldiers, and manufactured clay and copper reliefs depicting various events in the history of Christianity. The value of each object was determined, of course, according to its ability to ensure absolution from sin. Among them were relics that expiated their owner from sin for three to four years as well as those guaranteeing even twelve years of absolution.

Relics from Ein Karem from this period are still kept today in many European churches.

The enormous demand during the Middle Ages for objects from the holy sites in the Holy Land or for remains from the graves of the various saints was transformed by fast-thinking merchants into one of the most profitable branches of commerce in the East.

Saintly relics were thought to have remarkable powers, especially regarding everything related to healing various ills. The soil from the Mamre oaks near Hebron, for example, was considered a sure medication for any illness, since it was from this soil that the first man was formed.

An enormous trade in holy relics and souvenirs developed around the holy sites. The largest demand was for pieces of the True Cross, bits of the Holy Sepulcher, stone slivers carved out of the rock at Golgotha, pieces of wood from the table of the Last Supper, pieces from the pillar of the flagellation, and shreds of cloth from the robes of the saints. Less holy relics included pieces of rock or clumps of earth soaked in oil from the lamps of the Holy Sepulcher.

The large sums of money generated by the holy relic industry attracted a certain criminal element, which took advantage of the faith of the masses in the miraculous powers of the various objects and their admiration for the saints in order to manufacture counterfeit holy relics for all.

Special gangs who specialized in the relic business would also rob holy

Above: A bracelet vendor near the Church of the Holy Sepulcher, by P. Lortet.
Left: The mother-of-pearl souvenir industry in Bethlehem, by C.W. Wilson.

relics from the original burial places on demand. Thus, for example, such a band organized the removal of the body of Saint Mark from Alexandria to Venice, where the apostle was declared patron of the city.

Bishoprics Bloom in the Holy Land

Little Territory, Lots of Churches

The number of churches built during the Crusader period was so great that within the relatively small area of the Holy Land alone there were more than one hundred bishoprics. If the territory of each bishopric itself was small, this was because the number of churches in each city, especially in the large cities, was great. Most of the churches were built on or adjacent to holy sites.

The many churches belonged not only to various monastic orders but to different sects. The largest concentration of them was in the Patriarch's Quarter surrounding the Church of the Holy Sepulcher, and a great many were also built along the Via Dolorosa, which leads from the Mount of Olives to the Church of the Holy Sepulcher. Many churches also appeared in the Armenian Quarter and in the Jewish-Syrian Quarter in the northeast of the city.

Four of the most important concentrations of churches were granted the status of ecclesiastical seigniories—areas owned by the church. The central seigniory was in the royal capital in the quarter around the Church of the Holy Sepulcher referred to as the Patriarch's Quarter. A second ecclesiastical seigniory was in Lydda; the third was in Nazareth; and the fourth in Bethlehem.

Below: The seal of the Archibishop of Caesarea.

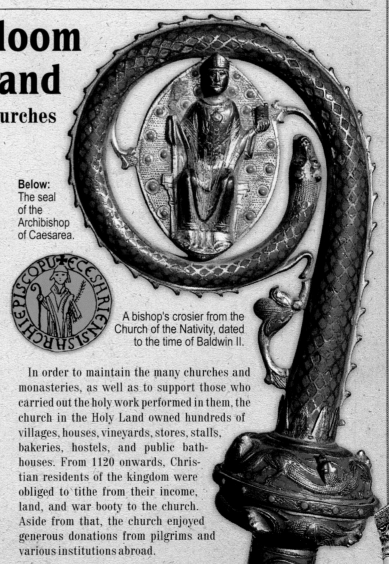

A bishop's crosier from the Church of the Nativity, dated to the time of Baldwin II.

In order to maintain the many churches and monasteries, as well as to support those who carried out the holy work performed in them, the church in the Holy Land owned hundreds of villages, houses, vineyards, stores, stalls, bakeries, hostels, and public bathhouses. From 1120 onwards, Christian residents of the kingdom were obliged to tithe from their income, land, and war booty to the church. Aside from that, the church enjoyed generous donations from pilgrims and various institutions abroad.

CRUSADER ARMY CRUSHED AT KARNEI HATTIN

Poor Military Judgment Results in Dreadful Defeat: 12,000 Muslim Cavalry Troops Trounce 1,200 Knights

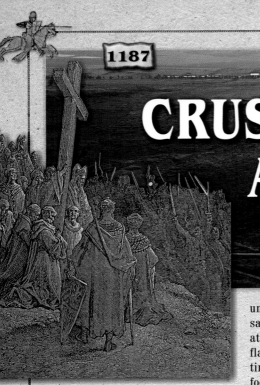

A fatal error by the Crusader military command at the Battle of Karnei Hattin brought about the defeat and annihilation of the army of the Kingdom of Jerusalem by the troops of Saladin and eventually led to the fall of the entire Crusader empire.

On June 30, 1187, Saladin crossed the River Jordan to the west at the head of an army of 30,000 soldiers, 12,000 of which were cavalry troops.

The Muslim army attacked the villages in the area and lay siege to Tiberias.

During earlier Muslim offensives, the Crusaders had dug in within their fortresses to bide their time until the Muslim army, which was not equipped to maintain an extended siege, withdrew. Only once, near Gezer, had the Crusader army clashed with Saladin's army, putting an end, once and for all, to his seasonal raids.

The Crusader army set out with a force numbering about 1,200 knights and 15,000 foot soldiers.

Saladin, who enjoyed the support of the local Muslim population, was prepared for the Crusaders. Almost from the beginning of the campaign, which took place in terrible heat,

units of his army followed the Crusader force. Mounted archery units attacked the Crusader army from its flank, forcing it to waste valuable time and manpower chasing the fleet-footed cavalry units.

On July 3, 1187, the Crusader army found itself without water, and its commanders ordered their forces to turn north in search of water instead of continuing east to Tiberias. Moving in a dangerously scattered formation, the Crusaders searched for sources of water. As they crossed the heights of Karnei Hattin, unprepared for battle, Saladin's soldiers suddenly attacked.

The Crusader army tried to regroup quickly and retreat over the hills, but the Muslim force, which had superior numbers, surrounded the Christians and separated the cavalry from the infantry, which fled to the top of the northern peak of Karnei Hattin.

Down below, the mounted knights fought a heroic battle but were exposed to a bombardment of arrows, against which their swords were useless. Only a small force of knights commanded by Raymond of Tripoli succeeded in breaking through the ring of siege. The remainder of the knights finally retreated to the heights of the southern summit of

Karnei Hattin and gathered around the king's red tent, next to which stood the True Cross.

Towards evening, the Muslims achieved the mountain's summit. On the northern hill, the thirsty and

Clockwise from upper left: The Holy Cross in the battlefield, by G. Doré; here, under Karnei Hattin, the Crusader army was crushed; Saladin orders the binding of the prisoners. A fourteenth-century manuscript; the battlefield; casualties at the foot of Karnei Hattin, by G. Doré.

exhausted infantry troops were either thrown off the cliff to their deaths or taken prisoner to be sold at Syria's slave market.

On the second summit, to the south, the last of the knights—about 150 out of the 1,200 who had set out for battle—awaited their fate, weak with thirst. The highest-ranking prisoners, Guy de Lusignan among them, were taken captive. Reynald of Chatillon was dispatched to meet his maker by Saladin himself. The remnants of the Templar and Hospitaler regiments were slaughtered by Muslim fanatics zealous to honor the commandment of Jihad.

Less than 1,000 Crusader warriors survived the disastrous battle. For all intents and purposes, the army of the Kingdom of Jerusalem had ceased to exist.

Saladin's Campaign

The catastrophic defeat at the Battle of Karnei Hattin left the Kingdom of Jerusalem with no defense force to speak of. The Crusader cities and fortresses were exposed to the whim of the Muslim enemy.

By 1189, more than fifty fortresses and all of the Crusader cities had fallen into Saladin's hands. Only the port city of Tyre, the fortress of Atlit, and a few strongholds in Galilee (including Belvoir and the virtually impregnable fortress in Safed) did not capitulate, and most of the refugees from the conquered cities gathered in them.

Convinced that the secret of Crusader power was their fortified cities and fortresses, Saladin razed the walls of all of those that he subdued until almost all of the Crusader kingdom had been leveled to its foundations. Only one fatal error prevented Saladin from achieving an ultimate victory over the Crusaders: he neglected to conquer the stubborn port city of Tyre. By allowing the continued survival of a Christian enclave on the coast, Saladin enabled the establishment of a Christian bridgehead for the landfall of the Third Crusade.

Jerusalem in Muslim Hands
Unconditional Surrender on October 2, 1187.
Pope Urban III Dies of Shock Upon Hearing the News.

The location of the Crusader government in Jerusalem contributed to the growth, prosperity, and relative tranquillity of the city, but its rulers, perhaps lulled into a false sense of security by the city's calm, neglected its walls, and in 1177 part of them collapsed. As the threat of an invasion by Saladin loomed, an annual sum of money was allocated for making the necessary repairs.

Eight years later, Saladin stationed his army at the city gates. He had already overcome the other cities of the Holy Land (aside from Tyre) by that time, and only Jerusalem remained to be conquered. During the battle for Ashkelon in September of 1187 a delegation from Jerusalem had already arrived at the Muslim camp in Ashkelon, hoping to negotiate terms of peace. (A full eclipse of the sun that occurred the same day was considered a bad omen.) Saladin offered tempting terms: the Crusaders could remain in the city and even continue to fortify it. An area within a fifteen-kilometer-radius around Jerusalem would remain under their control, and the sultan would supply them with food and money. This arrangement would continue until the following Pentecost. If by then the Crusader armies could get help to Jerusalem, it would remain in their hands; if not, they would surrender without a fight and return to their countries of origin.

The citizens of Jerusalem refused to accept the generous offer, though the city was without knights or armed warriors, all of whom had fallen or been taken captive at the Battle of Karnei Hattin. The delegation returned home and Saladin vowed to subdue Jerusalem by the sword.

The city's defense was entrusted to Balian d'Ibelin, the lord of Nablus, who arrived in Jerusalem from Tyre after fleeing there from the Battle of Karnei Hattin. He requested special permission from the sultan to enter Jerusalem to rescue his wife and children, who had fled there from Nablus. The sultan granted his request on the condition that d'Ibelin spend not more than one night in Jerusalem and swear that he would no longer bear arms against the Muslim ruler. Once d'Ibelin arrived in Jerusalem, however, the city leaders, led by Patriarch Heraclius, begged him to remain in order to stand at the head of the warriors. When Balian refused to break his vow, the patriarch formally released him from it.

Notwithstanding the patriarch's assurance, Balian sent a letter to the sultan asking him directly to release

The patriarch of Jerusalem, by G. Doré.

him from his vow. Having ensured the departure of his wife and children from the city for Tyre, Balian dedicated himself to defending Jerusalem. He demanded that its leaders recognize him as military commander, promise him their fealty, and pronounce him ruler of the city.

Finding only two knights in Jerusalem, Balian granted the title of knight to all noblemen over the age of sixteen as well as to thirty middle-class men. He sent units out of the city daily to bring food and supplies. At his command, the beaten silver and gold was removed from the Chapel of the Holy Tomb in order to strike coins with which to pay the wages of the army.

In mid-September the first Muslim forces arrived on the outskirts of Jerusalem. The villages and towns around the city were evacuated of inhabitants, who were concentrated behind the city walls. The number of people in Jerusalem reached sixty thousand—double that of peacetime. The hardest hours had begun.

The Muslims built siege machines and began to shell the city with grenades of Greek fire and arrows. Tens of thousands of horsemen gathered opposite St. Stephen's Gate in order to prevent the city garrison from bursting out of its portals. Muslim work details began to dig along the wall, undermining its foundations. Within two days a wide crack appeared exactly at the spot where the Crusaders had breached the wall to conquer Jerusalem in 1099. As the wall fell, the large cross that marked the spot of the Crusader victory also crashed to the ground. Attempts by the defenders to interrupt the destruction of the wall failed; they were forced to retreat from their positions and refused to return to them even after they were promised

large sums of money.

The fall of the city was now inevitable, and the wrenching decision to surrender was made. Balian left the city to negotiate with Saladin.

The night was passed in prayers and tears. In desperation, the women carried tubs of water to the Church of the Holy Sepulcher, baptized their daughters in them, and cut their hair. Priests and monks walked on the walls carrying a statue of the crucifixion and pieces of the True Cross belonging to the Syrians (the True Cross in the possession of the Catholics had fallen into enemy hands at the Battle of Karnei Hattin).

At their meeting, Saladin reminded Balian of his vow to conquer the city and avenge the blood of those massacred in 1099. Balian replied that if the surrender of the city was not accepted, the Crusaders would fight until their last drop of blood, slaughter their women and children, set fire to all their property, kill the five thousand Muslim prisoners of war they held, and not hesitate to destroy the

be sold into slavery. The Christians would be permitted to remove from the city any property they could carry. Meanwhile, the city gates would be locked—except for Jaffa Gate—and the keys given to Saladin. Officers would be posted in the city to maintain order, and the Muslims would be permitted to enter the city in order to buy property from Christians, who were in need of cash to pay the ransom. Balian obtained from the Hospitalers the amount required to free seven thousand of the city's poor from payment. After the sum was turned over to Saladin, Balian put two people on each street to make a list of those without means who were to be exempt from payment. The citizens either paid the ransom at Jaffa Gate or gave it to one of the Muslim officers in the city in return for a receipt.

After coming into possession of the city, Saladin did his best to remove any traces of Crusader occupation. The gold cross was removed from the Dome of the Rock, dragged through the streets, and melted down at the Cita-

The ruins of the Mirabel fortress.

city—including the Dome of the Rock and Al-Aqsa.

After lengthy negotiations, the terms of the surrender were fixed: the city's residents were to be ransomed—the Christians were given forty days to raise the ransom money and conclude their business. Anyone found in the city after that date would

del. The Church of the Holy Sepulcher was not harmed—only locked for three days. Thus ended 88 years of Christian rule in the holy city.

The fall of Jerusalem into Muslim hands shocked the West, and especially Christianity's foremost leader there; when Pope Urban III heard the news, he had a heart attack and died.

CHAPTER V

THE SECOND CRUSADER KINGDOM

1187-1270

After Saladin conquered the Holy Land, Tyre, which had been defended by Conrad de Monferrat, remained in Christian hands. The city was to become the center of the remnant of the Crusader body politic headed by the king Guy de Lusignan, and would later serve as a base for the military forces of the Third Crusade.

The lengthy siege the Crusaders laid on Acre from August 1189 to July 1191 and the subsequent conquest of the city by them marked the beginning of a renewed invasion of the Holy Land, this time led by Richard the Lionhearted. Due to disagreements between the kings of France and England, however, the rejuvenated effort yielded meager results. The Crusader state that was founded after Richard the Lionhearted and Saladin signed a peace treaty in September 1192 was situated in the area between Tyre and Jaffa (the Lydda-Ramla territory had been divided between the two opposing sides). The Christians secured the right of pilgrimage to Jerusalem, which remained in Muslim hands. Acre became, in effect, the capital of the kingdom.

With the death of Saladin in 1193, the Muslim empire was again divided, but the Crusaders were no longer able to exploit the opportune moment, despite the fact that their kingdom was in the process of being enlarged and would later take up various crusades, among them the German campaign that overwhelmed Beirut in 1197. The treaty of 1204 restored Jaffa (which had fallen to the Egyptians in 1197) to the Crusaders, along with Nazareth and part of the territory of Sidon.

The Fourth Crusade, which was intended to come to the aid of the ailing Crusader kingdom in the Holy Land, suddenly diverted its energies to the conquest of Constantinople. The result of this about-face was the deviation of crucial European military forces to the Byzantine Empire and Cyprus, which was conquered by Richard the Lionhearted in 1189.

The military campaign of the kings of Hungary and Cyprus in 1217 was wasted in unfocused operations in Galilee, Beit She'an, and on Mount Tabor: the sole positive results of it were the fortification of Caesarea and the establishment of Chateau Pelerins in Atlit. Afterwards, what remained of the regiments from this campaign joined a brave attempt by Jean de Brienne, the king of Jerusalem, to invade Egypt in an advance promoted as the Fifth Crusade, and, indeed, the march to Damietta in 1219 proved victorious. In exchange for Damietta, the Egyptian sultan was prepared to surrender all of the territories that had passed from the former Crusader kingdom to Egypt, but his proposal was rejected by the papal representative, and the subsequent attempt by the Crusaders in July 1221 to conquer Cairo ended in their defeat and retreat from the land of the Nile.

The Crusader East now awaited the arrival of Friedrich II, emperor of Germany and king of Sicily. His departure for the crusade was delayed until 1228, in which year he both reached Acre and was excommunicated by the pope. Meanwhile, the Crusaders conquered parts of Sidon, reconstructed the walls of Caesarea, and fortified the Montfort fortress. Thanks to Friedrich II's relationship with the sultan of Egypt, he secured the treaty of Jaffa (February 1229) without bloodshed, thus enlarging the territory of the Crusaders, and winning the holy city for them, although the Temple Mount remained in Muslim hands.

The Kingdom of Jerusalem was now comprised of two enclaves connected to the coastal plain: Nazareth and Jerusalem. Emperor Friedrich II, the son-in-law of Jean de Brienne, crowned himself king of Jerusalem, but after appointing civil servants to administer the kingdom, left the country. His unsettling departure dragged in its wake a civil war in the Kingdom of Jerusalem which spread from the Holy Land to the Kingdom of Cyprus. Leading the opposition to the absent monarch's rule was the noble house of Ybelin. The war, which lasted in fits and starts from 1231 to 1243, exhausted the strength of the Kingdom of Jerusalem. The Italian communes and the military orders conducted their own affairs according to their own policies, and the Holy Land remained without a real leader.

The 1239 crusade of Thibaut, the count of Champagne and king of Navarre, was debilitated by disputes among his leaders regarding whether to sign a treaty with Egypt or Damascus. The attempt of the Crusaders to restore the ruins of Ashkelon ended in their defeat at the Battle of Gaza.

Ismail of Damascus tried to persuade

the Crusaders to enter into an accord with him against Transjordan and Egypt, promising in return to restore to them Sidon and the Beaufort fortress, Safed, Tiberias in Galilee, and all the territories of the Holy Land under his control with the exception of Transjordan. The Crusaders departed Damascus, however, and when Richard of Cornwall appeared on the scene they fortified Ashkelon and procured a treaty with Egypt in 1241. As a result, a Crusader kingdom encompassing the coastal region (with Ashkelon), Galilee, and a strip of land from the coast into the mountains that included Beit Jibrin, Jerusalem, and Bethlehem came into being. The ruler of Transjordan, who had made a treaty with Damascus against Egypt, granted the Crusaders the Temple Mount in an effort to ingratiate himself with the Christian powers.

The new arrangement collapsed when the Templar Order and its allies approached Damascus with an offer of an alliance against Egypt, Friedrich II's traditional ally. Egypt appealed for help to the Khwarazmians, who were then fleeing the Mongols, and the two Muslim armies conquered Crusader Jerusalem in August 1244, crushed the European forces at Forbie near Gaza a few months later, and afterwards razed Galilee. Jerusalem, which was annexed to Egypt, was never to revert to the Crusaders; Judea and Samaria, which were annexed to Transjordan, were similarly lost forever. In 1247 the Egyptians conquered Tiberias and Ashkelon.

The divided nation, compressed to the coast, recovered once again for a brief moment when the crusade of

Louis IX, king of France, arrived in 1248 for an unforeseen stay of six years. His plan to conquer Egypt as the key to the takeover of the Holy Land commenced with the conquest of Damietta in Egypt, but the crusade eventually ended in disaster when the Crusader troops were taken prisoner together with their king in April of 1250.

Louis IX, who ransomed himself from his captors in exchange for Damietta and an enormous sum of money, then attempted to fortify the remains of the Crusader kingdom in the Holy Land—whose southern border was now in Jaffa—by rebuilding the walls of Acre, Caesarea, Jaffa, and Tyre. Despite his efforts, the days of the kingdom were numbered.

One last ray of hope appeared to the Crusaders with the arrival of a new factor in the Middle East—the Mongols, who conquered Baghdad in 1258. Initially, it seemed that a pact between the Mongols and the Europeans would be made (rumor had it that there were many Christians among the Mongols) to help the Crusaders repel the Muslim encroachment. But the kingdom was now in the midst of a different crisis—the wars of the Italian communes, who imported, among other things, their feuds from Italy to the shores of the Holy Land, had overwhelmed the last years of the Crusader kingdom by disrupting the trade and lifestyle of Christian residents. The local nobility and the military orders were divided in their support of the various communes, whose internecine quarrels dragged the Crusaders into a general civil war.

The Crusaders sat out the great clash between the Mongols and the Mamelukes of Egypt, careful to maintain neutrality. The Mamelukes victory of 1260 was accomplished without the Crusaders having intervened in the war in any way whatsoever, and as a result, what was left of the Crusader kingdom was eventually forced to face Baybars, the great Mameluke ruler of Egypt, alone. Slowly but surely, Baybars wrested fortress after fortress from the Crusaders. In 1263, Galilee, Mount Tabor, and Nazareth were attacked. In 1265, Caesarea, Haifa, and Arsuf fell into Baybars' clutches, in 1266—Safed and Toron, and in 1271—the fortress of the Teutonic Order at Montfort. The remains of the Kingdom of Jerusalem, unable to collaborate, made separate treaties with the conqueror in order to preserve what little property was left them.

Baybars and his successor Qalawun meanwhile liquidated the remains of the northern principalities: Antioch in 1287 and Tripoli in 1289. Acre fell into the hands of the Mamelukes in the spring of 1291. Upon hearing the news, the Crusaders evacuated Atlit and Tyre, whose inhabitants fled to Cyprus. The Crusader kingdom in the Holy Land was at an end.

1187

Three Kings—Third Crusade

Richard the Lionhearted, Philip II, and Friedrich Barbarossa Set Out to Liberate Jerusalem from Saladin

The three senior kings of Europe—Richard I (Richard the Lionhearted) of England, Philip II of France, and Friedrich I (Barbarossa), emperor of Germany— responded to the entreaty of Pope Gregory VIII to set out on a new crusade to liberate Jerusalem from Saladin.

The pope's request, perhaps his first official announcement after his coronation following the death of Urban III, was publicized on October 29, 1187, several weeks after Saladin's conquest of Jerusalem. Richard the Lionhearted of Britain responded immediately, and a short while later was joined by Philip II of France and Friedrich Barbarossa of Germany. Smaller forces led by various counts and princes from other European nations allied themselves with the armies of the three great kings.

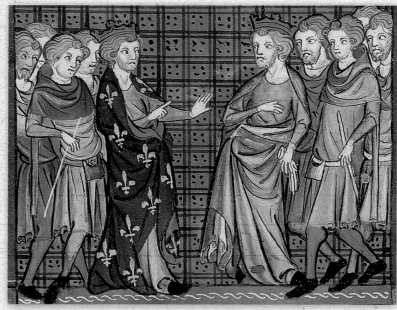

Richard I and Philip II quarrel. From a fourteenth-century French manuscript.

Friedrich Barbarossa in Crusader attire. From a twelfth-century manuscript.

The decision of the three most powerful rulers in Europe to stand at the head of the Third Crusade reflects the depth of the shock that shook Europe after the fall of Jerusalem. The three vowed that they would not return to their countries until they had liberated the holy city from its heretical occupiers and restored honor to the Kingdom of Jerusalem.

1190

String of Mishaps Delays Third Crusade

Kaiser Friedrich Barbarossa Drowns. English Force Arrives at Cyprus One Year Late.

The Third Crusade, for which the Christian world had such high hopes—especially given the three kings who led it and the preparations that preceded it—began with a series of misadventures that severely detracted from its momentum.

Richard the Lionhearted was delayed in London attending to the transfer of the kingdom to his hands after the death of Henry II, whose throne he inherited. The king of France, Philip II, was likewise held up at home with urgent matters of state.

Only at the beginning of 1190 did the first regiment finally depart on its way to the Holy Land. It was led by the German kaiser Friedrich Barbarossa, who guided his army on foot through Europe and Asia Minor until June 10, 1190, when he drowned while crossing a river in Asia Minor.

In July of 1190, the armies of England and France set sail for the East from Vezelay. Philip II's fleet sailed to Tyre in order to join the siege on Acre. Europeans amassed outside the city walls by land and sea, as fleets from Pisa and northern Europe as well as forces led by Henry of Champagne, Louis of Thuringia, Leopold of Austria, and a force from Cologne converged on the Muslim-held fortified city.

Above: The seal of Philip II.
Below: Leopold V, the duke of Austria, kneels at the feet of Emperor Friedrich Barbarossa, King Philip II, and King Richard I. From the family tree of the dukes of Babengers.

1189

Crusaders at the Gates of Acre

Sicilian Fleet Accompanies Force Led by Guy de Lusignan

Guy de Lusignan, freed from Muslim captivity in 1188 and despairing of returning to rule in Tripoli, mustered a force of 600 cavalry and about 7,000 infantry troops and set out in the direction of Acre. Thinking it would be easier to annihilate the Christian forces at close range, Saladin meant to let de Lusignan's men approach the city, but his hopes were dashed when the Crusader force seized a convenient position on a hill opposite the city gates and held it with all its might.

Saladin's forces surrounded the Crusader troops, forcing them to fight on two fronts. The Crusader warriors, demonstrating great courage, attempted to penetrate the city by means of ladders; the attack failed, though its impact embarrassed the Muslim camp.

The opposing sides had begun what was to turn out to be a three-year campaign that occupied many Crusader and Muslim soldiers. In the course of the standoff, a Danish fleet came to the aid of the Crusader force, as did a Flemish fleet and a regiment of French noblemen. After them came a German force that arrived by sea. Slowly, as a critical mass of reinforcements arrived, the ring of the Crusader siege around Acre tightened. Still, neither side was savvy enough to utilize its advantages for a definitive victory, and the campaign became a long-term trench war.

108

Richard the Lionhearted Conquers Comnenus' Cyprus

Saves Sister from Byzantine Bad Boy

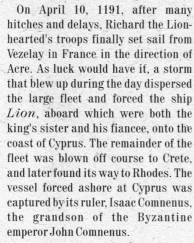

On April 10, 1191, after many hitches and delays, Richard the Lionhearted's troops finally set sail from Vezelay in France in the direction of Acre. As luck would have it, a storm that blew up during the day dispersed the large fleet and forced the ship *Lion*, aboard which were both the king's sister and his fiancee, onto the coast of Cyprus. The remainder of the fleet was blown off course to Crete, and later found its way to Rhodes. The vessel forced ashore at Cyprus was captured by its ruler, Isaac Comnenus, the grandson of the Byzantine emperor John Comnenus.

Emperor John Comnenus. A mosaic from the Hagia Sophia in Constantinople.

Richard the Lionhearted was unable to ignore the insult, and on May 6 landed on the Cypriot coast to take control of the island. From the moment the Crusaders occupied it, they realized the spot's strategic importance as a outpost for their future kingdom. The island was to remain under Western European rule for over three hundred years until falling into the hands of the Ottoman Empire.

Richard I, victorious over Saladin. 13th-century tiles from the Chertsey Abbey.

Richard the Lionhearted Lands on Acre's Coast

Acre's End at Hand

On June 8, 1191, Richard the Lionhearted's fleet reached the coast of Acre, marking the beginning of the end of the city's stalwart defense.

Shortly after Richard's arrival, the pace of the Christians' attacks quickened.

Soon, however, even he realized that it was no longer possible to save the city.

In return for granting the right of surrender and the safe exit of the besieged garrison and all of Acre's residents, the Christians demanded the territories of the Kingdom of Jerusalem prior to the Battle of Karnei

assault on the Christian camp in order to save Acre's inhabitants.

Finally facing the hopelessness of their situation, Acre's defenders surrendered on July 12, 1191. The Christians won the city and its property; its inhabitants were considered prisoners of war, redeemable in exchange for the liberation of Christian prisoners of war, a payment of two hundred thousand gold dinars, and the return of the True Cross.

The conquest of Acre inaugurated the second period in the history of the Kingdom of Jerusalem. The former property of communes, monastic

Richard I's shield.

orders, and churches in the city and its vicinity reverted to their Christian proprietors. Mosques switched back into churches. Thanks to the intervention of the king of France, longtime Christian residents of the city regained their property.

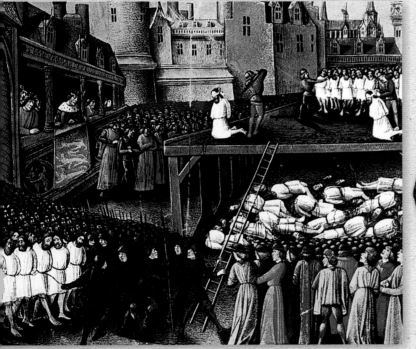

When not all of the Crusaders' demands were met after the conquest of Acre in 1191, Richard I gathered the 2,700 Muslim prisoners he had taken and executed them.

ened. The Muslim commanders of Acre reported on the worsening situation to Saladin and requested permission to contact the Crusaders in order to discuss the terms of surrender. Saladin, determined to hold on to the city at all costs, initially refused the request to enter into negotiations.

Hattin. They also requested the return of the True Cross, which had been captured at the Battle of Karnei Hattin, the liberation of the Christian prisoners of war, and payment for the redemption of Muslim prisoners. The conditions were rejected by Saladin, who subsequently attempted a final

Guy de Lusignan Crowned King of Jerusalem

Reduced Rights, but He's Still King

Jaffa's defeat having been achieved, the time had come for the political organization of the reborn Crusader kingdom. The governmental state of the country was somewhat complex: The queen, Sibylla, had died in 1190, and her husband, Guy de Lusignan, who had ruled until then by virtue of their marital status, technically lost his right to govern. Sibylla's rightful heir was her sister, who was forced to divorce her husband and marry the ruler of Tyre, Conrad of Montferrat, who insisted that the crown of the

Above: A coin of Guy de Lusignan.

Kingdom of Jerusalem belonged to him.

After exhausting negotiations that lasted almost two weeks, the kings and the noblemen decided that Guy de Lusignan would retain the title of king of Jerusalem for the rest of his life, though he would not enjoy the right of bequeathing it. His rights as king were also otherwise curtailed. Upon de Lusignan's death, the crown would pass to Conrad of Montferrat and his heirs. Should they both die, Richard the Lionhearted would appoint the next king of Jerusalem if he was still present in the Holy Land.

Stunning Crusader Victory at Arsuf

On August 22, 1191, the Crusader army commenced a march southward, the objective of which was to reoccupy Jerusalem and the other territories lost after the fiasco at Karnei Hattin. The campaign was to last an entire year and reach its conclusion without vanquishing the holy city.

On September 7, the force approached Arsuf. From the break of day it was clear that the Muslims intended to wage an intensive battle, and their forces shot a heavy barrage of arrows at the Crusader troops. Richard's strategy was to lead with a cavalry offensive, but his plan crumbled when some of his knights, upon seeing the approach of the Turkish cavalry, fled in fear, leaving both their honor and victory behind. Richard, witnessing the frenzy, charged into the field of battle at the head of the rest of his knights, brushing off the Muslim warriors.

The Crusader forces attacked the Muslims three times. When the third offensive drew to a close, the Muslim forces had disappeared from the horizon. The operation had broken the spirit of the Muslim ranks, who could no longer face a pitched battle with the Crusaders, and ceased striking at them. In a moment of poor military judgment, the Crusaders did not take advantage of the hiatus to march on Jerusalem: They would never again have such a promising opportunity.

Richard I, victorious in the Battle of Arsuf, by G. Doré.

Muslims Attack Jaffa

Saladin storms Jaffa, by G. Doré.

In the summer of 1192, Richard the Lionhearted was in Acre preparing to set out on his offensive against Beirut. Seizing his opportunity, Saladin carried out a daring attack on Jaffa on July 26.

The walls of Jaffa withstood the assault for five days, the Christian defenders within fighting for their lives. On the fifth day the city's eastern gate was breached and the Franks were forced to evacuate the city. They withdrew to the fortress above the port and sent a small boat to Acre to summon help, though they had already lost all hope of rescue and entered into negotiations regarding a surrender.

On August 1, just as the fortress was about to be transferred to Saladin's hands, the Muslims saw boats coming up over the horizon. Richard the Lionhearted had come to Jaffa's aid at the head of a fleet of vessels from Pisa and Genoa. A Frankish priest who jumped from the heights of the fortress onto the sand in front of the port succeeded in reaching Richard and giving him a full report on the situation.

Richard dove into the sea together with some comrades-in-arms, gaining the beach and climbing the steps leading to the fortress under a shower of arrows. With the added strength of his auxiliary forces, the knights from the fortress penetrated the city and expelled their Muslim foes. Jaffa remained a Crusader city, and was recognized as such in the peace treaty subsequently signed by both sides.

Richard I storms the Jaffa beach, by G. Doré.

SECOND KINGDOM OF JERUSALEM ESTABLISHED

Christian-Muslim Peace Treaty Signed

Even as Jaffa was being fortified, Richard the Lionhearted and Al-Malik al-'Adil, Saladin's brother, had already taken the first cautious steps towards the possibility of a peace treaty. Among the solutions brought to the table was the unusual proposal that Joan, Richard's sister and widow of the king of Sicily, marry Al-Malik Al-'Adil. After their nuptials, Richard and Saladin would turn the coastal area of the Holy Land over to them. The couple would live in Jerusalem, and priests from the Latin Church would serve in the churches of Jerusalem. When Joan vehemently refused to wed a Muslim, Richard the Lionhearted simply announced that al-'Adil would have to convert to Christianity. The peace treaty was signed on September 2, 1192, and a new Crusader kingdom spreading along the coast from Tyre to Jaffa was declared.

The Christians were assured the right to make unarmed pilgrimages to Jerusalem free of charge. On the other hand, Saladin insisted that the Crusader fortresses destroyed by him not be rebuilt. The Ayubbid leader's de-

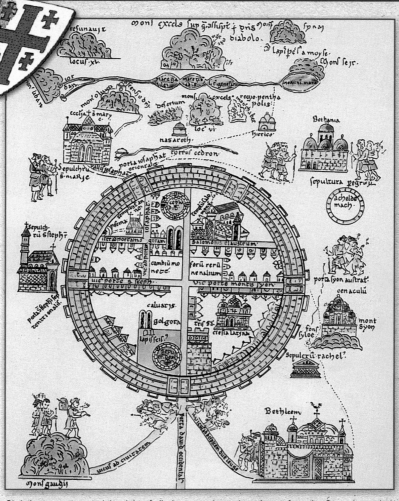

mand was intended to undermine the infrastructure of Crusader power—the fortresses—and eventually did exactly that.

The treaty was to be in effect for three years and three months. The Third Crusade, begun five years previously, had finally redressed the disastrous defeat at Karnei Hattin and set into motion a new Christian reign.

One month after signing the peace treaty with Saladin, Richard the Lionhearted set sail for home.

A meeting between Richard I and Saladin, by G. Doré.

Christians were granted the right of pilgrimage to Jerusalem. A map from the Crusader period.

Saladin Dies

Saladin.

On March 4, 1193, six months after coming to terms with Richard the Lionhearted, Saladin, the hero of the Ayubbid Dynasty, died, and his realm was hurtled into a series of struggles that was to continue for seven years. The three great centers of the empire—Damascus, capital of Syria and the Holy Land, Egypt, and Aleppo—were ruled by Saladin's sons. The remaining territories were divided among them, Saladin's brothers, and their offspring.

The Imperial Crusade

The peace treaty signed between Saladin and Richard the Lionhearted was due to expire in December 1195. The Crusaders feared that a call to jihad against the Franks would unify the Muslim forces in a renewed assault on the Crusader nation.

In Europe, Kaiser Heinrich VI, the son of Friedrich Barbarossa, was organizing another crusade, and the Germans were responding enthusiastically to his call. In September 1197, the first German regiments set sail for the Holy Land. They weighed anchor at Acre two weeks too late; Muslim forces had just attacked Jaffa and massacred its Christian inhabitants.

Disaster followed disaster: Henry of Champagne, the Crusader king of Jerusalem, fell to his death from a window of Acre's fortress into the moat. The kingdom was without a ruler. Succumbing to pressure from the Germans, the patriarch of Jerusalem married Henry's widow to Aimery de Lusignan, the king of Cyprus.

Aimery, taking advantage of the German military presence to enlarge the borders of his kingdom, conquered Beirut in October 1197 and then laid siege to the Turun fortress overlooking the road to Tyre. In the meantime, word of the death of the kaiser reached the

Holy Land. The leaders of the Crusader forces hastened to return to their homelands, and the siege came to an abrupt end.

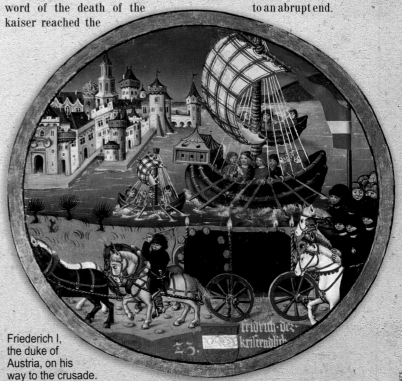

Friederich I, the duke of Austria, on his way to the crusade.

BYZANTINE EMPIRE FALLS!

Fourth Crusade Captures Constantinople!

1204

In August of 1198, Pope Innocent III announced a new crusade, the participants of which were to be transported by Venetian vessels for eighty-five thousand marks. But in October 1202, when the Crusader army was mustered in Venice, it was only half its expected size and its commanders had not managed to come up with enough money to pay the Venetians.

In lieu of cash the Crusaders agreed to help the Venetians regain control of the city of Zara, which had been taken by the Hungarians in 1186. In response to the pledge, the pope rescinded his patronage of the crusade, since he had stipulated that it was forbidden for the Crusader army to attack any Christian city.

In the neighboring Byzantine Empire, meanwhile, a civil war over the crown was taking place. The Byzantine emperor Isaac Angelus had been imprisoned by his brother Alexius III, who had also put out his eyes. Isaac's son, Alexius IV, promised the Crusaders that if they assisted him in freeing his father, he would pay them two hundred thousand marks, declare the unification of the Eastern Church with the Latin Church, and allocate a substantial force from the imperial Byzantine army for the

The coronation of Baldwin, the emperor of Byzantium, by A.V. l'Aliense.

planned campaign in Egypt.

The Venetians and most of the Crusader leaders agreed to the arrangement and on June 24 the Crusader force made landfall opposite Constantinople. Some three weeks later Alexius III fled from his palace and Emperor Isaac was liberated. The new emperor, Alexius IV, intended to fulfill

The conquest of Constantinople in 1204, by D.R. Tintoretto.

his commitments to the Crusaders, but was prevented from doing so by the residents of Constantinople, led by clergy from the Greek Orthodox Church. The anti-Crusader sentiment quickly turned violent, and in January 1204 an enraged crowd stormed the palace and murdered Alexius IV and his father.

Alexsius Comnenus requests the aid of the doge of Venice, by A.M. Vicentino

The next emperor, Alexius V, demanded that the Crusaders depart the country immediately. Incensed, the Crusaders stormed the Byzantine capital and vanquished it.

Prince Baldwin of Flanders was crowned at the cathedral of Hagia Sophia as the first Latin emperor of Constantinople.

1212

Children's Crusade Ends in Tragedy

The initiative of two youths, Stephen of France and Nicholas of Germany, who wanted to organize a crusade of children to the Holy Land, resulted in tragedy. The innocent and enthusiastic movement, calling for children and young people to depart for the Holy Land certain in their belief that God would help them succeed where kings and aristocrats had failed, managed to kindle the imaginations of many children throughout Europe.

At the last minute, the French authorities decided not to allow French children to join the campaign, though approximately twenty thousand German children arrived at Italian ports ready to set sail for the Holy Land. It later turned out that many of the children who went aboard the ships were taken prisoner by criminals and sold as slaves. Few of the children who left for the crusade ever returned home.

The Children's Crusade, by G. Doré.

Fifth Crusade Weighs Anchor in Holy Land

Forgoing Jerusalem, Crusaders Opt for Rapid Raids

At the Fourth Lateran Council in 1215, Pope Innocent III promoted the notion of a new crusade, declaring that he himself would be responsible for the idea's dissemination throughout the Christian world. A departure date of June 1217 was set.

The propaganda for the crusade was spread throughout Europe by special preachers and local clergy. Knightly tournaments were forbidden and the noblemen of Europe were enjoined to cease their bickering so that nothing would upset the organization of the crusade.

In the fall of 1217, the port of Acre filled with ships of pilgrims who had hearkened to the pope's call to save the Holy Land. The country was in the grip of a severe drought and urgent letters had been sent from Acre to Europe requesting those coming to bring a supply of food and horses, as there was no possibility of purchasing them in the Holy Land. After they arrived, the streets of Acre could not accommodate both the crowd of pil-grims and the Crusader regiments. By the end of 1217 an enormous camp had grown up in the city, its tents spreading out to the grazing land between Acre and Haifa.

The leaders of the crusade decided to waive an attempt to conquer Jerusalem in favor of a short-term crusade of knights. On November 3 the patriarch of Jerusalem, carrying the True Cross, left Acre for the Crusader tents—the Christian forces were on the move.

The Crusaders advanced across the Jezreel Valley, coming to a halt near Ein Jalud. When the Muslims saw that the Europeans did not intend to go up to Jerusalem, they avoided a direct confrontation. The Crusader forces continued on their way undisturbed, entered Beit She'an, sacked the city, and took many of its inhabitants prisoner. From there they advanced to Kursi: while an auxiliary force invaded the Golan, the main army made its way around the Sea of Galilee to the Benot Ya'acov Bridge, where the Crusader regiments regrouped and returned to Acre.

Pope Innocent III.

Crusaders Attack the Tabor

Two weeks after returning from their march around the Sea of Galilee the Crusaders attacked the massive fortress on Mount Tabor, a Muslim bridgehead to the interior of the Holy Land. The fortress' perimeter wall was over 1,800 meters in circumference, and it enclosed an area 1,200

Remains of the massive fortress on Mount Tabor.

long by 400 meters wide. Within it, Syria's finest troops were ensconced.

The Crusader offensive against Mount Tabor began on the last day of November, 1217. When the Syrian garrison exited the fortress in order to block the narrow path leading up the mountain, the Crusaders, led by Jean de Brienne, king of Jerusalem, overcame them. The remaining Muslim forces barricaded themselves inside the fortress, which was encircled by a deep moat.

The Crusader troops, though great in number, were not equipped with siege machines. Becoming discouraged after the Muslims set fire to the siege ladders they had brought up to Tabor's summit, they retreated to Acre.

Though the Crusader strike had failed, the Muslims realized that defending the stronghold from siege required troops, equipment, and supplies beyond their means. Over the course of the following year they deliberately dismantled the enormous fortress.

Giant Fortress Rears Its Head in Atlit

While half of the Crusader forces were re-fortifying Caesarea, the Templars, aided by the Teutonic Knights and several Crusader regiments, began to build a new fortress on the small peninsula near Atlit. According to the testimony of one of the builders, the Templars dug the foundations of the fortress over a period of six weeks. During the excavations, freshwater springs, an ancient wall, and a treasure trove of silver coins were unearthed.

Two towers were built at the front of the fortress out of enormous stones dragged to the site by two oxen. One hundred feet high and 74 feet wide, the towers had two stories; the height of the second story was double that of the first story. The steps ascending the towers were designed so that armed horsemen could negotiate them. A high wall was built between the two towers, and another wall, at a slight distance, connected two beaches and encompassed a freshwater spring on its inland side. The entire fortress was encircled by a high wall abutting the rocks of the coastline. The fortress compound included a church, palace, and numerous houses.

Chateau Pelerin, the giant Crusader fortress near Atlit.

The Crusade to Conquer Egypt

Having returned from the three abbreviated crusades to the Sea of Galilee, Mount Tabor, and the Lebanon Mountains, the Crusaders came to the conclusion that conquering Egypt would make it easier for them to overcome the Holy Land and eradicate a potential threat to the Crusader kingdom at the same time.

The preparations for the march on Egypt were time-consuming, and only in the spring of 1218 did the Crusader force finally set out for the land of the Nile, accompanied by a fleet of ships organized for this purpose in Europe. In May, the Crusader troops established a bridgehead on an island west of Damietta in Egypt, but they encountered zealous opposition from the Ayubbid army, and the situation remained unresolved for close to a year.

The Crusader fleet on its way to the Holy Land. From a medieval manuscript.

Saint Francis Visits Crusader Camp at Damietta

In the midst of the siege of Damietta, Saint Francis of Assisi arrived in the Crusader camp and implored the commanders to allow him to meet with the Egyptian sultan. The sultan agreed to receive the monk on the assumption that he had some message from the enemy camp. To the sultan's astonishment, Francis demanded the right to prove to him the truth of Christianity. This brave but futile attempt by the martyr from Assisi was engraved deeply upon the memory of the participants in the crusade to Damietta.

Above: Saint Francis before the sultan, by Giotto.

Crusader Siege Equipment
Firing Machines and Ramming Devices

There were two types of Crusader siege gear: the first included the *petraria* (Latin for "fire stones") —catapults that hurled large stones or arrows from a sling—and the *cattus* (cat), which fired anchor-shaped iron hooks attached to ropes at city walls. The barbs would catch hold of the stones in the wall and the warriors would then pull the ropes to collapse them. The name "cat" was undoubtedly related to its fearsome "claws."

The second sort of siege device included the battering rams—huge rods with an iron point at their tip that

Crusader siege implements, by G. Doré.

were operated on a pendular principle. The battering ram, which was housed in a wooden contraption that protected its operators, could fell even the strongest of walls.

Another implement of the Crusader arsenal was the moving tower *(berefredum)*, which served several purposes. As high as or higher than contemporaneous walls (or a modern five-to-seven-story building), these towers moved on wheels or round logs. Their bottom stories were equipped with a battering ram, and the upper stories held archers and catapults. Close to the top of the tower was a swinging bridge that could be

lowered onto a wall's ramparts. On the upper balcony stood elite archers who showered arrows onto the wall to scatter the defenders.

The Crusaders protected their war machines with hides and ropes that functioned as flexible shields, absorbing and deflecting the hail of stones fired at them by the Muslim forces.

Sultan Levels Jerusalem and Its Fortresses
Muslims Raze Their Own Holdings

In early 1219, Sultan Al-Malik al-Mu'azzam from Damascus, the brother of the sultan of Egypt, Al-Malik al-Kamil, decided to raze Jerusalem and its fortresses. A desperate act, it was intended to prevent the permanent establishment of the Crusader powers in the Holy Land in the event that they succeeded in conquering it.

The order to flatten Jerusalem amazed the commanders of the forces in the city, and they avoided implementing it until the sultan himself arrived. For the next two months the Muslims systematically destroyed the city's fortifications and houses, excluding only the Citadel at Jaffa Gate (David's Tower), the Church of the Holy Sepulcher, the Dome of the Rock, and Al-Aqsa Mosque. When they were done, Jerusalem's Muslim inhabitants

abandoned the ruined city.

The sultan's raze and burn policy included the fortresses of Galilee: the Banias fortress, the fortress at Tibnin, the fortress of Safed, and Belvoir were all left in ruins.

Safed. On the mountain's summit are the remains of the enormous fortress built by the Templars in 1240.

Crusaders Decline Sultan's Offer

Jerusalem Almost Handed to Christians on a Platter

In a desperate attempt to expel the Crusaders from Egyptian soil, the ruler of Egypt, Al-Malik al-Kamil, proposed a daring trade: Egypt would return to the Crusaders all of its territories on the western bank of the Jordan and sign a thirty-year peace treaty with them in return for the evacuation of Crusader troops from Egypt.

The proposal was rejected by the Crusaders, leading to an offer of additional concessions concerning the payment of reparations to provide for the restoration of the ruins of Jerusalem and the destroyed Crusader fortresses. Fumbling their chance to return to the Kingdom of Jerusalem without a battle, the Crusaders refused this proposal as well.

On November 5, 1219 the Crusaders stormed Damietta. The city was sacked and much of the local population sold as slaves.

Damietta, by the Comte de Forbin.

Muslims Conquer Caesarea
Atlit Stands Up to Arabs

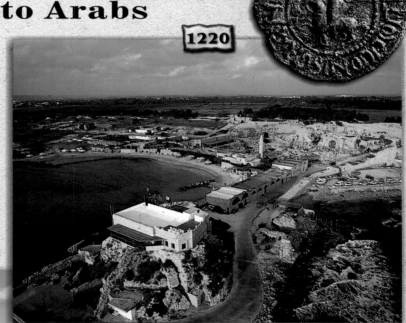

After conquering Damietta, the sultan of Damascus, Al-Malik al-Mu'azzam, departed for the Holy Land and laid siege to Caesarea. His three siege machines relentlessly pounded the fortress with stones day and night. The city's inhabitants escaped to the citadel, where, with the drawbridge raised, they were effectively severed from the city.

The fortress's fortifications proved to be weak, and the defenders needed help. The Genovese, who were interested in getting their hands on the city's port, proposed their taking over the fortress in exchange for delivering a shipment of supplies to the besieged Caesarea. Their proposal was accepted and the Genovese evacuated the garrison and sent in their regiments, but after four days their defeat was imminent as well. They fled by sea, and the Muslim forces that finally penetrated the city found it empty. The sultan commanded the destruction of the fortress, which had been built only four years previously.

After the conquest of Caesarea, Al-Malik al-Mu'azzam turned to the fortress of Atlit: the Muslim troops as-

Above right: A Crusader seal from Caesarea.
Above: An aerial photograph of Caesarea.
Left: The remains of Chateau Pelerin, the Crusader fortress in Atlit.

sumed positions along its entire facade. In order to defend themselves against an attack by the Crusader units, the sultan ordered a moat dug between the fortress and the Muslims' tents. He began bombarding the fortress walls, though their huge stones and towers proved fairly invulnerable.

Meanwhile, additional Crusader forces began to come to the aid of their brethren, and the sultan, who had suffered heavy losses, was forced to torch his equipment and withdraw. His retaliation, the destruction of Christian buildings in Nazareth and Safed, was harsh. Nor did Jerusalem escape his vengeance: its buildings were destroyed and its water cisterns blocked. Throughout the Holy Land, fruit trees and vineyards were uprooted.

Dreams of Conquering Egypt Drown in Nile

Christian POWs Swapped for Evacuation from Egypt

In June of 1221, the Crusader troops moved out of Damietta and headed south to conquer Cairo. Al-Malik al-Kamil's brothers, the sultans of Syria and Iraq, came to his aid. Meanwhile he commanded that the dams of the Nile be broken; the river, still swelling from the winter rains, flooded, leaving vast territories under water. The Crusaders found themselves wedged between the Muslim regiments and the Nile's spreading waters.

After three days, negotiations were opened and a treaty reached. The Crusaders agreed to surrender and evacuate all of their forces from Egyptian soil in exchange for their safe return to Acre and the liberation of all Christian prisoners held by the Ayubbid sultans. An eight-year cease-fire ensured the status quo in Syria and the Holy Land. The Crusaders maintained the right to discontinue the cease-fire in the event that Emperor Friedrich II, still deferring his departure from Europe on various and strange pretexts, appeared at the head of another crusade.

Friedrich II Excommunicated

Emperor Fakes Illness to Shirk Christian Duty

The summer of 1227 found Crusader warriors gathering at the ports of southern Italy in anticipation of the departure of the Sixth Crusade. German troops arrived towards the summer's end and, finally, the emperor himself appeared on the scene.

On September 8, 1227, the ships sailed south. Within a mere three days they stopped, however, when the emperor announced that, due to illness, he was forced to delay the crusade.

The real or imaginary ailment of the emperor was the last straw. The pope excommunicated the recalcitrant ruler and published a letter enumerating all of the emperor's postponements and evasions as well as their disastrous consequences for the Christian world. The excommunication and the epistolary battle that erupted between the papal and imperial courts scandalized the Christian world.

The coronation of Friederich II as king of Sicily. From a medieval manuscript.

Crusader Matchmaking

Kingdom of Jerusalem Heiress Weds Friedrich II

The wedding of Friederich II and Isabel. A thirteenth-century German manuscript.

Meetings held in 1223 between Jean de Brienne, king of Jerusalem, the pope, and Emperor Friedrich II resulted in the resolution to wed Princess Isabel, John's ten-year-old daughter, to the emperor. The pope, apparently the initiator of the idea, hoped the union would encourage the emperor to fulfill his commitment to embark on another crusade, and in 1225 he warned Friedrich that further delay of the crusade would result in his excommunication. The emperor renewed his vow, but pushed its date of implementation back to 1227. In the meantime, as proof of his earnest intentions, he sent a fleet of fourteen imperial ships to Acre to fetch his fiancee.

A leader of the Italian church in the Holy Land placed the emperor's wedding ring on Isabel's finger in the cathedral in Acre, which would later be the setting for her coronation as queen of Jerusalem. Since the fall of Jerusalem, the cathedral in Acre had served as an alternative to the Church of the Holy Sepulcher for inaugurating the kings of Jerusalem. From Tyre the convoy set sail for Brindisi, where the imperial wedding ceremony was repeated.

Immediately after the nuptials, Friedrich demanded that Jean de Brienne cede the Kingdom of Jerusalem, since the emperor was now the husband of the queen.

The seal of Jean de Brienne, king of Jerusalem.

Sixth Crusade Arrives in Holy Land

Orders Issued "In the Name of God and Christianity"

Ten years after vowing to spearhead a crusade to liberate Jerusalem from the Muslims, Friedrich II, the holy roman emperor and king of Sicily, led the Sixth Crusade to the Crusader kingdom.

Friedrich's arrival in Acre was fraught with tension. A papal decree delivered by the pope's emissaries forbade contact with him, impeding any meetings with the local aristocrats or knights of the orders. Seeking to escape the uneasy atmosphere in Acre and hasten the negotiations he was conducting with Egypt, the emperor announced his intention to fortify Jaffa, which the Christian regiments viewed as an important step toward conquering Jerusalem. The emperor himself claimed that a strengthened Jaffa would provide an easier approach as well as a shorter and more secure path for pilgrims bound for Jerusalem. Since Friedrich's excommunication, the heads of the military orders were prohibited from receiving direct commands from him and thus the Christian forces set out for Jaffa with the emperor commanding only the battalion of his men and the Teutonic Knights. The units of the other orders and the Holy Land regiments followed a short distance behind. Orders in the non-imperial camp were given not in the name of the emperor but "in the name of God and Christianity."

In Jaffa, a fortress was erected on the foundations of the walls that had been flattened in 1197, and a deep moat dug around it. The city itself was not rebuilt. The fortifications were completed within three months, by the end of which time Friedrich II had succeeded in signing a treaty with the sultan of Egypt.

Friedrich's Speech Slandered

Interdict Placed on Jerusalem. Emperor Confiscates Pilgrims' Offerings and Flees City

Friedrich II

Taking advantage of the infighting between Saladin's heirs, Friedrich II found an opportunity to achieve by diplomacy what his predecessors had failed to obtain on the battlefield. In 1229, he and the ruler of Egypt, Al-Malik al-Kamil, Saladin's nephew, negotiated a joint defense agreement according to which Friedrich II received control of Jerusalem and Bethlehem. The Christian holy places on the Temple Mount would remain under Muslim control, but all Christians were guaranteed free access provided that they behaved respectfully on the Temple Mount—a stipulation that included them removing their shoes in the precinct. The coastal area from Beirut to Jaffa would be one contiguous Christian territory from which two enclaves would extend: one comprised of Nazareth and a connecting strip to Tyre and a second including the road from Jaffa to Jerusalem via Lydda and Ramla, then south to Bethlehem. The accord was to be in effect for a decade.

One month after signing the agreement with Al-Malik al-Kamil,

Friedrich II entered Jerusalem and received the keys to the city. On March 18, 1229, the day after his arrival, he set out for the Church of the Holy Sepulcher dressed in his royal robes. Once there, he approached the altar, laid his crown upon it, and, after a pause, replaced it upon his head. No prayer service was held and the bells were not rung.

After the ceremony, a reception was held in the courtyard between the palace of the Hospitalers and the Church of the Holy Sepulcher. Friedrich delivered a speech that he had presented previously to the pope, but this time its conciliatory message was twisted by the time it reached his ears. Tension in Jerusalem peaked. The archbishop of Caesarea placed an interdict on the city, forbidding all religious activities therein. Churches that had opened just the day before were closed again, and religious services were held only outside the city.

During the afternoon of the same day, at a meeting between the emperor and the Christian leaders of the city, Friedrich proposed a plan for renovat-

ing the city walls. Because of the interdict, the meeting was held out of town. The leaders of the orders did not immediately respond, and requested a delay of one day. Their request angered the emperor, who ordered that all of the offerings brought by pilgrims to the churches of Jerusalem be forcibly transferred by his soldiers to the fortification fund. The following day at dawn he departed Jerusalem without waiting for the reply of the heads of the orders. A messenger from the Templars caught up with him on the road, bringing their agreement to

participate in the planned fortifications. The emperor replied evasively and refused to return to the city.

On May 1, the emperor departed the Holy Land despised and humiliated.

Crusader Kingdom Grows

In 1240 the Crusaders signed another defense agreement with the Muslims—this time with al-Kamil's rival, who ruled in the northern part of what remained of the Ayubbid kingdom. Tyre and the Beaufort fortress were transferred to Christian hands, and the capital of Galilee, Tiberias, fell under joint Muslim-Christian control. Later, following another crusade led by Richard of Cornwall, the brother of Henry III, king of England, the Christians received additional territories in Bethlehem as well

as an enclave that included Beit Jibrin and Ashkelon. The area of the Kingdom of Jerusalem was greatly enlarged and the new borders were easier to defend.

Quarrels and rivalries in the divided Ayubbid kingdom enabled the Crusader kingdom to expand. The Crusaders began to rebuild the fortresses of the Holy Land—Ashkelon in the south, Arsuf in the center, Tiberias in the east, and Safed in the north.

The remains of the Beaufort fortress.

Friedrich II Bungles Capture of Atlit Fortress

Templars Don't Take Him Seriously

On his way to Jaffa, then in the hands of the Templars, Emperor Friedrich II made a bid for the control of the Templar fortress of Atlit. Appearing at the gates of the fortress, he peremptorily demanded that the knights leave, relinquishing the place. The Templars had no intention of accepting such a demand from an excommunicated emperor who had entered the fortress accompanied by only a small regiment. The Templars closed the fortress gates and threatened to imprison the emperor inside. Having no other choice, Friedrich capitulated and left.

The Crusader fleet sets sail.

Anti-Egyption Coalition

Templars Bargain for Temple Mount

In the summer of 1244 a pact was made between the rulers of Damascus, Hamah, and Kerak against Egypt. The messengers of the new coalition appealed to the Franks to join the pact, and the treaty was signed in Jaffa, where the Templars were based. The Crusaders agreed to place their forces at the disposal of the anti-Egyptian coalition in a war against Egypt. In return, the Muslims agreed to relinquish control of the Temple Mount, in

their hands since the cease-fire agreement with Friedrich II. The Templar commanders, church leaders, and several of the barons of the Kingdom of Jerusalem signed the accord, though the Hospitalers and the Teutonic Order, as well as several of the barons, opposed it vehemently. The Muslims evacuated Jerusalem and the Temple Mount immediately. Al-Aqsa Mosque reverted to the Templars and became the Templum Solomonis again.

HORRIBLE DEFEAT AT BATTLE OF FORBIE

Crusader Army Massacred in Battle against Egyptians and Khwarazmians

The sultan of Egypt, searching for an ally against the coalition forming against him, turned for help to the Khwarazmian regiments camped along the Euphrates. The Khwarazmians were Turks who had been exiled from their homeland. They lived by the sword and were renowned for their cruelty.

On July 11, 1244, the Khwarazmians attacked Jerusalem. Although their first foray failed, the Christians were panic-stricken and decided to flee. On the night of August 23, seven thousand of the city's Christian residents abandoned Jerusalem accompanied by a security guard of knights.

On October 4, 1244, the Crusader army departed Jaffa for the south, intent on fighting the Khwarazmian and Egyptian forces. It was fairly strong, since all of the factions had set their rivalries aside in order to cooperate during this state of emergency.

On October 17, the Crusader camp and its allies encountered the Egyptian-Khwarazmian forces on the sands between Ashkelon and Gaza, near the village of Forbie. The Egyptian attack completely crushed the Crusader force, which consisted of 312 Templar Knights and 324 light cavalry, 328 Hospitaler Knights and 200 light cavalry, 400 Teutonic Knights, and an unknown number of knights from the Order of the Lepers of Saint Lazare.

Out of a total of approximately 1,000 knights and 700 light cavalry, only some 50 survived the catastrophic battle. Alongside them fought some 1,000 knights from Jaffa, Cyprus, and Tripoli and about 10,000 infantrymen, who all died in battle. Fifty-seven years after the Battle of Karnei Hattin, the Crusader military force had been exterminated once again.

The battle was referred to as "the second Hattin." In the wake of the defeat, the entire Holy Land was under control of the Khwarazmians, though their own end was also near: in the spring of 1246 the Khwarazmians were defeated by the sultan of Hamah, a formerly ally of the Crusaders.

Returning from crusade, by K.F. Lessing.

Louis IX in Egypt

Louis IX takes the cross before departing for the East. A medieval manuscript.

Louis IX's crusade to conquer Egypt began with wonderful victories and ended in total defeat when its hero fell into Egyptian captivity and was forced to surrender.

The Crusaders in the Holy Land, nearing total desperation, had looked hopefully towards Europe and especially towards France, where a savior did in fact appear—in the form of King Louis IX. Many French noblemen joined his crusade, which was led by three brothers.

In order to preserve the sanctity of the crusade, adventurers and criminals were prohibited from participating, though artisans, peasants, and workers were encouraged to enlist. Those taking part in the campaign were enjoined to preserve a Christian lifestyle and observe complete modesty both within the camp and outside of it. Drinking and profane language were prohibited.

Louis selected Cyprus as the gather- ▶

Saint Louis at the Battle of Mansourah. A medieval French manuscript.

Louis IX, in a work of the Flemish school.

ing point for the Crusader regiments, and turned it into his supply base.

The crusade's program was determined in France. It was decided to renew the strategy—initiated by Pope Innocent III—of conquering Egypt first. In May 1249, the Frankish forces set sail from Cyprus in the direction of Egypt. According to witnesses, the invading army had 2,500 cavalry and about 5,000 arbalest shooters. The entire army numbered around 25,000 people, who were transferred to Egypt

in 1,800 sailing vessels.

In May 1249, Louis and his army conquered Damietta but then became mired in the swamps of the Nile Delta, exactly as the previous Crusader force to penetrate the area had. An epidemic broke out in the Frankish camp, and Louis IX fell ill. The Crusaders began to withdraw, and the Egyptians chased them and massacred them. The incapacitated king, forced to surrender, was taken captive together with his noblemen in April 1250.

The Crusaders were compelled to accept Egypt's conditions, and they undertook to return Damietta and pay an enormous sum to redeem the Christian prisoners. Louis IX, ransomed, sailed with the few survivors back to Acre.

Over the next four years, the French king funded the re-fortification of Acre, Jaffa, Caesarea, and Sidon, whose walls had been destroyed by Saladin. The king of France believed that the fervor the Crusaders had

1254
St. Louis Goes Home

At the beginning of 1254, six years after he set foot on the Holy Land and four years after being released from captivity, King Louis IX decided to return home, and the Crusaders signed a cease-fire agreement with Damascus that was intended to be in effect until September 1256.

On April 24, immediately after Easter, the French king finally set sail from the Holy Land on his way back to his homeland, which had long been without him.

somehow lost since the Third Crusade could still be rekindled, and that when it was, the Christian armies would use the coastal towns he had fortified as a bridgehead for re-conquering the Kingdom of Jerusalem.

Left: A gate built by Louis IX in the wall of Caesarea. **Below:** The wall of Caesarea, surrounded by a deep moat.

The Kingdom of Jerusalem, rather than surrendering to external enemies, deteriorated into ruin from within.

The agreement between Friedrich II and the ruler of Egypt al-Kamil that was signed in 1229, returning Jerusalem, Nazareth, and Bethlehem to Christian control, and the coronation of Friedrich II as King of Jerusalem gave the Christian world the momentary illusion that the Kingdom of Jerusalem had returned to its days of glory. But Friedrich II, the holy Roman emperor and emperor of Germany, Sicily, and Jerusalem, abandoned his new kingdom almost immediately after his coronation, never again to return. His son Conrad, who inherited the crown after his death in 1243, did not even bother to visit the Holy Land.

Approximately twenty years after the Crusaders were banished from Jerusalem, the proud capital of the Crusader kingdom was no more than an abandoned town on the edge of the desert. In a letter sent from Jerusalem at the beginning of the 1260s, the holy city is described as having approximately 2,000 inhabitants, about 300 of them Eastern Christians.

In 1250 the Mamelukes deposed their Ayubbid masters and united the kingdom under their talented commander Sultan Baybars. The Crusader kingdom of Jerusalem, shoved over to the coastal towns by the Mameluke army, had become a burden to its owners, who gradually lost settlement after settlement.

In the absence of a central authority in the kingdom, it was managed by the local aristocracy and the military

Louis' Last Crusade
Saint Louis Dies on Way Back to Holy Land

When Louis IX saw that no one had taken up the cross in his place, he departed for a new crusade in March of 1267. This time as well, most of the participants (aside from 300 knights from England and a handful from Scotland) were from France. The force numbered about 10,000 warriors.

The renewed Crusader army's first stop was Tunisia. In July of that year, shortly after the fleet weighed anchor opposite the country's coast, an epidemic broke out in the Crusader camp, claiming many victims.

On August 25, Louis IX died in the epidemic; most of the Crusader force was dispersed. Only Prince Edward (the future King Edward I) continued at the head of his men to Acre. His brother, Edmund, joined him with reinforcements in 1271, but their combined army was still too small to achieve real results. In 1272, Prince Edward, after narrowly escaping an assassination attempt, decided to return home.

The Kingdom of Jerusalem at an End

orders. Internal strife, plots, and civil wars did much to hasten the deterioration of the Crusader kingdom from within.

The de Lusignan kings of Cyprus, who inherited the reduced Crusader kingdom in 1269, attempted, with the assistance of the military orders, to protect what remained of it. Even after 1277, when the crown of the Kingdom of Jerusalem was sold to Charles I of Anjou, the de Lusignan monarchs continued to protect it as if it were their property. But Baybars, who was victorious in 1260 over the

Mongols at the Battle of Ein Harod (Ein Jalud), found it easy to pick off the remaining Crusader cities one by one. Last to surrender was the Crusader capital of Acre; the king of Cyprus joined the military orders who defended the city heroically until all hope was lost. In 1291 the last of the Crusaders left Acre, leaving a wonderfully complete ghost town behind.

The Crusader kingdom had finally come to an end.

The refectory of the Hospitaler palace in Acre.

CHAPTER VI

THE MAMELUKE CONQUEST

1260-1516

The revolution of the Mameluke army commanders in Egypt in 1250 brought about the end of the Ayyubid dynasty. Their reign inaugurated by Saladin after his victory over the Crusaders, the Ayyubids had ruled in Syria, Egypt, and most of the Holy Land until the Mameluke revolt. As a result of the coup, the Mamelukes (Arabic for "white slaves") became the masters of the kingdom that had enslaved them and their forefathers for centuries.

The use of the services of the Mamelukes was introduced in the ninth century by the Abbasid caliphs of Baghdad, who were unable to trust their Arab army. They purchased young men, mainly of Turkish extraction, who had been taken prisoner along the border of Central Asia and the Caucasus, converted them to Islam, and trained them to be soldiers in the Abbasid caliphate guards. Eventually, the legions of Mamelukes who served as what amounted to a professional army under the Muslim rulers in the Middle East became the most powerful element in the region. It was with their help that Saladin succeeded in gaining control of Egypt when it was ruled by the crumbling Fatimid dynasty. The inheritance wars among the descendants of Saladin that split his kingdom finally convinced the chiefs of the Mameluke army that their Ayyubid rulers were not worthy of their position.

In 1250 the Mamelukes murdered the last Ayyubid sultan and crowned their leader Baybars, sultan of Egypt. Within a few years he had transformed the entire Ayyubid dominion into a Mameluke empire that was to endure for over 250 years.

The Mongols twice invaded Syria and the Holy Land at the beginning of the Mameluke period. The first time they penetrated the Holy Land was in 1260, and their success aroused new hope among the Crusaders, who still controlled several cities and fortresses along the coast and in Galilee. Feelers were sent out by the Crusader command to the Mongolian chiefs regarding the possibility of collaboration between the two armies against the Muslim forces. Almost no particulars about these contacts are available, but in the summer of 1260 the Mongolian army was welcomed at a fortress in Safed that was still under the authority of the Crusader Templar Order. A large tent was erected for the Mongolian command outside the fortress walls and the Mongolian army outfitted with supplies.

The Mameluke Sultan Baybars, who had already proven his military prowess in previous battles, beat the relatively small Mongolian army in a confrontation in the Jezreel Valley in September of 1260.

The second time the Mongols invaded Syria and the Holy Land was in December of 1299. This time, the Mongolian force, which was composed of thousands of cavalry troops and reinforced by Armenian and Georgian Christian soldiers, defeated the Mameluke army. The reversal triggered

Pervious pages: Interior of the chapel of Saint Catherine's in Sinai, by D. Roberts.
Background: The Land of Israel, by L.B. de Schass, 1475.

the collapse of the Mameluke army and the hasty retreat of its units in the direction of Egypt in order to regroup.

By the mid-1300s, the Mongols had apparently maximized the potential for looting in Syria and the Holy Land. Weighed down with booty, the Mongolian army returned eastward to its homeland. A short time afterward, the Mamelukes returned. Calling to account the collaborationist Christians who aided the Mongols in their invasion, they massacred the Armenians.

After the Holy Land had reverted to Muslim hands, it became a backwater for the next few hundred years. During that time, the Mamelukes erased all vestiges of the Crusader kingdom from the Holy Land and Syria, and razed Acre, Jaffa, and the other coastal cities for fear that they would serve as centers of support for new crusades. Jaffa remained in ruins until the end of the Mameluke period, though a small settlement arose in Acre in the fifteenth century. Tiberias and Ashkelon were also partially destroyed at the end of the Mameluke reign. Felix Fabri, who visited the Holy Land in 1480 and again in 1483, reported that Jerusalem had also suffered partial damage. During the early Mameluke period Ramla was a large city with flourishing trade, but those who visited it at the end of the fifteenth and beginning of the sixteenth century note that it too was being ruined. According to all of the historical sources, Gaza was a thriving trade city about twice as large as Jerusalem. By the end of the period, Gaza, Ramla, and Nablus were the largest cities in the Holy Land.

In 1310, Al-Malik en-Nasir Muhammad Ibn Qalawun rose to the Egyptian throne. During the period of his rule, which lasted thirty years, the Mameluke kingdom reached the pinnacle of its success. The governor Tankiz en-Nasiri, who was for a long while the omnipotent ruler of Syria and the Holy Land, brought order and security to the country, built water conduits, and erected public buildings.

Mameluke rule was weakened after the death of Ibn Qalawun, and at the beginning of the fifteenth century quarrels that broke out among the regime's senior ministers soon escalated into civil war. During the days of the sultans Barsbai and Jaqmaq in the middle of the century, the Holy Land once again enjoyed a brief period of well-being, but when their stewardship came to an end the Mameluke government crumbled at a rapid pace.

During the Mameluke period, Syria and the Holy Land were divided into large provinces, which themselves were divided into districts. At the head of each province was a naib (viceroy), and at the head of each district, a wali (governor). Accounts from the fourteenth and fifteenth centuries regarding the economic structure of the Holy Land testify that its organizational structure did not change significantly during the last centuries of the Middle Ages. After the last remains of the Crusader kingdom were destroyed, the Holy Land played no part in the international spice trade that in the past had brought large profits to its citizens. A Muslim traveler who visited the country in 1312 mentioned its fruits as export products. The fourteenth-century geographer A-Damasci and traveler Ibn Battuta report that olive oil and the soap made from it were the major products of the Holy Land. The Burgundian traveler Bertrandon de la Brocquiere, who visited the Holy Land in 1432, notes that cotton was cultivated in the Beit She'an Valley.

The security situation worsened in the Holy Land toward the close of the Mameluke period, as did the economy. The wars against the Ottomans forced the Mameluke government to seek extra sources of income and to recruit the Bedouin tribes into the army. Thus the authorities appropriated oil from farmers in the Nablus district, remunerating them inadequately, and forced the inhabitants of Jerusalem, Hebron, and Ramla to buy it at an exorbitant price. Policies like these sparked rebellions among local inhabitants and occasionally even impelled them to flee their hometowns. Natural disasters also contributed to the worsening of the situation: Arabic sources recount numerous plagues in the fifteenth century, a plague of locusts in 1484, and earthquakes in 1458 and 1497.

Though the Holy Land did not play a significant role in Arab cultural development during this period, the Mameluke authorities and their ministers continued to establish centers for religious study in the Holy Land and to set aside money for the upkeep of religious teachers and students. From a religious standpoint, the Holy Land became strictly Islamic, and the number of Shiites decreased. The distance of the Holy Land from the center of power, on the one hand, and the cultivation of religious fanaticism at the centers of Islamic scholarship on the other, caused unending religious debate.

The Mamelukes embarked upon a systematic destruction of prominent Christian religious structures while they simultaneously invested much effort and money in the erection of Islamic holy buildings. An intense effort was expended by the Mamelukes to cover over Jerusalem's Christian character. The rate of construction of mosques, seminaries, and other religious institutions during this period is greater than any Muslim period that preceded it. Much land and property were transferred to the communal Muslim endowment—the waqf. The dome of the octagonal Dome of the Rock at the heart of the Temple Mount was gilded, and its walls covered with magnificent mosaic work.

The Islamization of Jerusalem had begun previously, in the days of Saladin, who transformed Christian buildings into Muslim religious and educational institutions. In the course of his rule, the Church of Saint Anne, north of the Temple Mount near the Lions' Gate, was transformed into the Madrasa es-Salahiya, and the Church of the Assumption on the Mount of Olives converted into a mosque. The Mamelukes, who enlarged upon the policy of their predecessors, turned over to the waqf not only religious institutions but many other income-producing properties—stores in the market, lands and vineyards outside of the city walls—to provide a living for hundreds of religious elders, teachers, and legalists who came to Jerusalem from Syria, Egypt, and other countries.

The movement of Christian pilgrims continued even after the collapse of the Crusader kingdom, though their journey to the Holy Land was fraught with even greater difficulty than before. The Mameluke authorities considered the pilgrims hostile elements, and put many obstacles in their path. They were repeatedly arrested for document checks or otherwise hindered, and were usually forced to pay large sums of money as baksheesh in order to continue on their way.

Almost all of the traditional pilgrim routes were neglected and destroyed, and travel along the ruined roads was slow. Most of the pilgrim hostels had also been demolished, and the few caravansaries that were available stood on roads that had been paved or renovated by the Mamelukes. Intended for strategic and military needs, none of the roads the Mamelukes maintained really serviced the pilgrim routes. Not even the pilgrim routes from Jaffa to Jerusalem or Jerusalem to the River Jordan were in a reasonable state of repair.

During the Mameluke period, most of the pilgrims arrived from the East, but those few who came from western and central Europe, especially during the Easter season, wrote most of the travel descriptions that survive. Approximately two hundred travelogues have been preserved from between the years 1300 and 1500. The impressive quantity of descriptions, however, belies their importance. In those days, the journey of a pilgrim to the Holy Land was usually fairly curtailed: it covered Jaffa, Jerusalem, Bethlehem, and sometimes the River Jordan, from which they returned via Ramla to Jaffa. The trip took only a few days and most of the descriptions are short and routine, not mentioning much beyond the names of holy places and the indulgences granted for visiting them.

Nevertheless, a few travelers strayed from the regular route and braved longer trips; some even reached Mount Sinai. In the fifteenth century the main trade route from Egypt to the Far East passed through Sinai. Because of the economic value of the trade, the Mameluke rulers took care to enforce very stringent security measures on the Sinai Peninsula. As a result, a pilgrimage to the Holy Land included the possibility of continuing from Jerusalem via Gaza and the Sinai to Saint Catherine's Monastery, and from there to Suez and Cairo. In order to attract pilgrims to the monastery, the monks of Sinai offered pilgrims the attractive title of "Knight of St. Catherine," second only to the title "Knight of the Holy Sepulcher" granted by the Franciscans in Jerusalem. At the end of the fifteenth century, the trade route lost its importance, putting an end, for the time being, to pilgrimages to Sinai.

Mongol Cavalry Conquers Jerusalem

City Looted but Left Intact

A unit of Mongolian cavalry that arrived in Jerusalem in the summer of 1260 encountered no resistance upon entering the city, whose walls had been leveled on Saladin's orders several dozen years previously.

According to a Muslim historian who relied on the testimony of refugees from the city, the Mongols entered Jerusalem, looted it, and took prisoners. Since the main objective of the cavalry troops had been plunder, when they arrived in the city to find it had already been abandoned by most of its residents, they concentrated on making off with whatever possible before continuing on their way. Nevertheless, Jerusalem found it hard to recover from the Mongol invasion. In 1267, Ramban wrote that "In the city live only two thousand Christians. Since the Tatars [Mongols] arrived, [the Jews and the Muslims] fled, fearful of being killed by their sword."

A Mongol king in his Samarkand palace. A sixteenth-century Persian manuscript.

All-Out Mameluke Offensive to Expel Crusaders from Holy Land

Three years after his victory over the Mongols, the Mameluke Sultan Baybars began a widespread campaign for the final expulsion of the Crusaders from the Holy Land. The Mameluke army, having recovered from the heavy losses it incurred at the Battle of Ein Jalud, conquered Nazareth and the ports of Sidon, Haifa, Jaffa, and Ashkelon between 1263 and 1268. The conquests were followed by the razing of the sites' fortifications and ports, a decision arrived at by Baybars through mainly military considerations.

The devastation was not wanton; it was intended to prevent the Crusaders from being able to exploit their principle advantage—their excellent fleets of ships—in order to deposit military forces in the Holy Land for a new crusade. What may have appeared to be a prudent strategic measure shortly proved to be an economic disaster, however. Dismantling the ports severed the Holy Land from trade opportunities with Europe and the Mediterranean countries and badly disabled the economic backbone of its cities, which soon disintegrated. The coastal strip and the Sharon region, gradually abandoned by their inhabitants, were transformed into empty marshlands controlled by robbers and criminals. The havoc wreaked in the coastal cities also degraded the Holy Land's political importance, and its status gradually declined until it was really only a transit point between Syria and Egypt. The country was ruled by several governors, administrators, and a small garrison.

Right: Baybars' army massacring Christians, by G. Doré.
Left: The 1289 fall of Tripoli. From a sixteenth-century Italian manuscript.

Mamelukes Destroy Church of Annunciation

The Mameluke army under the command of Sultan Baybars invaded the Holy Land in 1263, wrested Nazareth from the Crusaders, and destroyed its Church of the Annunciation. The occupation of the city of Jesus and the devastation of its church and other holy Christian sites were manifestations of the Mameluke policy of eradicating the Christian identity of the Holy Land. The Mamelukes were to demolish churches and Christian structures in every settlement they would conquer. Churches, baptismal fonts, icons, and Christian mosaics were thrown away, altered, or defaced. Even the caves and huts of hermit monks in Wadi Kelt were ruined. Those sites that were not destroyed were retooled for Muslim use.

Nazareth in a Byzantine mosaic from the fourteenth-century.

Sheikh Shakes Up Monastery of the Cross

Church Converted into Study Center for Muslim Mystics

Sheikh Hachar, a confidante of the Mameluke ruler Baybars, was a religious fanatic from the mountains of Kurdistan. The two met in Syria after Baybars fled Ayyubid Egypt, and Hachar prophesied the end of the second man's tribulations and his subsequent rise to power. The accurate prophesy made a great impression on Baybars, and he later named his son after the fortune-telling sheikh, built him a special prayer cell in Jerusalem, and provided money for his living expenses.

Baybars partiality emboldened Hachar to harass the Jews and Christians living under Muslim rule. He vandalized their religious buildings in Damascus and Alexandria, and in 1272 broke into the Monastery of the Cross, confiscated the building, and transformed it into a study center for

Above: A whirling dervish.
Left: The Monastery of the Cross.

Muslim mystics. At the time, the monastery was under Georgian control, and the monks were suspected of collaborating with and spying for the Mongols, enemies of the Mamelukes. Hachar's deeds were sanctioned by Baybars.

Only at the beginning of the fourteenth century did the monastery revert to Christian hands.

Marco Polo Passes Through Jerusalem

empire. The three travelers went to Jerusalem before departing the Holy Land, but all that Marco Polo recorded about the holy city is that he passed through it in order to obtain holy oil from the Church of the Holy Sepulcher.

Marco Polo dictated the description of his trip to his cell-mate when he was being held by the Genovese as a prisoner of war. The Holy Land plays a minor part in his wonderful travelogue.

Marco Polo, the most famous traveler, real or otherwise, of the Middle Ages, visited Acre in 1272 when he was only seventeen. It was from there that he was to set out with his father and uncle on his grand twenty-year journey throughout the Mongolian

Left: Marco Polo, his father, and his uncle on their way to the East.
Right: At the Church of the Holy Sepulcher. An illustration for the fifteenth edition of *Book of Marvels*, by Marco Polo.

Crusader Capital Surrenders to Mamelukes: End of Kingdom at Hand

Templars Abandon Atlit Fortress

On May 18, 1291, after a siege of forty-four days, the Crusader capital of Acre capitulated to the Mameluke army. The legions of Muslim soldiers who entered the city found it nearly empty; most of the inhabitants and defenders had already been evacuated by sea to Cyprus and other points.

The fall of Acre clarified for the remaining Crusaders that the end of the Crusader Kingdom of Jerusalem had at last arrived. Residents of Tyre, Sidon, Beirut, and Haifa abandoned their homes and fortified bases and set sail in ships for the West. Only a

few hardy souls, like the Dominican monk Ricoldo de Monte Croce from Acre, decided to stay and continue their missions. Ricoldo, who knew Arabic well, turned eastward and struck out on a missionary journey among the Muslims.

On August 14, 1291, the last Crusader stronghold—the Atlit fortress—was evacuated. The Templar Knights, who had finished building the stronghold in 1218 and had never yet surrendered to an attacker, now capitulated to the tide of history and deserted the last Crusader outpost by ship. The curtain came down on the Crusader age in the Holy Land.

Acre, the Crusader capital.

Travelers' Choice: First Class, Business Class, or Pilgrim Class

Pilgrim-Class Conditions Harsh. Menu Monotonous and Skimpy.

It was on the pilgrim ships plying the route between the ports of Venice and Jaffa that the system of dividing travelers into different classes according to price was devised. First-class travelers were usually members of the aristocracy, wealthy merchants, and senior clergy. They stayed in the upper cabins and dined at the captain's table during the trip.

"Business-class" passengers were often merchants of lesser means. They stayed below decks, but the space set aside for them was roomier than that of the "pilgrim-class" travelers—the hoi polloi. The latter were crowded into the belly of the ship and each provided with just enough space to accommodate one supine body. Travelers in this class often relied upon the good graces of the rowers for the privilege of sitting a bit on their benches in order to stretch their bones.

The pilgrim-class menu did not make life any easier. According to the detailed description of the pilgrim Marino Sanuto, who set sail for the Holy Land in 1310, the monotonous daily menu of the average pilgrim included 750 grams of rusk, poor quality sweet red wine, an ounce of cheese, a few legumes and vegetables, and, every other day, a small portion of salt pork. After six to eight weeks of sailing, the pilgrims were ready to be saved by the Holy Land.

Pilgrims delousing themselves at a transit stop on the way to the Holy Land, by H. Wölffli, 1520.

Spies Disguised as Pilgrims

European Countries and Vatican Still Hoping to Organize New Crusade

Sanuto and the pope, by G. Doré.

Two hundred years after the Crusaders were forced from the Holy Land, the European countries and the Vatican still refused to accept their loss. Many in Europe believed that the inability to recruit masses of young people for a new crusade was only temporary and so took care to keep abreast about events in the Holy Land. If they kept their hand in, so they thought, the right moment to reconquer the Holy Land would surely come.

Apparently, some of the pilgrims who visited the Holy Land in the fourteenth and fifteenth centuries were actually spies in the service of European countries or the Vatican. In 1321, Marino Sanuto, the son of an aristocratic Venetian family, arrived in the Holy Land disguised as a pilgrim. His mission was to prepare a detailed plan for the reconquest of the Holy Land by Christian forces. Sanuto later submitted an extensive report including accurate maps of the Holy Land and its cities to the pope.

No one knows to whom the monk Jacob of Verona, who appeared in the Holy Land in 1335, reported, but it appears that he was in the service of a European ruler, perhaps even the pope. In any event, the "simple" monk's interests were not confined to holy places, and the people to whom he had recourse in the Holy Land and neighboring countries—in a private meeting with the king of Cyprus, for example—were not the usual acquaintances of a man of the cloth. Many of the details in the report subsequently written by Jacob comprise material crucial to military intelligence. He comments, for example, on Jerusalem's water system, reports

Mongols and Armenians Conquer Jerusalem

Mongolian Army Strikes Mercilessly. Armenians Cater to Christians.

In 1299 the Mongolian army conquered Jerusalem a second time. On this occasion, reports Mameluke historian Baybars al-Mantzuri, both Muslims and Jews were slaughtered. The Mongols got drunk with wine on the Temple Mount, perpetrated indecent acts, wrought destruction, murdered, looted, and took women and children prisoner.

A report of the same incident penned by an Armenian source describes it from another perspective. The Armenian, one of the men of Hayton II, the king of Little Armenia whose Christian army joined the Mongolian army on its march to the Holy Land, attempts to glorify the part played by the Armenian king on the journey and describes Hayton II's entrance into Jerusalem. The king apparently assembled Jerusalem's Christian inhabitants, who had been hiding in caves around the city, and held Christian ceremonies and prayers for fifteen days.

Solomon's Pools, part of Jerusalem's water system, by L. Mayer.

that Jaffa's walls had fallen into the sea, and notes that the latter city, virtually abandoned, was guarded by only six Saracens.

Holy City Kaput: Transformed into Provincial Town
Former Capital of Kingdom Answers to Gaza

Jerusalem, which in the twelfth century had been the bustling fortified capital of the Crusader kingdom, deteriorated during the fourteenth century into a ramshackle unwalled city of two thousand inhabitants run by a junior official. Pilgrims arriving in the holy city found it hard to conceal their disappointment in its appearance.

To the embarrassment of the Christian devout, the holy city—once a royal capital, the center of the world, a city of priests—was overrun by wild Saracens. The Irish pilgrim Symon Simeonis, who describes his 1323 encounter with Jerusalem, laments that the city's walls had toppled and its temple had been razed to its foundations.

At the time, the main city of the Holy Land was Gaza, the seat of the viceroy who also controlled Ashkelon, Jaffa, Hebron, and Jerusalem, according to the monk Jacob of Verona, who visited the Holy Land in 1335.

The Italian monk Nicolo da Poggibonsi, who visited Jerusalem in 1347, also bewails the fate of the most magnificent and aristocratic city in the world, asking after its walls and

The old town of Gaza, by H.B. Tristram.

gates of iron, "Where are the buildings that withstood the attacks of Vespasian and his six legions of horsemen for seven years?" In his day, he commented, two hundred horsemen could conquer the defenseless city.

Franciscans Settle on Mount Zion
Heads of Order in Italy Take Advantage of Conciliatory Atmosphere

The heads of the Franciscan Order in Italy were wise to take advantage of a time of goodwill among the Mameluke leadership to renew the presence of the Catholic Church in the Holy Land after a lengthy absence. The softening attitude of the Mameluke authorities vis à vis the Catholic order is attributable to the closer political and economic ties between the Mameluke government in Egypt and the kings of Aragon and Sicily.

Around 1335, under pressure from the Catholic nations of Europe, Sultan Al-Malik en-Nasir Muhammad Ibn Qalawun allowed the Franciscans to settle on Mount Zion and take charge of the Cenacle (room of the Last Supper), the Chapel of the Holy Spirit, and the Chapel of Saint Thomas on the mount.

Ibn Qalawun's acquiescence to the European request laid the foundation for governmental recognition of the Custodia de Terra Sancta—the preeminent Christian institution in Jerusalem from the Mameluke period until the present day. The sultans who came after him anchored the rights and privileges they awarded the Franciscan monks in written decrees. Among those rights, for which the Franciscans paid dearly, were the authority to hold mourning ceremonies that incorporated the drinking of wine, a waiver from the forfeiture to the Muslim state of the property of a Christian who died without heirs, entrance to the Church of the Holy Sepulcher without charge, and a general prohibition from harming Franciscans on the road from Jaffa to Ramla.

Pilgrims! Beware Big Fish!

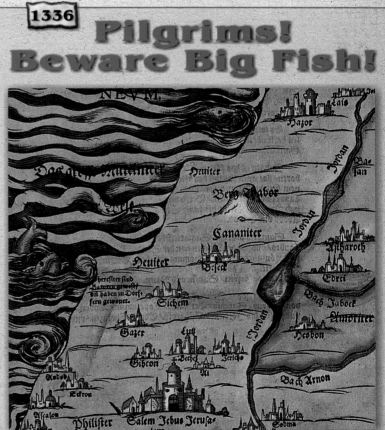

The humongous fish of the Mediterranean. A map of the Holy Land from 1545.

Three dangers threatened pilgrims during sailing, cautioned the German priest Ludolph von Suchen after his sojourn in the Holy Land from 1336 to 1341. They included running aground, dangerous storms, and...big fish. Backing up his warning graphically, von Suchen tells of three pilgrims who set sail in an Armenian boat only to have the craft sink during a tempest. As for his warning about the large fish, Ludolph notes that the peril only applied to small vessels. In one instance, he claims, an enormous fish attempted to swallow a whole boat. In another case, an oversized fish actually leapt onto the deck of one of the ships, killing one of the sailors.

Abandoned Acre—Heaven on Earth?

Delusional Description Belies Ramshackle Reality

With the fall of the Crusader kingdom, the trip to the Holy Land became much more expensive and dangerous than it had been in the past. Because of this, many of those who had already completed the pilgrimage saw it as their duty to describe not only their experiences but the places they visited as well. As it turned out, such writers were not always devotees of realism.

The priest Ludolph von Suchen, who visited Acre at the beginning of the 1350s, left an exuberant description of a splendid, bustling city. According to him, Acre was a wonderful city built of large hewn stones and fortified by minarets; all of its buildings were of equal height and had glass windows. Its houses were like palaces—built for a life of luxury. The king of Jerusalem and his brother lived in the city, as did the princes of Galilee and Antioch, the duke of Caesarea, the lord of Tyre, and the lord of Tiberias. The local noblemen wore crowns, were surrounded by servants, and all competed with one another in the magnificence of their attire.

Ludolph's description of Acre ignites the imagination with a vision of heaven on earth, but during the priest's era the place was actually a ruined ghost town. In truth, the fabulous city he depicts is much more beautiful than Acre ever was, even at the height of its glory before being sacked by the Muslims in 1291.

Strangely, Marino Sanuto, who visited the Holy Land thirty years before Ludolph, suffered from similar hallucinations.

While his detailed descriptions of Jaffa and many other places he visited are accurately rendered, his ability to distinguish between fact and fantasy ebbs when dealing with Jerusalem. On a map he sketched, Jerusalem appears surrounded by high ramparts—fortifications that had been razed almost one hundred years prior to his visit. In Sanuto's defense, it must be said that he at least wrote that his talents were insufficient to describe the sights of Jerusalem, and that when he began to do so his memory became cloudy and his eyes dim.

The beauty of Acre. A medieval Spanish manuscript.

Franciscans Establish Custodia de Terra Sancta

Pope Appoints Them Guardians of Holy Places and Pilgrims

In 1342 the Franciscans were officially appointed by the pope to serve as the Custodia de Terra Sancta and the representatives of Western Christianity in the Holy Land. Simultaneously, the Franciscan brothers were granted a permit to establish residences for themselves in the Church of the Holy Sepulcher in Jerusalem and the Church of the Nativity in Bethlehem, as well as to hold religious ceremonies in both places.

The renewal of Catholic activity in the Holy Land and the urgent need to provide essential services to pilgrims—especially those from Western Europe—brought about the Franciscans' establishment of the Custodia de Terra Sancta. The Franciscans were taking upon themselves the role of the orders of knights from the Crusader period, especially that of the Hospitalers. The main role of the Custodia, whose headquarters were in the Franciscan monastery on Mount Zion, was to care for pilgrims during their stay in the Holy Land and, more particularly, to escort them from Jaffa to Jerusalem as well as to the holy sites in the holy city and its vicinity.

The monastery on Mount Zion also served as a guest house for pilgrims. In 1392, the Franciscans added a hostel in Ramla and a hospital for pilgrims on Mount Zion.

The Franciscans attended to the lodging and well-being of the pilgrims, showed them around, and served as tour guides of the holy places for their groups.

The crest of the Custodia de Terra Sancta.

Make a "Donation to the Sultan" or Else!

No Forfeits and No Discounts. Pay or Be Beaten to Death.

In the mid-fourteenth century, every pilgrim visiting Jerusalem was forced to cough up "a donation to the sultan." Anyone attempting to avoid doing so, as the Franciscan monk Nicolo da Poggibonsi discovered personally, was subjected to corporal punishment.

During Nicolo's first visit to Jerusalem in 1346, he was brought, together with his traveling companions, who were also Franciscan monks, to the governor of the city. They were accused of not making the "donation to the sultan" that every Christian pilgrim was expected to come up with. The group's interpreter, a member of the Franciscan Custodia de Terra Sancta, tried to explain to the Mameluke governor that the brothers of the Franciscan Order were of modest means, and did not carry silver or gold with them. The governor did not even try to bargain; he immediately ordered his men to beat the interpreter in full view of the group. He warned the rest of the party that they would be beaten to death if they failed to pay the donation they owed. Poggibonsi, caught between two burly guards, prepared himself for death, but at the last moment the monks were saved by an acquaintance of the governor, a Christian merchant from Cyprus who happened by and promised to pay the Franciscans' debt. In order to avoid another such incident, Nicolo returned from Gaza straight to Damietta so that he would not have to pass through Jerusalem again.

Franciscan monks in the atrium of the Holy Sepulcher, by H.J. Breüning.

Pilgrims Prefer Roughing It

Christians in Caravansary with Cattle: No Beds and No Food

One pilgrim who visited the country in the mid-fourteenth century grumbled that during his visit he was forced to sleep on the hard ground most of the time, often under the stars. According to him, the bread in the Holy Land, improperly baked, was soft as dough. Since the Muslims drank nothing but water, it was also impossible to obtain wine in Jerusalem or its environs. Pilgrims, he claims, suffered greatly from the oppressive heat in which they were forced to rush from place to place.

Even in the khans (caravansaries) pilgrims were unable to rest from the rigors of the journey, as the few that stood along the pilgrim routes did not provide even basic services. Nicolo da Poggibonsi complained in 1347 about the conditions at the pilgrims' hostel in Jericho, where travelers were offered neither beds nor food. In most cases the pilgrims were lodged with animals, slept on the floor, and were forced to prepare their own meals. Consequently, even when there was an opportunity to stay in a khan, most of the pilgrims preferred to sleep out of doors.

Khan al-Ahmar near Jericho, by Bonfils.

Pilgrim's Advice: Prices, Perils, and Other Particulars

Use a Jewish Tour Guide

Above: Shepherds by the River Dan, by C.W. Wilson.
Below: Birket Ram on the Golan Heights.

What should the European pilgrim take with him to the Holy Land? Of what should he be wary, what should he wear, and what currency should he carry? Things that were obvious and common knowledge in the Crusader period, when Christian pilgrims enjoyed the hospitality and guiding services of the churches and the knightly orders, were cloaked in mystery and danger during the Ayyubid period. During the Mameluke period, after the final Crusader decampment from the Holy Land, pilgrims were even more at a loss.

Accordingly, pilgrims returning from the Holy Land included in their books recommendations and advice for those who would follow in their footsteps. In a guide for pilgrims written by Burchard of Mount Zion, who toured the Holy Land in the 1290s, pilgrim routes and holy places, geographical and historical information about the Holy Land, and guides to convenient but uncommon routes all appear for the first time. Burchard also mentions out-of-the-way sites like Birket Ram on the Golan Heights, whose water flows into the Dan River, and various Crusader fortresses, including Monfort and Belvoir.

For pilgrims who wished to visit the ancient cities and fortresses of the Holy Land, the fourteenth-century monk Jacob of Verona recommends employing Jewish tour guides, who he says were knowledgeable about the ancient sites that served as the background for the Bible and the stories of their forefathers.

According to the book Felix Fabri published upon his 1483 return from his second trip to the Holy Land, it was crucial to always have local currency. Regardless of religion, the merchants and money changers in Jerusalem had absolutely no scruples, and cheated Christian pilgrims any way they could.

Black Death Halts Pilgrimages for 25 Years

The tide of Christian pilgrimage to the Holy Land, especially from Eastern countries, that began in the Ayyubid period and rose at the beginning of the fourteenth century, was cut short in 1348 by the Black Death. The epidemic of plague that broke out felled even more victims in the East than in Western Europe, causing entire cities to be emptied of their inhabitants.

The well-known Muslim traveler Ibn Battuta, who visited Gaza a short time after the Black Death struck, relates that the huge number of deaths from the plague had left the city almost deserted. The *qadi* of Gaza told him that the mortality rate had reached 1,100 per day. The epidemic resulted in the total cessation of pilgrimages to the Holy Land for twenty-five years.

Pope Gregory the Great leads a procession to pray for the cessation of the plague. A late-fifteenth-century miniature.

Nicolo da Poggibonsi.

1349 Poggibonsi's Guidebook Tops Best-Sellers

64 Editions in 450 Years

The ultimate best-seller of guidebooks for pilgrims was written by the Tuscan monk Nicolo da Poggibonsi, who was in the Holy Land from 1346 to 1350. Sadly, the author never got to enjoy his immense success.

Poggibonsi traveled throughout the Holy Land, Sinai, Egypt, Damascus, and Mesopotamia, then upon his return to Italy wrote a book describing his journey. In the thirteenth chapter of his book he specifically asks that he be given credit for the work and the great effort invested in its writing. He even edited the book so that his name, his father's name, and his place of origin were spelled out by the opening letters of its chapters.

Poggibonsi's efforts were to no avail, however. About 150 years after his death, anonymous editors published his book as a pilgrim's guide to the holy places and retitled it "The Way from Venice to Holy Jerusalem," omitting the name of the original author. The guidebook had unprecedented success and became nearly the biggest best-seller of its genre ever published: the first edition came out in the year 1500 and led to 64 more editions with no changes. The last edition was printed in 1800—close to 450 years after Poggibonsi had completed his journey, Poggibonsi recovered his due glory recently, when he was revealed as the text's author.

1350 Women on the Move in Holy Land

Female Pilgrims Who Made an Impression: Bridget of Sweden and Margery of England

The improvement in pilgrimage conditions brought about not only a significant growth in the total number of pilgrims but also renewed the presence of Western women in the Holy Land. Most of the female pilgrims hailed from the European bourgeoisie, a fact that is reflected in the literature of the period. The Wife of Bath, for example, one of the heroines of Geoffrey Chaucer's *The Canterbury Tales*, written at the end of the fourteenth century, announces that she has been to Jerusalem three times.

The renewal of women's pilgrimages effected a reappearance of the feminine genre of pilgrimage literature after a hiatus of a thousand years. The prominent texts in the field are the books of the mystic Bridget of Sweden (1303-1373) and Margery Kempe of Norfolk, England (1373-1438).

Bridget, a member of the aristocracy in Sweden who wielded influence among the church leadership in Rome, and Margery Kempe, a member of the English upper middle class, were strikingly similar. Both were in their forties and mothers of a great many children (Bridget had eight and Margery fourteen) when they became ascetics. And both women experienced visions in which Jesus himself told them to make a pilgrimage to Jerusalem.

Both of the women, taking their respective visions to heart, decided to travel to Jerusalem. Leaving their homes and children, they dedicated themselves entirely to religious faith and experience.

The descriptions left us by the two women are set in the sites where Jesus suffered—Golgotha, the Holy Sepulcher, and the place on the Mount of Olives from which he ascended to heaven. In fact, the two women's identification with Jesus' afflictions was physically manifested. Bridget was the victim of weakness and aches, and Margery, who could not stop weeping during the entire three weeks of her stay in Jerusalem, had convulsions during her visits to the holy places, so that she could neither stand nor kneel.

Above: Pilgrims en route, by H. Burgmaar.
Left: Pilgrims bathing in the River Jordan, from a medieval manuscript.
Below: The Church of the Holy Sepulcher and the Dome of the Rock. A fifteenth-century miniature.

Venetian Fleet Acquires Rights to Transport Pilgrims to Holy Land

Package Tours with Shipowners, Franciscans, and Mamelukes

The Venetian merchant fleet received from the Mameluke authorities the exclusive right to transport Christian pilgrims to the Holy Land. According to the agreement, the port of Jaffa would serve as the principle anchorage for pilgrim ships: the city, entirely in ruins, was in any case unsuitable for the loading and unloading of goods.

The Mameluke agreement commissioning Venetian shipowners to bring pilgrims to the Holy Land emerged against the background of Venice's near-total control of marine trade in the eastern basin of the Mediterranean. The Venetians were especially powerful in trade with the East, and the land route passing through Egypt and northern Sinai was an important source of income for the treasury of the Mameluke kingdom. The Venetians had also renewed the trade in long-fibered cotton, which grew in the valleys of Galilee, and dispatched to the Holy Land merchants who concentrated their shipments in the ports of Acre, Tyre, and Sidon. Under the circumstances, the Mamelukes found it hard to refuse the Venetian request for a "monopoly" on the transport of pilgrims to the Holy Land.

Naturally, the agreement between the Venetians and the Mameluke authorities meant commercial profit

The port of Venice, by Canaletto.

for all concerned. The sailing contracts of the period quote the price paid by every pilgrim: it included—in addition to the cost of the journey—various "taxes," which the shipowners turned over to the governors of Jaffa, Ramla, and Gaza in exchange for licenses for going ashore, the right of passage from Jaffa to Jerusalem, and security guards to escort the pilgrim convoys during their stay in the Holy Land. In 1415 the sultan ordered the governors in the province of Palestine not to interfere with Christian pilgrims arriving on Venetian ships and to provide them with protection.

The pilgrim's impost included entrance fees to the Church of the Holy Sepulcher and escort services provided by Franciscan tour guides—members of the Custodia de Terra Sancta—who recounted stories of the holy places to their charges.

1393
King Henry IV Visits Jerusalem

Despite the harsh conditions that a trip to the Holy Land entailed, the percentage of European aristocrats among fourteenth-century pilgrims was relatively large. One of the more prominent was Henry IV, who visited the Holy Land in the winter of 1393. Six years after his trip to Jerusalem and the holy places, Henry was crowned king of England in place of his uncle Richard II.

Henry IV on his way to the Holy Land. A late-fourteenth-century manuscript.

Earlier, Henry IV had succeeded in evading his brutal uncle, who in his zeal to assume the crown systematically murdered all those who preceded him in the royal hierarchy. The English people, who despised their murderous king, supported Henry, who had found refuge in France. The English aristocracy also backed the exiled heir to the throne. In July 1399, Henry landed on English soil at the head of an army and deposed his uncle. His story was later commemorated in Shakespeare's well-known play.

1384
Local Tour Guides Collaborate with Robbers

Lead Pilgrims to Ambush and Share Booty

Towards the end of the fourteenth century, news spread of instances in which local tour guides hired by pilgrims collaborated with Bedouin robbers. Giorgio Gucci's party, which toured the Holy Land in 1384, was ambushed by a band of Bedouin robbers during a trip from Egypt to the Holy Land via northern Sinai.

According to Gucci, the robbers fell upon him and his companions with drawn swords and forced them to hand over all of their possessions. The group's guide and interpreter did not even attempt to conceal the fact that the attack had been coordinated with them. But while the Bedouin were busy looting the travelers, one of the leaders of the group, Leonardo Frescobaldi, a former army officer, the mayor of Castello, and a special emissary of the pope, surprised the traitor-

Bandits attack a pilgrim.

ous interpreter by putting a sword to his throat, and assured the robbers—frozen on the spot in surprise—that he would cut their colleague's throat if they did not desist. A long bargaining session by means of the now-inspired interpreter went on until the Bedouin agreed to return to the pilgrims all of their possessions in exchange for fifteen ducats. Gucci relates that the money was distributed between the guides and the robbers.

Most of the robberies did not end so cheaply, however; in many cases pilgrims lost all of their possessions. As time passed, it became clear that guides often cooperated with bandits, bringing their clients to a prearranged spot and subsequently sharing the spoils with the thieves. Sometimes they absconded after the robbery, leaving their charges alone with no means of assistance. In other cases they pretended to be surprised by the attack and "mediated" between the robbers and their prey, bargaining about the amount of the money demanded by the Bedouin in order to avoid bloodshed.

Tour of Holy Land: A Quick Trip with a Tight Itinerary

Baksheesh Always Helps

The usual pilgrim route began in Jaffa, passed through Lydda for a look at the Church of Saint George, visited Ramla—where one was forced to spend the night and avail oneself of the local Turkish bath—and went on to Jerusalem, Bethlehem, Jericho, and the baptismal site on the Jordan. Only in rare instances did Christian pilgrims reach the holy sites in remote Galilee, where even the Mamelukes found it difficult to provide full protection.

The timetable was rigid. According to their agreement with the Mameluke authorities, the Venetian ships were

Above: An exhausted pilgrim elevates his ailing legs. A medieval woodcut.
Right: Ramla's white tower, a mosque minaret built in 1318.

tains accompanied their groups of pilgrims. Special consuls functioning on behalf of the Venetian authorities in Ramla and Jerusalem were meant to ensure that the journeys proceeded without incident. Their principle duty was to arrange matters like the prompt release of pilgrims who were arrested for various reasons by local officers. In most cases such problems were sorted out by means of some well-placed baksheesh.

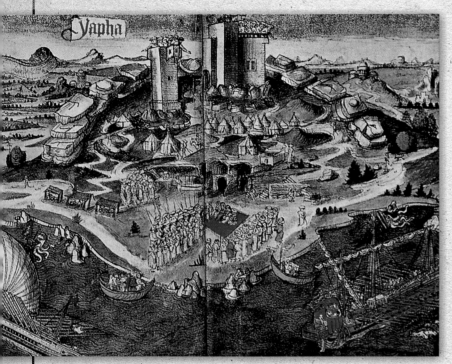

Vapha

Pilgrims arriving at the port of Jaffa in Venetian ships, by K.R. von Grünemberg.

allowed to anchor in Jaffa for only two or three weeks. The constricted time limit made the trip—which took place on donkey-back or on foot—into a speedy journey. In Jerusalem, even the pilgrim tours guided by Franciscan monks were rushed. The descriptions left by pilgrims of this period mainly enumerate the indulgences they earned from a visit to one site or another; seldom do they describe the sites themselves.

In order to see to it that the tight schedule was maintained, ship cap-

The bridge built by Baybars near Lydda, with his lioncel carved on it.

Pilgrims Praying by the Holy Tomb Worth Their Weight in Gold

Church Opened in Return for Gifts

The attitude of the Mamelukes towards Christian holy places was generally expressed through monetary means. Given such circumstances, pilgrims praying at the Church of the Holy Sepulcher were worth their weight in gold. The Russian monk Zosime discovered upon arriving at the church in 1419 that its gates were locked with the sultan's seal, but upon inquiring he was informed that in exchange for gifts presented to the emir the church doors would swing wide open.

If entrance into the church itself was for sale, however, prayer next to the Holy Tomb was subject to inflation: Zosime reported that fifteen Saracens stood next to the tomb and collected Venetian gold coins from everyone who wished to kneel before it.

Duke of Burgundy Philip the Good Dreams of a New Crusade

Agents in Holy Land Dispatch Descriptions

Philip the Good, the duke of Burgundy who later became king of England, dreamt of a new crusade to the Holy Land and sent several spies to the East in order to obtain detailed information on its inhabitants, rulers, and state of affairs.

In 1422 the duke dispatched Guillebert de Lannoy, an expert in fortifications from the duchy of Burgundy, to the Holy Land. De Lannoy submitted to his employer a thorough report on the strength of the cities and fortresses in the Holy Land, the number of soldiers and cannons in the hands of the Muslim garrisons, and the location of water sources in various areas. He writes that inside Jerusalem's western wall was a small fortress of lovely carved stone called David's Citadel. The Citadel, situated on a slight rise, was populated and guarded. Though it appeared to be almost impregnable from the outside, in the direction of the fields, it was much more vulnerable from inside the city. Standing as it did without moats and other fortifications, nothing prevented its capture.

Jerusalem itself, de Lannoy reports, was encircled by low, poorly-

Philip the Good, by R. van der Weyden.

constructed walls, and had no siege towers or moats worthy of the name. He estimates that the city, whose main strength was its location, was unable to withstand a serious attack. ▶

Acre, de Lannoy writes, had a superb harbor enclosed by an impressive rock and sand breakwater. He claims that though Acre was a ghost town, its houses could have been restored if the necessary effort had been made. On his way to the Holy Land, de Lannoy met with the king of Cyprus and the emperor of Byzantium, but details of the talks remain obscure.

Ten years later the duke sent Bertrandon de la Brocquiere to the Holy Land. Upon his return, de la Brocquiere wrote a comprehensive report that included detailed notes on the sites he visited. He relates that he visited the village where St. George was killed (Lydda), saw the stone that miraculously swallowed the infant John the Baptist (in the Church of the Visitation in Ein Karem), toured the place where Jesus resurrected Lazarus (Beit Hanina), visited the spot that had yielded the tree from which Jesus' cross was hewn (the Monastery of the Cross in Jerusalem), and saw the house and pillars that Samson demolished (Gaza).

Christians Lose David's Tomb and Cenacle
1452

At the beginning of the 1450s a debate erupted between the Jews and the Christians regarding ownership of the structure on Mount Zion in which the Tomb of David and the Cenacle, the room of the Last Supper, were located.

The Mamelukes, who were looking for a way to weaken and degrade the Christians, decided to appropriate the Tomb of David and the Cenacle. The sultan sent a delegation whose mandate it was to investigate rumors of "new" Christian construction—according to Islamic law, anything built since the days of Omar's conquest (in 638).

The delegation ruled that the suspicions had been substantiated. The building was taken from the Christians and further access to the holy places forbidden them.

David's Tomb, by Halbreiter.

Want to Be a Pilgrim? Show Me the Money!
1458

The local inhabitants of the Holy Land, like the authorities, saw the pilgrims first and foremost as a source of income, and they treated them accordingly. Pilgrims were required to pay for everything, and often had to add baksheesh as well. Often, the sums of money demanded from them represented blatant extortion based only on the greed of the local authorities. The fact that the pilgrims were "infidels" only made the thievery easier on the consciences of the Muslims.

The series of payments began even before the pilgrims touched land. William Wey, who arrived in Jaffa in 1458, reports that the disembarkation process was maddeningly slow and entailed the payment of steep bribes. The Franciscan monks who were always on the spot to assist pilgrims helped them haggle over the bribes and straightened out any misunderstandings, in many instances preventing violence. Wey also relates that he and his companions were not permitted to leave Jaffa on the day of their arrival despite the early hour. Instead of continuing on their way to Jerusalem, they were forced to sleep—and pay a large sum for the "privilege" of doing so!—in filthy and foul-smelling caves carved in the

Pilgrims pay a transit fee at port of Jaffa. An illustration copied from Sir. J. Mandeville's book.

mountain near the city's fortress.

Upon its arrival in Ramla, the party was again delayed on various pretenses so that the travelers would be forced to stop in the city and avail themselves of its services.

Not everyone put up with the manipulation. Roberto de San Severino, a highborn Italian pilgrim who also participated in the pilgrimage of spring 1458, was offended by the behavior of the donkey owner whose services he had employed. Refusing to listen to his Franciscan guide, who tried to convince him that a small bribe would provide him with better service, Roberto demanded an apology from the Arab. The ensuing argument delayed the convoy for three extraneous hours.

Pilgrims Vandalize Holy Sites
1458

For centuries, a great many pilgrims would break off pieces of stone from the holy places to take home with them as mementos. Obviously, the practice caused serious damage to the holy places. The Franciscan monks who guided the pilgrims repeatedly emphasized that it was forbidden to hack off parts of the holy structures, especially the Church of the Holy Sepulcher, but it appears that the warnings carried little weight. Thus in a travel book by William Wey, a graduate of Oxford University and a teacher at Eton who arrived in the Holy Land in 1458, appears a long list of the souvenirs he carried away with him: stone from Golgotha, stone from the Tomb of Jesus, stone from Mount Tabor, stone from the site of the Holy Cross, and stone from the Grotto of the Nativity in Bethlehem.

The grille that guards Golgotha.

Water of the River Jordan Causes Storms at Sea

One of the most popular souvenirs among pilgrims returning from the Holy Land was water from the River Jordan, which they would pour into special vessels brought with them for that purpose. But while filling the vials with the holy water was relatively easy, taking it back to Europe was more of a challenge. Medieval sailors believed that having waters of the Jordan on board was a sure prescription for a storm at sea. The instructions of the captains of all pilgrim ships were unequivocal: it was forbidden to bring water from the river aboard. When a flask of water from the Jordan was discovered among a pilgrim's belongings, it was wrested from him or her, and the contents poured out.

Even if a pilgrim managed to smuggle some holy water below deck, the precious cargo was not necessarily safe. Whenever a storm rose at sea,

crew members would break into the travelers' hall and rummage through their belongings in search of containers of water from the Jordan, which had clearly caused the storm.

A pilgrim who returned from the Holy Land in 1480 relates how his ship

was caught in a violent storm between Jaffa and Cyprus. Some of the pilgrims, accusing two Jewish passengers of performing magic and bringing about the storm, demanded that the captain throw them into the sea. The captain and his crew, rejecting

Above: A Byzantine lead ampule, usually containing holy water from the River Jordan.

Left: A ship in stormy water. From a medieval manuscript.

the pilgrims' demand, claimed that the source of the trouble was the river water they had brought aboard and forced them to cast their holy water overboard instead of the Jews. After they had done so, the sea calmed and the ship continued on to Cyprus.

Impossible Conditions in Jerusalem Hostel

Pilgrims Complain of Noise, Neglect, and Filth

Lodging conditions in Jerusalem for Christian pilgrims from the West were so degrading and intolerable that the wealthier among them tried to find

alternative arrangements in private homes, despite the fact that doing so was prohibited. During the Ayyubid period the only hostel available to

A pilgrim buys food in Jerusalem. From a medieval manuscript.

Tabor Slave Trade

Men and Women Sold at Weekly Market

The Belgian pilgrim Jean Adorno was amazed to discover that a slave trade was in full swing at the weekly market at the foot of Mount Tabor near Khan a-Tojar, which he described as a lovely caravansary constructed completely of marble.

Local residents brought their produce to market and merchants from faraway cities brought their wares, but Adorno relates that most of the activity revolved around the sale of people of both sexes, who were presented naked so that their worth could be better evaluated. Next to them, trade in animals, rice, sugar, and cotton occupied the rest of the crowd.

The remains of Khan a-Tojar at the foot of Mount Tabor.

European pilgrims was a stable that had previously sheltered the beasts of burden of the Hospitaler Order. The hostel, which was called "the Asneri" (from the Old French word *asne*—"donkey"), was located near St. Stephen's Church outside the walls of the city. The Ayyubids, fearing a renewed Crusader assault, took care to keep Western pilgrims outside of the walls, where they could not spy on the city. From the hostel the pilgrims were taken under heavy guard on daily tours of Jerusalem's holy sites.

In the 1340s the Mameluke authorities decided to turn an abandoned building in the Muristan area that had served in the past as a Hospitaler hospital into a hostel. When maintained by the Knights of St. John the place had apparently been a grand

building, according to a pilgrim who stayed there at the end of the century. In his day, unluckily for him, the hostel consisted of one long hall with columns in the middle, and was the only place Western pilgrims were allowed to stay in Jerusalem.

In July of 1480, almost one hundred years later, the French pilgrim Pierre Barbatre complained about the appearance and condition of the same hostel. He related that pilgrims were forced to purchase provisions from Muslim and Eastern Christian peddlers, and that they had to sleep on the floor. Felix Fabri, who stayed in the place in 1482, objected to the piles of trash, unpleasant odors, and noise.

The Donkey—Main Means of Transportation

Donkey Owners Fight Over Transport of Every Pilgrim

A pilgrim caravan on its way to Jerusalem, by H. Wölffli.

Almost the only means of transportation at the disposal of pilgrims during the Mameluke period was the donkey. Whenever a pilgrim ship dropped anchor in the port of Jaffa, hundreds of peasants awaited it in hopes of renting their donkeys to the Christians. The number of donkeys in demand was great—a convoy of two hundred pilgrims, for example, needed approximately four hundred donkeys to transport them and their luggage. Nevertheless, the supply was always greater than the demand, and it often happened that two or even three donkey owners latched onto a single pilgrim, each dragging him in a different direction.

The Franciscan monk Felix Fabri described just such a scene. A huge black Saracen began to drag him forcefully toward a group of donkeys. Fabri, who interpreted the man's zeal as an attempt at robbery, tried to free himself, but the Saracen caught him by the arm and ran until they arrived at his donkeys. Fortunately, the frightened Fabri ran into one of the Franciscan brothers who had come to welcome his party at the port. The monk told Fabri to calm down and haggle pragmatically over the price. A bargain was struck and Fabri rented what donkeys he needed from the Saracen.

Out of this "kidnaping" and the subsequent journey, a friendship between the pilgrim and the donkey driver was born. When Fabri arrived in the Holy Land a second time, on this occasion as a guide for a group of pilgrims, he searched the port of Jaffa for his "donkey man." The moment the Muslim laid eyes on Fabri he ran over to him, hugged him, laughed, and excitedly struck up a conversation, of which Fabri understood not one word.

Franciscans Grant "Knight of the Holy Sepulcher" Title

Taken with its role as guardian of the holy places on behalf of the Catholic Church, at the end of the fifteenth century the Franciscan Order began granting a title—"Knight of the Holy Sepulcher." Bestowed mainly upon persons of distinction who came to Jerusalem, it was intended to encourage important personages to visit the city and through them to increase the general awareness of pilgrimage to the Holy Land. The title, which after a short while was in great demand among European high society, indirectly contributed a great deal to encouraging pilgrimages from Europe and augmenting the church's income.

At the time, the head of the Franciscans in the Holy Land was the Italian Francesco Suriano, the son of a Venetian merchant family with connections in the East. He had joined the Franciscans at the age of 25, and at the beginning of the 1490s had been sent to serve in the Holy Land. Having traveled in the East previously, he spoke both Arabic and Greek. Upon his return from his first trip, he penned a description of the sites in the Holy Land. In 1493 he was again sent to Jerusalem—this time as head of the Franciscan Order and Guardian of Mount Zion, in which capacity he served for three years. At the end of his tour of duty he traveled widely throughout the East, returning to Jerusalem in 1510.

Left: The ordination of a Knight of the Holy Sepulcher, by H. Wölffli.
Below: The road to Jerusalem. An illustration from a manuscript prepared for Philip of Burgundy in 1455, based on an illustration by Burchard of Mount Zion.

Get Knighted in Sinai

At the end of the fifteenth century, the heads of Saint Catherine's in Sinai decided to grant dignitaries who visited their monastery the title "Knight of Saint Catherine's." This distinguished knighthood, second in importance only to the title "Knight of the Holy Sepulcher" that was granted in Jerusalem, was intended to encourage distinguished pilgrims to add the isolated monastery to their itinerary.

The decision to confer the honorary title on pilgrims was a result of the same sort of reasoning that had previously led to the establishment of a knighthood bestowed upon prominent visitors to Jerusalem's Church of the Holy Sepulcher. The monks of St. Catherine wished to draw to their monastery—located at some distance from the regular pilgrim route—pilgrims arriving in the Holy Land via Egypt and northern Sinai. The route had been a vital trade highway in the fifteenth century, and the many travelers along it had included pilgrims. At the end of the century, however, when the importance of the route to Sinai waned, the stream of pilgrims along the road ebbed, and only a handful of hardy pilgrims to the Holy Land dared to venture all the way to St. Catherine's. The monks were thus forced to concoct a reason for pilgrims to schlep all the way to St. Catherine's.

Bogislav the Bar-B-Que Hero

Bogislav X, the duke of Pomerania, an independent kingdom between Germany and Poland, departed on a journey to Jerusalem in 1496. Off the Greek coast, his ship was attacked by pirates. But after the Turkish vessel had overcome the pilgrim ship in a bloody battle, the pirates inexplicably withdrew, leaving the pilgrims to give thanks for their miraculous rescue.

The Turkish pirate ship approached the pilgrim vessel as it sailed opposite the coast of Greece on its way from Venice to the Holy Land. It appears that the Turkish pirates had prior knowledge of an important personage on board—the duke of Pomerania, Bogislav X—and were counting on their mission reaping them a large ransom in return for the release of the ruler of the small but wealthy duchy. When the duke decided to defend himself, many of his entourage and the other passengers followed suit. According to his own record of the events, a number of cowardly passengers who tried to hide in the ship's cabins were forced by Bogislav to face the enemy and fight, as he called on them to display a measure of bravery worthy of Germans.

According to the duke (who refers to himself in the third person in his account), when the battle was joined he fought with great courage at the head of his men, who struck at the enemy with all possible force. Having no helmets or shields, Bogislav's fighters were forced to improvise, using whatever was at hand. Some snatched up loaves of bread to defend themselves from Turkish arrows. The duke received a shield and helmet from the captain of the ship.

Meanwhile, the Turks mercilessly barraged the pilgrim vessel, firing many of their arrows in the direction of the duke, who was hard put to defend himself. At one point, fourteen arrows and spears simultaneously struck Bogislav's shield. As the Turks attempted to board the ship, the duke's men pushed them back. One of the Turks, a man of enormous dimensions, leapt upon the duke. Though Bogislav relates that he twice managed to throw the pirate into the sea, the Turk, a seasoned swimmer, recovered and reboarded the ship.

The waves of pirates continued their assault. Bogislav reports that he defended himself valiantly despite the fact that all of the Turks seemed to be fighting against him. Relying mostly on his sword, after it broke the duke was forced to defend himself for a long while with only his shield. Three of his companions, noticing that Bogislav was in mortal danger, came to his aid, defending themselves and him as best they could. Though one of them managed to kill a great many Turks, he was finally pierced by an arrow, and died a hero's death on the deck of the unlucky ship. The second man, wounded repeatedly, refused to surrender until he was at last shot in his eye and compelled to leave the fray. The third man was also mortally wounded.

The duke ran about in search of a new weapon, but to no avail. Suddenly, he found a skewer usually used for roasting chickens on the spit. Lacking any alternative, Bogislav grabbed the skewer and went to the aid of his three colleagues, one of whom was already dead and another who was close to death. Leaping forward in anger, disregarding his own safety, the duke wielded his skewer with such force that no one could withstand it. Many of the Turks died...

At exactly the moment it seemed that hope was lost, the duke relates, God saved the besieged pilgrims. The Turkish commander precipitously ordered his men to withdraw, and the pirates inexplicably sailed off as suddenly as they had come, leaving the pilgrims alone on the sea.

Duke Bogislav X's ship continued on its way east and anchored in the port of Jaffa in the summer of 1496. The duke headed to Jerusalem, where he was awarded the title "Knight of the Holy Sepulcher."

The Mamelukes' attitude toward Jerusalem was influenced by the fact that they were converts to Islam and not Muslims by birth. Their desire to emphasize their commitment to their new religion, its symbols, and its holy places contributed a great deal to the wave of Mameluke construction that overtook the city.

Sabil Qa'itbay.

200 Travelogues in 200 Years

The harvest of travelogues written by Western pilgrims between 1300 and 1500 is impressive; more than two hundred pilgrims from Western countries published books and essays about their journeys to the Holy Land during that time. Eastern pilgrims, on the other hand, were remarkably quiet—at least textually—about their adventures.

While during the Crusader period most pilgrims were Catholics from Western European countries, in the centuries after the Crusader fall and expulsion most of the pilgrims came from Eastern sects—the Greek Orthodox, Armenian, Georgian, Syrian, and Coptic Churches. Despite the fact that the number of Armenian pilgrims who arrived in the Holy Land (in large convoys that traveled overland) was much greater than the number of pilgrims from the West, the essay by King Hayton II of Little Armenia was the sole Armenian text from that period to describe a pilgrimage to the Holy Land.

Among pilgrims from the East who did write travel books, the Russian

Pilgrims at Saint Catherine's in Sinai. From a medieval manuscript.

travelers were prominent. The Russian archimandrite Grethenios, who toured the Holy Land in 1400, visited not only the holy sites, but Ramla, Jericho, Bethlehem, and Jaffa, proceeding afterwards to Gaza and Saint Catherine's Monastery.

From the description left us by a monk who arrived in the Holy Land from the city-state of Novgorod in 1456, and prepared for his parishioners an extensive report on the holy places, we learn that on the way to the Church of the Holy Sepulcher was a staircase with fourteen steps, each the width of eight pinkies. Before the church's portal, he related, stood a large round chapel. On top of its walls were slanted beams of wood overlaid inside by thin planks and surmounted by a leaden cupola open at its center like a jar.

Sultan A-Tahar Baybars, who gained control of the Mameluke kingdom immediately after its victory over the Mongols, arrived in Jerusalem in 1263 and examined the condition of the Temple Mount. He gave orders to install water cisterns, block up the spaces between the columns in the Dome of the Chain, and renovate the tiles on the outside of the Dome of the Rock. He also commanded the construction of the Khan a-Tahar west of the city, apparently to encourage Muslim pilgrimage to Jerusalem as a counterweight to Christian pilgrimage.

Emir Allah ed-Din, whom Baybars appointed head of the building campaign in Jerusalem, built a hostel in the city west of the Temple Mount, tiled the upper level of the Temple Mount compound, and attended to the water supply of the Temple Mount.

Above: The Madrasa el-Ashrafiya.
Right: Bab el-Qattanin.

Allah ed-Din retained his position throughout the days of Sultan el-Malik el-Mansur Qalawun, Baybars' son-in-law, during whose period he erected a second hostel opposite his first, and built, at Qalawun's orders, a mosque in the Christian Quarter—an architectural demonstration of dominance.

After Sultan Qalawun's death in 1290, several *madrasas* (colleges) were built in Jerusalem. In 1310, Qalawun's son, El-Malik en-Nasir Muhammad Ibn Qalawun, took the reigns of power for the third time. During this third term of rule, which began in 1310 and lasted thirty years, the country experienced its most intense phase of development. In Jerusalem the new age rode in on a wave of innovations and construction.

Two important governors ruled in Jerusalem during this era. The first was Sanjar al-Jawuli, who built a *madrasa* in the area of the Antonia, which served as a residence for the governors of Jerusalem until the end of the fifteenth century.

In 1320, Sanjar was replaced by the governor of Damascus, Tankiz en-Nasiri. Tankiz's achievements in Jerusalem were especially impressive. In 1327 he installed a water supply system for the city and restored the aqueduct leading from the

Al-Arub Spring to the city via Solomon's Pools. The aqueduct entered the city along the Street of the Chain and reached El-Kas (The Cup)—a marble pool encircled by seats and with a goblet in the center that is used to this day by Muslim faithful for washing their hands and feet before praying on the Temple Mount.

Next to the Temple Mount en-Nasiri built the Tankiziya—a two-story *madrasa* that served as a seminary, a place for entertaining notables, and a courthouse, eventually earning the name Mahkame (Place of the Law). He also built the Minaret of the Chain, and north of the Courtyard of the Chain, a hostel for women. Near the Temple Mount he established the Cotton Merchants' Market. In its southern wing he built two bath-houses and a khan; at its eastern end he opened an ornate gate in the wall of the Temple Mount—the Bab el-Qattanin (Cotton Merchants' Gate). A new commercial center had been added to the city.

Tankiz was also involved in restoration work on the Temple Mount and in gilding the domes of Al-Aqsa and the Dome of the Rock. He renovated the Citadel, redesigning it and repairing

the machicolations, the small galleries from which boiling oil could be poured on advancing enemies. As a contemporaneous Muslim geographer said of him, Tankiz restored to Jerusalem the rank of a city when it was a forgotten and neglected place.

Tankiz en-Nasiri's building spurt ended with the death of the sultan in 1341. The governors and sultans who followed invested their energies only in renovating the Temple Mount and constructing holy buildings in the city.

Another shift in the attitude of the authorities toward the city began in the days of the Circassian sultan Barkok, who aspired to return to Jerusalem its past glory. He revamped the city's aqueduct, built the Sultan's Pool, and established a royal khan (Khan a-Sultan, which was built in 1392) for merchants in the busiest part of the city. The income from the khan was dedicated to funding the activity of Al-Aqsa.

In the first part of the fifteenth century the emirs continued to erect holy buildings in Jerusalem—neglecting construction for other than religious purposes. During this period, tension between Muslims and Christians grew, and the Mamelukes, in an architectural power play, built

a tall minaret over the Khanqat Salahiya near the Church of the Holy Sepulcher, totally ignoring the Christian request that the structure not rise above the dome of the church.

In the second half of the fifteenth century, Sultan Qa'itbay came to power and ruled until 1496. It was in the period of his rule that the most impressive royal *madrasa* in Jerusalem—the Madrasa el-Ashrafiya—was built (1482). Expensive materials were invested in the building, and its beauty was often compared to that of the Dome of the Rock and Al-Aqsa. A year later, Qa'itbay ordered the local emir to repair the aqueduct and rebuild one of Solomon's Pools. The aqueduct ended at the Sabil Qa'itbay—a water fountain built opposite the Ashrafiya. Felix Fabri wrote of the project that it was grander than even that of King Hezekiah, and that there were those who thought that the capital of the Mameluke kingdom was about to be moved from Cairo to Jerusalem.

The sultans who came after Qa'itbay did not succeed in arresting the decline of the Mameluke kingdom, In 1516 the Ottomans defeated them and the Holy Land became part of the Ottoman Empire.

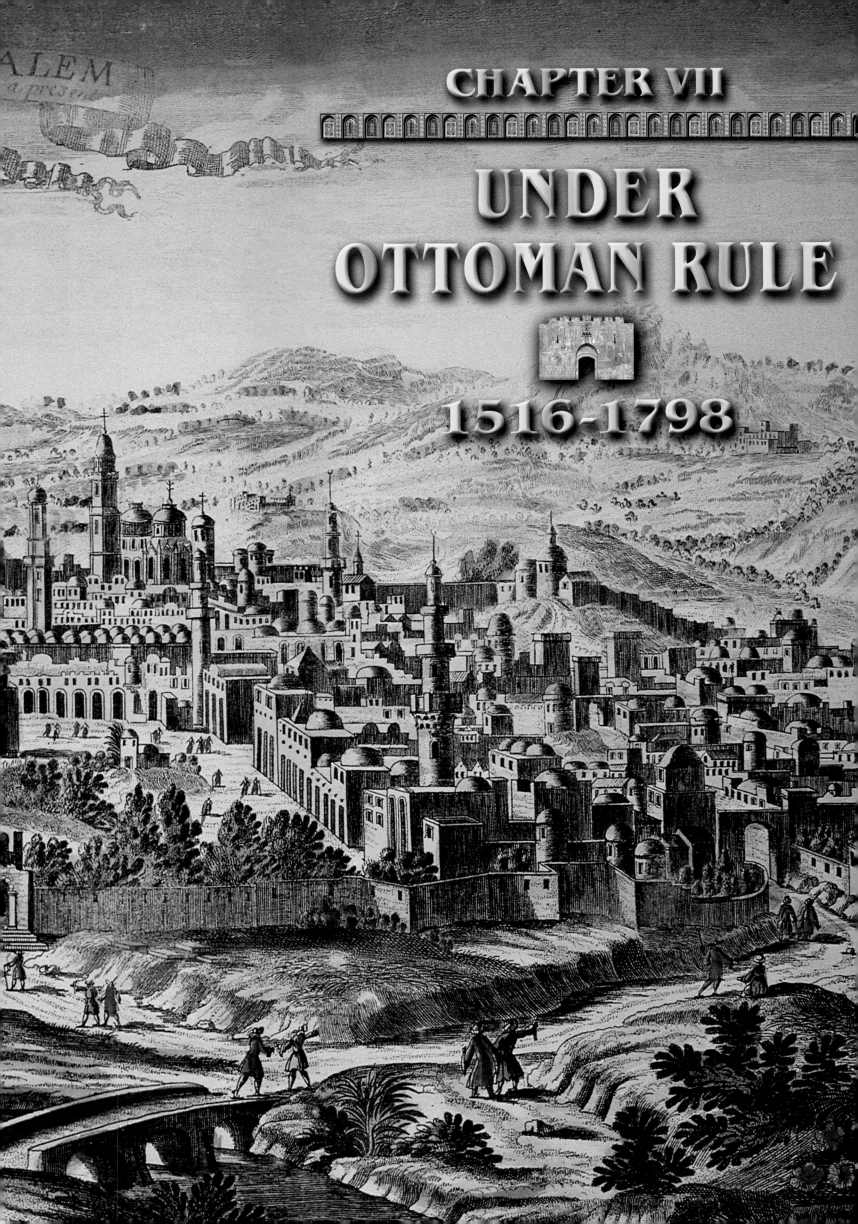

CHAPTER VII

UNDER OTTOMAN RULE

1516-1798

The Turkish conquest of the Holy Land in 1516 came as a complete surprise. Its roots lay far to the north, in the center of Ottoman Turkey. The Janissaries, Turkey's elite army units, were concerned about the nation's trend towards peace and the lessening interest of its rulers in wars and occupation. Through their intervention, Selim I, one of the few princes who wanted to perpetuate the expansionist wars, came to power in 1512.

After the conquest of Persia and Syria, the Turkish army advanced towards the Holy Land, occupying it without encountering any real resistance. At the end of the same year, Jerusalem fell into the hands of the Turks, who were warmly received by the city's residents.

The Ottomans ruled in Jerusalem and the Holy Land for four centuries, the longest period of continuous rule in the former's history. Surprisingly, the Ottoman reign bequeathed few changes in the city. Its buildings and infrastructures were neglected, including the walls and the holy buildings on the Temple Mount. The condition of the churches likewise deteriorated; some were abandoned while others were refurbished for different functions. Only the first years of Ottoman rule proved an exception to this general attitude of neglect, especially the period of Sultan Suleiman the Magnificent.

Suleiman II, "the Magnificent," came to power in 1520. The years of his rule are known as the golden age of the Ottoman Empire. He fortified Jerusalem, transformed it into his hub of power, and tried to restore it to its former glory. His projects included rebuilding the city walls, repairing the water supply system, and developing an economic and trade network. During Suleiman's era, Jerusalem was a vibrant and active commercial center.

At the end of the sixteenth century, a fundamental change occurred in the Ottoman Empire. English and Dutch ships penetrated the Indian Ocean and trade between Europe and the Far East shifted to the seaways around the Cape of Good Hope, abandoning the Mediterranean Sea and Turkish waters. The Ottoman Empire's economic downfall dragged a political and military decline in its wake. The powerful sultanate gave way to weak second- and third-rate rulers. The armies of Russia, Austria, and Persia began to reconquer territory from the Turks.

The weakening of the central government was pronounced in the provinces. Greedy provincial governors and judges replaced their superlatively efficient predecessors. The economic situation deteriorated. The fate of the minorities, the Christians and the Jews, was dismal; cruel governors like Ibn Farouk did not hesitate to oppress them and appropriate their property. Military forces became less disciplined, involving themselves in political intrigues. The state of security on the roads worsened drastically. The Turkish fleet floundered and left the high seas to pirates from Malta and Algeria.

The impotence of the central government brought a rise in the power of local rulers, between whom armed conflict often erupted. Oftentimes, these men were governors like Ibn Farouk, who was appointed by the government in Istanbul to rule in Jerusalem during the second decade of the seventeenth century and became famous for his great cruelty to the city's inhabitants. More often, these potentates were from local clans like the Radwan family in Gaza, which ruled as an autonomous dynasty and conducted independent foreign policy. The Radwans reestablished the port city of Jaffa in the mid-seventeenth century. The port served the majority of pilgrims who arrived during this period and who made a great contribution to the growth and prosperity of the city of Jaffa.

The most famous member of the Radwan family was the Druze ruler Fahr al-Din II, who ruled in southern Lebanon and even occupied Galilee in the seventeenth century. In order to strengthen his chieftaincy, he forged close relations with the dukes of Tuscany in Italy. When the Turkish government chased him from his land, he spent several years in the Tuscan court before returning to rule again in Galilee and Lebanon. Among al-Din's achievements were the resettlement of Nazareth and Acre in the north of the Holy Land, where Christian monasteries and churches were built during his reign. Al-Din even negotiated with representatives of the king of Spain regarding the establishment of a Christian nation in the Holy Land. In 1634 he was arrested by the Ottoman authorities, battered, and executed in Istanbul one year later.

The rise of religious fervor during the Counter-Reformation in the seventeenth century brought a sharp rise in the number of pilgrims to the Holy Land. They arrived mainly from Catholic countries: the French represented the majority of the pilgrims during this period and also wrote most of the travel books. Travelogues published in the period were written mainly by monks and clergy, but merchants who came to the Holy Land for purposes of trade also left records. They saw the Holy Land more realistically than did the devout pilgrims, and from their books one can learn a great deal about economic life in the country.

In the eighteenth century, European religious fervor waned and the number of Western pilgrims decreased. There was no variation in the amount of Eastern pilgrims, but since they contributed almost nothing to the corpus of pilgrimage literature, we know little about their experiences.

The pilgrims of the eighteenth century were of a different character than their predecessors. They exhibited an interest in the Holy Land's antiquities and inhabitants, its geography, flora, and fauna. Only fifty travel books survive from this period, as opposed to a collection of twice that number from the previous century, but the number of books with significant scientific and intellectual content is actually greater. Geographic treatments begin to appear among the texts of this period, their authors often basing their conclusions on extant travel literature without ever having visited the Holy Land.

Meanwhile, the power and status of the Ottoman Empire continued to decrease. Other nations made inroads in the empire's territory. The internal stability of Turkey was undermined. Unceasing plotting by the court eunuchs, religious leaders, Janissaries, and local governors caused ferment both in the center and in the periphery—disturbances that were also felt in the Holy Land.

Two regional leaders stand out from among those who ruled in the Holy Land in the eighteenth century: Dahir al-Omar and Ahmed al-Jezzar.

Dahir al-Omar (1688-1775),

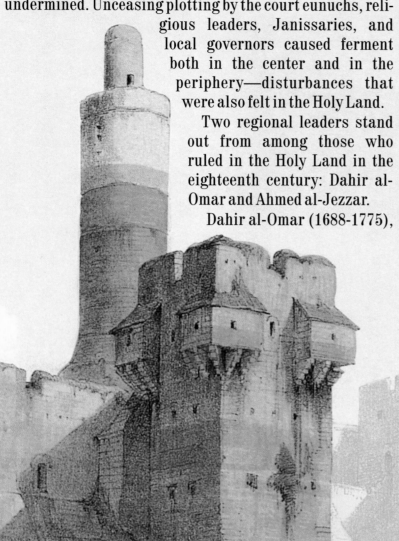

a Bedouin sheikh from the Zaidan family, was one of the most important Bedouin leaders in the history of the Holy Land. His rule, which lasted approximately sixty years, stimulated economic growth such as had not been seen in the Holy Land since the Crusader period. He made contacts with French merchants, facilitating their purchase of Galilee's cotton crop; in return, they supplied Dahir with money and arms. He resuscitated Tiberias and razed Haifa in order to rebuild the city in a more favorable spot. Dahir restored Acre and transformed it into his capital, initiating in it a period of growth that continued for a hundred years, until 1840.

Dahir viewed the Christians as a loyal element and encouraged their settlement in the cities under his control. Under his rule, development began in Nazareth: the number of its inhabitants grew, its economic situation improved, and its Christian character became pronounced. Numerous Christians settled in the village as it became a town: residential buildings, religious, and public buildings were erected. Among the churches that were reconstructed were the Franciscan Church of the Annunciation, the Greek Orthodox Church of Saint Gabriel, the Greek Catholic Synagogue Church, the Church of Saint Joseph, and the Mensa Christi Church.

The Ottoman government regarded Dahir as a rebel and commanded the pasha of Damascus to march against him. Dahir allied himself with Ali Bey, the governor of Egypt who had declared the independence of Egypt from Turkish rule, and the Russians, who had been at war with Turkey since 1768.

By 1771, almost all of the Holy Land was under the control of Dahir, who had conquered Gaza, Lydda, Ramla, and Jaffa. But in 1774 the Russians signed a peace treaty with Turkey and Dahir found himself somewhat isolated. The Ottoman authorities had also succeeded in causing a rift between Ali Bey and the commander of his army, Abu Dahab. The latter defected to the Turks and took over many of the cities in Dahir's possession. Abu Dahab conquered Jaffa after a 66-day siege, executed 1,500 of its citizens, and erected a memorial to his victory out of their skulls. His attempt to overcome Acre foundered when he suddenly died, apparently the victim of poison.

Dahir's battalions of mercenaries eventually betrayed their master by deserting to the enemy's side. In 1775, when the Turkish fleet arrived at the coast of Acre and began to bombard the city, some of Dahir's soldiers did not return fire and Dahir was forced to flee the city. As the 87-year-old sheikh awaited the most beloved of his wives, his former troops found and murdered him. That same day, Acre was conquered by the Turkish sultan's army

Ahmed al-Jezzar had previously served as Ali Bey's executioner in Egypt (hence his nickname *jezzar*, "butcher" in Arabic). During his subsequent service for the Turkish government, he was in command of Beirut during the battles against Dahir al-Omar. After the latter's death, al-Jezzar was appointed governor of Sidon, whose seat was in Acre.

Despite the fact that governors were traditionally appointed for one year only, al-Jezzar managed by various stratagems to retain the appointment for twenty-nine years until his death in 1804, in addition to being made governor of Damascus from time to time, since he was wealthy enough to fund the annual pilgrimage to Mecca. In this fashion, the Holy Land and Syria were united under one ruler. At times, the area of al-Jezzar's influence expanded even further afield; when his protégé Suleiman was appointed pasha of Tripoli, for example.

Al-Jezzar was an efficient if cruel governor. He levied heavy taxes on his estates, bringing to an end the period of prosperity that had its inception in the days of Dahir. With the large sums he collected, al-Jezzar marshaled a large private army that was far more competent than the other Ottoman forces. He also strengthened Acre and fortified its walls, which proved their worth in the days of Napoleon's siege.

Al-Jezzar's soldiers rebelled in 1789, looting his castle and raping his wives. The ruler armed the inhabitants of Acre with weapons from his store of arms, marched outside the walls, and crushed the traitors. His revenge was ruthless. He executed all of the miscreants as well as his wives, who had apparently collaborated with them.

Al-Jezzar was famous for his acts of brutality. He gave orders to have people put to death or shorn of various limbs without hesitation. After his death he was remembered not for his many talents as a commander and builder, but for his legendary iron fist.

Turks Rule Holy Land
Holy Land Divided Into Four Districts

Sultan Selim I.

Sultan Suleiman II.

The imperial Turkish governmental systems of the sixteenth century operated with great efficiency not only in the center, but in peripheral districts situated far from the capital as well.

The Holy Land was not a single administrative unit, but was divided into four districts: the Jerusalem district, the Gaza district, the Nablus district and the Safed district—each with its own governor. The Radwan dynasty ruled in the Gaza district, and hegemony passed from father to son. In the other districts, the governor was replaced every year or two. Sometimes one governor was appointed over two districts. From 1525 to 1526, for example, a single governor ruled Gaza as well as Jerusalem.

Alongside the secular government functioned a religious establishment headed by a judge, or *qadi*, the highest Islamic legal authority. All matters were heard in the Shariah courthouse. Christians and Jews had their own courts and appealed to the Shariah court mainly in instances of a disagreement between them and Muslims. The secular and religious governmental systems coexisted, functioning in a reasonable manner up until the end of the sixteenth century.

In the first half of the century, the economic situation was good. Woolen cloth was manufactured in Safed, glass products in Hebron, and souvenirs for Christian pilgrims in Bethlehem. Lively trade with neighboring countries, as well as with commercial centers in Europe, like Venice, thrived. In the second half of the century, exorbitant taxation resulted in an economic slump.

Tschudi: Jerusalemites Prefer Take-Out

1519

An Oriental stringed instrument, by the Comte de Forbin.

Ludwig Tschudi, a well-educated Swiss nobleman, arrived in Jerusalem in 1519. Since he had fallen out with the head of the Franciscan Order, he could not join the guided tours that the Franciscan monks gave in the city, and was forced to hire an Italian-speaking Arab guide.

Tschudi was fascinated by the customs of the local inhabitants, and his descriptions, free from the influence of the monks' prejudices, are original and interesting. He was impressed by the eating customs of Jerusalem's inhabitants, who did not cook at home but purchased prepared food in the market. According to Tschudi, the

Above: An Oriental dancer.
Left: Fruit and vegetable stands at a Jerusalem street market, by L.M. Cubley.

stores were brimming with wares. One could purchase anything one wanted, aside from wine, the sale of which was forbidden, though it could be obtained covertly. In the heart of the markets, fruits and other foodstuffs could be bought, and in some of the alleys, chefs offered for sale boiled, roasted, and baked goods; casseroles, fish, meat, and poultry. Some citizens had a permanent arrangement with cooks who would send food to their homes on a daily basis.

Tschudi also noted that the rooftops of the city, on which the Jerusalemites often slept at night, were flat and surrounded by a balustrade. When the Muslims had a celebration, the women danced on the roof accompanied by drums and stringed instruments different from those in use in Europe at the time. The women danced only with each other, however—men were permitted only to observe.

The gate of the Citadel.

Turks Raise Jerusalem's Walls

Fear of Charles V Crusade Mounts. City Fortified in All Due Haste.

After the Crusades, Jerusalem's walls lay in ruins until their reconstruction was necessitated by the rivalry between Muslims and Christians in the central Mediterranean.

Leading the opposing forces were two prominent figures—Sultan Suleiman the Magnificent (1520-1566) and Emperor Charles V (1519-1556). In 1535, Charles V set out at the head of a large landing force and occupied Tunis, destroying most of the Turkish fleet in its harbor and liberating thousands of Christian prisoners of war.

Suleiman's advisors panicked. It was common knowledge that Charles V was an avid supporter of the idea of renewing the Crusades. He had even met with the king of France, the Turks' ally, in an attempt to convince him to embark on a new crusade. The Turks feared that Jerusalem, unfortified as it was, would fall easily into his hands, severely damaging Turkey's prestige.

It was decided to fortify the holy city as quickly as possible, and the greatest of Ottoman architects, Sinan Pasha (1490-1588), was rushed to the Holy Land. Over a lifetime of service as the royal master builder, Sinan designed and constructed approximately 360 palaces, mosques, and fortresses—more than any other architect in history.

The reconstruction of the walls began in 1536 and ceased in 1541 before they were completely finished. The external part of each of the defense towers was completed, but the inward-facing sections were left incomplete, as were other details along the wall's circuit.

The project was halted as a result of a shift in the political and military situation. In 1541, Emperor Charles V landed a large military force near the city of Algiers. Winter storms shortly annihilated his fleet. In Istanbul, the opinion that there was no longer anything to fear from the emperor's designs on the Holy Land reigned. The order to stop the construction work was given despite the fact that the wall was almost totally finished.

The Turkish city wall, a reminder of the great achievements of the Ottoman Empire in the sixteenth century, encircles Jerusalem to this day.

Damascus Gate in Jerusalem's wall, by D. Roberts.

King Never Sees City

Emperor Charles V (1519-1556) inherited control of Austria, Bohemia, and various parts of Germany and Switzerland from his father, and was also elected emperor of Germany, thanks to his Hapsburg genealogy. From his mother he inherited the Spanish crown and, through it, dominion over the Netherlands, northern Italy, and the first European-occupied territories on the continent of America.

Charles V also inherited the title "King of Jerusalem," though he never visited the city. It remains unclear whether he ever actually planned to attack the Holy Land and occupy Jerusalem, as was feared in the Turkish capital. In any event, after his defeat in Algiers, Charles completely abandoned both the Mediterranean theater and his war with the Turks.

In following years, Charles V devoted himself to battling the Protestants in Germany, until, at the end of his days, he resigned from all of his political roles, bequeathing them to his son Philip II, and retired to a monastery in Spain.

Mount Zion Left Out in the Cold

The Turks either did not want to or could not assume the expenses connected with including Mount Zion within Jerusalem's walls, despite its strategic importance, and they appealed to the Franciscans for an immense sum so that they would be able to do so. The tight financial situation of the Franciscan monks did not allow them to take on the burden of payment, however, and Mount Zion was stranded outside of Jerusalem's walls.

Apparently, it was not easy for the Turks to forgo incorporating Mount Zion within the

walls, and it may be because of this that the construction of the southern wall was delayed to the last. According to testimony by Father Marcel Ladoire, a French clergyman who was sent to Jerusalem in 1719 to attend to the restoration of the Church of the Holy Sepulcher, rumor had it in Jerusalem that Sultan Suleiman was incensed that Mount Zion and David's Tomb had remained beyond the wall, and had issued an order that the architects who designed it be put to death. Another tradition recounts that the architects' execution was meant to ensure that another wall like Jerusalem's would simply never be built.

Above: According to tradition, the two architects executed by Suleiman were buried here, next to Jaffa Gate.
Left: Mount Zion in an aerial photograph.

Franciscans Arrested in Citadel

Authorities Suspicious of Monks. Catholic Property and Money Confiscated.

The Franciscans acted in Jerusalem as the representatives of papal interests regarding the holy sites—"Custodia de Terra Sancta"—and of European Christians in general. At the beginning of the sixteenth century, only twelve or thirteen monks served in the city's Franciscan monastery, but by the end of the century the number had risen to approximately fifty. The monks came to Jerusalem for three years each, after which time they were replaced. The majority of them came from Sicily, Naples, and Rome, though a few hailed from France and other countries.

The status of the Franciscans in the eyes of the authorities was ambiguous. On the one hand, they had connections with the government of Spain and the pope, and thus appeared seditious to the Ottoman authorities, requiring cautious and restrictive treatment. On the other hand, the monks had close ties with France, Turkey's main ally in Europe, with whom it had signed a capitulation agreement in 1535.

The original Franciscan monastery was established in Jerusalem in the fourteenth century close to the traditional Tomb of David and the room of

1539

The Citadel, also known as David's Tower, by P. Lortet.

the Last Supper above it. The Mamelukes confiscated both sites in the fifteenth century, leaving the Franciscans with the monastery and the Church of Mount Zion. In 1537, when war broke out between Turkey and Venice, the authorities in Istanbul regarded the monks on Mount Zion as a hostile element. The governor of the Jerusalem and Gaza districts,

Mustafa Bey, personally gave orders for their arrest and the confiscation of their movable property. Some of the money taken from the monks was used to finance the reconstruction of Jerusalem's walls.

Nine of the monks died in the Citadel. The rest were held for eighteen months, then set free and allowed to return to their monastery.

Muslim Women Bathe Three Times Weekly

1547

The pleasures of bathing in the East.

The French pharmacist Pierre Belon du Mans, who visited the Holy Land in 1547, was the first European traveler who dedicated his time to research on the country's natural world. His records mention 275 plants by name and contain illustrations of the various species of flora and fauna he observed. Belon was also interested in antiquities: in his writings are to be found the first Western description of the Ba'albek ruins in Lebanon.

Belon du Mans also demonstrated a typical European interest in exotic Easterners. Among other piquant details, he noted that Muslim women bathed three times a week, an insistence on hygiene that was not accepted practice in Western Europe at the time.

Franciscans Banished from Mount Zion

1551

The plan of the Turkish wall, which left Mount Zion and the Franciscan monastery outside of Jerusalem, worsened the Franciscans' plight, as the Turks began to fear that their monastery could be used as a base for a Christian military offensive against Jerusalem. In 1551 the monks were banished from their home and forced to take up residence in a shabby edifice near the room of the Last Supper.

According to Spanish pilgrim Juan Perera, who visited Jerusalem two years later, the Turks and the local Arabs had gradually taken over the Franciscan monastery and converted it into a mosque. Perera stayed with the displaced Franciscans: during the night they succeeded in bribing the guards, who allowed them to enter the monastery and visit the room of the Last Supper.

Mount Zion. A detail from an early-sixteenth-century map by C. Adrichom.

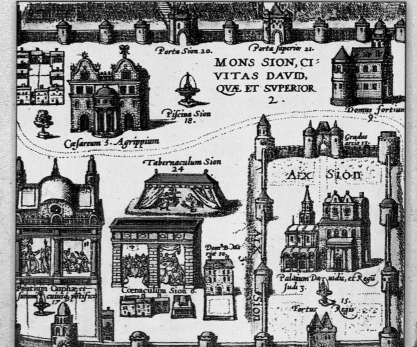

Catholic Priest Cautions: Don't Speak Spanish in Safed

1552

In the mid-sixteenth century, when a state of war existed between Spain and the Turkish empire, Spanish travelers to the Holy Land often attempted to hide their origins. Usually they pretended to be French, as France was an ally of the Turks.

In the north of the Holy Land, especially in the city of Safed, lived many Jews who had been expelled from the Iberian Peninsula, and Spanish travelers often entered into conversation with them in their native tongue. Juan Perera, a Spanish Catholic priest who visited the Holy Land in 1552, cau-

tioned against this practice, since it could reveal the traveler's origin to the Turks.

A description of Perera's trip is extant in two versions; one in Latin and one in Spanish. Since they are similar but not identical (and in the Latin version the author's name is missing), one cannot be certain that they were composed by the same man. One explanation for the discrepancies is that the two accounts were written by two travelers who were partners on a trip in the Holy Land but not on the voyages to and from the country.

Von Seydlitz Seized and Taken Hostage

Melchior von Seydlitz, a German nobleman from Silesia, visited the Holy Land in 1556. On the way from Jerusalem to Jaffa, he and his traveling companions were arrested by the Turks on suspicion that they were connected to an attack by Maltese pirates on a village near Jaffa during which seventy people had been kidnaped.

Seydlitz records that the local inhabitants appealed to the governor of Ramla in tears, claiming vociferously that Christians had taken their women and children and demanding that Seydlitz and his companions be kept as hostages until their relations were restored to their families.

The group was incarcerated in the Ramla prison. As was usual in such cases, the prisoners appealed for help to the Franciscan representa-tive in Jerusalem. Unfortunately, he refused to come to their assistance, saying that Lutheran infidels were among the prisoners. After several months in the Ramla prison, Seydlitz's group was transferred to Damascus in shackles. An exhausting trip, it nevertheless enabled Seydlitz to see Samaria and Galilee. In Samaria, he noted, large houses from days past stood along the road, empty of inhabitants. The Greek and Latin letters on their walls testified that they had been built by Christians when they ruled in the Holy Land.

From Damascus, Seydlitz and his friends were moved to Istanbul, where they remained in prison for two years, coming close to being sold as slaves. They were liberated in 1559.

A convoy of prisoners, by M. von Seydlitz.

Franciscans Purchase San Salvador Monastery

The Franciscans, compelled to leave Mount Zion, where they had been in residence since 1335, appealed to the Turkish authorities to install them in the Georgian monastery at the northeast corner of the city. They justified their request by pointing out that the Georgians had seven other monasteries in Jerusalem and that no great harm would be done to the small sect should it be required to relinquish one.

The Turkish authorities, softened by French gifts, found the Franciscan request justified and forced the Georgians to sell the monastery to the

The ancient jars of San Salvador's pharmacy.

Inside San Salvador's library.

Franciscans. After all, if the Franciscans were deprived of a place of their own they would be forced to move to Bethlehem, and would be unable to host pilgrims to the holy city. Were European visitors to be drawn away from Jerusalem, it would ultimately be the Turkish coffers that would suffer. The Franciscans bought the monastery from the Georgians in 1559 for 1,200 gold coins.

The monks were well pleased with their new monastery, which was located within the city walls and provided them with better protection from Muslim machinations. They retired the old name of the monastery and dubbed their new home "San Salvador" instead. The head of the order, however, continued to be called the Guardian of Mount Zion.

Both Catholic and Protestant pilgrims stayed at the San Salvador Monastery, which was famous for its progressive services. The monastery had a school where youths studied religion, manners, and a trade; a large central library and three smaller libraries; a hospital where pilgrims and local dignitaries received medical care; and a well-stocked pharmacy. The most famous item sold at the pharmacy was Jerusalem balsam, which was used as a treatment for various illnesses.

1,300 Christians Pay Taxes in Jerusalem

The Christian population in the Holy Land was concentrated mainly in the Jerusalem district. Most of the residents of Bethlehem and Beit Jala were Christians, the majority of whom belonged to the Greek Orthodox sect. There were also Christians in a few villages in the Gaza and Nablus districts, in Ramla, Transjordan, and Galilee.

In the mid-sixteenth century, 1,300 taxpaying Christians resided in Jerusalem: 557 Greek Orthodox, 216 Armenians, 176 Copts, and 92 Syrians. In addition, monks from the Franciscan and other orders dwelt in the city.

In 1519, the Swiss traveler Ludwig Tschudi had reported that the majority of the Greek Orthodox Christians in the Holy Land spoke Arabic and were

A Maronite monk in Jerusalem, by L. Mayer.

similar to the Muslims in their customs. According to Tschudi, their priests married and their faces were adorned with long, bushy beards. He also mentioned the Russian Orthodox, detailing the differences between their customs and those of the Greek Orthodox. He emphasized the good relationship between the Copts and the Catholics, as well as the hatred between the Armenians and the Greeks. In 1579, the traveler Jacob Breuning noted the presence of Nestorian, Syrian, and Maronite Christians in Jerusalem.

The naturalist Leonhart Rauchwolff claimed in 1575 that there were common theological points between the Armenians and the Protestants. He tried to speak to the Ethiopians through an interpreter, and praised them in his text: the rest of the Eastern sects he regarded as unbelievers.

New Medicinal Herbs Discovered

In 1575, Leonhart Rauchwolff, a German physician and plant researcher, visited the Holy Land.

Once the city doctor of Augsburg, Rauchwolff had been forced to move to Linz, Austria as a result of conflicts between Protestants and Catholics in his native town.

Rauchwolff set off for the East on behalf of his brother-in-law, whose business involved trade between Marseilles and the Levant. Rauchwolff's mission was to discover new medicinal herbs. In one of the more interesting sections of his book, he describes sailing in a ship on the Euphrates, disguised as a local merchant so as not to arouse the suspicion of the Bedouin. Later he was to visit the Holy Land.

Rauchwolff brought back about two hundred plants from his trip. They are kept to this day at the University of Leiden in Holland. Thirty-three of the species he described were considered in Europe to be scientific discoveries, and the appendix to his book includes drawings of many of them. After his death, the plant *Rauwollia* was named after him; in 1952, CIBA, the giant Swiss pharmaceutical company, extracted the drug Reserpin from it.

A specimen drawing by L. Rauchwolff.

Schweigger Draws Holy Land

Jerusalem, by S. Schweigger.

Salomon Schweigger was a German Protestant priest who set out for Istanbul with the Austrian ambassador to Turkey. Once there, he worked to strengthen his ties with the heads of the Greek Orthodox Church, which opposed the pope and the Catholic Church, as did he.

In 1581 Schweigger embarked on an extended tour of the Holy Land and Egypt. His travelogue, published twenty years after his return from the voyage, is illustrated with the many sketches he made in the course his travels. They depict the customs of the local inhabitants, their dress, eating habits, games, methods of punishment, and military parades.

A Turkish horseman and a *qadi*, by S. Schweigger.

Prince Radzivill Infiltrates David's Tomb

The frontispiece of Prince Radzivill's book.

The Polish prince Nicolai Christopher Radzivill was the scion of a distinguished Polish family. A relative of his even married one of the kings of Poland. The prince, upon having been cured of a serious illness, vowed to make a pilgrimage to Jerusalem, but was forced to delay his departure until 1583 since the Polish king would allow him to set out on the journey only after he had participated in the ongoing Polish wars. Radzivill's education, befitting a prince, is reflected in his descriptions of his travels.

While staying in Jerusalem Prince Radzivill disguised himself as a monk-pharmacist and succeeded in penetrating David's Tomb (then serving as a mosque), entrance to which was forbidden to non-Muslims. Apparently, he was also the first Christian to make it all the way to the top of Mount Hermon.

Upon his return to his homeland, Radzivill was first appointed head of the Polish court and then governor of two Polish duchies. His family continued to maintain its prominent social rank in following generations: one of his descendants married Jacqueline Kennedy's sister.

Pilgrims kissing the ground of the Holy Land, by H. Wölffli.

Belgian Mayor Visits Jerusalem

1586

Johann Zuallart, the son of an eminent Belgian family who served as a mayor in his homeland, arrived in Jerusalem in 1586. Though he spent only twelve days in the Holy Land, he managed to sketch Jerusalem a number of times.

Zuallart's resulting travel book was very successful, and was translated into several other languages. His illustrations, even more popular than his book, were copied by other travelers without reference to the source. Among them was the first modern map of Jerusalem, itself lifted by Zuallart from the map of a Franciscan monk, Antonio degli Angeli.

Viri Galilaei and the Church of the Ascension on the summit of the Mount of Olives, by J. Zuallart.

Holy Land Hostels Not Fit for Humans

1598

The Dutchman Johann van Cootwijck did not hesitate to candidly express his feelings when forced to spend the night at a Nablus khan. According to the record he left, the caravansary was falling to pieces. Its dirt floor was strewn with pig excrement, its roof leaked, and there were no windows or doors that could be closed at night. The terrible stench was practically unbearable. As far as van Cootwijck was concerned, the place was not worthy even of the name hostel.

Van Cootwijck should perhaps be considered the father of archaeological research in the Holy Land. While he did not actually carry out excavations, he was the first to express interest in the country's antiquities, and he described them relatively accurately. During his visit to Jerusalem he examined the Jehoshaphat Valley and the Ecce Homo Arch, described the remains of the Antonia tower, and conducted a complete survey of the Tombs of the Kings. Van Cootwijck also penned a profile of the ruins of ancient Samaria and copied an early Greek inscription that he found in Nablus.

The Tombs of the Kings in Jerusalem, by L. Mayer.

Stopping for the night at Khan el-Bireh (the biblical Be'erot).

Morison: Turks Drug Soldiers with Opium

1596

Fynes Morison was a member of a wealthy English family. His father was a member of the House of Commons and he himself was a graduate of Cambridge University.

Morison arrived in the Holy Land in 1596 to find adverse conditions and an oppressive regime. He recounted that the Turks pumped their soldiers full of opium in order to instill in them a fighting spirit. Even stranger, he claimed the authorities supplied their camels with opium too.

As were all other pilgrims, Morison was required to leave his weapons in Venice so as to avoid an armed confrontation with Muslims in the Holy Land. During their stay, he and his traveling companions assumed Eastern dress in hopes of reducing the chances of being held up by Bedouin.

Morison complained that he had to fear not only the Bedouin but his Franciscan hosts as well: he recounted an episode involving six English and Dutch Protestant pilgrims, some of whom had been taken sick and others who had been injured in a brawl. According to Morison's testimony, instead of proffering them medical aid, the Franciscans let the pilgrims die, even hastening the process by poisoning them.

Franciscans and Greek Orthodox Clash Over Holy Places

Church of Holy Sepulcher and Church of Nativity Change Hands. Greek Orthodox Patriarch Moves to Jerusalem. French Apply Pressure to Turks.

In the seventeenth and eighteenth centuries, the Franciscans and the Greek Orthodox wrestled for control of the holy sites in Jerusalem and Bethlehem. In 1605, the Greek Orthodox solidified their grip on the northern portion of the rock of Golgotha in the Church of the Holy Sepulcher, after which the conflict revolved around the proprietorship of the Stone of the Anointing, the arches on the northern and western sides of the rotunda, and in Jerusalem as well as the Church of the Nativity and its gardens in Bethlehem.

The Greek Orthodox sect became the dominant Christian entity in the whole of the Holy Land. In the 1650s, its stature was such that it managed to gain control over the property of the Ethiopian Church and temporarily evict the Armenians from the Monastery of Saint James.

The second round between the Fran-

Above: The Franciscan cloister in the Church of the Nativity.
Left: The Catholicon—the Greek Orthodox prayer hall in the Church of the Holy Sepulcher, by D. Roberts.

ciscans and the Greeks took place at the end of the seventeenth century. The Ottoman Empire, which had suffered losses to Austria, was in need of France's help. As part of the accord, the French ambassador to Istanbul demanded that a new *firman* be issued, returning to the Franciscans their rights to the holy places. In the edict published by Suleiman II in 1690, the Catholics regained control over Stone of the Anointing, the arches in the rotunda, half of Golgotha, two domes, and the Chapel of the True Cross in the Church of the Holy Sepulcher, as well as the Grotto of the Nativity and the gardens at the Church of the Nativity in Bethlehem.

the northern portion of the Crusader church.

A war was also waged over the keys to the Grotto of the Nativity in the Church of the Nativity in Bethlehem. The keys were held by the Franciscans, and the Greek Orthodox, who comprised the largest Christian sect in Jerusalem and were directly subordinate to the Ottoman government, considered themselves the victims of discrimination. In 1631, the Greek Orthodox patriarch of Jerusalem, who had lived until that time in Istanbul, moved to Jerusalem, where he embarked on an intensive campaign to bribe the governors and *qadis* of the city to transfer supervision of the holy places to the Greek Orthodox. After six years of disputes and schemes, Sultan Murad IV published a definitive *firman* (preceded by eleven such decrees, each contradicting the other) giving the Greek Orthodox authority over the Church of the Holy Sepulcher

Christian Prays at Temple Mount Mosque

Johann Wild, a German mercenary who was taken prisoner and sold into slavery, visited the Temple Mount and prayed at the site of Solomon's Temple in 1608. He was one of the first Europeans to describe the mosques and precinct of the Temple Mount, which were off-limits to Christians and Jews on pain of death. Wild, accompanying his Muslim masters on their travels, also visited Mecca and Medina, the Muslim holy cities.

In 1516, a Maronite Christian disguised as an Arab had been caught on the Temple Mount and forced to convert to Islam in order to save himself from execution. In 1539 a Greek bishop had stolen into the complex escorted by a few Muslims, but they betrayed him and he was put to death. In 1557, the *qadi* of Jerusalem had himself executed a Sicilian monk discovered in the holy compound. At the end of the sixteenth century, a Christian Spanish woman who had entered the forbidden area was condemned to death, and in 1599 a Spanish monk was burned to death for the same offense.

Despite the fact that he refutes the charge in his book, Wild probably converted to Islam and was only thus allowed to enter the Temple Mount. He participated in prayer at the mosque in the precinct, though he claims that in his heart he prayed to God, not Allah. He reports that the walls of the mosque were decorated with alabas-

Johann Wild.

ter stones on which Arabic inscriptions were written in gold. On the floor were embroidered rugs, and hundreds of lamps hung from the ceiling. Ornate tomes lay on lecterns standing throughout the mosque.

Wild moved with his masters from Jerusalem to Cairo, where after several years he was allowed to purchase his freedom.

Franciscan Monk on the Temple Mount

Jean Boucher at prayer.

In his book *Le Bouquet Sacre* (The Holy Bouquet), the Franciscan monk Jean Boucher chronicles two interesting escapades from his visit to the Holy Land. As his ship sailed northwards along the Holy Land's coast, Boucher espied the vessels of Muslim pirates from North Africa commanded by Barbarossa ("Red Beard"), a Christian convert to Islam.

Panic gripped the ship. Its passengers and crew escaped to the port of Haifa and hid among the ancient ruins of the city, home to only dogs, ravens, snakes, and lizards at the time. Having eluded the pirates, they feared leaving their hiding places and falling into the hands of highway robbers, and only after twenty-four hours did they dare return to the ship and set sail for nearby Acre.

Boucher's adventures did not end there. In 1612, while the Frenchman was staying in Jerusalem, the mufti of the city, who resided in the Temple Mount complex, fell ill. Since the two local Muslim doctors were absent, the medic from the Franciscan monastery was asked to care for the mufti. Boucher took advantage of the opportunity, and after promising the Franciscans that no harm would befall them, accompanied the physician as his assistant.

The fanatic guards of the Temple Mount, by C. de Bruyn.

Boucher and the doctor left the monastery accompanied by two translators, the head of the dervishes, two servants, and two Janissaries.

Boucher reports conflicting feelings of fear and joy; joy upon seeing the rare treasures of the forbidden precinct, and fear that he and his companion would be harmed. As the latter treated his patient, Boucher took the opportunity to survey the Haram al-Sharif (Temple Mount) area from the window of the apartment. Afterwards, a dervish led the visitors to a small vestibule, where for half an hour Boucher was allowed to gaze out over the entire Temple Mount complex. In his book, he includes a detailed description of everything he saw.

When they left the Temple Mount, about thirty men who had noted their entrance to the holy place gathered near the gate. They threatened Boucher and his entourage, pointing at them with daggers and calling them dogs, pigs, infidels, and wicked men who had defiled the holy place. The group was rescued by its escorts and returned unharmed to the monastery.

Bare-Bottomed Scotsman Beholds Bedouin Attack

Travelogues were usually written by members of the upper class or the educated middle class. The Scotsman William Lithgow, who visited the Holy Land in 1612, was one of the exceptions. A member of the lower class, he wrote in a crude and simple style. In his book's forward he informs potential critics of his book, especially Catholics, that he wishes the hangman's rope for them. Finding it difficult to recall the names of the places he visited, Lithgow made up nicknames for them, apparently relying upon the ignorance of his readers. Despite some glaring faults, his book was a best-seller that came out in a dozen editions and was sold for over two hundred years.

Lithgow set out on his journey after being caught in flagrante delicto by the brother of one of his mistresses, who cut off both of his ears as a warning. He paid for the cost of his trip in various bizarre ways. On his way from Holy Land to northern Egypt, for example, he befriended six Germans: coincidentally, three of them died of thirst on the road, and the other three met the same fate after a four-day drinking bout. Lithgow inherited their money—420 pounds sterling, a hefty sum in those days.

Lithgow later witnessed an attack along the River Jordan, when a group with whom he was traveling was set upon by Bedouin. The bandits failed to notice Lithgow, who had just returned from a swim in the river and was about a quarter mile from the party. Lithgow, who heard the shots and saw the struggle, fled naked, carrying with him only his head covering and his staff. When he subsequently tried to rejoin the party, one of the soldiers accompanying the group wanted to kill him as punishment for having abandoned them. Lithgow eluded him by hiding among the pilgrims. The leader of the Franciscans gave him a leather shirt so that he could cover

William Lithgow.

himself, and the commander of the pilgrim party finally succeeded in calming the furious Arabs with promises of payment.

Franciscans Make a Play for Ein Karem Church

From the fourteenth century onward, the Franciscans attempted to regain control over the holy places in Ein Karem, traveling once a week from Jerusalem to hold ceremonies there. In the fifteenth century they even cleaned and renovated the Crusader church several times, though they were repeatedly forced to relinquish the structure to the local Arabs, who used it as a vegetable market and a pen for livestock.

In 1621, the Franciscans finally managed to gain a foothold in the church, whose purification and refurbishment entailed much labor and great expense. The monks took up residence in the building, but after several months were compelled to return it to the Arabs, who once again turned it into a barn.

The Church of Saint John the Baptist in Ein Karem, by C. de Bruyn.

Sharp Rise in Number of French Pilgrims

In Catholic countries, especially France, the age of the Counter-Reformation brought with it a renewed religious fervor that caused a sharp rise in the number of seventeenth century pilgrims. The French pilgrims, many of whom were monks and clergy, wrote the majority of travel books in this period.

Fahr al-Din Gives Grotto of Annunciation to Christians

1620

Fahr al-Din was known for his good relations with Christians. When he conquered Nazareth, he collected only a modest head tax from the Christian community there and in 1620 even transferred the Grotto of the Annunciation to the authority of the Franciscan monks, allowing them to build a church and monastery on the spot.

The construction of the monastery and church took thirty years and contributed much to the development of Nazareth and its holy sites. As the village grew, the number of Christian inhabitants there gradually increased. At first, Maronite Christian families came from Lebanon, and later a Greek Orthodox family arrived with its own priest. The Franciscans, pleased with the newcomers, allowed the Greek Orthodox to pray in the grotto above Mary's Spring.

Above: Fahr al-Din, by E. Roger.
Right: The Grotto of the Annunciation, by D. Roberts.

Second Attempt to Navigate Siloam Tunnel Fails

Operation Foiled by Extinguished Candle. Monks Make It Through Entire Tunnel 50 Years Later.

1626

Francesco Quaresmio, one of the most important Franciscan researchers of the history of Jerusalem and its surroundings, was in the Holy Land from 1616 to 1626 and wrote a huge book of about 2,000 folio pages. Though his account deals primarily with the history of the Holy Land, Quaresmio occasionally touches upon contemporaneous events.

The Siloam Tunnel was dug in 701 BC during the days of King Hezekiah in order to connect the Gihon Spring—called "the Virgin's Spring" by European Christians—to the Siloam Pool in an attempt to ensure the supply of water to Jerusalem during wartime. According to Quaresmio, at the beginning of the seventeenth century a monk named Julius succeeded in negotiating the length of the tunnel. Later, a friend of

Above: Jerusalem from the Mount of Olives, by F. Quaresmio.
Left: The Pool of Siloam, by L. Mayer.

Francesco's failed in an attempt to repeat the feat.

Quaresmio's friend started out at the Virgin's Spring. Crawling on all fours, he was at times forced to prostrate himself completely in order to progress along the tunnel. When his candle flickered out, he was unable to rekindle it, and crawled back to exit the tunnel soaked and filthy. The following day he made a second attempt from the Siloam Pool at the lower mouth of the tunnel, but was again stymied.

Only in 1674, many years after Quaresmio wrote his book, did two Franciscan monks succeed in forcing a passage through the tunnel. According to the description they left, fallen stones had almost completely blocked the passage.

Carmelites Back on Mount Carmel
Prosper Builds Monastery in Mountain Tunnels.

Jerusalem and Bethlehem were the principle objectives of most pilgrims, but not all. For the Carmelite monks, Mount Carmel was the primary destination in the Holy Land.

The Carmelite Order was founded during the Crusades. Its first monastery was built on the western portion of Mount Carmel, but abandoned at the end of the thirteenth century when the Carmelites moved to Europe, where they established numerous monasteries. At the beginning of the seventeenth century the Carmelites considered returning to the Carmel, and in 1629 the monk Filippo della S.S. Trinita visited Mt. Carmel, not even bothering to journey to Jerusalem and Bethlehem. His travel book contains a description of the mountain and the remains of the old monastery.

Two years later, the heads of the order dispatched another monk, by the name of Prosper, to organize the monastery's revival, and he managed to arrive at an agreement with the local authorities. In 1634 Prosper was sent to the Holy Land a second time to reestablish the monastery in the tunnels beneath the crest of the mountain. In following generations the monastery was known as "Prosper's Monastery"; it survived for 130 years.

The monastery on Mount Carmel in a photograph from 1887.

Higher Power Saves Monk Bernardin Surius

The Belgian monk Bernardin Surius arrived in the Holy Land in 1644 for a stay of four years. He traveled throughout the Holy Land, visiting Tyre, Sidon, Acre, Haifa, Sepphoris, Nazareth, Tiberias, Galilee, Safed, Ramla, Hebron, the Dead Sea, and many other places and sites. A comprehensive description of his journey was published in 1664.

On his return voyage to Europe, Surius' ship was approached at great speed by three large Turkish pirate vessels. The Corsairs had departed Algeria three days previously with 75 cannons and 425 armed Turks on board— Surius' ship held only 30 people and 4 cannons.

The ship's passengers, believing their fate was to be either death or slavery, began to sink into despair. The officers, nonplused by the encounter with the pirates, could only pray to a merciful higher power for a wind blowing in a favorable direction. And indeed, the wind suddenly rose, sending the ship scuttling away from the Turks. With the assistance of the elements, Surius' vessel arrived within range of the cannons of the city of Sciacca on the coast of Sicily, and was saved.

An aerial photograph of Sepphoris.

Christians Permitted to Return to Mount Tabor

In 1631, the emir Fahr al-Din allowed the Franciscans to return to Mount Tabor. In 1644 the order received additional permission to erect a church and monastery on the spot, but was forced to relinquish such plans in the face of opposition by Muslims who blocked up the entrance to the church in an effort to eject the Franciscans from the site.

The French traveler Jean Doubdan, who visited Mount Tabor in 1652, testified that the place was full of refuse. His record also depicts three partially destroyed chapels, one of which contained an altar.

The chapel on Mount Tabor, by J. Doubdan.

Greeks and Armenians Defend Franciscan Monastery

Jerusalem Governor Recruits 6,000 Peasants to Destroy Monastery and Murder Monks

The governor of Jerusalem.

The Franciscan monk Electus Zwinner, who resided in Jerusalem from 1651, recounts in his book how the governor of the holy city conspired against the Franciscan monastery, only to be foiled by a miracle.

In 1652 the governor promised gifts to 6,000 peasants if they would kill the city's *qadi*, monks, and major merchants, as well as fall upon a Christian convoy as it made its way back from the River Jordan. The peasants assembled in Solomon's Stables and prepared to stone the *qadi*, but he sought refuge in his palace. The peasants, turning their anger on the Franciscan monastery, were determined to loot it, raze the building, and massacre the monks.

The monastery and its inhabitants were saved by the unexpected help of the Greek Orthodox, Armenians, and other Christians in the city, who though they were usually enemies of the Franciscans, set out against the attackers and stoned them. Fortunately for the Christians, none of the peasants was seriously hurt, since if they had been the Catholics would have been in great danger of retaliation by the authorities. According to Zwinner, hundreds of people with burning eyes and bright swords had appeared to the rioters at the monastery, and they had run away in a panic.

The riots continued for four days until help came in the form of the governor of Gaza, an old friend of the Franciscans who had just been appointed governor of Jerusalem.

1666
Von Troilo's Holy Land Adventures
Twice Saved from Bedouin Robbers, Twice Captured by Pirates

Franz Ferdinand von Troilo, a minor German aristocrat who arrived in the Holy Land in 1666, seems to have had more adventures than all of the other writers of Holy Land travelogues put together.

On his way from Ramla to Jaffa, von Troilo was set upon by a band of robbers. The two Turkish soldiers who were supposed to be guarding the convoy fled, and he and his translator fell into the hands of the bandits, who made do with eating all of the party's food.

Another time, von Troilo joined a large convoy of Armenian pilgrims on its way from Jerusalem to Damascus. Near Jenin, their march was halted by Bedouin from the Turbai tribe, whose emir demanded a ransom of six piasters for each of the members of the convoy. When they refused, he ordered sixty of the company's most distinguished members whipped. The Armenians capitulated; every one of the 1,200 Christians in the convoy paid the required amount, and were then allowed to continue on their way.

The Armenians were attacked again near the customshouse at the Benot Ya'acov Bridge over the Jordan. Von Troilo relates that as dawn broke, the surrounding hills blackened with spear-wielding Arab horsemen. Other riders had amassed around the customshouse, and they galloped in all directions, making sport with their spears. Von Troilo notes that he had never seen such beautiful horses nor such ugly and cruel riders. Many of the latter wore only swatches of fabric over their chests. Instead of saddles, they used rough goatskins. They shoved their way among the members of the convoy, gnashed their teeth, and threatened to beat the travelers.

The terrified Christians, encircled by a thousand armed Arabs, capitulated without a peep. Their weapons were taken from them, as was their money. Those who did not have the required sum were stripped to their underclothes. Von Troilo was lucky—his Arab escort knew one of the attackers and succeeded in extricating himself and von Troilo from the attack unscathed.

Von Troilo's adventures did not soon come to an end: he fell twice into pirates' hands. The first time was in 1668, when he sailed south from Alexandria to Tripoli. On the ship was a group of boys and girls who had been

A Barbary pirate, by P.F. Mola.

taken captive by the Tatars in Russia and bought by the ship's captain in the Istanbul slave market. The captain arrested von Troilo in hopes of adding him to the slave shipment, but at the port of Tripoli von Troilo managed to extricate himself with the help of an acquaintance who was the secretary of one of the local consuls.

The second incident occurred during von Troilo's passage from the island of Malta to Europe, when his ship was attacked by three frigates of Muslim pirates from North Africa. Von Troilo and his friends defended themselves at great peril, killing many of the attackers in the process. Though the first two attacks were repelled, upon the third the pirates succeeded in boarding and taking control of the ship. Troilo sustained a head injury and part of his ear was torn off. Those who were badly wounded and had no chance of survival were bound by the pirates and decapitated with the slice of a sword.

Von Troilo was taken to the port of Algiers and sold as a slave for the embarrassingly low price of 20 tallers. His purchaser treated him well in order to make the most of his investment, and then sold him for 350 tallers. In 1670 von Troilo by chance met yet another old friend, who ransomed him for a reasonable sum, allowing him to return home.

1674
Renovation Work in Ein Karem Monastery Completed

Local Inhabitants React Violently. Monks Shell Out Cash to Keep Them Quiet.

In 1674 the Franciscans once again finagled permission to live in the church in Ein Karem, and members of the order have resided there continuously since that time. But the reinstallation of the Christians in Ein Karem aroused the wrath of its Arab inhabitants, and approximately two years after the monks took up residence, riots erupted. In order to quell the disturbances, the pasha of Jerusalem expelled the monks from Ein Karem, and only with great effort did they secure the sultan's leave to make yet another comeback at the site.

Over the following years, the monks purchased the houses adjacent to the monastery, enlarging their property. They also erected a wall around the monastery to aid in defending themselves against attacks by local Muslims. In 1694, the restoration of the church was completed and new wings added to the monastery. At the time, the Church of Saint John the Baptist was considered the most ornate Franciscan church in the Holy Land.

In 1699, dozens of Arabs broke into the church, pulverized everything in their path, and beat the monks. The *qadi* of Jerusalem agreed to mediate between the sides in return for payment, but within the month riots convulsed the spot again. The *qadi*, playing the role of go-between for the second time, demanded that the monks pay the locals a large sum of

The Grotto of the Nativity of John the Baptist *(above)* and the Church of Saint John the Baptist *(left)* in Ein Karem.

Pirating Pays: Sea Scourges Pocket 300,000 Tallers in 6 Months

Otto Friedrich de Gröben.

At the age of eighteen, the Prussian Otto Friedrich de Gröben joined the Maltese pirates in order to earn enough money to set out on a journey to the East and the Holy Land.

De Gröben relates that the Order of the Knights of Malta had twenty-four ships at its disposal. While the vessels did not belong to the Maltese order, in exchange for the right to fly the order's flag their owners paid it one tenth of their booty, accepted upon themselves the order's discipline, and rendered it assistance when necessary.

Among the shipowners were many Knights of Malta as well as wealthy mariners and regular citizens. Often, three four or five knights would get together, invest 50,000 tallers, and buy a ship. They would outfit it with rifles, ammunition, and provisions, man it with soldiers and experienced seafarers, and obtain the order's permission to fly its flag. The ships would set out for the Mediterranean, where they would lay in wait for Turkish vessels. Frequently, a fleet of five or six pirate ships invaded Turkish-held territory, kidnaping men, women, children, sheep, and anything else of value. It sometimes happened that the pirate ships were disabled by the Turks and their crews taken captive.

According to de Gröben, with a bit of luck a pirate could earn between 200,000 to 300,000 tallers in half a year. Though many of the knights become wealthy in this manner, others lost all of their property.

Within a year, de Gröben earned enough to continue on his travels to the Holy Land, which he reached in 1675. As luck would have it, on his way home he was taken prisoner by Maltese pirates. The fact that he had served with them previously was apparently meaningless, and for six months the young Prussian was forced to participate in pirating sallies without receiving a share of the profits.

A naval battle between Turkish and Venetian ships. A Venetian woodcut from the sixteenth century.

De Bruyn Paints the Holy Land

Cornelius de Bruyn was a Dutch painter who made his living by journeying to distant places and capturing their land- and city-scapes in his work. Upon his return home he would publish his paintings in huge volumes accompanied by textual descriptions of the sites. The first serious artist to pursue such a vocation, de Bruyn was not to inspire an heir until the nineteenth century. His paintings, equal in descriptive value to many volumes of written records, depict the streets of Jerusalem and Bethlehem as they were in the seventeenth century. De Bruyn visited the Holy Land in 1679, painting many of its cities and holy sites. A few years ago, when archaeologists began to dig in the courtyard of Acre's fortress, they used one of de Bruyn's books to locate a staircase the artist had portrayed three hundred years previously.

Above: Cornelius de Bruyn's portrait; the staircase in Acre's fortress today.
Left: The same staircase in C. de Bruyn's painting.

Greek Orthodox and Armenian Dispute Delays Holy Fire Ceremony

Qadi Orders Joint Ceremony. Excited Masses Throng to Obtain Holy Fire, Ignoring Cudgels of Turkish Soldiers.

According to the testimony of Henry Maundrell, in 1697 the Ceremony of the Holy Fire at the Church of the Holy Sepulcher was delayed as a result of an attempt by the Greek Orthodox to prevent Armenian participation.

Maundrell was an Oxford-educated priest who had become embroiled in a love affair. In order to extricate him, his family sent him to serve as priest to English merchants operating out of Aleppo, Syria. He set out in 1697 on a journey to Jerusalem with the inten-

tion of writing a book that would help him advance, and kept a detailed diary for two years. His book became the biggest best-seller of all the travel books written in English until the nineteenth century, though Maundrell did not enjoy its success, as he died of an illness at the age of thirty-six.

According to Maundrell, the Greek Orthodox and the Armenians brought their dispute to the *qadi*, who ruled that they must hold a joint ceremony, as in previous years. The Greek Ortho-

dox set out first in a procession around the Holy Tomb, and immediately after them came the Armenians. Thus they encircled the tomb three times, wearing sumptuous robes and carrying crosses and flags. At the procession's conclusion, a dove flew

Above: The Turkish *qadi*.
Left: The patriarch brings out the Holy Fire.

to the dome of the church, at which a great cry escaped from the mouths of the celebrants. According to Maundrell, the Catholics claimed that the dove was sent to symbolize the descent of the Holy Spirit.

After the procession, the Greek Orthodox deputy patriarch and the Armenian bishop entered the chapel where the annual miracle of the sparking of the Holy Fire occurred. When they emerged with burning torches, the masses crowded around them, jostling each other in order to be the first to light their candles with the Holy Fire. Though Turkish guards struck them with clubs, the excited believers apparently did not feel the blows. Those who managed to get hold of a flame brought it close to their faces and chests in order to demonstrate that it was not real fire, though Maundrell noted that they could not do so for long. Torches and candles were lit on all sides until the church galleries looked as if they were going up in flames.

Three Christian Hostels in Jaffa

Michael Eneman, the priest of the Swedish embassy in Istanbul who was sent on a journey to the Holy Land in 1712 by Charles XII, king of Sweden, later composed a description of the ruins of Jaffa's impressive walls.

Eneman noted that on a hill by the sea was a small square fortress that did not strike him as very strong. It was equipped with four or five cannons that were fired from time to time to frighten the Bedouin.

According to Eneman, Turks and Christians lived around the fortress. The Turks collected taxes on imported goods of three percent of the merchandise's value. The customs officer and the governor billeted a force of 120 troops in the fortress.

Eneman further relates that the Franciscans ran a small pilgrims' hostel opposite the sea, and had at their disposal one or two translators who took care of collecting taxes from the travelers. The Greek Orthodox likewise maintained a modest house across from the Franciscan hostel, and the Armenians boasted the biggest Christian hostel in town. Travelers usually sojourned at hostels until they made arrangements to leave with a convoy for Jerusalem.

Eneman, a specialist in Oriental studies familiar with the languages of the region, wrote a comprehensive and important work about the situa- ▶

Imaginary Jaffa, by O. Dapper, 1677.

tion in the Holy Land that was never published in full. A short excerpt of it was printed in 1740, and in 1889 a fairly large book was published including much, but not all, of the work.

Eneman was not the only emissary sent to the Holy Land by Charles XII. The Swedish monarch (1697-1718) had ascended the throne at the age of sixteen only to be immediately attacked by Denmark, Poland, and Russia. Much to their surprise, the boy king defeated the three countries and set out on a tour of conquests that extended to Central Europe. Charles was finally defeated by the Russian czar Peter the Great and exiled to Turkey. While there, he succeeded in causing a rift between the Ottomans and Russia, eventually bringing about a war between the two empires.

The young king had plans of his own, of course, and he dispatched three officers to the Holy Land, headed by Colonel Cornelius Loos. They returned with detailed reports of the Holy Land and its fortifications accompanied by drawings and sketches. After their return, relations cooled between Charles XII and the Turks until actual battle erupted between the two camps in 1713, when the king and his comrades in exile defended their quarters with swords against a Turkish attack. Charles' rooms went

up in flames, taking with them most of the reports and drawings his officers had brought from the Holy Land. (A few, including the first political map of the region, survived, eventually making its way to the Swedish national archives.) In 1715 Charles sent the archbishop of Sweden on a journey to the Holy Land, and a few of his letters have also been preserved.

Charles was killed during an attempt to conquer Norway in 1718.

Jaffa, by H.B. Tristram.

Apparently, his subjects had had their fill of unceasing war—the bullet was probably fired from the Swedish side.

1719

Church of Holy Sepulcher's Dome Repaired
Despite Cupola's Disrepair, Strong Opposition from Christian Sects.
Mufti of Jerusalem Tries to Murder Ladoire.

In 1719, Marcel Ladoire, a clergyman sent by the French court to attend to the repair of the dome of the Church of the Holy Sepulcher, arrived in Jerusalem.

The condition of the church's cupola was such that it was in imminent danger of collapse. The Turks took advantage of the opportunity to make

work on the church conditional upon the liberation of five hundred Muslim prisoners of war who were currently toiling as oarsmen on French ships. During the course of negotiations, the French haggled the number of liberated slaves down to 150.

The consent of the Turkish authorities did not completely clear the way

The renovated dome of the Church of the Holy Sepulcher, by L. Mayer.

however. In those days, though the Catholics held the senior position in the Church of the Holy Sepulcher, the Greek Orthodox, the Armenians, and other small sects also wielded rights in the church. As it happened, the

Greek Orthodox vehemently opposed the renovation, fearing that the project would augment the influence of the Catholics within the holy site. The mufti of Jerusalem also opposed the repairs, as did the dervishes from Hebron, who claimed that the site was holy to Islam as well.

When Ladoire arrived in Jerusalem, the mufti loosed three hundred fanatic Maghrebi guards of the Temple Mount upon him with orders to murder him and his escorts. Trying to break into the Franciscan monastery where Ladoire was staying, they fired into it in an attempt to kill the monks. According to Ladoire, the shots barely missed the head of the pharmacist. When it seemed as if the mufti's men would indeed force their way into the monastery, Ladoire ordered the monks to retreat to the church. A minute later they were informed that the pasha had arrived to rescue them in the nick of time.

Only after the authorities in Istanbul sent supervisors to oversee the repairs and forced the governor of Jerusalem to quell the Maghrebi guards was it possible to start renovation work on the church. The restored dome lasted until the great fire of 1808.

752 Catholics Live in Bethlehem

Elzear Horn, a German Franciscan monk who spent from 1724 to 1744, the last twenty years of his life, in the Holy Land, occupied himself by collecting details on and preparing illustrations of the holy sites in Jerusalem and Bethlehem. His illustrations, though not extraordinarily beautiful, show a marked attempt at precision of detail. Horn's sketches have acquired a particular importance as the sole evidence of many sites within the Church of the Holy Sepulcher that were destroyed by the fire of 1808.

Horn's descriptions excel in their realism. Bethlehem, according to his rendering, was a ruined city whose pitifully poor inhabitants lived almost like animals. Horn could distinguish between them by religion but not lifestyle or costume, and said that fights and spats abounded in the city.

There were eleven family groups in the city—seven of them Muslim and four Christian. Of the 752 Catholics residing in Bethlehem, 500 were men. They were divided into two clans: one

A street in Bethlehem, by L. Mayer.

Franciscan monks in the Church of the Holy Sepulcher, by E. Horn.

of longtime Christians from whom the translators of the Franciscan monastery in Bethlehem were chosen, and the second of converts, many of whom did not wholly believe in their adopted faith and were more interested in the material benefits of being Christian than the salvation of their souls.

The snow that fell in Jerusalem in the winter of 1730 awakened in Horn a longing for his homeland, though he visited Europe only in 1739, taking with him a stone from the rock in the Church of the Holy Sepulcher as a gift to the church of his birthplace. Upon his return to the Holy Land, he served one year at a monastery in Nazareth, and died in Acre. A collection of his illustrations and writing was published only in the twentieth century.

Greek Orthodox Patriarch Chrysanthos Notaras Visits Jerusalem

Though nearly all of the Holy Land travelogues were written by Europeans, a few exceptions exist. In the eighteenth century, two or three books written by Greeks appeared, though they were descriptions of the Holy Land, as opposed to real travelogues.

The Greek Orthodox patriarch Chrysanthos Notaras, who visited the Holy Land in 1727, had studied at the best European universities and was considered one of the most important Greek Orthodox theologians of the eighteenth century. His book revolves around sites in the Holy Land, particularly the Church of the Holy Sepulcher. Especially of interest is the frontispiece, which depicts the author standing on Golgotha, trumpet in hand, his figure overwhelming the nearby Church of the Holy Sepulcher.

Jerusalem, by C. Notaras, who portrayed himself standing on Golgotha.

Franciscans Build Church of Annunciation

The Church of the Annunciation, by D. Roberts.

In 1730, after years of strife with the inhabitants of Nazareth and nearby villages, the Franciscan monks built a new Church of the Annunciation on the ruins of a former church to serve Christian pilgrims as well as locals who had joined the Catholic sect. The church was decorated with pictures, altars, and an imported European organ.

1738
Christian Pilgrims Avoid Hebron

Mountain climber and antiquity scholar Richard Pococke, who toured the Holy Land in 1738, reported that in the wake of the Christian murder of an Arab, Christian pilgrims were no longer traveling to Hebron for fear of retribution by its citizens.

Pococke was an English clergyman and one of the most learned British scholars of his generation. He was also an avid climber, and his writings helped turn various mountains into popular tourist sites. During his sojourn in the Holy Land, Pococke was interested mainly in antiquities, and left a great many records of them. He visited Jerusalem, Bethlehem, and Hebron, toured Acre, Haifa, and Tiberias, climbed Mount Tabor, and saw Galilee and Safed. The chronicle of his journey, published in two huge volumes with many illustrations, was widely distributed in England.

Herodion, by R. Pococke.

1750
Construction Starts on Greek Orthodox Church of Annunciation

The Greek Orthodox Church of the Annunciation in Nazareth.

The conflict between the Franciscans and the Greek Orthodox over the question of ownership of Mary's Spring in Nazareth dragged on for years. At first the site was under Franciscan control, but in 1741 Dahir al-Omar transferred its guardianship to the Greek Orthodox. In 1750 the Greek Orthodox began to build the present-day church on top of the ruins of the Church of Saint Gabriel. Construction of the Church of Saint Gabriel, also called the Church of the Annunciation, was completed in 1763.

1772
Russians Participate in Siege of Jaffa
Attempt by Russian Officers to Torch Boats in Jaffa Port Foiled. Russian Fleet Harasses City.

We learn of the assistance proffered by the Russians to Dahir al-Omar and Ali Bey from the book of Lieutenant Sergei Pleschtsjeew, a Russian naval officer who participated in the Russian fleet's maiden voyage to the Mediterranean during the war with Turkey. He left a book of his experiences that included his eyewitness testimony regarding the long siege laid by Dahir and Ali Bey on Jaffa.

The Russians sent a ship to help the besiegers in 1772. On board were two Russian officers: a cavalry captain and Lieutenant Pleschtsjeew. Their mission was to gather information about the situation in Jaffa, but at their own initiative the two officers took an active part in the siege instead. They set out at night in a boat full of incendiary material to set fire to the vessels in the port of Jaffa, but the townspeople shot at them, leaving them no choice but to withdraw.

The cavalry captain later took command of a battery of three 12-pound cannons south of Jaffa, and together with his Norwegian servant, bombarded the houses and walls of

ered letters from Ali Bey to the commander of the fleet and the Russian empress requesting their continued assistance. Accordingly, a Russian fleet was dispatched to Jaffa to

The port of Jaffa, by O. Dapper.

the city. Standing up to assess the damage he had done, he was shot by a sniper and killed. The Russians continued to assist the attackers, and transferred to them three of the cannons from their ship, which were used to assault the walls of Jaffa from a northeasterly direction.

At this stage, Pleschtsjeew deliv-

harass the city for several days. Soldiers from the fleet even participated in an offensive on the city during which several vessels in the port were torched. Nevertheless, the fate of Jaffa was not sealed at this stage, and the siege ended after the Russian withdrawal.

1732
Pallbearers Passing Citadel Lower Caskets

According to Elzear Horn, a Franciscan monk who arrived in Jerusalem in 1724 for a stay of several years, when Christians marching in a funeral procession to Mount Zion passed the Citadel, the pallbearers removed the casket from their shoulders and carried it in their hands until reaching the eastern gate of the stronghold. Only at the water hole in the center of the street were they permitted to raise the casket to their shoulders once again.

Elzear Horn, who as an amateur artist had a sharp eye, relates that the Citadel's lamentable fortifications would have been unable to prevent the city's conquest. Aside from the prominent round tower at its heart, the Citadel was protected by neither walls or stockades, and was encircled by only a waterless moat.

Numerous cannons protruded from the fortress' walls, but Horn notes that they were not in good repair, as the Muslims were aware that the Christians had lost hope of ever again occupying the city. On Muslim holidays or when an important personage visited the city, the Citadel's canons customarily fired honorific salutes.

Dahir al-Omar's Men Raze Carmelite Monastery

Soldiers on a Spree.
Prosper's Monastery Dismantled.

Carmelite monks near their monastery on the Carmel, by C.W. Wilson.

The Carmelite monk Giambattista di S. Alessio, who was sent to the Holy Land in 1765, recounts that the potentate of Acre, Dahir al-Omar, clashed with a few local chiefs from the villages at the foot of the Carmel and in 1761 sent soldiers to Haifa in order to demolish the city. Because of the unanticipated nature of the attack, the Carmelite abbot did not have sufficient time to appeal to the French ambassador and have him send soldiers to defend the monastery.

Dahir's soldiers razed old Haifa, which was little more than a village lying east of the present-day city. (In place of the ruined city, Dahir founded a new Haifa behind the Carmel ridge in a spot sheltered from winds and more convenient for boat anchorage. The new location encouraged the development of what was to be the largest city of the northern Holy Land during the nineteenth and twentieth centuries.)

The soldiers also went up to Mount Carmel and vandalized the monastery, though they had not been issued orders to do so. Having looted everything in their path, they removed their booty to Acre, where some of it was repurchased by French merchants who returned it to the monastery.

Attempts to rebuild the Carmelite monastery were unsuccessful—it was worked over again by Dahir's soldiers during one of his later campaigns. It was clear that a new monastery needed to be constructed in place of the old "Prosper's Monastery," and the monks themselves dismantled what was left of their former home. Giambattista, an architect by trade, was sent to the Holy Land to erect the Carmelites' new refuge.

The cornerstone for the new monastery was laid in 1767—this time at the head of Mount Carmel—but the construction encountered many difficulties and Giambattista was compelled to travel to Paris to enlist the support of the French king's daughter, who was a Carmelite nun. At her request, the French put pressure on Dahir to allow the work to be completed unhindered. The small monastery that resulted from the episode served the Carmelites until the beginning of the nineteenth century.

Greek Orthodox Establish Mount Tabor Church

In 1737, the scholar Richard Pococke visited Mount Tabor, where he said the Greek Orthodox celebrated mass on the site of the early Greek Orthodox church on the northern side of the mountain. From 1760 the Greek Orthodox referred to the spot as Saint Elias, and they constructed a new church over the ruins of its predecessor. The new structure was designed along the contours of the ancient church, though a few changes were introduced. The Greek Orthodox gradually settled the entire northern part of the mountain, which remains under their control to this day.

The St. Elias Monastery on Mount Tabor.

Dublin to Jerusalem and Back in Less Than a Year

Wagered He Would Get to Jerusalem and Back in Two Years—and Won 15,000 Pounds Sterling

Buck Whaley in his youth.

The gambler Buck Whaley was the son of a wealthy Irish family who had his gambled his fortune away. His trip to Jerusalem was one of the few instances in which his gambling proved profitable. It began during an argument between Whaley and his friends as to whether Jerusalem really existed and whether one could actually get there. Whaley bet 15,000 pounds sterling (an enormous sum in those days) that he could make it to Jerusalem and back to Dublin within two years.

Whaley won his bet in less than a year. Upon his return, the residents of Dublin welcomed him with burning torches. After presenting a letter from the head of the Franciscans in Jerusalem certifying that Whaley had indeed visited the holy city, the gambler also received the money owed him.

The account of Whaley's trip was only published in the twentieth century. In it is a description of the Irishman's meeting with the cruel governor of Acre, al-Jezzar, during which Whaley was amazed at the behavior of the British consular representative, who went down on his knees, his whole body trembling and his expression revealing painful evidence of the fear so obviously gripping him.

Whaley recounted that over three hundred people were working in the garden during the encounter, but they dared not raise their heads. One of the workers nevertheless annoyed al-Jezzar, however, and the governor ordered the man brought before him. Glowering, al-Jezzar ordered him stripped and brought out from behind his back a silver hammer weighing about four pounds. Whaley leaves no doubt as to the purpose of the hammer—when al-Jezzar occasionally spared someone's life, he had him lie on a plank and would crush his spinal cord with the hammer, paralyzing the poor victim for life.

Luigi Mayer Draws the East

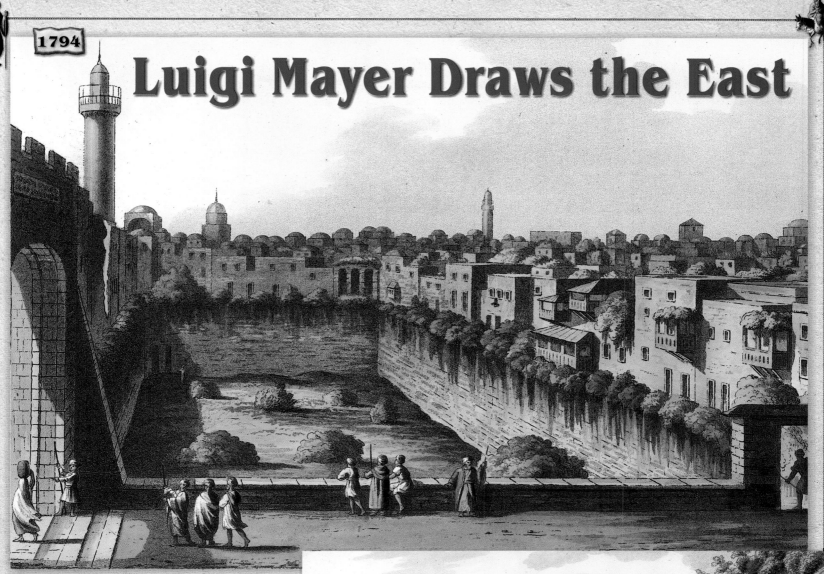

From the drawings of L. Mayer: The Bethesda Pool *(above)*; the village of Bethany and the Dead Sea *(right)*; tombs in the Jehoshaphat Valley *(below)*.

Luigi Mayer was a Swiss or German artist educated in in Italy. From 1796 he served as an escort for the British ambassador in Istanbul and traveled on the latter's behalf in the Holy Land, Syria, Asia Minor, and the Balkans. Throughout his journeys, Mayer prepared prints of the landscapes and sites he witnessed.

All in all, Mayer completed 167 pictures, which were published in various collections at the beginning of the nineteenth century. Unfortunately, his representations of the Holy Land are not very precise, and it is often hard to identify the places to which they refer. Most of the pictures were printed as aquatints, and were hand colored. Out of the dozens of works Mayer completed, only twenty-four illustrations were printed in his volume on the Holy Land.

Building the Mensa Christi Church

During the early years of al-Jezzar's rule, the condition of Christians in the Holy Land was satisfactory. In 1777, the Franciscans purchased the right to collect taxes in Nazareth and five villages in its vicinity, and in 1781 they began to built the "Church of the Rock," better known as the Mensa Christi.

The tradition connected to the rock originated in the seventeenth century. Pilgrims who came to the site would break off a piece of the rock as a souvenir or inscribe their names on it. The French traveler Jean Doubdan, who visited the site in 1652, believed he saw the signs of Jesus' body imprinted on the stone to a depth of four fingers.

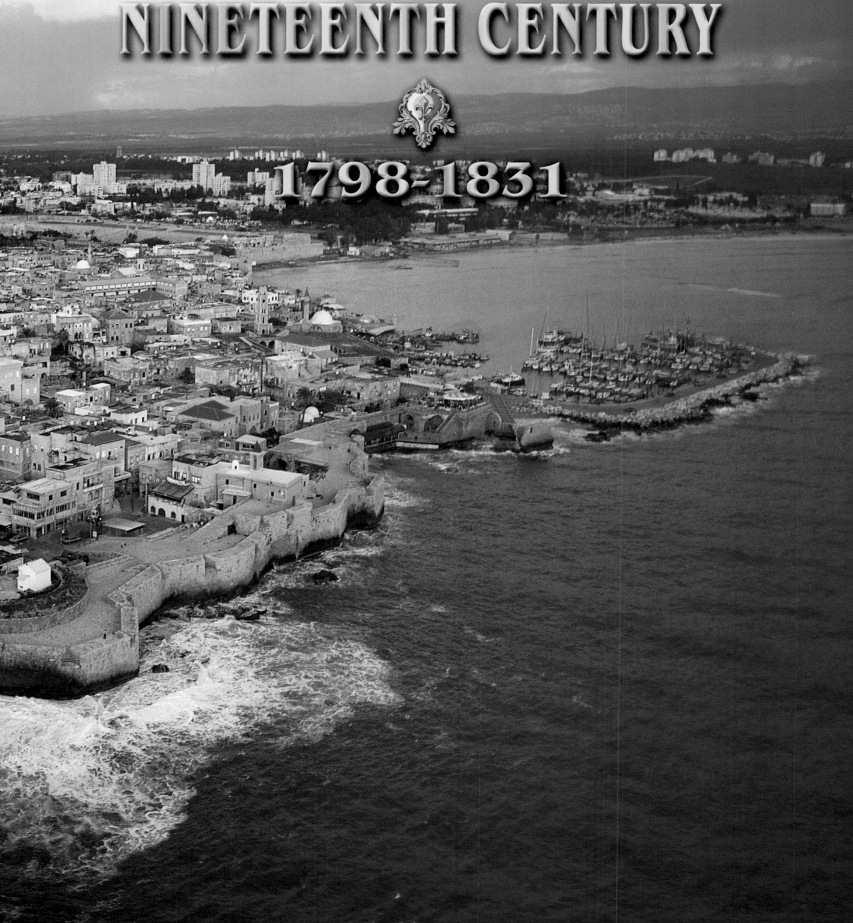

CHAPTER VIII

INTO THE NINETEENTH CENTURY

1798-1831

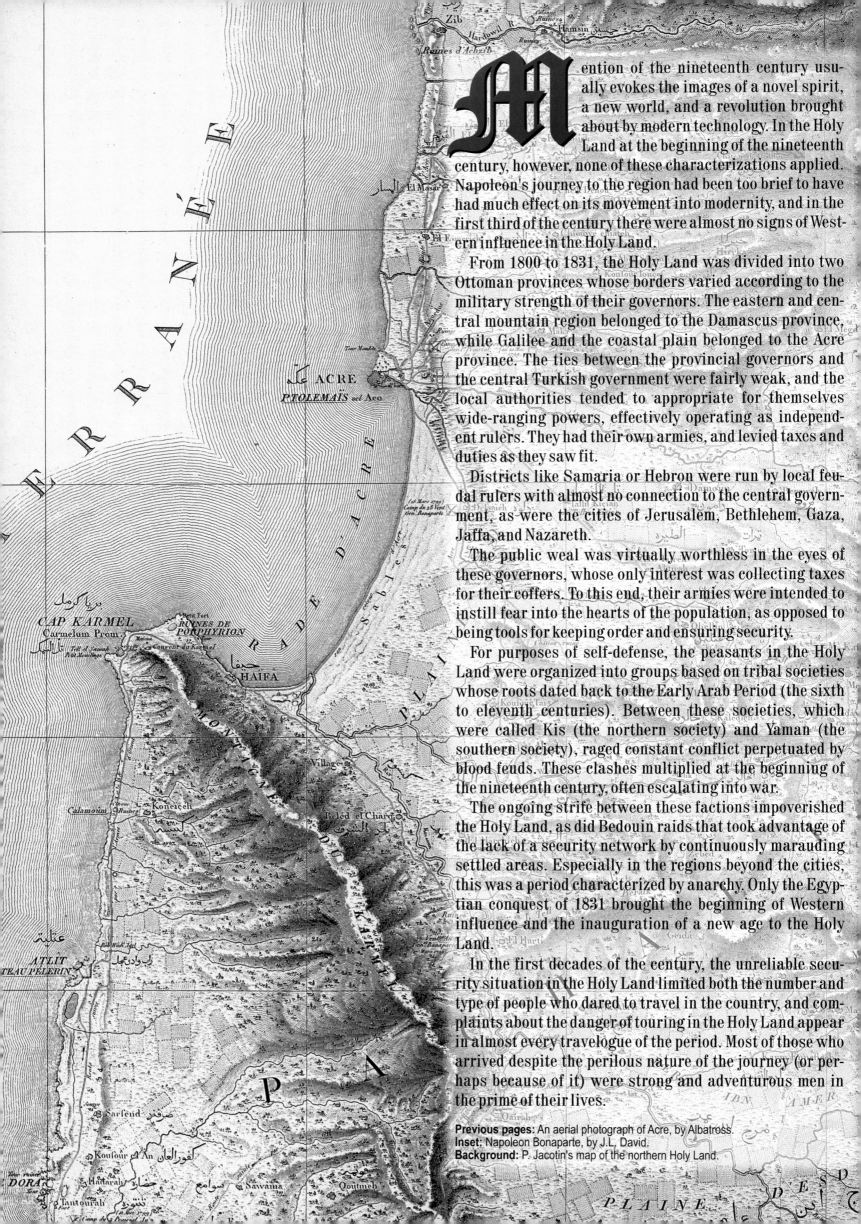

Mention of the nineteenth century usually evokes the images of a novel spirit, a new world, and a revolution brought about by modern technology. In the Holy Land at the beginning of the nineteenth century, however, none of these characterizations applied. Napoleon's journey to the region had been too brief to have had much effect on its movement into modernity, and in the first third of the century there were almost no signs of Western influence in the Holy Land.

From 1800 to 1831, the Holy Land was divided into two Ottoman provinces whose borders varied according to the military strength of their governors. The eastern and central mountain region belonged to the Damascus province, while Galilee and the coastal plain belonged to the Acre province. The ties between the provincial governors and the central Turkish government were fairly weak, and the local authorities tended to appropriate for themselves wide-ranging powers, effectively operating as independent rulers. They had their own armies, and levied taxes and duties as they saw fit.

Districts like Samaria or Hebron were run by local feudal rulers with almost no connection to the central government, as were the cities of Jerusalem, Bethlehem, Gaza, Jaffa, and Nazareth.

The public weal was virtually worthless in the eyes of these governors, whose only interest was collecting taxes for their coffers. To this end, their armies were intended to instill fear into the hearts of the population, as opposed to being tools for keeping order and ensuring security.

For purposes of self-defense, the peasants in the Holy Land were organized into groups based on tribal societies whose roots dated back to the Early Arab Period (the sixth to eleventh centuries). Between these societies, which were called Kis (the northern society) and Yaman (the southern society), raged constant conflict perpetuated by blood feuds. These clashes multiplied at the beginning of the nineteenth century, often escalating into war.

The ongoing strife between these factions impoverished the Holy Land, as did Bedouin raids that took advantage of the lack of a security network by continuously marauding settled areas. Especially in the regions beyond the cities, this was a period characterized by anarchy. Only the Egyptian conquest of 1831 brought the beginning of Western influence and the inauguration of a new age to the Holy Land.

In the first decades of the century, the unreliable security situation in the Holy Land limited both the number and type of people who dared to travel in the country, and complaints about the danger of touring in the Holy Land appear in almost every travelogue of the period. Most of those who arrived despite the perilous nature of the journey (or perhaps because of it) were strong and adventurous men in the prime of their lives.

Previous pages: An aerial photograph of Acre, by Albatross.
Inset: Napoleon Bonaparte, by J.L. David.
Background: P. Jacotin's map of the northern Holy Land.

Napoleon Sets Out to Conquer East

After his victory in northern Italy in 1797, Napoleon found himself without serious rivals in the European arena. Redirecting his desire for glory at a new frontier, he set out on an adventurous campaign to the East. He conquered Egypt with relative ease in 1798, but the British Admiral Nelson subsequently sank his fleet, stranding Napoleon and his army in the Holy Land.

Napoleon launched another expedition: a journey further east in the footsteps of Alexander the Great. His

Napoleon Bonaparte, by A.J. Gros.

intention was to isolate the Ottoman Empire and advance by way of Persia to India, most of which was then ruled by the hated English. A number of obstacles stood in his way. Firstly, he had little time at his disposal; the British-Turkish invasion would land on the coast of Egypt at the end of spring, 1799. Secondly, an advance north along the eastern coast of the Mediterranean would expose him to the intervention of the British fleet. Thirdly, though the Holy Land did not appear to be a serious challenge to Napoleon's march north, he had not taken into account Ahmed al-Jazzar, a cruel, tenacious, and savvy ruler.

Journey to the Holy Land
Delay at El Arish Spoils Surprise. Plague Strikes Soldiers.

Napoleon's strategy was to reach the Holy Land quickly and to attack it without warning, but from the outset things did not develop as planned. The French expeditionary force, which was composed of four infantry divisions, some cavalry, engineers, scouts, and camel riders (a total of 13,000 people), got into trouble on its way to the Holy Land.

The French, who had thought that El Arish was undefended, were surprised to encounter a well-fortified citadel equipped with a dozen cannons. Though the military force sent to the aid of the city by Ahmed al-Jazzar was defeated by one of Napo-

leon's generals during a night battle, the citadel did not succumb as quickly, and two precious weeks passed until Napoleon was able to conquer it and proceed on his way north.

The delay cast a shadow over the rest of the Corsican's campaign: he had lost the element of surprise. Meanwhile, the pasha of Damascus had mustered a large force to block Napoleon from the north and al-Jazzar had concentrated his forces in the fortresses of Jaffa and Acre. A British fleet commanded by Sir Sidney Smith beat Napoleon to Acre, and to make matters worse, at El Arish the French were infected with the bubonic plague.

Jaffa Vanquished

From El Arish Napoleon proceeded to Gaza, which surrendered to him after a short battle on February 24, 1799. He turned to Ramla and Jaffa. Meanwhile, some of his scouts approached Jerusalem, though they did not enter the city.

The siege of Jaffa was short, and lasted less than a week in early March. The French forces penetrated the city from the south, massacring many of its inhabitants, looting their homes, and raping the women. One eyewitness related that everything was annihilated in a spectacle of fire and blood. The soldiers killed unceasingly, without taking into consideration the age or sex of their victims. Only fatigue finally compelled them to end the slaughter.

Napoleon, who was well acquainted with the nature of his men, did not intervene in the atrocities, letting the soldiers find an outlet in a sea of blood for the tension that had accumulated over the previous long weeks of hardship and danger.

A great deal of booty fell into the hands of the French: 15 ships, 50 cannons, 400,000 rations of biscuits, 100 tons of rice, 13,000 containers of wheat, numerous barrels of olive oil and vinegar, and a large quantity of soap and tobacco.

The French troops sustained only a few casualties—approximately 30 dead and 20 injured. On the opposing side, around 2,000 soldiers were

killed and 3,000 taken prisoner. Some of them surrendered only after receiving an explicit promise that they would not be harmed; a promise that was not kept. Though the soldiers of Egyptian extraction were assigned to French army work details, all other enemy troops were executed. The carnage was unusual; In other military campaigns, Napoleon had been less vicious. Probably for that reason, the memory of the massacre of the prisoners of war in Jaffa has been well preserved.

Eight hundred prisoners of war were executed on March 8, around 600 more the next day, and on March 10, 1,041 prisoners were killed. The executions were carried out on the beach south of Jaffa. Several of the prisoners attempted to escape by running into the sea and swimming to the nearby reefs, but the French chased them in rafts and executed most of them.

As if in divine punishment for the horrors they had inflicted on Jaffa's population, an epidemic of the bubonic plague broke out in the French army. The sick were hospitalized at the Armenian hospital in Jaffa and Napoleon himself came to visit them. The doctors attempted whenever possible to conceal the true nature of the disease from the soldiers. Touching them in order to demonstrate his opinion that what afflicted them was not the plague, Napoleon even helped move the body of one of the dead.

Napoleon visits the plague victims at the Armenian hospital in Jaffa, by A.J. Gros.

The Siege of Acre Begins

After the conquest of Jaffa, the French army moved north, vanquished the local regiments at the battle of Cacon, and took the city of Haifa without a siege. But when Napoleon ascended the Carmel in order to catch a glimpse of his primary objective, the port city of Acre, he was amazed to see a British flotilla—Sir Sidney Smith's fleet—anchored nearby. The English soon captured Napoleon's siege equipment, which had been sent to him on several small, unprotected ships. The cannons that fell into the hands of the British would be used against him during the siege of Acre.

The siege lasted two months, from March 19 to May 21, and the French stormed the walls of Acre on March 28. Their cannons were not heavy enough to destroy the city's thick walls, however, and their ladders were too short to cross the moat, which al-Jazzar had made eight meters deep. Spurring his soldiers on, al-Jazzar himself stood at the scene of the French attack and threatened to shoot anyone who dared flee the field of battle.

The French realized that there was no possibility of conquering the city without a true siege. Heavy cannons and ammunition were brought from Egypt, but since the French could not unload their arms at the port of Haifa, which was under the control of Sir Sidney Smith's ships, they were forced to bring them ashore at the small port of Tantura and transfer them overland to Acre. A great deal of time slid by, giving the besieged the opportunity to carry out sorties against the French camp and strengthen their fortifications.

Right: Napoleon's soldiers lay siege to Acre, by N. Charlet.

Below: The British warship *Le Tigre* opposite Acre's coast, by F.B. Spilsbury.

Head of the Class: Phelippeaux vs. Napoleon

The commander of the French cannons held by the British was Colonel Phelippeaux, a French Royalist who had fled to England during the days of the revolution, joined the British army, and set out with Sir Sidney Smith for the East.

Phelippeaux, who was even shorter in stature than Napoleon, had studied at the French school for artillery officers, where he had been a classmate of Napoleon's. Phelippeaux had been first in his class, and Napoleon third.

The ultimate contest between the two rivals occurred opposite the walls of Acre. Phelippeaux, demonstrating his skill as an artillery officer, situated the French cannons at his disposal on either side of Acre outside the city ramparts and shelled the French troops whenever they attempted to storm the city. Phelippeaux's luck did not hold, however, and he died of an illness on May 1, 1799, too early to witness the withdrawal of his former classmate from Acre.

Victory at Tabor
Despite French Disadvantage of 7 to 1

General Kléber.

The Battle of Tabor was one of Napoleon's great victories. In other clashes from which he emerged triumphant, he took the field with numbers of troops at least equal to those of his enemies, but at Tabor, and only at Tabor, he bested an enemy when the balance of forces was 7:1 to his disadvantage!

The opposing forces were those of the pasha of Damascus, who advanced toward Acre and then turned south and descended to the Jezreel Valley. There they were joined by soldiers from the Nablus area and apparently from Jerusalem as well.

Napoleon dispatched some of the forces concentrated around Acre

The Battle of Tabor, by H.F. Phillippoteaux & L. Cognie.

gles from the Nazareth ridge. He ordered his men to descend to the valley and advance south, not directly toward the enemy but some distance to the west, in order to close in on the Arab forces from the rear.

When Napoleon saw that Kléber was combining his two quadrangles into one with the clear intention of withdrawing, he gave the command to fire the cannons and attack. The Muslims, startled, fled in all directions—the forces from Nablus to the south and those from Damascus to the

east. But when the latter group attempted to ford the Jordan they discovered that the Benot Ya'akov Bridge was already in the hands of the French and their allies, cutting them off from the north. Many of them were slaughtered or drowned in the river.

The French casualties were slight compared to the losses of the Turks and Arabs.

As a result of the victory, the Maronites and the Druze of southern Lebanon announced that they were joining the French.

General Murat's camp near the Benot Ya'akov Bridge, by F.B. Spilsbury.

against the pasha's troops. The infantry, under the command of General Murat (who later married Napoleon's younger sister and was appointed king of Naples), invaded Galilee, took the city of Safed, and defeated a force commanded by the pasha's son in a battle near the Benot Ya'akov Bridge over the River Jordan.

Napoleon's childhood friend, General Andoche Junot, advanced to the Lower Galilee, overcame Nazareth (to the delight of its Christian inhabitants, as it was the first time since the Crusades that a Christian force had ruled the city), and clashed with one of the lesser forces of the Damascus army. He was joined by an entire division from Acre, commanded by the French General Kléber.

When the Turkish forces had amassed in the Jezreel Valley, Kléber

decided to surprise them, attacking them there, south of Mount Tabor, by night.

But the nocturnal advance took longer than Kléber had planned, and he did not surprise the Turks and the Arabs, who subsequently surrounded him. The French force was arrayed in defensive quadrangles, one commanded by Kléber and the other by Junot. Their chances looked slim.

Luckily for Kléber, the previous day he had sent his plan of attack to Napoleon. Napoleon, who was equipped with Pierre Jacotin's maps, immediately realized that Kléber's plan could not be implemented and that his force was in any case too small for the mission. Taking with him an additional division and a cavalry force, he set out after Kléber. On the morning of April 16, Napoleon saw the French quadran-

A Thanksgiving Prayer in Nazareth

Napoleon spent the night between April 17 and 18 in the Franciscan monastery in Nazareth, where his soldiers offered up a prayer of thanksgiving to the accompaniment of an

organ. The French wounded were hospitalized in the monastery.

On April 19, Napoleon returned to his camp in Acre after having been absent for five days.

Terra Sancta, the Franciscan monastery in Nazareth, by D. Roberts.

Napoleon: "At the Gates of Acre, My Luck Ran Out."

Despite Napoleon's victory at the Battle of Tabor, Acre did not capitulate. At the point at which any other commander might have surrendered, al-Jazzar doubled the rate of his sorties.

After the French forces were again concentrated around Acre, they had to wait several more days until their heavy guns arrived from Egypt. Unfortunately for them, the guns arrived at the same time as Turkish reinforcements for the besieged. As a result of pressure from Sir Sidney Smith, al-Jazzar allowed the Turks to enter Acre despite the fact that he suspected their intentions.

During the days of the decisive French attack (May 7-10), al-Jazzar relied upon the element of surprise. He allowed the French to penetrate the city by means of a corner tower in which he had, unbeknownst to his enemy, erected an internal wall. As the French made their way inside the tower, al-Jazzar shelled them from cannons he had placed on the wall. The French losses were great, and several of Napoleon's best commanders were killed or wounded. Al-Jazzar, not even bothering to repair the destroyed portion of the wall, killed more French soldiers every day in Acre.

French spirits continued to fall throughout the final attacks, during which Napoleon was forced to send officers along with his soldiers in order to ascertain that they would continue to fight. Finally, Napoleon discontinued the siege. In his camp, his commanders and soldiers were shouting contemptuously at him. Many of them had fallen ill with the plague and died. Napoleon also feared an Anglo-Turkish attack on Egypt. He gave orders to fire all of the remaining heavy ammunition into Acre and then declared that there was no point in conquering a city that had been hit so hard.

On the night of May 20, the French quietly retreated from Acre. In the summer heat, the withdrawal became a nightmare. Warriors from Mount Samaria attacked the French repeatedly. Many of the wounded and sick were abandoned along the way.

After a short stopover in Jaffa, the French reached Sinai. The soldiers rested and received new uniforms, so that when they entered Cairo they at least looked like a conquering army.

The French recovery was speedy. On July 25, Napoleon repulsed the Anglo-Turkish naval invasion of Egypt. Immediately afterwards, he secretly returned to France, leaving his army in Egypt. Only the victories of the young general had reached the ears of the French, and when the government fell a mere five months after his disgraceful retreat from Acre, the regime passed into Napoleon's hands.

A British sailor buries the body of a French general, probably Caffarelli, at the foot of Acre's wall, by F.B. Spilsbury. General Caffarelli was killed during the French siege on Acre. Several years ago, his bones were recovered and repatriated to France.

The Horrors of the Retreat

Louis de Bourienne, a childhood friend of Napoleon's, accompanied him as his secretary to Egypt and the Holy Land, and described in his memoirs (written, naturally, only after Napoleon's fall) the atrocities of the retreat from Acre.

De Bourienne relates that the wounded were carried on stretchers, horses, donkeys, and camels. During the retreat it became known that the soldiers stricken by the plague who had been left at the Carmelite monastery had been massacred by the Turks.

The unbearable thirst, the heat, and the journey through the sands lowered the morale of the French troops and gave rise to incidents of horrible and inhumane egotism. Officers with amputated limbs were thrown from stretchers despite orders to evacuate them. Bribes were paid to the stretcher bearers. The amputees, the wounded, the ill, and those suspected of having been infected with the plague were cast on the roadside and left to die.

The journey was lit by torches that also served to set fire to the wheat fields, towns, villages, and farms along the way. The frustration of the French soldiers at their military failures and final defeat found its expression in horrific acts of destruction. Marauders and arsonists abounded. The dying lay at the roadside, begging for help in feeble voices. To prove that they were only wounded, rather than ill with the plague, they exposed their old wounds or wounded themselves afresh. Nevertheless, no one paused for these unfortunates.

As the French made their way back to Jaffa, the bright sun of the Holy Land was often obscured by the smoke that arose from the conflagrations. To the right of those retreating lay the sea and home; to their left and behind them remained the wasteland they had created with their own hands.

Colonel Pierre Jacotin's Maps

Colonel Pierre Jacotin was the commander of the French Geographical Engineering Corps that accompanied Napoleon on his journey to the Middle East. During the brief military foray, the colonel managed to carry out important and extensive cartographic work, and the map of Galilee that he prepared is considered to be the best of the period. It assisted Napoleon in pinpointing the weakness of the French General Kléber's plan, and so clinched the glorious French victory at the Battle of Tabor.

On the other hand, Jacotin erred seriously in his map of Sinai when he drew the peninsula between Eilat and Aqaba. The mistake was only discovered in 1822, when the German researcher Eduard Rüppell arrived in Aqaba.

The Man Who Would Be King

Francois Bernoyer, the head tailor of Napoleon's camp, kept a diary that was published only a few dozen years ago. According to Bernoyer, rumor in the French camp reported that Napoleon's extreme ambition was leading him to plan the establishment of an independent government once the conquest of Acre was complete. After triumphing over the kingdom of Persia, so camp gossip had it, Napoleon would crown himself king.

According to the tailor, the plan suited Napoleon's overweening character but displeased his troops, especially those who were attached to their homeland and those, like the tailor, who had wives they loved and did not want to lose, even for all the crowns in the world.

We hear firsthand of Napoleon's intentions from a phrase he penned years later in his book *Journal de Saint Helene*: "It would have been better if I had stayed in Egypt. Today I would be the emperor of the East…"

Al-Jazzar: Ruler, Judge, and Hangman

His Name Strikes Fear into Hearts throughout the Holy Land

Edward Daniel Clarke.

Edward Daniel Clarke, an educated English priest, described his 1801 visit to Ahmed al-Jazzar's palace in a book he wrote upon his return to England.

Al-Jazzar, explained Clarke, was the prime minister and ruler, chief of staff, minister of finance, secretary, chef, gardener, judge, and hangman of his realm. Nevertheless, the supposed holders of these positions were at their liege's service: Clarke saw several of them standing by the door of al-Jazzar's residence—some with amputated noses, others with missing limbs, a few with only one ear or eye.

They had all been subject to punishment by al-Jazzar, who considered them branded. Clarke tells of al-

Al-Jazzar sentences an accused subject to having his eyes put out. Second from left is Haim Farhi. By F.B. Spilsbury.

Jazzar's Jewish secretary, Haim Farhi, whose face al-Jazzar ordered mutilated; his nose was cut off and one of his eyes put out. Once, Clarke

continues, when al-Jazzar was suspicious of his wives' fidelity, he killed seven of them with his own hands. His sobriquet "al-Jazzar," on which the

ruler prided himself, was derived from the word "butcher," as he himself explained to Clarke—only a hint of the acts of mayhem he perpetrated in his time.

According to Clarke's record, al-Jazzar retired to his harem daily during the early evening hours, passing through three sturdy gates that he locked himself. Anyone who knocked, even upon the outer gate, risked execution.

Nobody in Acre knew how many wives al-Jazzar had. From time to time he received female slaves as gifts, and he installed them in his harem, though no one knew whether they remained alive, as those who entered the harem never left it.

When Clarke met him, al-Jazzar, who was past sixty, was inordinately proud of his virile masculinity. He bragged many times to Clarke and his companions of his great strength, rolling up his sleeves to show them his powerful muscles.

Ahmed al-Jazzar's Last Days

Al-Jazzar Gains Control of Southern Holy Land—Appointed Pasha of Damascus and Governor of Cairo

The grand vizier meets Sir Sidney Smith in his tent, by F.B. Spilsbury.

Ahmed al-Jazzar, though already an old man when the French left the Holy Land, was nevertheless still powerful. In 1800, the Turkish army, with the grand vizier at its head, passed through the Holy Land on its way to Egypt to fight the French. The pasha Abu Marak, who was one of al-Jazzar's

enemies and had a good relationship with the grand vizier, was appointed by the latter to command the districts of Jerusalem, Jaffa, Gaza, and Ramlá.

It was the Turkish authorities' hope to forge in the southern Holy Land a counterweight to al-Jazzar's strength in the north. But al-Jazzar, fresh from his unexpected victory over Napoleon, saw the appointment as infringing upon his rights, and did not hesitate to openly disobey, for the first and only time in his life, an order of the authorities in Istanbul.

From the end of 1801 until March 1803, al-Jazzar's army besieged Jaffa, where Abu Marak lived. Though letters of complaint arrived from Istanbul, military forces did not. A letter of June 11, 1802 even declared al-Jazzar a rebel and ordered him killed—but to no avail. Finally, Abu Marak was forced to evacuate Jaffa and the southern Holy Land, which reverted to the direct rule of al-Jazzar.

In 1804, the Turkish government, openly admitting its own helplessness, appointed al-Jazzar to an additional term as pasha of Damascus and finally as the governor of Cairo as well. Had he in fact undertaken the final appoint-

ment, al-Jazzar would have ruled over nearly all of the Mameluke empire of the Middle Ages, but he died that year without becoming embroiled in the internal wars then consuming the land of the Nile.

Al-Jazzar's Heirs Fight over Rule in Acre

Haim Farhi—Banker and al-Jazzar's Secretary—Aids Suleiman Pasha

The district of Acre (formally the district of Sidon) remained the center of power in the Holy Land even after al-Jazzar's death. Though in other districts governors were replaced annually, in Acre they were apparently appointed for life.

Initially, Ismail Pasha attempted to be al-Jazzar's inheritor, but he was bested in 1805 by Suleiman Pasha, the former governor of Tripoli and a past associate of al-Jazzar. Suleiman was aided by Haim Farhi, a Jewish banker and al-Jazzar's former secretary, who supplied Suleiman with contacts in Istanbul and funds to hire mercenaries.

Suleiman ruled the district of Sidon from 1805 to 1818. The opposite of al-Jazzar in character, he was easygoing and peace-loving, and let Farhi handle most matters of

The Abu Nabut Fountain in Jaffa, by C.W. Wilson.

policy. From 1808 to 1811, Suleiman was also appointed pasha of Damascus, and though the appointment was not afterwards renewed, since his close associates continued to serve as governors of the southern districts of the Holy Land (which were subordinate to Damascus), the entire country remained essentially under his control. During those years, the pashas of Damascus were too impotent to risk becoming his adversaries.

At the outset of his rule, Suleiman was forced to suppress a rebellion by Abu Marak, who took control of Jaffa again in 1805. Suleiman dispatched an army to besiege his forces, and Abu Marak retreated to Damascus. Suleiman appointed as governor of Jaffa the Mameluke Abu Nabut, who proved similar to Abu Marak in his cruelty, his flair for orderly administration, and his love of building. He earned the nickname *nabut* (club) by his indulgence in excessive brutality. Abu Nabut ruled in Jaffa from 1807 to 1822, erecting a mosque, a new city gate, markets, a new quay, and various public buildings, parts of which still exist.

Ulrich Seetzen Converts to Islam—Becomes Great Explorer

First Western Tourist to Reach Dead Sea, Dahab, and Gulf of Eilat

Ulrich Jaspar Seetzen, considered the greatest nineteenth-century explorer of the Holy Land, studied medicine and natural science in Germany. Upon concluding his studies, Seetzen carried out geological research in his homeland. Lucky to be coming of age at the beginning of the industrial revolution, he took advantage of his scientific knowledge to construct a factory for the production of building materials and to carry out extensive research on the possibility of extracting salt from seawater. After a time, he decided to retire from these pursuits in order to dedicate his life to research trips abroad.

Seetzen set out on his travels in 1802, and after a period of preparation in which he converted to Islam, arrived in Transjordan in 1805 already comfortable in his new role as a Muslim. He had neatly disposed of the major obstacle preventing other Western travelers from traveling as they wished throughout the Middle East.

Seetzen's Muslim name was Musa al-Hakim—"Moses the Doctor." He was the first European of the modern age to arrive in the Bashan, travel in the Ajlun region, visit Amman, and circumnavigate the Dead Sea.

On his way to the Dead Sea, he arrived at a cloven, bare mountain, from which layers of salt—characteristic of the saline composition of the Dead

ney, Seetzen was also able to take in Ein Gedi and Sedom.

Leaving the Jordan Valley, Seetzen continued on to Jerusalem, Hebron, and the western Holy Land. He traveled to Galilee, visited the ancient synagogue of Bar'am, and was the first Western traveler to climb the heights of the Gilboa. Afterwards, he returned south. Though he had heard of Aqaba and Petra, he did not manage to reach them, though he made his way to the Sinai Peninsula and was the first European since the Middle Ages to traverse its desert from north to

The ancient synagogue in Bar'am.

Napoleon's Agent Spies in Holy Land

Tours the Middle East Disguised as a Muslim, then Reports to Superiors

Ali Bey al-Abasi.

Ali Bey al-Abasi was an unusual and mysterious figure. Actually not a Muslim, al-Abasi was a Spanish Christian whose real name was Domingo Badia y Leblic. Apparently, he was also a spy—at first for Spain and later for Napoleon. His disguise as a Muslim was so perfect that even his memoirs contain no hint of any other identity.

His duplicity was revealed in a book written by a member of Napoleon's court, Count Bausset. According to the nobleman, al-Abasi was recruited by the Spanish to work for the transformation of Morocco into a Spanish colony.

After the conquest of Spain by Napoleon, Domingo became one of the emperor's supporters, and went to work in his service. Napoleon sometimes preferred that the supervision of important agents remain in his hands instead of those of the head of police or the director of intelligence services, and he accordingly appointed people from his court to direct them. Al-Abasi was Count Bausset's operative.

The Spaniard's espionage mission meant traveling throughout North Africa and the Middle East and reporting to his superiors regarding developments in the region. As a supposed Muslim, al-Abasi visited Mecca as well as Muslim sites in the Holy Land such as the Cave of the Machpela and the Haram al-Sharif (the Temple Mount) in Jerusalem. Later, without mentioning the true nature of his expedition, he was to write a travel book—an unusual step for a spy.

Al-Abasi's death was as enigmatic as his life. Bausset relates that he was executed in 1807 by the governor of Damascus, but Lady Hester Stanhope claims that the Spaniard continued to operate as an spy until 1818, when he was poisoned and died. The French scholar F. de Saulcy claims the secret agent died a natural death in Paris in 1836.

Sea area—protruded. The salt, whose hues varied from white to earth-colored and red, filled the caves, crevices, and cracks of the mountain. Seetzen wrote that he had never seen such a furrowed mountain. To his surprise, he discovered that there was no vegetation in the Dead Sea, and that only snails were to be found on its beach. During the course of his jour-

south on his way to Saint Catherine's Monastery in southern Sinai. He was also the first Western traveler to reach the shore of the Gulf of Eilat and the beaches of Dahab.

Seetzen's complete memoirs were only published forty years after his death, postponing the accolades he deserved as the greatest modern explorer of the Holy Land.

Disaster in Church of Holy Sepulcher: Rotunda Set on Fire

1808

Christian Sects Sling Accusations. Greek Orthodox Receive Permission to Renovate Church.

On October 13, 1808, a fire broke out in the Church of the Holy Sepulcher. The edifice surrounding the tomb, though it was damaged, survived, but the dome of the rotunda caught fire and collapsed. The overall loss was enormous.

The fire apparently started as a result of carelessness, and the various Christian sects in Jerusalem blamed one another. The Catholics claimed that the Greek Orthodox and Armenians had intentionally burned the church down. The Greek Ortho-dox—as well as the rest of the Christian sects—blamed the Armenians (in whose section of the church the fire appears to have started), accusing them of arson.

That same year, Napoleon invaded Spain and the affairs of Jerusalem were far from the hearts of European states. The main beneficiaries of the church's calamity were the Greek Orthodox, who quickly obtained permission to repair the structure before the other sects could get involved. The Greek Orthodox began to rebuild the Church of the Holy Sepulcher at the beginning of the 1820s, but Muslim fanatics and the local Turkish garrison, who opposed the church's renovation, laid siege to the house of the governor of Jerusalem and attacked the Greek patriarchate as well as the employees of the church. With the intervention of the governor of Damascus, everything was soon put aright, however, and the leaders of the rebellion executed.

During the reconstruction, the Greek Orthodox took their revenge on the Catholics and completely destroyed the tombs of the Crusader kings buried beneath Golgotha.

The tombs of the Crusader kings in the Church of the Holy Sepulcher.

Ancient Nabatean City Discovered in Petra

1812

A rock-carved tomb in Petra, by D. Roberts.

Johann Ludwig Burckhardt.

Antiquities of Petra and Altar of Aaron the High Priest Are the Pinnacle of Burckhardt's Discoveries

Johann Ludwig Burckhardt was a native of Basel, Switzerland and the son of a wealthy merchant family. After completing his studies at a German university, he decided to move to England. There he offered his services to a company established in 1788 for the purpose of exploring Africa, and set out in 1809 on its behalf for the East. At first, Aleppo served as Burckhardt's base. He had planned on a period of acclimatization and study of the Arab language and eastern customs before embarking on his true mission—an expedition to central Africa. He converted to Islam and chose a native name—"Sheikh Ibrahim."

Burckhardt set off in 1812 from Damascus southward past the Bashan and Jabal al-Druze to northern Transjordan and Jerash, and went on from there to the Golan, the Hauran for a second time, Galilee, Safed, and Tiberias. He did not visit Jerusalem.

Reentering Transjordan, he made his way south via Amman to Wadi Musa and Petra. His discovery of the antiquities of Petra, his visit to the nearby altar of Aaron, and his accurate identification of those sites were the acme of Burckhardt's work.

Unfortunately, the Swiss explorer did not leave a complete description of the antiquities he had located. He traveled dressed as an Arab in a desert wilderness where no traveler had ever been seen, and had he examined the structures closely, he later explained, he would have aroused the suspicion that he was a sorcerer looking for treasure. He feared that he would be detained, prevented from continuing on his trip to Egypt, and relieved of even the bit of money he had with him, or worse, his travel journal.

Seetzen Murdered in Yemen

1811

In 1809, Ulrich Seetzen arrived in Mecca on his way south to Yemen; after preparing for the next leg of his journey there, he planned to set out on his discovery of central Africa.

But Seetzen was apparently too daring. A large convoy of camels carrying the antiquities he had collected thus far on his journey accompanied him, and perhaps they tempted the Bedouin who happened upon his caravan. It might also have been the knowledge that Seetzen had drawn an accurate picture of the Kaaba in Mecca that led to his demise by arousing the ire of religious fanatics. Or perhaps the European's eastern disguise was less than perfect and he struck fear in the hearts of local Arab rulers who suspected him of being a Turkish spy.

Whoever harmed him, in October 1811 Seetzen was murdered in Yemen, where his journey ended prematurely, just short of realizing his plan to explore the dark continent.

Princess of Wales Visits Holy Land

Great Excitement in Holy Land: Adultery Scandal in Europe

Great excitement prevailed in Jerusalem and Acre when Lady Caroline, wife of the heir to the English throne, the future King George IV, arrived for a visit in the Holy Land.

Lady Caroline set out on her journey in order to distance herself from her husband. George IV was in the habit of taking mistresses, and Lady Caroline could not reconcile herself to his adulterous affairs.

Lady Caroline began her journey in 1814 by visiting her homeland of Germany and continuing from there to Italy, where she took on new servants. Among them was an attractive young man named Bartholomeo Pergami. When rumors of an intimate relationship between the two reached England, George IV decided to take advantage of the opportunity. In order to force Caroline to divorce him, he appended spies to the princess' entourage with orders to collect evidence that would enable him to put her on trial for adultery.

Lady Caroline's visit to the Holy Land in 1815 was something of an

and her entourage while seated on the edge of a gold-embroidered sofa, smoking a diamond-encrusted hookah. All of his officers stood around him in total silence, listening to their master's instructions with arms folded. They did not even dare to smile at the antics of the court jester.

Coffee was brought in diamond-encrusted gold cups. The pasha asked only a few questions of the princess's party, but warmly invited them to tour Acre's new fortifications and to see his Arabian horses.

Not content with the standard visits to places like Jaffa, Ramla, Jerusalem, and Jericho, Lady Caroline also ventured to more remote spots like Nazareth, Nablus, and Ashkelon. The security situation in the Holy Land at the time was rendered irrelevant by the size of her entourage, which comprised almost two hundred people by this time, besides the security officers placed at her disposal by local governors.

Upon her return from the East, Caroline spent time in Italy, Austria,

George IV's spies, as well as others who testified against the queen, expounded in some length on the sleeping arrangements aboard ship. Due to the sweltering heat within the vessel, Lady Caroline had lived in a tent erected on deck. The witnesses claimed that Pergami often slept in the tent, though other witnesses, testifying in Caroline's defense, denied the allegation. According to the final opinion of the House of Lords, the

Lady Caroline, Princess of Wales.

queen's guilt had not been proven. Lady Caroline did not have much chance to enjoy her victory, however, as she died a short while later.

Lady Hester Stanhope's Treasure Hunt

Lady Hester Stanhope was the daughter of a respected English family. Her grandfather had served as Britain's prime minister, as had her uncle, Pitt the Younger, during the Napoleonic wars. Since Pitt was unmarried, Lady Stanhope served as his official hostess. After his death she set out on a journey to the East, and never again returned to England.

While in Malta, Lady Stanhope fell in love with Michael Bruce, a Scotsman from a wealthy family. Bruce's father footed the bill as the two traveled to the East with a large convoy of escorts and Bedouin guards.

After digging for several days, they reached the cellar they had been seeking, only to discover that the place had been looted.

When her love cooled and the elder Bruce was no longer willing to pick up the tab, Lady Hester embarked on a treasure hunt in the Holy Land. Having purchased an old Italian manuscript disclosing the location of an ancient treasure buried in Ashkelon, she departed for the spot accompanied by one of the Turkish sultan's men.

Arriving in Ashkelon, they discovered that the mosque in which the treasure was supposed to have been hidden had been destroyed, and that only a wall was left of the magnificent building, which had served in different periods as a temple, a church, and a mosque. After digging for several days, they reached the cellar they had

been seeking, only to discover that the place had been looted a long time previously. Lady Hester maintained that the cellar could have indeed contained the three million gold coins mentioned in the manuscript.

During the party's excavations, lovely columns and floors were unearthed, as well as a huge headless statue. Stanhope gave orders to have the latter smashed into thousands of pieces so that it would not be said of her that she had come to the Holy Land in pursuit of statues for her countrymen. Fortunately, the archaeologists who followed after Lady Hester related differently to their discoveries.

Disappointed, Lady Hester left Ashkelon and withdrew to the Leba-

Lady Hester Stanhope, who called herself the "Queen of Lebanon."

non Mountains, where she found shelter in a castle to the east of Sidon until her death in 1839.

European visitors to the Holy Land have always seen Stanhope as a romantic figure, and she is often mentioned in books on travel to the East.

![Acre's bazaar in the early nineteenth century, by F.B. Spilsbury.](image)
Acre's bazaar in the early nineteenth century, by F.B. Spilsbury.

event, as she was the first member of the British royal family to arrive there since the Middle Ages. The local inhabitants proved completely uninterested in her worsening relations with her husband, and she was greeted everywhere with royal honors.

The ruler of Acre, Suleiman Pasha (1805-1818), was especially welcoming, and invited Lady Caroline to visit his palace: the entire meeting is described in a book on Caroline's journey written by an unknown member of her party. Suleiman received the lady

and Germany until her husband ascended the throne in 1820. She decided to return to England then in order to realize her rights as queen. George IV, displeased with Caroline's reappearance in England, immediately put her on trial before the House of Lords with the intent to divorce her on the grounds of her improper behavior with Pergami, who had meanwhile been dismissed. The trial became one of the greatest royal scandals in Europe during the entire nineteenth century.

Brothel Discovered in Jerusalem

1816

Scam exposed: While an unsuspecting man visits a prostitute's home, a "Turkish soldier" arrives, claims the stranger has broken the law, and orders him to pay a large fine. The cash is later split by the woman and her partner.

James Silk Buckingham.

James Silk Buckingham was an adventurer's adventurer. At the tender age of nine he had already left his homeland as a sailor on a ship plying the high seas. At ten he was taken prisoner on a Spanish vessel and imprisoned in Portugal. In the course of later travels he reached America, Egypt—where he learned Arabic— and even India.

He arrived in the Holy Land in 1816 an experienced traveler. He toured the Holy Land, the Hauran, and Transjordan. The spiciest story in his book is his testimony about the existence of a brothel in Jerusalem, the supposed holy city.

Buckingham, according to his account, visited the house of ill repute only in order to discover if there was any truth to the rumor. He hinted to his guide that he had heard of the "women's institution," and slipped him three piasters. The guide swiftly

An Arab woman in her room.

pocketed the money, winked meaningfully, and led Buckingham to the spot.

It was late afternoon, and Gabriel (the guide), waited in the yard while Buckingham ascended a winding staircase leading from the dark street to an open courtyard above, and walked up an additional set of steps to a private residence. There he was met by an man of about fifty who spoke to him in Arabic. Buckingham told him that he was an English traveler who was passing by with a companion on his way from the Coptic monastery. The door immediately opened and he was led into a room with a mattress and pillows arranged on the floor, little children playing on them. A woman of about thirty, the mother of the children and the wife of the man who had admitted him, appeared, and was presented to Buckingham as "Theresa." The man and children left the room, leaving Buckingham and Theresa alone. Suddenly a loud knock was heard. Theresa cried "Who's

there?" and put her finger to her lips, signaling Buckingham not to make a sound. At the second knock she opened the door, and Musa, Buckingham's Ethiopian friend, entered, livid. Musa insisted that he needed Buckingham urgently and refused to budge until he came with him.

It seems that Musa, happening by downstairs, saw Gabriel near the door, suspected that Buckingham was inside, and came to rescue him. He claimed that the place's usual scam was to make the stranger's stay as lengthy as possible while arranging the entrance of the husband, a brother, or another man, dressed as a Turkish soldier. The "soldier" would claim that the Christian was breaking the law and demand immediate payment of a large "fine"—later split by the prostitute and her partner.

Napoleon's Sister's Lover Paints Holy Land

1817

Upon His Return to France, His Pictures Are Printed Using a New Technique—Lithography

The Church of the Holy Sepulcher, by the Comte de Forbin.

A statue of Pauline Borghese, by A. Canova.

Louis Nicolas Philipe August, Comte de Forbin, was one of the fathers of lithography. The count was a well-known society painter in Paris and a student of David, but he won fame in his youth as the lover of Maria-Paulette, the most beautiful of Napoleon's sisters and the wife of Prince Borghese, a member of the famous Borghese family. (At the Villa Borghese in Rome there still stands a statue of the naked Maria-Paulette in the image of Venus—the work of the sculptor Antonio Canova.)

Gossip in Napoleon's court had it that the wild Maria-Paulette, who was

dissatisfied with her husband, found comfort in the arms of the count. Unfortunately, de Forbin was so virile that Maria-Paulette became ill from the overwhelming effort his energies compelled her to expend.

After Napoleon fell from power and Maria-Paulette was no longer young and attractive, de Forbin left her in the arms of a famous Italian composer and set out on a journey to the East. Unwilling to settle for just the usual pilgrim route—Jerusalem and Bethlehem—he brought with him upon his return the first sketches of Gaza and Ashkelon, interesting renderings of Acre, the Sea of Galilee, bathing in the Jordan, and, of course, the requisite pictures of Jerusalem. De Forbin published his work in a huge volume, for which a new technique— lithography—was used.

De Forbin's drawings were celebrated less for their beauty than their good fortune at having been the first lithographic works to be printed.

First Archaeological Excavations in Jerusalem

William John Banks, a member of the British House of Commons and an experienced traveler and scholar, was the first person to carry out archaeological excavations in Jerusalem.

While in Istanbul, Banks attempted in vain to receive permission to excavate the Tombs of the Kings in Jerusalem. Since the governor of Jerusalem also refused to allow him to dig there, Banks excavated secretly. He was joined by several friends: the English travelers Thomas Legh, Charles Irby, and James Mangles. The latter describes the adventure in a book he wrote with Irby.

Each member of the group set out alone one night to met his colleagues near the Tombs of the Kings. They were accompanied by five servants, two of them deck hands from the entourage of Lord Belmore, the governor of Ireland. They toiled vigorously throughout the night, clearing away the earth until morning, when they hit a huge rock that they were unable to budge.

They returned to their clandestine work the following evening and managed to shatter the rock, but were discovered by the Turks and forced to abandon the site. In order to prevent the continuation of the excavation, the governor of the city ordered a wall erected on the spot.

Left: Charles Irby in Middle Eastern attire.

Below: The Tombs of the Kings, by D. Roberts.

Abdalla Pasha Rules Holy Land
Fights Unceasing Wars until Defeated by the Egyptians

Arab warriors from the mountains of Samaria, by D. Roberts.

Jerusalem, and, once there, raked the city with his cannons. When he finally offered them lower taxes and pardon, the rebels capitulated.

In 1826, great changes shook Istanbul's administration. Mahmoud II dispensed with the Janissaries and their allies among the Muslim religious elders, ensuring himself full control of the government, and then embarked on a program of reforms, including the suppression of feudalism in distant semi-autonomous regions and the forceful submission of the large feudal families.

Mahmoud II chose the young Abdalla Pasha to execute his policy in the Holy Land, appointing him pasha of Tripoli and governor of the districts of Jerusalem, Gaza, Nablus, and Jaffa. Now the governor of Acre was in control of the entire Holy Land and Lebanon as well.

Abdalla ruled his territories with an iron fist until Egypt intervened and his government tumbled.

Suleiman's successor was Abdalla Pasha (1818-1832), whose reign was fraught with unceasing wars. He had Haim Farhi executed, as a result of which the governors of Damascus and Aleppo went to war against him, besieging Acre in 1822. Only by bribing and assassinating his opponents did Abdalla free himself from the encirclement. The south of the country was temporarily lost to him during this confrontation, but he continued to rule in Acre and Galilee.

From 1823 to 1826, tax burdens ignited rebellions in the districts of Jerusalem and Samaria. In 1825 an open revolt broke out in Jerusalem and Nablus, and the local governor was ousted. The pasha of Damascus failed to gain control of the situation, and the sultan was compelled to ask Abdalla, the governor of Acre, for assistance.

Abdalla departed with his army for

Englishmen Assist Franciscans Attacked by Greeks

On April 30, 1818, a group of Franciscans holding a service at the Church of the Holy Sepulcher was surrounded by Greek Orthodox, who attacked and injured several of them. William John Banks, Thomas Legh, James Mangles, and Charles Leonard Irby came to the aid of the Franciscans, whose lives were in grave danger. The Englishmen appealed to the governor of the city, compelling him with shouts and threats to put the city garrison at their disposal. With the help of the garrison and their drawn swords, the foreigners extricated the Franciscans and expelled the Greek Orthodox from the church.

Dressed as Arab Woman, Englishwoman Steals into Mosques

Discovered, She Flees to Egypt

Above: The mosques on the Temple Mount, by the Comte de Forbin.
Right: On Mount Zion, by L. Mayer.

The Englishwoman Mrs. Belzoni was the wife of a well-known Italian Egyptologist. Visiting Jerusalem on her own, she proved that the spirit of adventure beat within her heart as well. Though entrance to the area of the mosques on the Temple Mount was forbidden, she decided to infiltrate the compound.

Near the Franciscan hostel where she was staying lived Christian Arab workers—builder-artisans who had been brought to the Holy Land to

1818

Disguised Englishmen Penetrate Petra

Charles Leonard Irby, James Mangles, Thomas Legh, and their party visited Petra disguised as Bedouin six years after its discovery. They hired a guide from a Bedouin tribe camping near Jericho to escort them to the ancient city of red rock. Their most worrisome enemies turned out to be the tribes camping in Petra itself, who feared the Christians' evil eye and well-known tendency to locate treasures in ruins and remove them.

One conflict reached the stage of mutual threats, as first voices and then hands were raised. The Bedouin mustered four hundred warriors, and it appeared that the matter would be settled by a real battle. After a few days of arguments and quarrels, however, a compromise was reached and the English were permitted to enter Petra. Mangles wrote a detailed description of the area of the antiquities and prepared the first map of the site. The publication of Legh's and Mangles' impressions of Petra caused a sensation not only in the scientific community but also among wider circles in England. Throughout the nineteenth century, a journey to Petra was the heart's desire of anyone who purported to be an expert in the lands of the Near East.

renovate the mosques in the Haram al-Sharif. Belzoni befriended them and they promised to take her to the Temple Mount dressed up as one of their wives. The artisans first took the disguised Belzoni to David's Tomb on Mount Zion, where entrance was also forbidden to non-Muslims. Attracting no attention, Belzoni entered the outer courtyard of the tomb and could have, according to her account, continued on inside in exchange for one dollar. She only wished to enter the Haram, however—or perhaps she didn't want to waste the dollar—and did not take advantage of the opportunity.

Unfortunately for the adventuress, the artisans' job at the Temple Mount came to an end and they were no longer able to smuggle her into the sacred precinct. Not willing to give up, Belzoni attempted to bribe the person responsible for the Haram trust. Much to her disappointment, he did not keep his word.

By her third attempt, Belzoni had resolved to rely on nobody. She dressed up as an Arab Jerusalemite woman, hired an Arab girl of about nine years old to accompany her, and entered the Haram, where she visited the Dome of the Rock and Al-Aqsa Mosque. The adventure ended quietly, with no unfortunate discovery, but afterwards the fact of the visit became known in Jerusalem, and in order to escape harm Belzoni was compelled to leave the city hastily and return to her husband in Egypt.

Bedouin horsemen at the foot of Petra, by D. Roberts.

Price of a Good Seat at Holy Fire Ceremony—8,000 Grush

The price of a good spot near the tomb for the Ceremony of the Holy Fire at the Church of the Holy Sepulcher could reach eight thousand *grush* in the early nineteenth century, according to the account of Franz Wilhelm Sieber, who visited Jerusalem in 1818. Sieber relates that in anticipation of the holy fire celebration, the leaders of the Greek Orthodox sect would sell off the best seats near the Holy Tomb to the highest bidder.

According to calculations, the Greek Orthodox earned about five hundred *grush* per pilgrim at the annual ceremony—an enormous sum of 1.5 million *grush* per year—in addition to their income from payments for lodging, confessions, the selling of indulgences, entry fees to heaven, etc.

The Armenians, Sieber states, also sold seats to the Holy Tomb, and on St. James' Day even exchanged the right to remove the cloth covering the head of the saint for one thousand golden ducats!

Given such accounts, it is no surprise that the Protestant doctor Robert Richardson, who visited Jerusalem in 1818, recounted later in wonder that the Armenian monastery was the most magnificent in the city and its monks habits the most ornate.

The Armenian monastery was the most magnificent in Jerusalem. The Church of St. James at the Armenian patriarchate.

The burial place of the head of Saint James in the Armenian Church of St. James.

First Modern Map of Jerusalem Drawn

Risky Map Prepared in Opposition to Sultan's Orders

Franz Wilhelm Sieber prepared the first modern map of Jerusalem by means of on-site measurements.

Sieber was a merchant of exotic plants and rare works of art who lived in Prague. He stayed in Jerusalem and its environs forty-two days, putting himself at great risk while sketching and carrying out his measurements, since both were contrary to the sultan's orders and not much to the taste of the fanatic Muslim population.

Sieber disguised his preparatory work as nature hikes for botanical research. He stayed in Jerusalem for the scorching month of July, and purposefully went out to measure during the hottest noon hours, when the field workers were resting from their labors. He was usually accompanied by a local Christian assistant, who, carrying a few plants as an alibi, warned Sieber whenever he saw a Muslim approaching.

Muslim rider demanded to know what was written on it, but Sieber deftly managed to switch it for a letter in Arabic that he had received in Cairo. The rider calmed down as soon as he saw the Arabic script.

Another time, Sieber met a resident of the village of Siloam armed with a rifle. His trusty escort immediately ran away, at which point, according to the account in Sieber's book, the Arab aimed his rifle at him and cocked the trigger, his face glowing with arrogance. He appeared to be enjoying alarming Sieber, who quite reasonably believed that his life was about to come to a premature and unpleasant end.

At the fateful moment, Sieber threw a fistful of coins between the Arab's legs. Fortunately for the cartographer, they were new coins, and they flashed

The village of Siloam, by D. Roberts.

The two experienced moments of real danger. Once, a local Arab rode up to them on horseback, galloping at such speed that Sieber did not have time to hide the paper in his hand. The in the sunlight. The Arab took his hand off the rifle and demanded that Sieber gather the money for him. In response, Sieber threw more coins at his attacker's feet, and as the Arab was busy gathering them up, escaped with his life.

Warning: European Dress Dangerous

Wear Arab Costume to Avoid Attack

William Rae Wilson, the closest friend of the duke of Kent, father of Queen Victoria, learned the hard way how dangerous it was to travel in the Holy Land in European dress.

While staying in Jerusalem in 1819, Wilson decided one day to tour outside the city walls. He abandoned his eastern costume in order to walk about more easily, and resuming his usual form of dress, set out on his hike as the proper Englishman he was. As he approached the city upon his return, however, a sudden shower of stones whistled around his ears, one of them almost striking him. Wilson hastily returned to the monastery where he was staying and recounted his story to the resident monks.

They confirmed that the anonymous assailant's intention had indeed been to kill him and advised him not to venture out again in European dress, but to wear eastern garb in order to protect himself from harm and insult—the expression of the hatred of Christians lurking in the Muslims' hearts.

Sir Frederick Henniker Departs for Sinai Peninsula: Miraculously Rescued from Bedouin

Robbed and Wounded During Journey to Jericho

Sir Frederick Henniker was an English aristocrat with a taste for adventure. Dissatisfied with the usual pilgrimage itinerary, he set out on a journey through the central Sinai Peninsula such as very few had made before him in the nineteenth century.

As was accepted practice, Henniker traveled disguised as a Muslim, but in one of the Bedouin encampments where he stopped, the fact that he was a European Christian was discovered. The members of the tribe wanted to murder him on the spot. His Bedouin escort only barely succeeded in saving him by threatening the murderers with retaliation by his own tribe. At another Bedouin encampment, the situation was reversed and Henniker's entourage was attacked because of their Bedouin escort, who apparently owed their host fifty head of sheep and several camels.

In another incident that occurred while he was attempting to reach Jericho with insufficient escort, Henniker was assaulted by eight bandits. The servant and Turkish soldier accompanying him fled, and in the fray one of the bandits cut

Henniker's ear and slashed one side of his face with his sword. They then stripped him bare, robbed him of all his possessions, and made their getaway. Henniker's servant and the Turkish soldier had him transported to Jerusalem, where the pharmacist from the Franciscan monastery cared for him for several weeks (as there was no permanent doctor in the city). Meanwhile, negotiations were held with a representative of the bandits, and most of Henniker's possessions were returned to him, with the exception of a book and a pair of trousers.

Not surprisingly, Henniker came away with a somewhat negative view of the Holy Land in general and of Jerusalem in particular: he described the streets of the holy city as narrow and neglected, its houses as dirty and in disrepair, and its few stores as untended. Nowhere, he reported, was there a sign of trade, comfort, or wealth.

Entry to the Temple Mount was still forbidden to Christians and Jews. Not long before, Henniker reported, a man had robbed a tourist and then fled to the Temple Mount as if to a place of

A Bedouin warrior in full dress, by D. Roberts.

sanctuary. Shortly afterward, a Greek Orthodox man who entered the area of the mosque while accompanying his Turkish master was required to convert; upon his refusal he was mur-

dered by the crowd. His body was cast outside the Temple Mount precinct, where a Muslim who passed by it kicked its head, crying "So shall be done to all Christians!"

Acre's Inhabitants Recruited to Work on Fortifications

Rich and Poor Alike Forced to Labor Immersed in Water

John Carne, the son of an English banker, spent time in Acre while Abdalla Pasha was preparing for an upcoming war. The pasha decided to surround his city, in addition to the double walls, with moats, and he recruited all of Acre's inhabitants to provide the labor force for the job.

According to Carne, one could see soldiers beating passers-by and idlers into reporting for work digging the canal, and the city was almost completely emptied of inhabitants. When he visited the canal site one day, Carne found people from all walks of life toiling on its construction—wealthy people, merchants, servants, and, of course, the city's poor.

Some of them stood working in water up to their chins. Everyone had a basket in hand; they filled them with dirt from the bottom of the moat and then tossed the contents on the bank. Overseers supervised all the work.

At noon, bread and water were distributed to the laborers, and only at evening were they allowed to return to town. The wealthy strode away first, the poor trudging along behind. Among all of them were those lacking either a nose or an ear—victims of the days of al-Jazzar. The mountain people, who were also forced to come and work, brought up the rear singing their mountain songs in good-natured humor.

People from all walks of life toiled during the construction of Acre's walls.

Greek Orthodox Sect Faces Bankruptcy

Church of Holy Sepulcher Renovations and Greek War of Independence Break the Bank

Renovating the Church of the Holy Sepulcher required enormous financial investment, and the Greek Orthodox Church, despite its celebrated wealth, was forced to borrow huge sums from Jews and Muslims.

In 1821, a rebellion broke out in Greece and the flow of contributions and pilgrims from there to the Holy Land turned into a trickle. The Greek Orthodox, finding themselves unable to repay their creditors, were forced to sell silver and gold utensils from their churches in order to make good on their debts. The creditors even demanded that the Ottoman authorities compel the Greek Orthodox to sell monasteries in order to reimburse them.

In 1829, at the end of the Greek War of Independence, the authorities decided that the creditors would have to be content with ten percent of the original debt per year without interest, thus saving the Greek Orthodox Church from bankruptcy.

The Holy Sepulcher, by the Comte de Forbin.

Existence of Peninsula between Eilat and Aqaba Refuted

Eduard Rüppell.

Pasha Muhammad Ali Asks Rüppell to Reseach Natural Resources of Sinai Peninsula

The fortress of Aqaba.

Eduard Rüppell, the first European since the Crusades to arrive in Eilat and Aqaba, was a native of Frankfort on the Main and the scion of a wealthy family. His father was a well-known banker who put at his son's disposal enough financial resources to ensure that he did not ever have to worry about supporting himself.

Rüppell made a journey to Sinai in 1817 and one year later published an article on the research he had conducted during the trip. Afterwards, he studied science for several years at the University of Pavia in Italy and trained in the use of optical instruments for determining geographic location.

In 1822, Rüppell traveled again to Egypt, where he was asked by the pasha Muhammad Ali to help research the natural resources of the Sinai Peninsula. The pasha equipped Rüppell with an entourage of thirteen people, enabling him to travel freely through wild regions divided between hostile Bedouin tribes. He followed the Darb al-Haj (the Pilgrim Route) to Mecca from west to east. (Burckhardt had been the first European to travel this route, though in the opposite direction.)

On April 30, 1822, Rüppell reached Eilat and Aqaba, where he was received with great pomp by the Egyptian garrison. He stayed there four days and determined the exact geographical location of Aqaba with his instruments. Because of the absence of ships in the gulf at the time, he was unable to perform depth measurements of its waters. According to him, the local inhabitants fished with palm fronds that they lashed together.

It was during this visit that Rüppell once and for all dispelled the myth of the existence of the peninsula between Eilat and Aqaba that had been appearing for dozens of years on most maps of the Middle East.

At the conclusion of his journey, Rüppell recommended to Muhammad Ali that he not mine the veins of copper in the northwest part of the Sinai Peninsula, mainly because of transport problems and the difficulty of supplying the fuel necessary for operating the smelting ovens.

Pasha Muhammad Ali in his palace.

Richard Robert Madden Bests Bandits

1826

Irishman Extricates Himself from Trouble Four Times

Richard Robert Madden was a native of Ireland and a physician. He toured in the guise of an Easterner, his long beard adding an authentic touch to his getup. His appearance was so convincing that bandits who took him captive on his way from Suez apologized to him and returned the Turkish coins they had stolen from him.

On his way from Nazareth to Jaffa, Madden fell into the clutches of thieves four times. From the first three incidents he emerged more or less unscathed and the bandits allowed him to continue his journey in return for payment. The fourth attack, however, which took place between Nazareth and Acre, was more treacherous. Eight Bedouin, armed with spears and rifles, fell upon him and his servant. Madden succeeded in escaping, but the servant and all of Madden's belongings were captured. He watched from afar as his property was spread out on the ground to be divided amongst the thieves, and then, extraordinarily, returned to confront the robbers face to face.

One of the Bedouin caught the reins of his horse and commanded him to dismount. Madden shoved him away, turned to the man who appeared to be the chief, and told him that since they had chased him but had not succeeded in catching him, he had now come to them of his own free will—as a guest. And a man who raised a hand to his guest was not an Arab but a Turk and an infidel!

Finished with his speech, which made quite an impression on the bandits, Madden sat down on the ground and lit a pipe using a small magnifying glass, which struck the Bedouin as miraculous. Madden's servant warned them that his master was a miracle worker who could either summon fire from the sky and rain curses down on them or invoke a blessing upon those who treated him as an Arab.

In the account of his travels, Madden relates that he had never been surrounded by such a repulsive and frightening collection of faces as at that moment. Murder and robbery were etched on their foreheads. While speaking to them, he anticipated a blow to the head at any moment. Nevertheless, in an amazing expression of

Richard Robert Madden examines a Muslim patient.

self-possession, he drew a package of laxative powder from his headdress, divided the contents into eight equal portions, and gave one to each of the bandits together with instructions to use the powder only when ill...

Madden did not give the robbers much time to recover from their shock: he shoved a large quantity of tobacco and coffee at them, scooped up his recovered belongings, and beat a hasty retreat.

1827

French Flag Flies over Coral Island Crusader Fortress

Marquis de Laborde Investigates Coral Island, Paints Petra, and Prepares Map of Region

Marquis Léon Emmanuel Simon Joseph de Laborde, who visited the East from 1827 to 1828, was the son of a family that had been both well-connected and wealthy for many generations. His grandfather, who

Left: The Marquis de Laborde.
Below: The Crusader castle on Coral Island.

had been the leading banker in the court of the French King Louis XV, had aided in funding the French involvement in the American War of Independence. In recognition of his services, he had been granted his aristocratic title. His son Alexander (Léon's father) published illustrated travel books:

De Laborde followed in his father's footsteps. In 1827 the two set out with a few companions on a journey to Asia

The ancient ghost town of Petra.

Minor, Syria, the Holy Land, and Egypt. The father soon tired, however, and his son continued on to the most interesting portion of the journey by himself. He arrived via Suez at Saint Catherine's Monastery on the Sinai Peninsula, whence he continued to the Gulf of Eilat and Aqaba.

Young de Laborde was the first European traveler since the Crusades to set foot on nearby Coral Island. He landed there on a primitive raft he had fashioned from palm fronds, flew the French flag high above the island's Crusader fortress, and outlined a sketch of the island on a piece of paper he carried under his hat to keep from getting wet.

De Laborde then sent messengers from Aqaba to the Bedouin tribes around Petra, and with their assistance succeeded in both reaching the ancient ghost town and avoiding the obstacles that had hindered the explorers who had traveled the same way before him. He had time to draw Petra's antiquities carefully, prepare a good map of the region, and ascend to those ruins that his predecessors had not reached.

The Frenchman's drawings were published with explanations in a huge volume that was issued to great acclaim and made him famous throughout the world. Soon de Laborde took upon himself the publication of a second book, describing his travels with his father in Asia Minor, Syria, and the Holy Land—the prelude to his journey to Petra. The two volumes are the largest and heaviest (the first weighs 15 kilograms) travelogues on the Holy Land ever published. In fact, the giant volumes proved to be so inconvenient that only a few copies were ever actually sold.

During the period of the empire of Napoleon III, de Laborde was first appointed director of the Louvre and later director of the imperial archives. He also published books on various fields of art.

Armenians and Franciscans Clash over Golgotha Altar

In 1827, the Armenians attempted to expel the Franciscans from the altar at Golgotha, but the Franciscans forcibly ousted the Armenians from the place instead.

After a series of clashes, the matter was brought to the governor to decide. Since it was clear that his decision would favor whomever offered him the largest bribe, both sides paid the governor a substantial sum.

At the time, the Irish physician Richard R. Madden was treating the governor, and he took advantage of the opportunity to inquire of him how much he had received from each side. Apparently, the Armenians had paid eight thousand *grush*, and the Fran-

The altars at Calvary—Stations XI, XII, and XIII on the Way of the Cross.

ciscans only six thousand. Madden transmitted the information to the Franciscans, who raised their offer by three thousand *grush* and won the contest. The altar has remained in Franciscan hands to this day.

Activity of Austrian Consulate in Acre Recommences

Count von Osten Convinces Abdalla Pasha to Return Confiscated Property to Austrian Consul

In 1829, the governor of Acre, Abdalla Pasha, incarcerated the Austrian consul, extracted a great deal of money from him through blackmail, confiscated his property, and expelled him and his family from the city. The Austrian authorities, having decided not to remain silent about the insult, sent Count Anton Prokesch Ritter von Osten to the Holy Land to negotiate with the malevolent ruler.

Von Osten describes the meeting with Abdalla in his travel book. Upon his arrival in the city, a large delegation of officers came to fetch the count to the pasha. Along the street leading to the palace and within the palace itself, soldiers stood in rows. An army of servants was arrayed up to the very door of the hall in which the meeting took place.

Von Osten writes that he anticipated meeting a man of grave countenance whose clothes could not be wiped clean of bloodstains. Instead he found a smiling and good-natured fellow who presented him with a bouquet of roses when he sat down. The pasha, reports von Osten, was not more than thirty-three years old, and his face was slightly pockmarked from smallpox. His attire was simple, but rich. He wore a type of North African cloak secured in front by a diamond-encrusted clasp, and a pearl-encrusted dagger was stuck into his belt.

Count Anton Prokesch Ritter von Osten.

In conversation with the Austrian, Abdalla spoke knowledgeably about various matters, European rulers, and the sultan. Von Osten gradually brought the conversation around to the subject that had occasioned his arrival. Abdalla expressed his regret about what had transpired, promised to return the sum of money that had been taken, agreed that the work of the consulate be renewed, and even gave permission for the Austrian flag to be hoisted anew the following day. To all the rest of von Osten's demands, which were presented as requests, the pasha acceded equally graciously.

In the East, the count concluded, every transaction depends upon its outward form, and even the most difficult thing can be achieved if one only knows how to present it, leaving its image intact.

Acre in 1819, by the Comte de Forbin.

Banks of the Jordan. April 2nd 1839.

CHAPTER IX

THE ADVENT OF THE MODERN AGE

1831-1876

ince the second millennium BC, every powerful Egyptian ruler has attempted at one time or another to gain control of the Holy Land. At the beginning of the nineteenth century it was Muhammad Ali, who rose to greatness in the military during the expulsion of the French and gained control over the entire land of the Nile, where he introduced European administrative methods and established a modern, well-organized army. When the Turkish sultan called upon Ali's assistance in his attempt to overcome the Greek freedom fighters, he promised to transfer the Holy Land and Syria to the Egyptian ruler's control. When the sultan failed to fulfill his promise, Muhammad Ail decided to take the territories by force.

Leading the conquering army was Ibrahim Pasha, Muhammad Ali's nephew and adopted son who was also his best commander. Acre, Abdalla Pasha's place of residence, was the primary target of the campaign. In the fall of 1831, the Egyptian infantry and naval forces moved north, capturing Jaffa and Jerusalem. Acre, always a difficult place to win, remained beyond their grasp.

The walls that even Napoleon had not been able to overcome had been doubled during the last years of Ahmed al-

Previous pages: Pilgrims immersing themselves in the River Jordan, by D. Roberts.
Inset: The officers of the Palestine Exploration Fund survey the Holy Land.
Background: The Mount of Olives, by E. Pierotti.

Jazzar, and the city's fortifications strengthened by both Suleiman and Abdalla. Only at the end of May 1832, after half a year of offensive forays, did Ibrahim Pasha manage to take Acre. The city ceased to be the capital of the Holy Land, and served afterwards only as the district capital.

When Ibrahim Pasha had completed the conquest of the Holy Land and Syria he began to institute far-reaching changes. His goal was to establish a strong centralized administration according to the Egyptian model. As he did so, the state of security in the Holy Land began to improve and resolute steps were taken against the Bedouin tribes and bandits.

At first the new regime enjoyed local sympathy, but within a short while opposition arose to Egyptian rule. The centralized system of administration common to Egypt did not suit the Holy Land: its inhabitants opposed the regular payment of taxes; the conservative Muslim fundamentalists opposed the equal rights granted to Christians and Jews; the ancient feudal families opposed the various limitations placed upon them; the Muslim clergy opposed secular amendments (such as the establishment of nonreligious courts); and the peasants opposed the labor forced upon them. By far the most hated Egyptian imposition, however, was the introduction of a general compulsory draft.

The dissatisfaction caused the explosion in May 1834 of the broadest popular rebellion the Holy Land had seen in many generations. Despite the fact that it is known as the Peasant Rebellion, it was led by the great feudal lords, who this time collaborated against the foreign regime. The rebellions occurred in Jerusalem, Bethlehem, and Hebron, but the longest-lasting and most dangerous erupted in the mountains of Samaria.

On May 19, rebel peasants from Hebron and Mount Samaria amassed around Jerusalem. The Egyptian garrison repelled their first few attacks, but on the night of June 6 the rebels succeeded in penetrating the city through one of its sewage pipes, and the garrison retreated to the Citadel.

The city changed hands several more times until June 29, when Muhammad Ali himself arrived in the Holy Land at the head of fifteen thousand experienced troops. The huge force frightened most of the feudal lords, who quickly surrendered. The uprisings in most places were quashed in July, and the Egyptian government once again ruled the Holy Land. The Egyptian regime never became more popular, however, and its presence in the Holy Land was seen as an enemy occupation. The compulsory military service in particular continued to arouse opposition. In 1838, a new revolt broke out—this time among the Druze in the Hauran. Though the rebel forces managed to reach Safed, the Egyptians eventually crushed that rebellion as well.

The great powers finally intervened. Britain had decided to reinforce the Ottoman Empire so that it would be able to provide an efficient buffer against southward expansion by Russia. The other European powers agreed, only France offering a mild protest to the British scheme.

In 1840, a large British fleet was dispatched to the Middle East together with a few Austrian and Turkish vessels.

It came first to the aid of the uprising against the Egyptians in the Lebanon Mountains, its forces routing the Egyptian infantry and conquering Beirut. Eventually, Ibrahim Pasha was forced to withdraw from Lebanon and to relinquish Syria and Anatolia as well.

After the conquest of Acre by the British and the Austrians, the entire Egyptian military operation in the area collapsed and Ibrahim Pasha quickly retreated with his army via Transjordan to Gaza and Egypt. The Holy Land returned to Turkish rule.

In the last years before the Egyptian conquest, the publication of travel books on the Holy Land had slackened, attesting to the ebbing wave of travelers from the West. Due to the domestic strife on one hand and the aggression of external enemies on the other, few Western travelers and pilgrims dared to set out on such a dangerous journey.

At the completion of the Egyptian conquest, however, the situation changed dramatically. The Egyptian government opened the gates of the Holy Land to Western travelers and Western influence alike. In Europe, meanwhile, elite society was embracing a novel intellectual trend. The rationalist opposition to religion characteristic of the eighteenth century succumbed to a wave of renewed Christian faith, nostalgia for the Middle Ages, and an appreciation of the historical past. The Romantic movement transformed the Holy Land, the land of Jesus, into a focal point for those who were able to afford long-distance travel.

Furthermore, in the mid-1830s there was a revolution in sea travel: steamboats began to replace small sailing vessels, and travelers' time aboard ship was greatly reduced. The state of security on the seas improved, and pirates began to disappear. Within several years, the journey to the Holy Land was transformed from a perilous adventure into a routine summer entertainment.

As the security situation on the roads of the Holy Land also improved, Palestine became an appropriate destination for not just young, armed adventurers but the elderly, women, and children. Protestant missionaries began to settle in Jerusalem, and in 1839 the first consular representative—an Englishman—arrived on the scene.

Tourism in the Holy Land flourished. Europeans could now move about in their usual attire. Commerce flowered. European goods—watches, photography equipment, modern weapons, steamships, pumps, and oil lamps for light and heating—appeared in all the markets. Cheap cotton cloth from England and metal products from the Continent were sold in large quantities.

The Europeans who settled in the Holy Land brought with them household goods such as furniture, bed linens, and even pianos. But Western influence was not solely material. Western culture, languages, and medicine began to penetrate the Holy Land. Western historians, including the Swiss Titus Tobler and the American Edward Robinson, appeared on the scene. The Austrian Joseph Rusegger laid the foundations for geological research in the Holy Land. The Irishman Christopher Costigan was the first scholar to sail the Dead Sea, though he drowned in the attempt. In 1837, the German Gottfried Heinrich von Schubert and the Englishmen George Henry Moore and Charles Beke discovered that the Dead Sea, the River Jordan, and the Arava were all below sea level. A nearly perfect map of the Holy Land was sketched by Heinrich Kiepert as a result of Robinson's journey. The landscape of the Holy Land became famous the world over as the pictures of David Roberts, J.H. Bernatz, William Henry Bartlett, Count Joseph d'Estourmel, and Ulrich Halbrieter were published.

◈

In 1840—the year that Turkey returned to rule the Holy Land—the Ottoman Empire was in the midst of a process of renewal and reform. Sultan Muhammad II, who had initiated a novel Westernizing trend in order to rescue his empire from imminent decline, died in 1839, but his sons Abdul Majid (1839-1861) and Abdul Aziz (1861-1876) proceeded along the lines of the program he had formulated. It was in this spirit that new edicts were published in Istanbul.

Not all of the decrees made their mark immediately in the outer provinces like the mountains of Hebron or Samaria. In Jerusalem and Jaffa, however, where the westward turn was especially apparent because of the rush of Europeans to the traditional centers of the Holy Land, the tenor of the age was increasingly palpable. The changes were slow but significant, and gradually the profile of the Holy Land rose. The consuls of the great European powers that began to display an interest in the country often wielded great influence in Jerusalem and its vicinity.

The greatest achievements of the Tanzimat regime in the Holy Land were related to issues of security. After the departure of the Egyptians, the conflicts between feudal families, as well as between the Kis and Yaman factions, were renewed, especially in the mountains of Hebron and Samaria. Eventually, a series of massacres and rebellions resulted in strong protests by the Continent's most influential powers, whose flags were burnt in Nablus by the raging crowd.

The Turks decided to bring order to the region, and set out to complete Abdalla Pasha and Ibrahim Pasha's work. From 1858 to 1859 they forcibly took control of the two relevant districts and brought about both the final capitulation of the great feudal families and the elimination of the conflict between the Yaman and Kis.

The last local despot to control the Jezreel Valley and the Lower Galilee was Akili Aga. Aga operated at times for the Turkish powers and at times against them. He had good connections with the Western world. He accompanied an American scientific mission to the Dead Sea, entertained the prince of Wales in his tent in 1862, and received an award from Napoleon III for rescuing Christians in Galilee from a massacre in 1860. Ultimately, however, he was forced to retreat to Transjordan.

From 1860 onwards, the security situation in the Holy Land improved. Bands of marauders still operated here and there, but in contrast to the past, they were the exception and not the rule. Tourists and explorers from the West could now visit all of the sites in the Holy Land in relative safety, and their numbers grew.

War Oriental Style: Egyptians Besiege Acre

Tourist Arrives at Acre during Siege and Is Arrested

Henri Cornille, who arrived in the Holy Land on a leisurely summer trip, happened into an Egyptian camp as it besieged Acre. The Egyptians, suspecting he was a spy, did not allow Cornille to leave for several months.

His misfortune was history's boon, however, since he detailed the turn of the siege in his later travel book.

Cornille describes Ibrahim Pasha, commander of the siege; appearing to be about forty-five years old, he was

short in stature, with a hard, wild gaze and heavy brows. His light-toned beard looked like a dishrag hanging on his chin. An old, long, brown coat covered his broad chest and part of his short limbs. Thus Cornille provides us

The ruler of Lebanon honors Ibrahim Pasha at the gates of Acre.

with an idea of the mien of the hangman of Greece.

The Egyptian camp did not much impress Cornille either. It was comprised of low white Arab tents arranged in three rows. A number of filthy, sickly soldiers sat around a cauldron cooking rice. Others cleaned their weapons or stood guard. The commanders went from row to row, beating the soldiers on the back with their sticks.

The pashas, beys, and bimbashas (regimental commanders) galloped among the forces, the soldiers falling to the ground to bow to them. Camels passed through the crowd, grunting nostalgically for the desert and chewing cud. The muezzin issued his call to prayer. In the background was the sound of cannons exploding in the city—an eastern style war.

Military exercises near Acre, by D. Roberts.

Two Weeks of Rain Pours over Haifa Homes

Major Thomas Skinner.

Officer Skinner Swims into Haifa, Finds Shelter from Flood in Carmel Monastery.

Major Thomas Skinner, a British officer who arrived in Haifa in 1833 in the midst of a storm that had already lasted several days, was amazed to discover that the city had almost entirely disappeared. Haifa, he relates, was encircled by a wall. It had one small gate facing the sea, but the

storm had rendered it almost impassable, as a river three-feet deep flowed through it, carrying with it planks and stones.

Skinner was forced to take off his trousers and shoes, wrap them in his wet coat, and plunge into the water. With a great deal of effort he managed to pass through the gate, only to find himself up to his waist in the middle of what appeared to be a lake, surrounded by the debris that had been caught up in the waters of the river and had piled up within the portal of the wall. Skinner was actually in a courtyard, though the only structure still standing was a tower. At its foot Skinner found a door leading into a dark room, in which he found temporary shelter.

Later, Skinner encountered two Jews who had crawled in under the ruins of a hut. They told him that all of Haifa's houses had been swept away in the rains that had been pelting the city for two weeks straight.

Skinner succeeded in finding the house of the consular agent, where he was invited to dry his clothing and warm himself. But right when he and his host sat down to eat a hot meal, the

agent's home began to collapse, leaving the Englishman once again exposed to the elements. Skinner finally arrived on the Carmel, where he took refuge at the Carmelite monastery.

The bay of Haifa during a storm, by C.W. Wilson.

Sabil Qa'itbay on the Temple Mount, by P. Lortet.

English Architects Make First Temple Mount Measurements

A Risky Refusal to Comply with Prohibition on Entering Temple Mount

Muslim worshipers in the Haram al-Sharif, by C.W. Wilson.

In 1833, three young English architects by the names of Catherwood, Bonomi, and Arundale embarked on an extensive journey to the East. From Egypt they passed through the Sinai Peninsula to St. Catherine's Monastery, and from there traveled north, traversing the Darb al-Haj and arriving in Gaza. From Gaza they continued on to Jerusalem, where adventure awaited them.

Entrance to the Temple Mount was forbidden to non-Muslims for the entire period of Ottoman rule. Though some Europeans nevertheless succeeded in penetrating the precinct, they did so under conditions that did not allow them to provide accurate descriptions of it, not to mention any measurements, drawings, or sketches. Catherwood, Bonomi, and

Arundale decided to try their luck. One day, Catherwood, the leader of the group, donned the uniform of an Egyptian officer and entered the Temple Mount accompanied by a servant. Trying to maintain his pose as an Egyptian army man, he took a pad out of his pocket and began to draw.

After a short while, the Arabs in the Haram noticed Catherwood, who recounts how they approached, surrounded him, and cursed him loudly. As their number grew, the Englishman's chances of escape shrank. His servant Suleiman screamed at those crowding around that he would tell the governor what they were doing and even dared to beat the crowd with his whip. The moment was fateful—the crowd, incensed, would tear the travelers to pieces at any moment.

Just then, the governor of the city and his entourage appeared. A dervish appealed to him, demanding that the infidel be punished for defiling the holy place. The governor, who knew Catherwood and was certain that the visit was taking place with the approval of the ruler Ibrahim Pasha, began to calm things down. He told the Arabs that the mosque was in poor shape and that their master Muhammad Ali had sent "this effendi" to carry out measurements in order to repair it. There was no alternative but to employ whomever could carry out the task, and so he requested that they disperse. Catherwood thanked the governor and for the next six weeks he

and his two friends, whom he recruited as his assistants, made use of the opportunity to carry out surveys, drawings, and sketches of the entire Temple Mount.

Thus the first thorough, modern survey of the Temple Mount precinct was prepared by Christians during a period when entrance to non-Muslims was forbidden. Only when the three learned that Ibrahim Pasha was about to visit the city did they decide it would be best if they decamped posthaste. Strangely, the expert team's extensive surveying work was never assembled and published, despite the great risk the three had incurred in order to carry it out.

Sophisticated Trick Wins Jaffa

1831

Ibrahim Pasha Fools Jaffa Citizens Visiting His Ship and Enters City with Army

Marie-Joseph de Geramb.

The Egyptian viceroy Ibrahim Pasha gained control of Jaffa by means of a sophisticated gambit that presented itself to him by chance but which he was wise enough to quickly exploit.

He had set out with several sailboats to attack Acre. When he passed Jaffa, several of its distinguished citizens thought they ought to pay him a visit. The moment they boarded the ship, Ibrahim forced the skippers who had brought them to navigate a few of his warships to the beach. He landed fifteen hundred of his troops in Jaffa and took control of the city as the surprised soldiers of the local pasha fled without firing a shot.

The story of the ploy was recounted later by Marie-Joseph de Geramb, who arrived in Jaffa several days after Ibrahim Pasha's victory. De Geramb was a former Austrian officer who had been taken prisoner during the Napoleonic wars. At the conclusion of the wars, he had joined the Trappist order of contemplative monks.

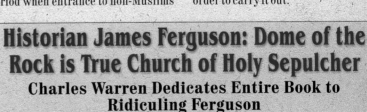

Historian James Ferguson: Dome of the Rock is True Church of Holy Sepulcher

Charles Warren Dedicates Entire Book to Ridiculing Ferguson

The well-known architectural historian James Ferguson purchased the sketches and drawings of the Temple Mount prepared by the architect Fredrick Catherwood and his colleagues. From this material and other documents he gathered, Ferguson came to an extraordinary conclusion: the original Church of the Holy Sepulcher was not to be found in the place known today by this name: The Dome of the Rock was the true Church of the Holy Sepulcher, built by Emperor Constantine the Great. Stranger still was the amount of attention accorded Ferguson's theory. Only the renowned scholar Charles Warren succeeded in laying the farfetched proposal to rest once and for all by dedicating an entire book to its ridicule.

Disaster at Ceremony of Holy Fire in Jerusalem

Crowd Rushes Candles Lit by Patriarch.
Crazed Christians Crushed: Guards Stab the Devout.

Waiting for the Holy Fire at the Church of the Holy Sepulcher, by H.A. Harper.

Robert Curzon, a member of the British Parliament, visited Jerusalem during Easter in 1834 and was among the survivors of the disaster that occurred at the Church of the Holy Sepulcher during the Ceremony of the Holy Fire.

Curzon left a description of the catastrophe. The behavior of the worked-up pilgrims was wild. The crowd was so large that people began to crawl on top of each other and stand on one another's shoulders. Because of the press of people and the lamps, the heat soon became unbearable.

Ibrahim Pasha finally arrived and was led to his spot. The Greek patriarch entered the tomb to perform the miracle of lighting the candle. The excitement of the pilgrims peaked. They cried out, the multitudes moving back and forth like sheaves in the wind. Finally, light was seen shining from the tomb, and the patriarch emerged with beeswax candles from which those present would light their own candles.

A raging battle ensued. Everyone wanted to receive the holy fire, and would even extinguish their neighbor's candle in an effort to try and light their own. The flames spread quickly. The chapels, vestibules, and every corner that could accommodate a candle appeared as if they were on fire. Suddenly, disaster struck. Three people fell to their deaths from the balconies. An Armenian girl died in her place from heat and exhaustion. Heavy smoke shrouded what was happening in the church.

When Curzon and his friends tried to leave the church at the end of the ceremony, they encountered piles of

The chapels, vestibules, and corners of the church appeared as if they were on fire.

human bodies. Curzon, who led the way, relates that he progressed among the corpses as best he could until they were stacked so high that he was forced to step on top of them. It took him some time to realize that the people he was passing were all dead. Initially he had thought they were tired from the ceremony and had lay down to rest, but when he looked more closely at them he saw to his horror that their faces wore the unmistakable mask of death.

The panic-stricken crowd had apparently begun to press and mill outwards, everyone wishing to escape the church. The Muslim guards outside, alarmed by the general frenzy, thought the Christians were assaulting them, and the commotion became a battle. The soldiers killed many of the fainting people emerging from the church with their daggers. Blood spurted onto the walls. Anyone who fell was immediately trampled underfoot. The struggle became so desperate that even the pilgrims appeared as if they wished to annihilate each other

in their frantic attempts to save themselves.

Curzon himself was almost trampled in the confusion, but fled the worst of the melee by retreating into the church, where he noted about four hundred corpses. Even Ibrahim Pasha barely managed to escape the mob.

Rebel Peasants Storm Jerusalem

American Pilgrim: "They're Similar in Temperament to the Indians"

On May 19, 1834, rebel peasants from Hebron and the mountains of Samaria amassed around Jerusalem. The Egyptian garrison repelled the first attack. An American eyewitness described the scene as follows:

Within a few days, Jerusalem was encircled by a crowd of twenty thousand people who had gone totally berserk. They did not have enough ammunition and they did not have cannons, but they deployed themselves on the surrounding hills, perhaps in the hope of starving out the garrison, coming up with a stratagem, or, more probably, without knowing at all what they were doing nor how to go about it. The situation of Jerusalem's inhabitants, who found themselves surrounded by a wild and unrestrained throng, was obviously unpleasant.

To the American, who noted their skin color, attire, and temperament, the peasants appeared to resemble Indians.

English Artist Bartlett: Acre in Shambles After Siege

Painter's Picture-Perfect Travel Book: Portraits of Jaffa, Haifa, and Acre

The Englishman William Henry Bartlett was one of the most successful painters and writers of the genre of illustrated travel books. He published books on, among other destinations, Sicily, North America, Malta, and Gibraltar. But to no other country was he so attached as to the Holy Land.

Bartlett first visited the Holy Land as a young man in 1834, when he was dispatched to prepare illustrations for a large multi-volume publication. Though the texts were written by John Carne, who had toured the Holy Land about ten years previously, today the books are called by Bartlett's name, as

W.H. Bartlett's paintings:
Right: Khan al-Omdan in Acre.
Below: Saint Catherine's Monastery.

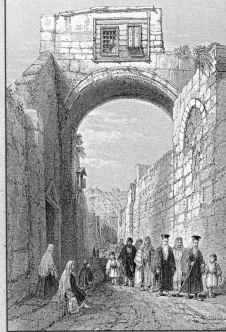

The Ecce Homo Arch, by W.H. Bartlett.

it was his pictures that imbued them with their special character and brought about their great commercial success. Bartlett did not prepare the pictures of Jerusalem and its environs for the publication, however; his contribution was made up of drawings of the region of the Dead Sea, Galilee, Syria, and Lebanon, as well as renderings of Jaffa, Haifa, and Acre.

In a book he published twenty years later, Bartlett describes Acre's appearance after the siege of Ibrahim Pasha from 1831 to 1832. The famous city, so embattled throughout history and the most important fortified site in the Holy Land, had been utterly destroyed: entire streets had turned to heaps of rubble, the roofs of the mosques had been demolished, the fountains had dried up, and even the massive fortress rebuilt by the ruthless Ahmed al-Jazzar with walls fifteen feet thick had been badly damaged by the cannonballs that had rained down upon it throughout the six-month siege. Those residents of the city who remained alive had begun to repair their crumbling houses, and little by little the ruined market showed the first signs of renewed trade.

Bartlett visited the Holy Land three more times—in 1842, 1845, and 1853—and published many more books about it. His pictures were extremely successful, and were reprinted in many other books about the Holy Land, usually with no mention of the original artist.

After his last trip Bartlett compiled a book in which he surveyed the penetration of Western influence in Jerusalem, the growth of its European colony, the beginning of the religious conflict that resulted in the Crimean War, the establishment of the first printers in Jerusalem, and the discoveries of the missionary James Thomas Barclay at various sites in the city. The main beauty of the book was its illustrations—evocative images in a small format, with slim lines and great delicacy. It may be because of their tiny dimensions (and the difficulties such dimensions presented to printers) that these works did not become as popular as their predecessors and were copied less by others.

Bartlett did not live to see the book published. He died a fitting death for an artist-traveler on the deck of the boat *Aegyptus* on September 13, 1854, as the vessel was making its way between Malta and Marseilles.

Count Abraham Noroff.

Russian Minister Visits Abdalla Pasha's Summer Palace in Acre

Splendor, Grandeur—and the Sound of Thousands of Frogs Croaking

Count Abraham Noroff was a Russian aristocrat who served as the czar's minister of education. When he visited the Holy Land in 1835, touring most of its principle sites, he reported at length on the holy city's thirteen Greek monasteries, which Western travelers did not usually discover.

Ibrahim Pasha allowed Noroff to visit Mount Moriah. His willingness to permit the count to be the first Christian traveler to do so was a sign of his appreciation of his guest's status as a Russian minister, but because of the sensitivity of the matter, the visit was conducted in an inconspicuous manner. Noroff wore Eastern dress and was accompanied by a *kawas* (escort) in order not to arouse the suspicions of the fanatic Muslim crowd.

When he reached Acre, Noroff was invited to visit the summer home built by Abdalla, the city's previous pasha.

Noroff relates that his interpreter proposed that he lodge at the villa, which was located half an hour from the city.

It was already dusk when they arrived. While the interpreter informed the pasha of the Russian's

The summer home built by Abdalla Pasha belongs to the Baha'i today.

presence, Noroff waited in a field, overwhelmed by the wonderful scent of the fruit trees that surrounded the palace walls. The manservant quickly returned, bringing with him an invitation from the pasha to stay the night, together with his apology that he

could not greet his visitor, as he had already retired to the harem.

Noroff was pleasantly surprised by the magnificence he encountered upon entering the mansion. Opposite the gate was a marble staircase leading to a wide terrace built entirely of white marble, on which four grand pavilions stood. In the middle of the terrace was a fountain with a square pool, in which the twilight was reflected. At the foot of this splendid edifice, closely-planted orange, myrtle, and pomegranate trees swayed in the breeze, slim palms and cypresses rising behind them. Next to each of the pavilions were fountains, and the sound of the trickling water harmonized with the rustle of the sweet-smelling trees. Despite his fatigue, Noroff strolled for a long while in the enchanted garden.

At a late hour he laid down on a soft couch and dozed to the sound of the water in the fountains. Sleep eluded him, however, as he soon became aware of a noise that grew steadily louder. At first he thought the source of the noise was the water in the many fountains, but it soon became so intrusive that he decided to get up and investigate. The moon lit his way.

The moment Noroff opened the door to the pavilion he was overwhelmed by the mighty croaking of the millions of frogs living in the pools in the pasha's garden. With a touch of a magic wand, the fabulous house had turned into a frog kingdom, and the Russian count did not sleep a wink all night.

Governors of Hebron and Safed Healed with Laxative

It's a Known Fact: All Westerners Are Doctors

In 1836, John Lloyd Stephens, an American attorney who had arrived in the Holy Land for reasons of his health, was detained in Hebron. The governor, who had fallen ill himself, asked for his help, claiming it was a known fact that all Westerners were expert physicians. Stephens feared acceding to the demand: though he had once dispensed medication to a simple Arab, he had never been asked to diagnose a governor. He decided to test his skill, however, and gravely inquired of the governor as to the symptoms of his disease. He checked his pulse, asked him to stick out his tongue, and looked at his throat and eyes. At the end of the "examination," Stephens told the governor in all

seriousness that he would soon send him medication with the appropriate instructions.

Stephens relates that he was able to deal with the governor's illness only because he realized that the ruler had nearly killed himself with overeating. The only thing he needed was to clean out his stomach. Stephens, who knew he was leaving the city towards daybreak, sent the governor a double portion of laxative with instructions to take it that evening.

Only afterward did Stephens hear that though at first the governor had been sullen and displeased with him, in the morning he had felt so much better that he had been ready to grant Stephens half his kingdom.

A similar incident occurred upon Stephens' arrival in Safed: The governor, ill, announced to Stephens that God had sent him to act the physician. Since his successful episode with the governor of Hebron, relates Stephens, he had begun to consider himself an expert in curing ailing governors. This time too, Stephens checked the governor's pulse, asked him to stick out his tongue, and acted according to the principle that what was good for one governor was good for the next. He gave the governor a laxative that, though it almost removed his intestines, cured him completely.

Stephens' humorous style of writing drew a large reading audience to his travel book, which sold over twenty

John Lloyd Stephens.

thousand copies in two years. Stephens' income from it reached about twenty-five thousand dollars—a vast sum in those days. With the money, the American funded a trip to Central America, where he discovered the remains of the Mayan civilization and brought himself worldwide fame.

Scientific Sensation: Dead Sea 600 Feet below Sea Level

Naturalist Von Schubert, Father of Climatology in Holy Land, Lays the Foundations for the Understanding of the Jordan Valley

Gottfried Heinrich von Schubert, a native of Germany and a professor of science, was the father of climatology in the Holy Land. Initially employed at Erlangen University and later at the University of Munich, von Schubert published books on the philosophy of science in which he attempted to find a common denominator between science and the humanities.

Von Schubert decided to set out on a trip to the East when he was well past

The Dead Sea. A tinted photograph from the late19th century, by Bonfils.

men; Charles Beke and George Henry Moore. On his way north, von Schubert found that Tiberias was also below sea level, and he subsequently laid the foundations for the understanding of the nature of the entire Jordan Valley depression.

His discoveries allowed von Schu-

> **To his immense surprise, he read on his barometer that he was at a depth of ninety-one feet below the level of the Red Sea.**

bert to develop a new approach to the climate of the Holy Land, and especially of Jerusalem. In his book he notes that from a climatic point of view, for each 100 meters of difference in altitude between two points in the region, it is as if they were removed from one another by one geographical degree of latitude. Thus the difference in climate between two nearby cities like Jerusalem and Jericho is the same, according to him, as the difference between the climates of Rome and London, which are quite distant from each other. Thus he also explains the very different floral worlds of the heights of Jerusalem and the lowlands of Jericho. Von Schubert, ever since dubbed the father of climatology in the Holy Land, was the first to explain the different vegetation in various parts of the country on the basis of their climatic conditions.

his youth. With him on his journey he took a painter by the name of Barnetts, and after their return the two published books together. Their volumes of pictures from the Holy Land and its vicinity became bestsellers that were issued in many editions. On the other hand, von Schubert's detailed book on his trip, which is considered a serious and reliable treatment, was much less of a commercial success.

In the latter work, von Schubert describes his journey via Egypt to the Sinai Peninsula. In the town of A-Tur in southwest Sinai, he witnessed the sale of oil—not yet produced in A-Tur, but brought from the Egyptian coast opposite—to Muslim pilgrims traveling in boats anchored at the port.

From there he went on via Saint Catherine's Monastery in a northeasterly direction, noting the various geological formations he saw along the way. From Aqaba, von Schubert made his way to the red stone city of Petra.

When he returned from Petra to the Holy Land, von Schubert lit upon one of the most sensational discoveries in the history of Holy Land research. To his immense surprise, he read on his barometer one evening that he was at a depth of ninety-one feet below the level of the Red Sea. Progressing northwards, he realized that the plain continued to descend deeper and deeper below sea level. In his book he describes the strange experience of incredulously watching the mercury

Tiberias. A tinted photograph from the late19th century, by Bonfils.

rise ever upward in his barometer.

Calculations confirmed that the floor of the valley von Schubert was traversing was indeed ninety-one feet below the Red Sea—a fact that was substantiated later by measurements in the lower Jordan Valley. But either von Schubert's instruments were imprecise or he simply did not believe his eyes, as through his calculations he arrived at the conclusion that the Dead Sea lay at 600 feet (about 200 meters) below sea level—less than half its true depth.

Von Schubert's findings caused a sensation in the scientific world and were later confirmed by two English-

Roberts' Books of Lithographs

Queen Victoria, Russian Czar, Austrian Kaiser Register to Purchase

David Roberts, a Scottish painter (1796-1864), visited the Holy Land in 1839. Roberts' journey to the East was planned with great pomp by the publishing house for which he prepared his pictures. He set out from Egypt, and continued via Sinai to Aqaba and Petra. From there he traveled north to Jerusalem and throughout the Land of Israel and Lebanon.

issued a less expensive series on a smaller scale that had a wide distribution. Roberts' pictures were copied repeatedly.

Not everyone was impressed, however. A Swiss scholar wrote of the volumes that they were so heavy and unwieldy that he had been compelled to transfer them to his home in two separate trips. Complaining that only

a few of the pictures were proximate representations of the landscapes they purported to depict, he claimed that the publications were intended for the fashionable world of the wealthy nobility, for whom the authenticity of products is always less important than ostentation. Further, he was certain that the scientific world would not benefit from the series,

David Roberts in native costume.

which excelled mainly in its external grandeur and its high price.

Despite their Swiss critic, Roberts' lithographs have great success even today, and appear in many books, on calendars, greeting cards, and postcards.

David Roberts' lithographs:
Left: The Temple Mount with the Dome of the Rock.
Below: The Church of the Holy Sepulcher.

Upon Roberts' return to Scotland, his Holy Land drawings served as the sketches for enormous lithographs, some of which were printed in two or three tones and some of which were colored under the supervision of Roberts himself after the original printing. Roberts' colored lithographs are still considered among the most magnificent of lithographic creations.

Following their success, the lithographs were printed in two series of three volumes each: one series of Syria, the Holy Land, and nearby regions, and a second series of Egypt. A pre-publication sale that was announced even before the books were printed received an enormous response: 634 people registered to purchase the volumes, among them Queen Victoria, the archbishops of York and Canterbury, the Austrian kaiser, the Russian czar, the king of France, and the king of Prussia. The names of all of those who ordered in advance were printed in the third book of each series.

The two series were issued from 1842 to 1849 with such great success that from 1855 to 1856 the publisher

Jerusalem Photographed for the First Time

French Painter Goupil Fesquet Photographs Jerusalem from Mount Scopus Two Years After Invention of the Daguerreotype

Jerusalem from the Mount of Olives. A daguerreotype photograph by F. Goupil Fesquet.

A daguerreotype camera.

Nazareth *(above)* and Acre *(below)* in daguerreotype photographs by F. Goupil Fesquet.

Two short years after the Frenchman Louis Jacques Daguerre introduced his innovative method of photography, Jerusalem was photographed for the first time. Daguerre, after whom the early photograph—the daguerreotype—was named, employed copper plates covered with silver iodide to capture images. When the plates were exposed to light inside the camera, an invisible negative was achieved. Mercury vapor was used to turn it into a visible positive. The equipment necessary for the process was very cumbersome, but it was nevertheless tested in the Holy Land for the first time only two years later.

The Frenchman Frederic Goupil Fesquet was a drawing teacher who set out for the Holy Land after joining the party of the well-known artist Horace Vernet. The French optician Lerebours outfitted Goupil Fesquet with the necessary daguerreotype equipment, which he brought with him to the Holy Land. He used it for the first time on the slopes of the Mount of Olives, where, after encountering numerous difficulties, he finally managed to take a picture of Jerusalem's Old City.

Just as Goupil Fesquet set up his daguerreotype device, the wind began to blow, upsetting its balance: the image of the landscape would be blurry as a result. Next, two Jews who were strolling in the area stopped right in front of the camera despite the fact that Goupil Fesquet gestured to them to move. They refused to budge, and one of them, beginning to laugh, positioned himself directly in front of the lens. The photographer, angry, caught the man by his shoulders and shoved him aside, but his companion took the spot he had vacated. Goupil

Fesquet renewed his attack, and raining blows on them with his fists, banished the two men from the spot.

Amidst these and other disturbances, the first photograph of the Holy Land was prepared: a view of Jerusalem from the Mount of Olives on the southeast. But the Frenchman's trials were not yet at an end. In order to develop the image, he needed distilled water, which, it turned out, was impossible to find in sufficient amounts in Jerusalem's pharmacy. Since his companions planned to continue on their journey the next day, Goupil Fesquet spent the night distilling the water he needed and developed his picture.

Three of Goupil Fesquet's pictures—of Jerusalem, Nazareth, and Acre—were included in a collection of photographs from all over the world that Lerebours later published. These early images do not really look like the photographs we know today. Since they were incised on copper, they resemble engravings, albeit engravings especially faithful to reality.

Finn, First English Consul in Jerusalem, Enjoys High Status and Great Influence

England First to Appoint Deputy Consul. Other Nations Follow.

1839

Above: The English consul James Finn.

Right: The German consulate's *kawas*.

In 1839 England became the first European country to appoint a deputy consul in Jerusalem. The other powers followed in her wake—Prussia (present-day Germany) in 1842, Sardinia (present-day Italy) and France in 1843, the US in 1844, Austria in 1849, and Spain in 1854. Consuls soon replaced deputy consuls in the Holy Land, and in 1857 the Austrians appointed a consul general.

The English consul, James Finn, wielded the most influence, both because of his personality and the assistance England rendered the Turks in the war of 1840 as well as in the Crimean War (1854-1856). Finn, who served in Jerusalem from 1846 to 1863, enjoyed a singular status, and many of the political strings and intrigues in the city passed his way. Since the pashas changed often but Finn remained in his position for almost two decades, his influence in the city and in all of the Holy Land grew unprecedentedly strong. In his book *Stirring Times* he presents himself as the strongman of Jerusalem, whom everyone obeyed and to whom even the governor was second in actual power.

During his last years in Jerusalem Finn was in conflict with his superiors, his protégés, the other consuls, and the city's Protestant bishop. Beset by financial troubles too, he finally went bankrupt. In 1863 Finn found himself on his way back to England.

1840

British Fleet Conquers Acre

The decisive battle between the British fleet and the Egyptian infantry that held Acre's fortress took place on November 3, 1840. Considered an important moment in the history of naval warfare, this clash was the first time that steamboats were operated under battle conditions and that explosive cannonballs were fired.

After a three-hour bombardment, the main Egyptian munitions warehouse exploded. The destruction was terrible; approximately fifteen hundred soldiers and civilians were killed, and the portion of Acre's wall that even Napoleon had not succeeded in breaching was pulverized.

The next night, a force of eighty Austrians led by an archduke of the imperial family landed on the beach and reached the city's fortress under cover of darkness. The Austrians quickly raised their flag—it had not flown in Acre for 660 years, since the British under Richard the Lionhearted had removed it. This time, the Austrians made sure they raised their flag first, preempting the British.

The Egyptian munitions warehouse explodes, by R.D. White.

1840

King George IV's Adopted Daughter Complains:
Jerusalem's Markets Pitiful

No Cups, Plates, or Knives. No Beef or Vegetables. Not Even Pudding.

The most well-known of the mistresses of King George IV of England was Mrs. Fitzherbert. Fitzherbert took in and raised a young girl, Minny Seymour, who had been left an orphan. George IV, who was fond of Minny, evinced more fatherly sentiments towards her than he did towards his real daughter. When the child grew up, she married Colonel Dawson-Damer and bore him five children, all the while maintaining her ties to the royal family and the English aristocracy.

In 1839, their children being grown, Minny Dawson-Damer and her husband set out on a journey to the Mediterranean, eventually arriving in the Holy Land. The travel book Minny penned after the trip includes descriptions of everything she saw, and excels in its portrayal of lifestyles and customs.

Minny had little good to say about the markets of Jerusalem, which she thought were narrow, poor, and their merchandise pitiful. According to her, neither cups, plates nor utensils for the buffet could be found. In place of a knife for cutting food, she was able to find only a dagger. Aside from mutton and goat—and even this was often sold spoiled—no meat was available. The local residents had apparently never heard of beef, and vegetables were so expensive that cauliflower was a sensation in the kitchen. In place of potatoes, Jerusalemites ate rice, the main staple of the populace.

Minny also relates that the citizens of the city drank only out of ceramic vessels, and that rice was served on one tray to the entire family. Rough bread, poorly baked, was eaten by most of the Syrian and Arab population, and Minny believed it impossible to find a cup, glass, or plate in the home of any of the Muslims.

The Dawson-Damers brought with them to the Holy Land, at their own expense, a French painter by the name of Chacaton. Some of his paintings were added as illustrations to Minny Dawson-Damer's travelogue, and they

A Bedouin encampment in northern Sinai. A painting by Chacaton for Minny Dawson-Damer.

provide the book with an especially original character. One of Chacaton's pictures was later exhibited in the Louvre.

Patriarchs Return to Jerusalem

Out of all of the Christian patriarchs residing in Jerusalem in the late Middle Ages, only the Armenian patriarch remained in the city when Crusader rule in the Holy Land came to an end. It was only in the nineteenth century that European interest in Jerusalem motivated the reestab-

Bishop Alexander.

Jews Societies. Missionary circles were influential in England, and they had a say in the appointment of Britain's first deputy consul, Young, in 1839. Next, the king of Prussia, Friedrich Wilhelm IV (1840-1861), turned to the British government and the Anglican Church with a proposal to establish a joint bishopric in Jerusalem. The Prussian king, very much a man of the romantic age, wished to

1847 Pope Pius IX appointed the Frenchman Valerga Catholic patriarch. During his long tenure from 1847 to 1872, Valerga enlarged the Catholic community in the Holy Land and created a foundation for its stable organization and future development.

The Greek Orthodox Church always had a Jerusalem patriarch, but he had resided for generations in Istanbul. When a new patriarch, Cyril II, was installed in 1845, it was determined that he would serve in the holy city. Cyril II was a man of many talents, and his influence on events in Jerusalem and all of the Holy Land was felt for dozens of years until the end of his appointment in 1872.

The Greek Orthodox patriarchate in Jerusalem.

Christ Church, the first Anglican church built in the Middle East, stands opposite David's Tower in Jerusalem's Old City.

lishment of the bishoprics and patriarchates. The first to return to the holy city in an official manner were the Protestants, who formerly had not maintained any institutions of their own in Jerusalem. Their interest, among other things, lay in protecting the relatively large number of Protestant missionaries who were active in the city.

Most of the missionaries were sent by one of two British societies: the Church Missionary and the London

renew contact with the holy city of the Crusades, albeit this time in a peaceful fashion. The Prussian offer was happily received, and the first joint bishop, Michael Solomon Alexander, appointed. The bishop, his wife, children, and entourage were transported to Jaffa in a British warship, a sign of his official status.

The presence of the Anglican bishop in the city prodded the Catholic and Greek Orthodox Churches to renew their presence in Jerusalem, and in

1842
Walling Up the Church of the Nativity

During renovations made in the Basilica of the Nativity to repair damage from the earthquake that struck the Holy Land in 1837, the

Greek Orthodox built a wall separating the nave from the altar. The wall was dismantled during the British Mandatory Period.

The Greek Orthodox wall in Bethlehem's Basilica of the Nativity.

1843
Warburton: First European to Achieve Hermon's Summit

Eliot Warburton was the first nineteenth-century European to reach the summit of Mount Hermon, the highest mountain in the Holy Land. He left a description of the treacherous climb.

Warburton and his companions set out at dawn through valleys so choked with grapevines that they were difficult to navigate. Leaving their horses at a hut in one of the vineyards, they set out towards the mountain. Though Warburton had climbed mountains in the past, this ascent was to be the most difficult he had ever experienced.

Their guide, who had received explicit instructions from the local emir to lead the party to the mountaintop, was determined to fulfill his orders, and when he thought the Europeans were straggling, would draw himself

up to his full height and cry "Puka! Puka!" ("Up! Up!").

To the great disappointment of the members of the expedition, not a drop of water was to be found along the way. Though there is always some snow on the Hermon, in the summer it is usually sparse, and the first patch the Europeans reached sufficed only to moisten their lips. Their guide broke off chunks of ice and placed them in the sun, providing precious liquid for the travelers' parched mouths.

After six hours of arduous hiking, the expedition reached the mountain's summit. According to Warburton, no view in the world is more thrilling. They caught several goats, milked them, and drank the milk. Going on, the

party came upon a small spring on a snowy hill. Warburton remarks that only someone who has climbed a nine-thousand-foot mountain in the burning Syrian sun can appreciate the delight to be had in a small spring's water.

Right: Eliot Warburton. **Below:** Mount Hermon, by Bonfils.

Ancient Copy of New Testament Discovered at Saint Catherine's

Lobgott F.C. Tischendorf.

1844

The German researcher Lobgott Friedrich Constantin Tischendorf specialized in deciphering ancient manuscripts of the New Testament. The crowning glory of his research was his discovery of the *Codex Sinaiticus*, the earliest version of the New Testament ever found.

Tischendorf first set out for Saint Catherine's Monastery on the Sinai Peninsula in 1844. He writes that he was astounded to find himself surrounded by men with long beards and black robes within the walls of a hospitable, orderly, and well-organized monastery situated in the heart of a stark desert.

The head of the monastery put Tischendorf up in a suite consisting of a spacious reception room, a bedroom, and a room that served as a dining and work room.

In the courtyard of the monastery was a fountain covered by thick grapevines, and every morning after the bell rang a monk named Cyril would stand beside it. Tischendorf became friendly with Cyril, who eventually allowed him to take any manuscripts he liked from the library to his room.

In the course of his exploration of the library, Tischendorf found a box of papers meant to be burnt; among them were 129 large pages of parchment with texts from the Septuagint. The monks presented him with 43 of the precious pages as a gift.

Upon Tischendorf's return to Germany he discovered that he had in his possession the most ancient pages of the Septuagint ever found. He did not disclose their source to anyone, however, and in 1853 returned to Sinai, though he did not meet with much success on his second visit. In 1859 he set out on a third trip to Saint Catherine's Monastery, this time funded by the Russian czar. The German's status as an emissary of the czar improved his reception, and he found, besides the remaining 86 of the pages he had seen the first time, additional portions of the Septuagint and an ancient Greek text of the New Testament. The approximately 300 pages of the Septuagint Tischendorf never located may have been burnt in 1844 before he discovered the treasure.

Tischendorf traveled to Cairo and managed to obtain permission to bring all of the finds to the Russian czar and prepare them for publication.

Monks in the courtyard of Saint Catherine's Monastery in Sinai, by D. Roberts.

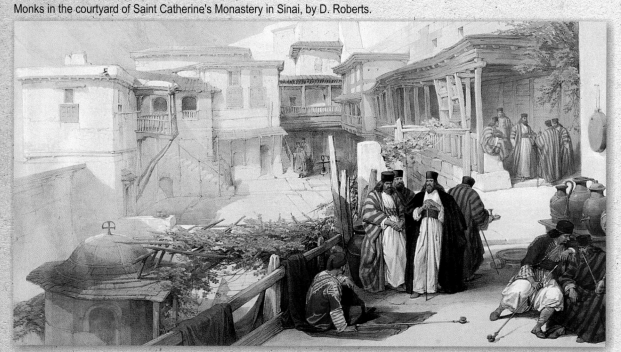

Titus Tobler Takes Measure of Jerusalem
Swimming Swiss Researcher Learns Eleven Languages in Order to Review the Literature on Jerusalem

1845

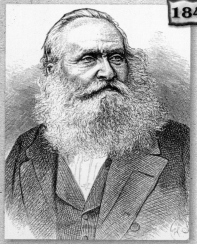
Titus Tobler.

Titus Tobler is considered the greatest nineteenth-century researcher of Jerusalem and its environs. A scholar of literature and travel books as well as a field researcher, after his arrival in the Holy Land Tobler utilized his time efficiently, never wasting a moment. The German scholar Johann Sepp mentions seeing Tobler at work in the Church of the Nativity in Bethlehem. As Sepp stood entranced before the birthplace of Jesus (next to a murderer who had escaped from Egypt and was kneeling before the altar), he suddenly noticed that to his left was a man soberly measuring the steps descending to the holy spot—Titus Tobler.

Among Tobler's discoveries in the field was Wilson's Arch, the only remains of the bridge that connected the Temple Mount to Jerusalem's western quarter in the days of Herod. Tobler was the first to thoroughly investigate the ancient cemeteries around Jerusalem, list the names of the alleys of the Old City, and descend to the Pool of Saint Helena beside the Church of the Holy Sepulcher to measure it while swimming. The Swiss scholar was also among the first to explore Zedekiah's Cave to the north of the Old City.

In the books he wrote after his journey Tobler combined his field discoveries with a comprehensive survey of all of the ancient sources for each and every site. In order to have access to such an extensive body of literature, he learned eleven languages fluently, and his bibliography serves the scientific world to this day.

Wilson's Arch, the remains of a bridge from the days of Herod, by W. Simpson.

Women Forbidden in Mar Saba Monastery

Ladies Spend Nights Locked in Tower Outside Monastery

The Austrian Ida Pfeiffer, a renowned world traveler who published books about her journeys, chose the Holy Land as her first destination. In the course of her trip she was aided by the English painter William Henry Bartlett. They describe, each in his or her own book, how Mrs. Pfeiffer was not allowed to enter the Greek Orthodox Mar Saba Monastery in the desert between Jerusalem and the Dead Sea.

According to Mrs. Pfeiffer, the masters, servants, Arabs, Bedouin—everyone else in her party, that is—entered the complex, but just as her turn came, the cry to close the gate was sounded! Finding herself alone in the wilderness outside the monastery, Pfeiffer feared she would have to spend the night out of doors—an unencouraging thought given the security situation in the area. Finally, the monks' servant appeared and pointed to a lone tower in which she would apparently spend the night.

He brought a ladder, and the two climbed up it together to a small portal in the tower's wall. Wooden steps led upwards to two tiny rooms. In one was an altar; the second served as a bedroom for female pilgrims. A wooden couch was the only piece of furniture in the room. Pfeiffer, though safe for the night, felt like a captive princess for whom escape was impossible, as her guide carefully locked the

Mar Saba Monastery. On the right is the Women's Tower, in which the monks lodged women pilgrims. By W.H. Bartlett.

creaking door after him and removed the ladder.

In his book Bartlett includes a drawing of the tower in which Ida Pfeiffer stayed, describes how he accompanied the monks who went to visit her, and applauds her tranquillity and bravery: She sat on a low couch, a serene expression on her face. Bartlett imagined that the dusky and neglected appearance of the tower room on the upper floor, the total

darkness below, and the terrible silence all around could affect anyone's nerves, awakening frightful thoughts. He relates that when Captain Bill Hall and his daughters visited Mar Saba the ladies refused to stay locked up in the tower and kept escaping from it until they were finally permitted to enter the monastery complex.

Not so the brave Ida Pfeiffer, however, who apparently declared that

she had never felt more comfortable, and refused Bartlett's offer when he proposed staying on the lower floor and watching over her.

Russian Author Gogol Visits Holy Land

Nikolai Gogol.

Nikolai Gogol (1809-1852), one of the greatest pre-revolutionary Russian writers, lived from 1836 outside of his homeland. He resided for the most part in Rome, where he sank into melancholy and mysticism. In 1848 he made a pilgrimage to Jerusalem. Despite the fact that he left no record of his journey in book form, a sheaf of letters he wrote from the holy city has been preserved—testimony to the inner workings of a sick man within whom the Holy Land induced only gloom.

As time passed, Gogol became the victim of serious mental illness. He died prematurely in Moscow at the age of forty-three.

Price List for a Journey from Cairo to Jerusalem

Countess de Gasparin, a Calvinist Protestant from Switzerland, was married to a French count who was the representative of Corsica in the French house of representatives. When he was not reelected to government in 1846, the two decided to set out on a tour of the East.

The countess recorded her impressions of their trip in a travelogue. At the end of the book are details of the journey's expenses—expenditures for travel, lodging, and camel-hire. The party paid 150 piasters for camels

The Piasters Flow: Camels, Horses, Escorts, Hostels, and Bribes

for the trip from Cairo to Saint Catherine's Monastery in Sinai. Another 200 piasters were disbursed for the next leg of the trip from Sinai to Hebron. The convoy numbered a total of sixteen camels, a relatively large herd in those days.

The countess also details the payments and bribes that she says had to be shelled out at the monastery in Sinai, in Hebron (300 piasters to the sheikh who guided them), and in Jerusalem. From Hebron onwards they abandoned both camels and Bedouin, hiring an interpreter-guide who put horses at their disposal instead. For each horse they paid 25 piasters a day. The hotel in Jerusalem cost 70 piasters per day per person.

A camel caravan at rest in Sinai, by D. Roberts.

The United States' Expedition to the River Jordan and the Dead Sea

At the beginning of the nineteenth century, several attempts were made to carry out a serious study of the River Jordan and the Dead Sea. The American naval lieutenant William Francis Lynch was the first to actually succeed in doing so.

Lynch's substantial party, dispatched under the auspices of the American navy and consisting of five officers and nine sailors, landed in Acre on April 1, 1848. From there they turned towards the Sea of Galilee, then proceeded along the River Jordan to the Dead Sea. The members of the expedition carried with them two metal boats and one wooden boat, which they affixed to wheels and hitched to camels. The wooden boat was to crash almost immediately in the whirlpools of the Jordan.

The journey on the river lasted eight days, during which time the party carried out scientific observations and made the first depth measurements of the Dead Sea. The party visited Masada, Kerak in Moab, and afterwards made its way back through Jerusalem, Jaffa, Haifa, and Galilee to Beirut before sailing home to the United States.

Part of the expedition's success was due to the attention Lynch devoted to issues of security. He was assisted by the escort of a guard unit at the head of which stood Akili Aga—one of the powerful figures of Galilee in those days—a Bedouin leader who ruled over an expansive territory, sometimes with the agreement of the Ottoman authorities and sometimes after revolting against them. The presence

The tents of Lynch's delegation at Ein Gedi, by R. Aulick.

of Aga and his men, not to mention the well-armed soldiers of the American navy, ensured that the Bedouin kept their distance.

Lynch published his adventures in a book written in the form of a travelogue, from which the following descriptions were excerpted.

The Bathing Place of Pilgrims

Monday, April 17. At 9.30 P.M. we arrived at "El Meshra," the bathing place of the Christian pilgrims, after having been fifteen hours in the boats. This ford is consecrated by tradition as the place where the Israelites passed over with the ark of the covenant; and where our blessed Saviour was baptized by John. Feeling that it would be desecration to moor the boats at a place so sacred, we passed it, and with some difficulty found a landing below.

My first act was to bathe in the consecrated stream, thanking God, first, for the precious favour of being permitted to visit such a spot; and secondly for his protecting care throughout our perilous passage. For a long time after, I sat upon the bank, my mind oppressed with awe, as I mused upon the great and wondrous

Pilgrims bathing in the Jordan, by Lieutenant Dale.

events which had here occurred. Perhaps directly before me, for this is near Jericho, "the waters stood and rose up upon an heap," and the multitudinous host of the Israelites passed over,—and in the bed of the stream, a few yards distant, may be the twelve stones, marking "the place where the feet of the priests which bare the ark of the covenant stood."

Tradition, sustained by the geographical features of the country, makes this also the scene of the baptism of the Redeemer. The mind of man, trammelled by sin, cannot soar in contemplation of so sublime an event. On that wondrous day, when the Deity veiled in flesh descended the bank, all nature, hushed in awe, looked on,—and the impetuous river, in grateful homage, must have stayed its course, and gently laved the body of its Lord.

In such a place, it seemed almost desecration to permit the mind to be diverted by the cares which pressed upon it—but it was wrong—for next to faith, surely the highest Christian obligation is the performance of duty...

Tuesday, April 18. At 3 A.M., we were aroused by the intelligence that the pilgrims were coming. Rising in haste, we beheld thousands of torchlights, with a dark mass beneath, moving rapidly over the hills. Striking our tents with precipitation, we hurriedly removed them and all our effects a short distance to the left. We had scarce finished, when they were upon us:—men, women, and children, mounted on camels, horses, mules, and donkeys, rushed impetuously by toward the bank. They presented the appearance of fugitives from a routed army.

Our Bedawin friends here stood us in good stead;—sticking their tufted spears before our tents, they mounted their steeds and formed a military cordon round us. But for them we should have been run down, and most of our effects trampled upon, scattered and lost. Strange that we should have been shielded from a Christian throng by wild children of the desert—Muslims in name, but pagans in reality. Nothing but the spears and swarthy faces of the Arabs saved us.

I had, in the mean time, sent the boats to the opposite shore, a little below the bathing-place, as well to be out of the way as to be in readiness to render assistance, should any of the crowd be swept down by the current, and in danger of drowning.

While the boats were taking their position, one of the earlier bathers cried out that it was a sacred place; but when the purpose was explained to him, he warmly thanked us. Moored to the opposite shore, with their crews in them, they presented an unusual spectacle.

The party which had disturbed us was the advanced guard of the great body of pilgrims. At 5, just at the dawn of day, the last made its appearance, coming over the crest of a high ridge, in one tumultuous and eager throng.

In all the wild haste of a disorderly rout, Copts and Russians, Poles, Armenians, Greeks and Syrians, from all parts of Asia, from Europe, from Africa and from far-distant America, on they came; men, women and children, of every age and hue, and in every variety of costume; talking, screaming, shouting, in almost every known language under the sun. Mounted as variously as those who had preceded them, many of the women and children were suspended in baskets or confined in cages; and, with their eyes strained towards the river, heedless of all intervening obstacles, they hurried eagerly forward, and dismounting in haste, and disrobing with precipitation, rushed down the bank and threw themselves into the stream.

They seemed to be absorbed by one impulsive feeling, and perfectly regardless of the observations of others. Each one plunged himself, or was dipped by another, three times, below the surface, in honour of the Trinity; and then filled a bottle, or some other utensil, from the river. The bathing-dress of many of the pilgrims was a white gown with a black cross upon it. Most of them, as soon as they were dressed, cut branches of the agnus castus, or willow; and, dipping them in the consecrated stream, bore them away as memorials of their visit.

In an hour, they began to disappear; and in less than three hours the trodden surface of the lately crowded bank reflected no human shadow. The pageant disappeared as rapidly as it had approached, and left to us once more the silence and solitude of the wilderness. It was like a dream. An immense crowd of human beings, said to be 8000, but I thought not so many, had passed and repassed before our tents and left not a vestige behind them.

On the Dead Sea, by Lieutenant Dale.

A Storm on the Dead Sea

Tuesday, April 18, At 1.45, started with the boats, the caravan making a direct line for Ain el Feshkah, on the north-west shore of the Dead Sea, the appointed place of rendezvous...

At 3.25, passed by the extreme western point, where the river is 180 yards wide and three feet deep, and entered upon the Dead Sea; the water, a nauseous compound of bitters and salts.

The river, where it enters the sea, is inclined towards the eastern shore, very much as is represented on the map of Messrs. Robinson and Smith, which is the most exact of any we have seen. There is a considerable bay between the river and the mountains of Belka, in Ammon, on the eastern shore of the sea.

A fresh north-west wind was blowing as we rounded the point. We endeavored to steer a little to the north of west, to make a true west course, and threw the patent log overboard to measure the distance; but the wind rose so rapidly that the boats could not keep head to wind, and we were

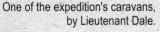

One of the expedition's caravans, by Lieutenant Dale.

obliged to haul the log in. The sea continued to rise with the increasing wind, which gradually freshened to a gale, and presented an agitated surface of foaming brine; the spray, evaporating as it fell, left incrustations of salt upon our clothes, our hands and faces; and while it conveyed a prickly sensation wherever it touched the skin, was, above all, exceedingly painful to the eyes. The boats, heavily laden, struggled sluggishly at first; but when the wind freshened in its fierceness, from the density of the

> ## At times it seemed as if the Dread Almighty frowned upon our efforts to navigate a sea, the creation of his wrath.

water, it seemed as if their bows were encountering the sledge-hammers of the Titans, instead of the opposing waves of an angry sea.

At 3.50, passed a piece of drift-wood, and soon after saw three swallows and a gull. At 4.55, the wind blew so fiercely that the boats could make no headway; not even the Fanny Skinner, which was nearer to the weather shore, and we drifted rapidly to leeward: threw over some of the fresh water, to lighten the Fanny Mason, which labored very much, and I began to fear that both boats would founder.

At 5.40, finding that we were losing every moment, and that, with the lapse of each succeeding one, the danger increased, kept away for the northern shore, in the hope of being yet able to reach it; our arms, our clothes and skins coated with a greasy salt; and our eyes, lips, and nostrils, smarting excessively. How different was the scene before the submerging of the plain, which was "even as the garden of the Lord!"

At times it seemed as if the Dread Almighty frowned upon our efforts to navigate a sea, the creation of his wrath. There is a tradition among the Arabs that no one can venture upon this sea and live. Repeatedly the fates of Costigan and Molyneaux had been cited to deter us. The first one spent a few days, the last about twenty hours, and returned to the place from whence he had embarked, without landing upon its shores. One was found dying upon the shore; the other expired in November last, immediately after his return, of fever contracted upon its waters.

But, although the sea had assumed a threatening aspect, and the fretted mountains, sharp and incinerated, loomed terrific on either side, and salt and ashes mingled with its sands, and foetid sulphurous springs trickled down its ravines, we did not despair: awe-struck, but not terrified; fearing the worst, yet hoping for the best, we prepared to spend a dreary night upon the dreariest waste we had ever seen.

At 5.58, the wind instantaneously abated, and with it the sea as rapidly fell; the water, from its ponderous quality, settling as soon as the agitating cause had ceased to act. Within twenty minutes from the time we bore away from a sea which threatened to engulf us, we were pulling away, at a rapid rate, over a placid sheet of water, that scarcely rippled beneath us; and a rain-cloud, which had enveloped the sterile mountains of the Arabian shore, lifted up, and left their rugged outlines basking in the light of the setting sun.

Hebron Quarantine Halts Travelers Arriving from Egypt

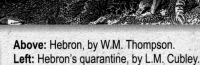

Fear of Egyptian Plague Strikes

At mid-century, tourists who could not somehow manage to circumvent it were compelled to spend a week in quarantine in Hebron for fear they were carrying the plague from Egypt into the Holy Land. Apparently, the pasha of Egypt, copying the French custom, forced travelers coming from Turkey to be placed in quarantine. The Turkish sultan, in order to take his revenge, made those coming from Egypt do the same.

Thus it happened that a certain Count Charles de Pardieu who was traveling from Egypt to Sinai, visiting Saint Catherine's Monastery, ascending the summit of Jabal Musa, and then continuing on to Dahiriya and Hebron, found himself imposed upon for a week. The quarantine station had just recently been completed, and the count and his companions were its first guests. The rooms they were given were actually cells, their exposed limestone floors not even covered by mats. De Pardieu and his companions preferred to set up a tent in the courtyard and live there.

In the early hours of the morning it was very cold, especially for those who had just emerged from the heat of Egypt, but during the day the air

Above: Hebron, by W.M. Thompson.
Left: Hebron's quarantine, by L.M. Cubley.

warmed up and the tent became a furnace, making it impossible to remain inside it. The nobleman and his companions were forced to seek refuge from the scorching heat of the day in a shady spot outside, from which they looked out over the city of Hebron.

The count describes Hebron as a long, narrow city located at the bottom of a valley, with grey block-like houses surmounted by domes set in the middle of roofs that doubled as balconies.

Dutch Naval Officer Van De Velde: Writer, Painter, and Cartographer

1851

In his youth, the painter and naval officer C.W.M. Van de Velde served in the Dutch navy in Indonesia, which at the time was a Dutch colony. His talent for drawing expressed itself early in a fifty-page volume of his renderings of Indonesia. Van de Velde, a devout Protestant, wished to put his abilities and experience at the service of Holy Land exploration. All of his attempts to enlist public support and find companions for his journey proving futile, he decided to set out alone and at his own expense.

Van de Velde left from Beirut, making his way south along the most

Above: Nazareth.
Left: Nablus and Mount Gerizim, by C. Van de Velde.

common routes but visiting remote spots as well, so that he would be able to include them in his map. He recorded cartographic measurements and painted watercolors throughout his tour, in the course of which he surveyed the Jezreel Valley, northern Samaria, and the Holy Land's coastal plain. Afterwards, Van de Velde visited Jaffa and Jerusalem, where he met Edward Robinson.

Following his return home, the Dutchman published three works: a two-volume description of his journey that, while not particularly well-written, is a detailed text that includes much important and interesting material, especially about places other explorers had not yet reached; a map of the entire Holy Land with a scale of nearly half an inch to the mile (1:315,000); and an enormous volume of illustrations similar to Roberts' and Barclay's books but including villages and untouched corners that the other painters did not see. The last volume contains the most beautiful and precise pictures of the Holy Land's landscape left us by the nineteenth century.

Jerusalem Literary Society Established for Holy Land Information
Fascinating Friday Meetings Ignored by Travelers

Elizabeth Finn.

The Jerusalem Literary Society was established in 1849 by a group of friends who resided in the holy city. The members of the society, who had lived in Jerusalem for a number of years, believed that the antiquities, literature, and customs that surrounded them would be of great interest to European scholars, especially those engaged in studying sacred texts. They imagined that instead of writing of these matters in their correspondence it would be more useful to concentrate the information in a manner that made it available to all.

The Dutch painter C.W.M. Van de Velde relates that the group established a library and small museum for the especial use of travelers. At the society's meetings, which took place every Friday evening, its members presented interesting material that had come into their hands. The circle of founders even intended to recruit subscribers in London in order to publish a quarterly in which the lectures would appear as articles.

The president of the society, James Finn, was the consul of the queen of England in Jerusalem. Rogers, his deputy, served as secretary. Bishop Gobat and the earl of Aberdeen were patrons, and the archbishop of Canterbury enjoyed the position of head patron.

Van de Velde participated twice in these Friday meetings, much to his enjoyment. According to him, the efforts of Finn, Rogers, and Finn's wife Elizabeth were deserving of special praise and renown. Ironically, the travelers who reached Jerusalem were usually too busy to visit the society's library and avail themselves of its documents.

Holy Land Harems Full of Fleas and Filth

Lacking Mirrors, Jealous Women of the Harem Give Each Other Makeup "Tips"

Princess Christina Belgiojoso (1808-1871) was born into an aristocratic and wealthy Lombardy family. At the age of sixteen she married the Italian prince Belgiojoso. They were both ardent patriots, and although they parted after four years, Christina's struggle against the Austrian occupier and for the liberation and unification of Italy continued throughout her entire life.

After the Italian defeat in the war with Austria in 1848—a war in which Christina actively participated—she voluntarily left to live in exile, embarking on an extended journey throughout the Mediterranean and the Middle East. During her travels she dispatched articles to newspapers like the Parisian *Le Monde* and New York's *Tribune*.

Of special interest are Christina's articles about the living conditions of people in the Holy Land and life in the Turkish harem, which she tried to describe realistically. Belgiojoso stayed in several harems, where she suffered the incredible filth and flea infestations prevalent in such places. She describes the cracked walls covered with soot, ceilings decorated with cobwebs, and well-used, dirty sofas stained with fat and beeswax.

Christina relates that since the women of the harem had no mirror, they would "assist" each other in beautifying themselves with cosmetics. Since they were also in competition, however, they often led each other's makeup regimens astray, giving one another advice leading to ridiculous results.

According to the Italian noblewoman, women in the harems lived in shadows alleviated by only the occasional ray of sun. Bored, their only way of passing the time was to smoke, drink tea, and beat their children.

Left: Princess Christina Belgiojoso.
Below: The bored women of the harem.

The Return of the Silver Star

A fourteen-pointed silver star that had marked the site of Jesus' birth in the Grotto of the Nativity since 1717 mysteriously disappeared in the mid-nineteenth century—yet another episodes in the string of incidents that accompanied the Franco-Russian rivalry over control of the holy places in the Holy Land and eventually led to the outbreak of the Crimean War in 1853. In 1852, after the Turkish sultan exercised some governmental pressure, the Greek Orthodox installed a new silver star in place of the one that had vanished.

Edward Robinson Identifies Eight Biblical Cities

1852

Greatest Holy Land Scholar of All Time

The well-known American scholar Edward Robinson (1794-1863) identified the locations of most of the places mentioned in the Bible.

Robinson found that in many instances the biblical name was preserved in the nineteenth-century Arabic name of the given village or site. In this manner, from the top of the hill of Ma'an (present-day Ma'on) near Hebron he identified no less than eight of the biblical cities of Judea. In the course of a two-day journey northwards from Jerusalem he also identified the sites of Anatot, Geva, Michmash, and Beit El. Among his many identifications were Beit Shemesh, Maresha, Emek Ha'elah,

Above: Edward Robinson.
Left: Beit El. A tinted photograph from the late nineteenth century, by Bonfils.

which he felt more tense and excited than during that journey. The answer to a question of great historical significance depended upon his getting to Idhna by eight o'clock. If his party arrived on time, its lengthy search for Heleutheropolis would come to a ▶

and Masada. He also identified the Crusader fortress of Monfort.

A meticulous scholar who was cautious in his determinations, Robinson was unwilling to conclusively identify places in the absence of evidence other than the sound of the name. Thus, for example, he confirmed the location of the city of Heleutheropolis mentioned in Greek and Roman literature. He thought it must be Beit Jibrin (present-day Beit Guvrin), but proof of his hypothesis was dependent upon the distance

Above: The hills of Beit Jibrin, by C.W. Wilson.
Right: The Monfort Fortress.

between Beit Jibrin to Idhna, since one of the Roman-period sources said that Heleutheropolis was six miles from a place whose name was similar to the name Idhna. Since there were still no precise maps of the Holy Land, in order to prove his theory Robinson had to travel the distance himself.

Robinson admits in his account that he does not remember an instance in

successful conclusion; if not, they would have to begin again.

They headed in a southeasterly direction in a gradually-narrowing wadi. On both sides rose verdant hills. At 7:50 they arrived at the mouth of the wadi, where they found a large public well. Only ten minutes were left to them and they had seen no sign of Idhna. When they reached the top of the hill, however, there was the village laid out before them on the other side. They entered Idhna exactly at eight o'clock and dismounted in front of the sheikh's home.

Robinson forged the tools by which the Holy Land is investigated to this very day. Many of his heirs, far less restrained than he, were to arrive at all sorts of exaggerations in identifying sites by employing his methods in a more liberal fashion. In his generation, Edward Robinson contributed more than any other person to the clarification of the Holy Land's biblical topography. Today he is considered its greatest scholar.

An aerial photograph of Masada.

1852 Robinson's Contribution to Archaeological Research

The ancient synagogue at Capernaum.

Robinson's contribution to the archaeological research of the Holy Land was equally impressive. He was the first to point out the arch in the wall of the Temple Mount that today bears his name. He was also the first to identify the remains of Jerusalem's third wall and the ancient synagogue in Capernaum.

Robinson was among the first to crawl through the Siloam Tunnel, in which he made very precise measurements. He also emphasized the importance of the residential city at Petra, while his predecessors had concentrated mainly on the area of the tombs. His three-volume book, *Biblical Researches in Palestine, Sinai and Arabia Petrea*, which summarizes his work, was received with great enthusiasm in scientific circles, among which it was considered to be more important than all of the research that had preceded it.

In 1852 Robinson set out on another journey to the Holy Land during which

he attempted to visit those places he had not managed to see previously. His impressions from this final trip served as the basis for a new map of the Holy Land that was prepared by the German geographer Heinrich Kiepert and was superior to all of its predecessors. After returning to the United States, Robinson wanted to write a definitive book on the historical geography of the Holy Land, but died before he could complete it. Only one volume of this project, which was intended to be the crowning work of his oeuvre, was published.

The ruins of the synagogue at Capernaum. A tinted photograph from 1875, by Bonfils.

Robinson's Arch is a remnant of the large arch that supported the staircase leading from the street into the Temple precinct in ancient times.
Above: A model of the arch and staircase.
Right: Robinson's Arch as it looked at the end of the 1860s, by C. Warren.

Belgian King Leopold II Visits Temple Mount

Pasha Tricks Guards of Forbidden Holy Site

In the mid-nineteenth century, the number of visitors to the Holy Land from among Europe's royalty grew. Leopold II, the Belgian heir to the throne, was among them. Since these were the years of the Crimean War, when Turkey was dependent on support from the European nations, the sultan granted Leopold and his wife a *firman* permitting them to enter the Haram al-Sharif (the Temple Mount area), which until then had been officially closed to Christians, although there had been tourists who had used deception to sidestep the prohibition.

The pasha of Jerusalem was asked to organize a formal visit to the forbidden precinct for the royal party, but he was worried about the reaction of the guardians of the holy site—Islamic fanatics renowned for their violence. Since the tour happened to fall on the day of a Muslim festival, the city was also full of fanatic dervishes and pilgrims—all of which convinced the pasha to keep the event a secret from the Muslim population.

The fact of the visit was known, however, to the numerous European tourists who had arrived in Jerusalem for Easter, and many of them requested of their consuls permission to participate in the historic moment. Their number being large, the pasha declared that only the most important among the consuls, the Anglican bishop, a lord who happened to be in Jerusalem, and others of similar rank were invited to join the party.

On the morning of the proposed day, the governor invited the entire corps of Haram guards to his palace on the pretext of giving them a message from the sultan. Once they had gathered in one of the rooms of the palace he locked the doors and stationed Turkish soldiers to guard them. The remainder of his troops were dispatched to ensure the safety of the many visitors who were to enter the Temple Mount precinct.

The British consul James Finn described the royal visit. Everyone had arrived at the holy place; Turkish soldiers armed from head to toe awaited the distinguished visitors. The procession entered the complex, the pasha and his senior officers striding in front of the royal entourage. The group passed into the huge courtyard and moved towards its center. Squarely in the middle of the plaza were stairs leading to the raised platform on which Solomon's Temple had once stood. The members of the party paused to remove their shoes at the foot of the steps, and then ascended them to the edifice called the Dome of the Rock, which Europeans mistakenly refer to as the Mosque of Omar. Inside the shrine, under its large dome, they saw an enormous rough gray rock encircled by a railing and covered by a fabulous canopy draped with green and gold silk. According to Finn, the group's initial awestruck reaction to the site of the glorious Temple turned into complete astonishment at the splendor of the colored windows, the lush silk canopy, the wealth of gold, the arabesques, the mosaics, and the rich marble columns.

Following the visit, arrangements for visiting the site became possible even for non-Muslims.

The summer pulpit on the Temple Mount.

The enormous gray boulder in the Dome of the Rock.

First Modern Travel Guide to Holy Land and Syria

J. Murray Publishing House Sends Porter to Write Updated Guide

John Leech Porter (1823-1889) received his education at the universities of Glasgow and Edinburgh in Scotland. At the conclusion of his studies he left for the East, arriving in Beirut in 1849 as a missionary. The following year he settled in Damascus, which had been closed until then to settlers from the West, and stayed for five years. Later he was to publish a book on his life in Damascus in which he also describes his trips in the region and presents updated maps. In England, Porter was considered an expert on Middle Eastern affairs.

When the London publishing house of J. Murray decided to print the first modern guide to the Holy Land and Syria, its executives turned to Porter to write it. The guidebook, called *A Handbook for Travelers in Syria and Palestine*, was a great success and was issued in many editions from the late fifties to the seventies of the nineteenth century.

Starting in 1879 Porter served as president of Queen's College in Belfast, Ireland. During his tenure he published two ornate books filled with pictures of the Holy Land (most of them taken from the French doctor Paul Lortet's popular book about his own years in the country).

Barclay Discovers Mouth of Zedekiah's Cave

Ancient Gate under Maghrebi Gate Dubbed "Barclay's Gate"

James Barclay.

members of the Peachtree Christian Church of Dr. James T. Barclay, Medical Missionary in Julia S. Barclay, both faithful missionaries from America. Disciples of Christ.

The missionary James T. Barclay, who lived in Jerusalem from 1855 to 1859, was an American doctor who mainly treated Muslim patients.

Barclay spent several weeks in the Haram al-Sharif making careful measurements. In the book he published on his experiences in the East, he claims that he was the first Westerner to penetrate Zedekiah's Cave, after its mouth east of Damascus Gate was discovered by his dog.

Wishing to further explore the grotto, Barclay left Jerusalem with two companions at dusk after the city gates were closed so that no one would meddle in their mission.

They enlarged the hole he had found until they could crawl through it into the cave. As they did so, they realized that their path was blocked by a giant heap of soft clay close the entrance. The clay had hardened in several spots, however, and the three men managed to climb over it. They found themselves in a huge dark room that their lamps could not illuminate. Paralyzed by admiration and fear, they stood for a time not knowing how to progress. The descent from the entrance into the cave was very steep in some places.

Barclay found that the distance from the entrance to the back of the cave in a straight line was 750 feet, that its circumference was over 2,000 feet, and that it was supported by a good number of natural rock pillars. At the southern end of the grotto was a deep abyss in which the three explorers found a man's skeleton. Someone had apparently fallen into the depths of the cave and broken his neck.

There was water everywhere in the grotto: it dripped from the high ceiling, creating small stalactites and stalagmites—some very beautiful, but too delicate to be removed. Hundreds of bats gripped the ceiling, letting out bloodcurdling cries. Numerous crosses were carved on the walls, evidence that despite the fact that the cave was unknown to Christians in Barclay's time, earlier pilgrims had frequented it.

Another discovery of Barclay's was an ancient gate beneath the Maghrebi Gate leading to Mount Moriah. The gate was almost invisible, concealed as it was by the house of one of the city's notables that abutted the wall at the site. Barclay's precise description of the ancient gate was rewarded with an extraordinary honor: scholars have since referred to the ancient portal as Barclay's Gate. Today the gate is hidden under a mound of dirt leading to the Maghrebi Gate, and is not mentioned very often, even in several of the more detailed guides of Jerusalem.

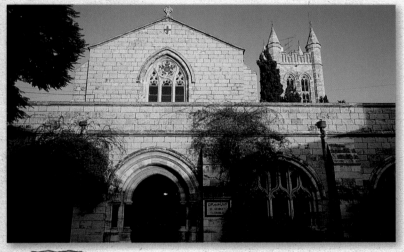

Left: St. George's Cathedral in Jerusalem.
Above: The stained glass windows of the church dedicated to James Barclay.

Crusader Church of Saint Anne Returns to Christian Hands

In the wake of the Crimean War, Saint Anne's Church was given to the French in gratitude for the help they rendered the Turks during the conflict. The French government transferred the church to the Order of the White Fathers, which controls it to this day. The church was later renovated, though most of its original form has been preserved.

The renovated Church of Saint Anne.

Adventure in David's Tomb, Holy to Muslims

American Woman in Turkish Costume Penetrates Guarded Tomb

Sarah Barclay, a young American woman, first arrived in Jerusalem with her father, the missionary James Barclay. She lived in the city several years, became friendly with the daughters of local families—especially the well-known Husseini clan—and learned fluent Arabic. Her command of the native language enabled her to set out on one of the most daring adventures of her time—an intrepid penetration of the

Christians were forbidden to enter David's Tomb since the fifteenth century, though many pilgrims attempted to sneak in. David's Tomb, by L.M. Cubley.

Tomb of David. At the time, the site was in Muslim hands, and guards were posted at the gate to prevent the entrance of Christian "infidels."

One morning during the Ramadan fast, one of Sarah Barclay's friends, a member of the local aristocracy, paid

her a visit. He said that he and his sister were willing to assist her in surreptitiously visiting David's Tomb, and she eagerly accepted the offer. Shortly afterwards, the two arrived at the home of the man's sister. Sarah Barclay was disguised in a dress and trousers of damascene silk, with a wide cashmere belt girding her waist. Under her dress she wore a flowered blouse. Fortunately, Barclay's hands had been dyed with henna during a visit to the Mosque of Omar, and had retained a deep orange hue without which her costume would have been imperfect. Even her face, recently tanned by the Syrian sun, was appropriate to her Turkish attire.

Barclay hid a sketchbook and pencil in her clothes, and the group set out on its way. Leaving the Old City via Zion Gate, they made their way through halls and corridors until they arrived at the holy site, which was blocked by

a double iron gate. An old dervish lay on the cold stone floor before the gate and gazed at the tomb through the iron bars. Even Muslim clergymen were seldom given permission to enter. Fortunately, Sarah Barclay's companions were relatives of the person in charge of the tomb.

The Muslims' maid was sent to fetch the key with the excuse that her lady wanted to pray in the holy place, and she soon returned with another maid-servant. Fear of detection gripped Barclay. The servant peeked under her veil, asked a brief question, and, apparently believing Barclay's companion when she explained that Barclay was a friend from Istanbul, left them at the site.

After wandering around the place for over an hour and even managing to draw it, Sarah Barclay and her companions left, delighted with the success of their mission.

English Royal Family Visits Holy Land
Consul's Wife Outfits House in Royal Luxury

In 1859, the duke of Connaught and Prince Alfred, the second son of Queen Victoria, arrived in the Holy Land. The latter, still quite young, was serving as a cadet on a British ship anchored in the port of Jaffa. It was decided to arrange a few ceremonies in honor of his visit, during which he was put up at the home of the British consul in Jerusalem.

The consul's wife, Elizabeth Finn, describes in her memoirs how she emptied the two best rooms in her

Jerusalem, by W.M. Thompson.

house, had her children stay with friends, and outfitted the chambers anew with furniture and other fixtures lent to her.

The French consul gave her all of the glass and silver serving pieces he had in his house, and ornate china was obtained from Jaffa. The consulate's Jewish interpreter, Rafael Pinhas, outdid himself, bringing from home magnificent coverings for sofas and

beds, checked cushions embroidered with gold thread, a small table covered with a gold-embroidered cloth that had been given to his great-grandfather by Sultan Selim, and a gorgeous curtain from one of the synagogues in the city. A tent was erected next to the house, in which the

prince's companions were lodged.

It remains unclear whether the young prince appreciated the tremendous effort invested in preparing for his visit: he may simply have believed that the Finn family was accustomed to always living in such royal splendor.

Permission Granted for Ein Karem Belfries

In 1857, the sultan in Istanbul gave the churches in Ein Karem permission to erect belfries, and the Franciscans began building a bell tower at the Monastery of Saint John the Baptist. The king of Spain sent four enormous bells to the monastery as a gift, each bearing its own name: The Visitation, John, Elizabeth, and Zechariah.

At the time, a new road was being paved from Jerusalem to the Monastery of Saint John the Baptist, and the small trickle of a few dozen pilgrims a year soon turned into a steady stream of hundreds and thousands.

The bells tolled for 120 years at the monastery, their sound overpowering the voice of the muezzin in the nearby mosque. In 1977, when the elderly monks could no longer climb the tower to clean them, the sound of the bells was stilled.

The belfry of the Monastery of Saint John the Baptist.

Archduke Builds Russian Compound in Jerusalem

Home to Russian Pilgrims

Archduke Constantine Nikolaievich (1827-1892), the second son of Czar Nicholas I and the younger brother of Czar Alexander II, served for a time as the commander of the Russian fleet. Part of his role was the management of the Russian shipping companies, and he helped establish a firm whose vessels set sail for Istanbul and the Holy Land. The government supported this company with significant financial backing, enabling it to inexpensively bring large numbers of Russian

Russian pilgrims in the dining room of the Russian Compound's hostel.

pilgrims to the shores of the Holy Land every year at Easter.

Once in the Holy Land, however, the Russian authorities had no means to lodge the pilgrims properly. Although there were Greek Orthodox monasteries at all of the holy sites, the heads of the Russian Orthodox Church felt that the Russians pilgrims disembarking in the Holy Land were not receiving enough assistance. A plan was proposed to establish in Jerusalem an entire block of buildings with the sole purpose of servicing Russian pilgrims. The site selected for the compound was northwest of the Old City, outside of the walls that still demarcated the city limits. At the time, the land beyond the wall, almost completely undeveloped, was empty of buildings aside from those on Mount Zion.

The archduke Constantine himself set out in 1859 for the Holy Land in order to decide where to purchase the land. Not a personal pilgrimage like those of other princes and kings who came to the Holy Land, his was a journey meant to further the imperialist goals of czarist Russia in the region. Constantine was received with the pomp due him, and the Greek Orthodox patriarch Cyril held an especially grand ceremony in his

honor at the Church of the Holy Sepulcher. Constantine himself negotiated the purchase of the plot, having eventually decided upon a site that included land formerly used as a parade ground for the Turkish garrison of Jerusalem and for the excursions of local residents. The area became known as the Russian Compound, and buildings intended to cater to the needs of the Russian Orthodox pil-

The Russian Compound.

Above: The Russian cathedral today.
Above left: The construction of the cathedral in the Russian Compound.

grims were erected in it.

The Russian Compound was the first expansive precinct constructed outside of the walls of ancient Jerusalem. It included a church where the *episcopus* sat, a hospital, a consulate, and two hostels—one for men and one for women. In order to ensure the pilgrims' safety, the site was enclosed by a wall.

The Russian government donated half a million rubles for the complex's construction; 600,000 additional rubles were collected as donations from the Russian people. The money was not quite enough to cover the extensive building work, however, and Constantine was compelled several times to raise the additional amounts necessary for the project's completion.

French Fleet Day in the Holy Land

Amateur Painter Vice Admiral Paris Takes Sailors Sightseeing

Francois Edmond Paris served as a vice admiral in the French fleet. In 1861, having set sail in the Mediterranean, he resolved to organize a visit to the Holy Land for his sailors, and was assisted in the realization of his plan by the French consuls of Jaffa and Jerusalem. The sailors began their tour in Jaffa, where they had dropped anchor. From there they proceeded to Jerusalem, where they visited the Church of the Holy Sepulcher and went up to the Temple Mount for a tour of the Dome of the Rock and Al-Aqsa Mosque. Their next stop was Bethlehem, where they took in the Church of the Nativity.

Paris, an amateur painter, decided to award his sailors with a souvenir of their visit to Jerusalem, and prepared an ornate picture album, *Souvenirs de Jerusalem*, commemorating their tour of the holy sites. The album was published in 1862.

Vice Admiral Paris and his sailors touring the rotunda of the Church of the Holy Sepulcher, by F.E. Paris.

1862

The prince of Wales under the pine tree where Godfrey de Bouillon pitched his tent.

Prince of Wales, Edward VII, Arrives in Holy Land
Turks Formally Open Hebron's Cave of Machpelah

In 1862, the prince of Wales (1847-1910), Alfred's eldest brother and the future King Edward VII, visited the Holy Land on an official tour. He was led through the country by the senior British cleric Dean Stanley, who had written a best-selling book about the Holy Land and would later be known as one of the founders of the Palestine Exploration Fund.

In Jaffa the members of the royal party were greeted by the local governor and the deputy British consul from Lebanon. The consul James Finn and his wife met the prince at the Church of Saint George in Lydda and accompanied him on the rest of his journey.

Because of the size of the prince's entourage, a tent camp was set up near a large pine tree north of Jerusalem where, according to tradition, the Crusader Godfrey de Bouillon's tent stood during his 1099 conquest of the city. In a photograph that has survived to this day (the work of Francis Bedford, who participated in the expedition and at its conclusion published a book of 172 photographs from the Holy Land and Egypt) the prince of Wales can be seen standing next to the tree.

In view of the gesture made earlier by the Turkish authorities in honor of the Belgian heir to the throne by allowing him to tour the Haram al-Sharif, it was deemed fitting that the future king of an enormous power like England, who deserved no less, would be permitted to visit the Cave of Machpelah in Hebron.

The Cave of Machpelah was even more perilous than the Haram. Hebron's population was known for its religious fanaticism, and there were almost no covert penetrations by Europeans in Muslim dress at the site, as was known to have occurred in the Haram. The pasha of Jerusalem attempted to dissuade the prince from visiting the site up until the last minute, but to no avail—the prince insisted on the right promised him in a *firman* of the sultan.

The pasha concentrated all of the military forces at his disposal in Hebron, and on April 7, 1862, the gates of the Cave of Machpelah were officially opened for the first time to visitors from the West. Dean Stanley took advantage of the opportunity to make detailed notes and sketches of the Cave of Machpelah, and he later described the visit in his second book: The prince and his entourage, striding in pairs between two lines of soldiers, passed the ancient pool of Hebron and ascended the steps to the new city.

Faces of Hebron's residents were scarcely visible as they passed; only here and there could a guard be seen near a window or on the flat roof of a tall residential building, securing the group from any object that might be thrown at them. What was effectively a curfew had been ordered in the city by the army.

The procession finally arrived at the southeastern corner of the massive retaining wall of the edifice built above the cave. They ascended the outer steps up to the top of the structure, where they saw the wall from the inside for the first time. They were received with great ceremony by six senior Muslim clerics who were representing the forty traditional guards of the mosque.

From that time on, Westerners, and especially important Western dignitaries, were occasionally allowed to enter the cave, though unlike the Haram it was not actually opened to the European public at large.

The prince of Wales returned to his homeland, but not for long. In 1868 he once again set out on a journey to the East and the Holy Land, this time accompanied by his wife.

The Cave of Machpelah, by S. Munk.

Ecce Homo Arch Uncovered

During construction work at the Convent of the Sisters of Zion, the engineer Ermete Pierotti (at center under the small arch), an Italian who served as Jerusalem's city engineer from 1854 to 1866, discovered a small arch flanking the central arch of the Ecce Homo gate. According to tradition, it was here that Pontius Pilate presented Jesus to the people *(John 19:5)*. Today the small arch has been incorporated into the Ecce Home Chapel in the Convent of the Sisters of Zion on the Via Dolorosa. A lithograph according to a photograph from 1861.

Revolutionary Proposal: A Canal from Haifa Bay to Jordan Valley
Mediterranean's Water to Fill Valley

After a short visit in the Middle East and the Holy Land, William Allen, a senior officer in the British Royal Navy, wrote a travel book of 768 pages in which he included, along with descriptions of countries and sites he had visited, a revolutionary proposal to dig a canal from the Haifa Bay through the Jezreel Valley to the Jordan Valley. Allen's thought was that the waters of the Mediterranean would flow through to the Jordan Valley, filling it up to the level of the Mediterranean.

According to the Englishman's program, the Dead Sea, the Sea of Galilee, and most of the River Jordan would disappear, leaving in their stead a huge lake stretching from Galilee to the southern Arava. Allen claimed it would not be difficult to connect this lake to the Red Sea by canal, creating a sea passage between the Mediterranean, the Red Sea, and the Indian Ocean. The result would be a direct and convenient sailing route from Britain to its largest colony, India, rendering the long and arduous journey around Africa unnecessary.

The scheme fired the imaginations of the English, and was spoken of for many years. Its implementation was not undertaken for many and various reasons: the obvious engineering obstacles, religious sentiment (such a lake would inevitably submerge holy sites like Capernaum and Tabgha), the fact that the area was settled, and political stumbling blocks—some of the sultan's lands were in the proposed underwater area.

Haifa Bay and the Sea of Galilee. A revision of a map from the Baedeker guide.

The Palestine Exploration Fund

In the last third of the nineteenth century, the exploration of the Holy Land began to pass from the hands of individual explorers to research institutions, of which the Palestine Exploration Fund was the first and most important.

At mid-century, a special affection for the Bible and the geography and native people of the Holy Land took hold of England. In that context, the Syrian Improvement Committee, which attempted to enlist support and raise funds for the realization of a program organizing the supply of water to Jerusalem, was established at the beginning of the 1860s. With the assistance of this committee and a private donor, enough money was collected to enable the project's initial stage—dispatching an officer of the British Royal Engineers to carry out a preliminary survey of Jerusalem. Captain Charles Wilson volunteered for the mission, and he spent the years of 1864 and 1865 carrying out the task.

Wilson prepared a map of Jerusalem that was better than any previous attempts and

A tunnel beneath the Temple Mount.

published a comprehensive report on the city—including sketches, maps, and photographs—that was issued in three volumes. Though the problem of Jerusalem's water supply was not resolved because of opposition by the Ottoman authorities to any engineering project by foreign forces within its realm, Wilson's survey served as the motivation for the establishment of the Palestine Exploration Fund in London in 1865.

The fund was a private society whose income relied on donations from its members: Since Queen Victoria's name led the list of donors, however, the fund enjoyed great popularity and for many years succeeded in footing the bill for most of the best research activity in the Holy Land. Among the fund's many activities worth mentioning was an additional survey carried out by Captain Charles Warren from 1865 to 1866, this time mainly in the north of the country. As a consequence of it, many new sites were identified and the objectives of the fund's future work—including Warren's excavations in Jerusalem from 1867 to

1870—were determined. Despite the enormous obstacles presented by the local authorities, who opposed the PEF's program, and despite neglect by the members of the fund, who did not send Warren money, compelling him to pay for some of the excavations out of his own pocket, he managed to carry out far more crucial and interesting excavations than many that occurred later under far easier conditions.

As a result of Muslim opposition, Warren did not dig openly near the walls of the Temple Mount, but utilized an ancient system of underground shafts, from which he dug tunnels, to gain access to the walls and foundations of the Temple Mount. Due to the unstable nature of the ground in the area, Warren's system was dangerous, and only by chance was no one hurt. The excavations drew the attention of many tourists in Jerusalem, and Captain Warren took them on guided tours, simultaneously recruiting from

A gallery under the Temple Mount, by C. Warren.

C. Warren excavating near the Western Wall. This illustration, drawn by Warren, was reproduced for years on the cover of the PEF's *Quarterly Review*.

Lieutenant Herbert Kitchener.

them donations to pay for the fund's future projects. The highlight of the learned society's work was the first accurate mapping of western Palestine that was carried out from 1871 to 1877. A number of English officers, the most active of whom were Lieutenants Claude Renier Conder and Horatio Herbert Kitchener, handled the project. Working together with them were British NCOs, members of the Royal Engineers. Together with its survey work, the PEF also uncovered archaeological sites, produced sketches, and identified biblical locations according to the names of extant Arab settlements, much in the style of Robinson. The total expenses for the survey work came to 17,039

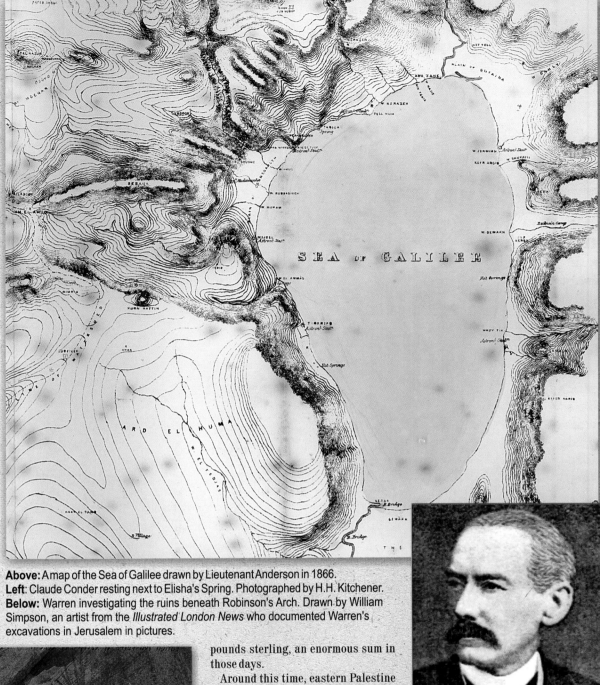

Above: A map of the Sea of Galilee drawn by Lieutenant Anderson in 1866.
Left: Claude Conder resting next to Elisha's Spring. Photographed by H.H. Kitchener.
Below: Warren investigating the ruins beneath Robinson's Arch. Drawn by William Simpson, an artist from the *Illustrated London News* who documented Warren's excavations in Jerusalem in pictures.

Charles Wilson.

pounds sterling, an enormous sum in those days.

Around this time, eastern Palestine was briefly slated to be explored by an American company similar to the Palestine Exploration Fund. Though the organization sent a small team to the region, it did not persist in its work and was soon disbanded. Thus from 1881 to 1882 Conder led a British attempt to survey eastern Palestine, though he was stopped after a short time by the Turkish authorities, who were angered by the English invasion of Egypt. From 1883 to 1884 a delegation was sent to the Arava to survey that region, which had not been included in the original map of the Holy Land.

After 1890 the fund devoted most of its resources to archaeological excavation, so that the PEF was heavily involved in the introduction of scientific archaeological research in the Holy Land. Its other achievements included the survey by the French researcher Charles Clermont-Ganneau from 1873 to 1874 of Jerusalem and Judea, and that of Lawrence of Arabia in 1914 of the Negev and Sinai.

The fund published its findings in large, ornate books. It printed, for example, a deluxe volume of pictures of the Roman frescoes discovered by its officers in a cave at Maresha. Since the frescoes were subsequently defaced by Bedouin and visitors, the PEF's book is the only surviving record of these singular works of art.

The fund renewed its archaeological activities (especially in Jerusalem) after World War I, though they were of less import than those that had preceded them. Competitors to the PEF had meanwhile appeared on the scene; one of them was a German society that operated in the Holy Land from 1877 onwards and issued a yearbook of its own. Later, research delegations of the French Dominicans as well as the Americans and various organizations also arrived in the Holy Land. The rise of these rival scientific expeditions was at least partially attributable to the enormous success of the PEF.

Pleasure Excursion to the Holy Land

1867

In the year 1867, gigantic advertisements announcing an expedition to Europe and the Holy Land appeared in the newspapers of the United States. In June of that year, the American steamship *Quaker City* set sail with an assemblage of passengers equipped with holy and historical books. Accompanying the group was Mark Twain, who described the pilgrims' expedition in a series of witty and venomous articles that were published in a number of American newspapers and collected afterward into the book *The Innocents Abroad*. The American journey was portrayed by the celebrated author thus:

The Frenzied Final Preparations

We sailed from Smyrna, in the wildest spirit of expectancy, for the chief feature, the grand goal of the expedition, was near at hand—we were approaching the Holy Land! Such a burrowing into the hold for trunks that had lain buried for weeks, yes, for months; such a hurrying to and fro above decks and below; such a riotous system of packing and unpacking; such a littering up of the cabins with shirts and skirts, and indescribable and unclassable odds and ends; such a making up of bundles and setting apart of umbrellas, green spectacles, and thick veils; such a critical inspection of saddles and bridles that had never yet touched horses; such a cleaning and loading of revolvers and examining of bowie-knives; such a half-soling of the seats of pantaloons with serviceable buckskin; then such a poring over ancient maps; such a reading up of Bibles and Palestine travels; such a marking out of routes; such exasperating efforts to divide up the company into little bands of congenial spirits who might make the long and arduous journey without quarreling; and morning, noon, and night, such mass-meetings in the cabins, such speech-making, such sage suggesting, such worrying and quarreling, and such a general raising of the very mischief, was never seen in the ship before!

But it is all over now. We are cut up into parties of six or eight, and by this

Twain's party of eight.

time are scattered far and wide. Ours is the only one, however, that is venturing on what is called "the long trip"—that is, out into Syria, by Baalbec to Damascus, and thence down through the full length of Palestine. It would be a tedious, and also a too risky journey, at this hot season of the year, for any but strong, healthy men, accustomed somewhat to fatigue and rough life in the open air. The other parties will take shorter journeys.

Camping in the Holy Land

Shortly after six, our pack-train arrived. I had not seen it before, and a good right I had to be astonished. We had nineteen serving men and twenty-six pack mules! It was a perfect caravan. It looked like one, too, as it wound among the rocks...I had camped out many and many a time before, and knew just what was coming. I went off, without waiting for serving men, and unsaddled my horse, and washed such portions of his ribs and his spine as projected through his hide, and when I came back, behold five stately circus-tents were up—tents that were brilliant, within, with blue and gold and crimson, and all manner of splendid adornment! I was speechless. Then they brought eight little iron bedsteads, and set them up in the tents; they put a soft mattress and pillows and good blankets and two snow-white sheets on each bed. Next, they rigged a table about the center-pole, and on it placed pewter pitchers, basins, soap, and the whitest of tow-

els—one set for each man; they pointed to pockets in the tent, and said we could put our small trifles in them for convenience, and if we needed pins or such things, they were sticking everywhere. Then came the finishing

"Pewter pitchers, basins, soap, and the whitest of towels..."

touch—they spread carpets on the floor! I simply said, "If you call this camping out, all right—but it isn't the style *I* am used to; my little baggage that I brought along is at a discount."

It grew dark, and they put candles on the tables—candles set in bright, new, brazen candlesticks. And soon the bell—a genuine, simon-pure bell—rang, and we were invited to "the saloon." I had thought before that we had a tent or so too many, but now here was one, at least, provided for; it

> ### Knives and forks, soup plates, dinner plates— everything, in the handsomest kind of style... And they call this camping out.

was to be used for nothing but an eating saloon. Like the others, it was high enough for a family of giraffes to live in, and was very handsome and clean and bright-colored within. It was a gem of a place. A table for eight, and eight canvas chairs; a tablecloth and napkins whose whiteness and whose fineness laughed to scorn

Stepping Over the Border

the things we were used to in the great excursion steamer; knives and forks, soup-plates, dinner-plates—everything, in the handsomest kind of style. It was wonderful! And they call *this* camping out. Those stately fellows in baggy trowsers and turbaned fezes brought in a dinner which consisted of roast mutton, roast chicken, roast goose, potatoes, bread, tea, pudding, apples, and delicious grapes; the viands were better cooked than any we had eaten for weeks, and the table made a finer appearance, with its large German silver candlesticks and other finery, than any table we had sat down to for a good while, and yet that polite dragoman, Abraham, came bowing in and apologizing for the whole affair, on account of the unavoidable confusion of getting under way for a very long trip, and promising to do a great deal better in future!...

They call this camping out. At this rate it is a glorious privilege to be a pilgrim to the Holy Land.

And as the evening drew near, we clambered down the mountain, through groves of the Biblical oaks of Bashan (for we were just stepping over the border and entering the long-sought Holy Land), and at its extreme foot, toward the wide valley, we entered this little execrable village of Banias and camped in a great grove of olive trees near a torrent of sparkling water whose banks are arrayed in fig-trees, pomegranates, and oleanders in full leaf. Barring the proximity of the village, it is a sort of paradise...

The incorrigible pilgrims have come in with their pockets full of specimens broken from the ruins. I wish this vandalism could be stopped. They broke off fragments from Noah's tomb; from the exquisite sculptures of the temples of Baalbec; from the houses of Judas and Ananias, in Damascus; from the tomb of Nimrod the Mighty Hunter in Jonesborough; from the worn Greek and Roman inscriptions

set in the hoary walls of the castle of Banias; and now they have been hacking and chipping these old arches here that Jesus looked upon in the flesh. Heaven protect the Sepulchre when this tribe invades Jerusalem!

The ruins here are not very interesting...trees and bushes grow above many of these ruins now; the miserable huts of a little crew of filthy Arabs are perched upon the broken masonry of antiquity, the whole place has a sleepy, stupid, rural look about it, and one can hardly bring himself to believe that a busy, substantially built city once existed here, even two thousand years ago. The place was nevertheless the scene of an event whose effects have added page after page and volume after volume to the world's history. For in this place Christ stood when He said to Peter: "Thou art Peter; and upon this rock will I build my church, and the gates of hell shall not prevail against it. And I will give unto thee the keys of

the Kingdom of Heaven; and whatsoever thou shalt bind on earth shall be bound in heaven, and whatsoever thou shalt loose on earth shall be loosed in heaven."

"As soon as the tribe found out that we had a doctor in our party, they began to flock in from all quarters."
Twain´s Dr. B. treats the ill at Banias.

A Miracle at Lake Ginnosar

Just before we came to Joseph's Pit, we had "raised" a hill, and there, a few miles before us, with not a tree or a shrub to interrupt the view, lay a vision which millions of worshipers in the far lands of the earth would give half their possessions to see—the sacred Sea of Galilee!...

During luncheon, the pilgrim enthusiasts of our party, who had been so

Fisherman on the Sea of Galilee. A late-nineteenth-century photograph by Bonfils.

light-hearted and happy ever since they touched holy ground that they did little but mutter incoherent rhapsodies, could scarcely eat, so anxious were they to "take shipping" and sail in very person upon the waters that had borne the vessels of the Apostles. Their anxiety grew and their excitement augmented with every fleeting moment, until my fears were aroused and I began to have misgivings that in their present condition they might break recklessly loose from all consid-

erations of prudence and buy a whole fleet of ships to sail in instead of hiring a single one for an hour, as quiet folk are wont to do...These men had been taught from infancy to revere, almost to worship, the holy places whereon their happy eyes were resting now. For many and many a year this very picture had visited their thoughts by day and floated through their dreams by night. To stand before it in the flesh—to see it as they saw it now—to sail upon the hallowed sea,

and kiss the holy soil that compassed it about; these were aspirations they had cherished while a generation dragged its lagging seasons by and left its furrows in their faces and its frosts upon their hair. To look upon

> ## I began to have misgivings that they might break recklessly loose from all considerations of prudence and buy a whole fleet of ships.

this picture, and sail upon this sea, they had forsaken home and its idols and journeyed thousands and thousands of miles, in weariness and tribulation. What wonder that the sordid lights of work-day prudence should pale before the glory of a hope like theirs in the full splendor of its fruition? Let them squander millions! I said—who speaks of money at a time like this?

In this frame of mind I followed, as fast as I could, the eager footsteps of the pilgrims, and stood upon the shore of the lake, and swelled, with hat and voice, the frantic hail they sent after the "ship" that was speeding by. It was a success. The toilers of the sea ran in and beached their bark. Joy sat upon every countenance.

"How much?—ask him how much, Ferguson!—how much to take us all—eight of us, and you—to Bethsaida, yonder, and to the mouth of Jordan, and to the place where the swine ran down into the sea—quick!—and we want to coast around ▶

(cont.) A Miracle at Lake Ginnosar

everywhere!—all day long!—I could sail a year in these waters!—and tell him we'll stop at Magdala and finish at Tiberias!—ask him how much!—anything—anything whatever!—tell him we don't care what the expense is!" [I said to myself, I knew how it would be.]

Ferguson—(interpreting)—"He says two napoleons—eight dollars."

One or two countenances fell...

"Too much!—we'll give him one!" I never shall know how it was—I shudder yet when I think how the place is given to miracles—but in a single instant of time, as it seemed to me, that ship was twenty paces from the shore, and speeding away like a

frightened thing! Eight crestfallen creatures stood upon the shore, and oh, to think of it! this—this—after all that overmastering ecstasy! Oh, shameful, shameful ending, after such unseemly boasting!...

Instantly there was wailing and gnashing of teeth in the camp. The two napoleons were offered—more if necessary—and pilgrims and dragoman shouted themselves hoarse with pleadings to the retreating boatmen to come back. But they sailed serenely away and paid no further heed to pilgrims who had dreamed all their lives of some day skimming over the sacred waters of Galilee and listening to its hallowed story in the

Eight crestfallen creatures stood upon the shore...

whisperings of its waves, and had journeyed countless leagues to do it, and—and then concluded that the fare was too high. Impertinent Mohammedan Arabs, to think such things of gentlemen of another faith.

Between Capernaum and Magdala

Capernaum lies close to the little sea, in a small plain some five miles long and a mile or two wide, which is mildly adorned with oleanders which look all the better contrasted with the bald hills and the howling deserts which surround them, but they are not as deliriously beautiful as the books paint them. If one be calm and resolute he can look upon their comeliness and live.

One of the most astonishing things that have yet fallen under our observation is the exceedingly small portion of the earth from which sprang the now flourishing plant of Christianity. The

longest journey our Savior ever performed was from here to Jerusalem—about one hundred to one hundred and twenty miles. The next longest was from here to Sidon—say about sixty or seventy miles. Instead of being wide apart—as American appreciation of distances would naturally suggest—the places made most particularly celebrated by the presence of Christ are nearly all right here in full view, and within cannonshot of Capernaum. Leaving out two or three short journeys of the Savior, he spent his life, preached his gospel, and performed his miracles within a

compass no larger than an ordinary county in the United States. It is as much as I can do to comprehend this stupefying fact. How it wears a man out to have to read up a hundred pages

of history every two or three miles—for verily the celebrated localities of Palestine occur that close together. How wearily, how bewilderingly they swarm about your path!

The Ancient Village of Magdala

In due time we reached the ancient village of Magdala...

Magdala is not a beautiful place... The streets of Magdala are anywhere from three to six feet wide, and reeking with uncleanliness. The houses are from five to seven feet high, and all built upon one arbitrary plan—the ungraceful form of a drygoods box. The

rated by carefully-considered intervals—I know of nothing more cheerful to look upon than a spirited Syrian fresco. The flat, plastered roof is garnished by picturesque stacks of fresco materials, which, having become thoroughly dried and cured, are placed there where it will be convenient. It is used for fuel. There is no timber of any

Our Guard

In the early morning we mounted and started. And then a weird apparition marched forth at the head of the procession—a pirate, I thought, if ever a pirate dwelt upon land. It

"A pirate, I thought, if ever one dwelt upon land." A tinted photograph by Bonfils.

was a tall Arab, as swarthy as an Indian, young—say thirty years of age. On his head he had closely bound a gorgeous yellow and red striped silk scarf, whose ends, lavishly fringed with tassels, hung down between his shoulders and dallied with the wind. From his neck to his knees, in ample folds, a robe swept down that was a very star-spangled banner of curved and sinuous bars of black and white. Out of his back, somewhere, apparently, the long stem of a chibouk projected, and reached far above his right shoulder. Athwart his back, diagonally, and extending high above his left shoulder, was an Arab gun of Saladin's time, that was splendid with silver plating from stock clear up to the end of its measureless stretch of barrel. About his waist was bound many and many a yard of elaborately figured but sadly tarnished stuff that came from sumptuous Persia, and among the baggy folds in front the sunbeams glinted from a formidable battery of old brass-mounted horse pistols and the gilded hilts of bloodthirsty knives.

The hovels of Magdala, by Bonfils.

sides are daubed with a smooth white plaster, and tastefully frescoed aloft and alow with disks of camel-dung placed there to dry. This gives the edifice the romantic appearance of having been riddled with cannonballs, and imparts to it a very warlike aspect. When the artist has arranged his materials with an eye to just proportion—the small and the large flakes in alternate rows, and sepa-

consequence in Palestine—none at all to waste upon fires—and neither are there any mines of coal. If my description has been intelligible, you will perceive, now, that a square, flat-roofed hovel, neatly frescoed, with its wall-tops gallantly bastioned and turreted with dried camel-refuse, gives to a landscape a feature that is exceedingly festive and picturesque, especially if one is careful to remember to stick in a cat wherever, about the premises, there is room for a cat to sit.

The Girls of Nazareth

This "Fountain of the Virgin" is the one which tradition says Mary used to get water from, twenty times a day, when she was a girl, and bear it away in a jar upon her head. The water streams through faucets in the face of a wall of ancient masonry which stands removed from the houses of the village. The young girls of Nazareth still collect about it by the dozen and keep up a riotous laughter and sky-larking. The Nazarene girls are homely. Some of them have large, lustrous eyes, but none of them have pretty faces. These girls wear a single garment, usually, and it is loose, shapeless, of undecided color; it is generally out of repair, too. They wear, from crown to jaw, curious strings of old coins, after the manner of the belles of Tiberias, and brass jewelry upon their wrists and in their ears. They wear no shoes and stockings. They are the most human girls we have found in the country yet, and the best natured. But there is no question that these picturesque maidens sadly lack comeliness.

The Fountain of the Virgin.
A tinted photograph by Bonfils.

At the Gates of Jerusalem

After a while we came to a shapeless mass of ruins, which still bears the name of Beth-el. It was here that Jacob lay down and had that superb vision of angels flitting up and down a ladder that reached from the clouds to earth, and caught glimpses of their blessed home through the open gates of Heaven.

The pilgrims took what was left of the hallowed ruin, and we pressed on toward the goal of our crusade...

At last, away in the middle of the day, ancient bits of wall and crumbling arches began to line the way—we toiled up one more hill, and every pilgrim and every sinner swung his hat on high! Jerusalem!

Perched on its eternal hills, white and domed and solid, massed together and hooped with high gray walls, the venerable city gleamed in the sun. So small! Why, it was no larger than an American village of four thousand inhabitants, and no larger than an ordinary Syrian city of thirty thousand. Jerusalem numbers only fourteen thousand people.

We dismounted and looked, without

Right: Mark Twain at the Church of the Holy Sepulcher.
Below: Jerusalem gleamed in the sun. A tinted photograph by Bonfils.

speaking a dozen sentences, across the wide intervening valley for an hour or more; and noted those prominent features of the city that pictures make familiar to all men from their school days till their death...

There was no call for tears. Tears would have been out of place. The thoughts Jerusalem suggests are full of poetry, sublimity, and more than all, dignity. Such thoughts do not find their appropriate expression in the emotions of the nursery.

Just after noon we entered these narrow, crooked streets, by the ancient and the famed Damascus Gate, and now for several hours I have been trying to comprehend that I am actually in the illustrious old city where Solomon dwelt, where Abraham held converse with the Deity, and where walls still stand that witnessed the spectacle of the Crucifixion.

Charles Warren.

Charles Warren at the Ceremony of the Holy Fire

Charles Warren, a lieutenant in the British Royal Engineers, was first sent to Palestine in the year 1867. He was to remain in the country for the next four years. Under the auspices of the Palestine Exploration Fund, he was the first to carry out archaeological excavations in Jerusalem's Old City, and it is after him that Warren's Shaft and Warren's Gate in the area of the Temple Mount are named. In 1876, Warren's book _Underground Jerusalem_, an account of his four years in the city, was published. Within is a description of the Ceremony of the Holy Fire at the Church of the Holy Sepulcher in the year 1869.

Little do we know as to when this fire first was displayed in the Church of the Holy Sepulchre, but it is suspected to have commenced in the time of Charlemagne, about A.D. 800. Bernard the Wise, about A.D. 867, appears to be the first to mention it, and states that on Holy Saturday, while the Kyrie Eleison is being chanted, an angel lights the lamps over the sepulchre of our Lord...

Sir John Maundeville, in A.D. 1322, relates, "And there is one lamp which hangs before the sepulchre which burns bright; and on Good Friday it goes out of itself, and lights again by itself at the hour that our Lord rose from the dead"...

On Good Friday all lamps burning with sacred fire within the chapels of

> **As the crowd tightens its clasp, the wail of infants is heard, fainting women are pushed out of the way, and all become expectant, for the hour is drawing nigh.**

the central church, and also in those of Bethlehem and others, were extinguished; and during the interval until the afternoon of the following day, the church gradually filled with pilgrims and devotees, who, collecting together in groups, passed the night around the Holy Sepulchre: a strange company!

As morning dawned, all the city became astir. Soldiers assembled in the narrow streets, and pilgrims traversed the city in bands according to their religion. Gradually they converged on the church, and filled its court yard. Our gallery was easily reached from a side entrance, and then what a tumult met our gaze!...

The gallery we were in extended round the Rotunda, and was crowded: above again was another gallery, swarming with life; and high on top of the dome were to be seen pilgrims looking down with telescopes and

After the patriarch enters the Holy Tomb, the door is sealed with wax.

glasses. Every vantage post was filled; Russian women lined the wooden beams of a scaffolding high above us to our left; and even the projecting cornices might boast of statuary drawn to the life. Soon irregular fits of excitement troubled the living sea of mortals, and strife ensued. Then came the guardians of the church, the Turkish soldiers; joining hand and hand in great good humor, they separated the combatants, and acted as a cordon between them. Soon mirth succeeds to passion, and the most playful antics are observed. Men coursing lightly along the heads of the crowd, running one after another. Then, as the crowd tightens its clasp, the wail of infants is heard, fainting

women are pushed out of the way, and all become expectant, for the hour is drawing nigh.

For a while the soldiers relax their vigilance, and a curious game of leap-frog commences, initiated by the native Christians; in the excitement real athletic feats may be observed, ending with a stampede round the building; men with men on their shoulders. This cannot continue without a fight, and again the soldiers come to the rescue and enforce order. Shortly after an armed company of soldiers is marched in, drawing a cordon round the sepulchre, and separating it from the multitude, for the miracle is about to be performed, and there must be no chance of collusion on the part of

outsiders. Round and round the stout, hearty, old Turkish Kaimakam may be seen strutting, cheerfully flogging the Christians into their places. While this is going on the natives sing the following refrain in chorus:

> _Christ came to us._
> _With His blood hath_
> _He ransomed us._
> _To-day we are glad._
> _And the Jews are unhappy._
> _The Saturday of the Light is_
> _our fête._
> _This is the tomb of our_
> _Saviour._

But now a struggle is to be witnessed, the Latin lookers-on must give way and allow the Greek procession to emerge from their church, in grand procession. The bishops of the Greek Church can be counted by tens; but where is the Bishop of Petra, the "Bishop of Light" as the Arabs call him? He is not! He died last year, and has not been replaced...

Priests and monks accompany the bishops and Patriarch, the procession commences to tour around the sepulchre, against the course of the sun. They are preceded by banners, which have descended from time immemorial to the ancient or more wealthy Christian families of the city. The sight of these banners arouses long-standing jealousies, and free fights

> **Shortly after an armed company of soldiers is marched in, drawing a cordon round the sepulchre, and separating it from the multitude, for the miracle is about to be performed.**

commence for their possession, put down by the strong arm of the Turk. Make way for the Christian Patriarch, who is about to perform the ancient _towâf_ around the sepulchre! The mob press hither and thither, and a

have, for he could not suppose I believed in his miracle.

I was ushered in, and in order to introduce the subject thought it desirable to make a statement about the handkerchief of St. Veronica. This at once gave the proper opening: he was eager to show that I knew nothing about the subject, and very kindly described how it all happens. It is as follows. After he is thrust in to the

As he prays more fervently the fire becomes stronger, springing up in a soft flame about half an inch high.

inner chamber of the sepulchre he finds himself alone; he kneels down in front of the stony couch, facing north, and as he prays that the fire may be manifest, it gradually appears. It does not descend from heaven, but appears on and emanates from the stone itself. As he prays more fervently the fire becomes stronger, springing up in a soft flame about half an inch high; this he collects together with both hands and carefully places it in a goblet, which fills itself up to the brim with the flame. He then hands it out of the sepulchre into the vestibule, and those waiting, who should be a Greek, an Armenian, and a Syrian, receive a little in each of their goblets, and they hand it out through the holes to the assembled multitude. I asked him if there was no truth in the story of the handkerchief: he said none at all.

narrow lane is opened to admit the procession, and then it closes over it. Thrice is the *towâf* executed, and then the Patriarch, paler than usual with excitement and emotion, reaches the east side of the sepulchre, fronting the door, which has been duly sealed by the Turks, after the interior has been examined for presence of lucifer matches, or flint and tinder, and such

Round and round the stout, hearty, old Turkish Kaimakam may be seen strutting, cheerfully flogging the Christians into their places.

like. The Patriarch also himself has been examined and searched, for, strange to say, it is the Turks who attest the truth of the miracle...

What are those Russians doing up in that gallery? Some are trimming their lamps, lighted with the Holy Fire, which they are about to carry away and keep up until their dying day. But what else are they about? The fire cannot burn (so they say) therefore the fire-eaters put it into their mouths, until their hollow cheeks glow; they pass it under their arms, through their hair, between their legs; soon we find it does burn, for singed hair is smelt all around, and not a few lose some of the greasy locks which adorned their heads. The women in the general enthusiasm forget all decency, and pulling up their petticoats on high pass the fire about their legs, as a cure for the rheumatics...

I was curious, however, to know how the fire really was obtained, and made many inquiries; at last I found

the following as a result from the various accounts. The miracle in the previous year was performed by the Bishop of Petra. It is well known that there is a handkerchief of Saint Veronica in Europe, at the Vatican, I believe; but perhaps it may not be known that the Greeks suppose that they possess this same handkerchief. It is this that the bishop took into the sepulchre, within a silver case, and laid on the couch of the sepulchre. On this the fire collected, and then, by picking it up by its four corners, the fire was in a bag,

Believers light their candles with the Holy Fire.

and could be ladled or poured into the goblet. I was most anxious to know whether the venerable Cyril would endorse this account, accordingly I paid him a visit soon after Easter.

I had always been very friendly with the old Patriarch, only I could not kiss his hand, as he expected all visitors should do: however, I explained to him that it was not the custom for Englishmen to do so, and he forgave me. On this occasion, however, I felt very doubtful as to what reception I should

The patriarch leaves the Holy Tomb after lighting the Holy Fire.

Kaiser Friedrich III of Germany Purchases Muristan in Jerusalem

Friedrich III (1831-1888) visited the Holy Land for the opening of the Suez Canal when he was the heir to the Prussian throne. On his way to Jerusalem he obtained from the Ottoman authorities a parcel of land known as the Muristan within the Old City of Jerusalem. The Anglo-German Church of the Redeemer adjacent to the Church of the Holy Sepulcher was later built on the site.

A certain amount of competition existed for this piece of property, since Emperor Franz Josef of Austria wanted it in order to build a Catholic church. Also on a visit to the Holy Land at the time, he arrived in Jerusalem too late; despite the fact that Friedrich's rank carried less weight than that of the Austrian emperor, the former had already gotten hold of the rights to the Muristan.

The Church of the Redeemer, built in the Muristan in 1897.

MacGregor and Rob Roy Taken Captive by Bedouin

John MacGregor, an Englishman of Scottish extraction and the son of Sir Duncan MacGregor, a general in the British army, was an enthusiastic traveler. He made his most famous journeys on the rivers of France,

Above left: MacGregor and the *Rob Roy* being taken captive.
Above: MacGregor and his captors in the Bedouin encampment, by L.M. Cubley.

Germany, Austria, and Switzerland in canoes he successively named *Rob Roy*. He recounted his adventures in a book that quickly became a bestseller and made its author a celebrity.

In 1869 MacGregor set out on a journey along the River Jordan in his fifth *Rob Roy*, a canoe built especially for him that was not only a sailing vessel and floating hotel, but a traveling companion. MacGregor speaks of the *Rob Roy* with love and admiration—almost as if it were a human being.

One day as the Englishman was sailing in the Hula swamp, Bedouins jumped him, grabbed him and the *Rob Roy*, and carried them away to their tent camp on the banks of the Jordan. Only after lengthy negotiations and the payment of a bribe to the local sheikh were MacGregor and his pal liberated and permitted to sail away.

Henry Baker Tristram, a priest and orientalist, visited the Holy Land for the first time in 1858 and was deeply impressed by the country. In 1863 he set out again, this time on a one-year research mission, in the wake of which he published a book. He made another visit to the Holy Land in 1869, and then penned *Scenes in the East*, which included twelve colored photographs (among them the picture of Bethany below). In 1879 Tristram received an offer to serve as the bishop of Jerusalem, which he refused.

Isabel Burton.

An Unpleasant Welcome for English Consul and His Men

Sir Richard Burton, who is considered the greatest explorer of the nineteenth century, toured and wrote books about numerous exotic countries. Only about the Holy Land, which he visited, did he write nothing.

During his tour of duty as consul general in Damascus, Burton visited Nazareth together with his wife,

Showdown between Richard Burton and Angry Greeks in Nazareth

1871

Isabel. During their stay, a quarrel broke out between their servants and a local resident from the Coptic sect. According to Isabel Burton, it was a trivial spat that no one would ordinarily have paid any attention to, forgetting it immediately. Unfortunately for the Burton party, however, just at that moment Greek Orthodox worshipers were leaving their church, and upon overhearing the contretemps, decided to intervene on behalf of the Copt against the foreigners. The Copt took advantage of the opportunity to flee, leaving the Greeks, who numbered 150, confronting Burton's servants, a mere six in number.

When Captain Burton and his countryman Charles Tyrwhitt Drake heard voices raised in argument, they ran half-dressed out of their tent to see what was happening. Trying to defuse the situation, they were pelted by a rain of stones the size of melons. One of the Greeks, wealthy and well-known, cried, "Massacre them! I'll pay the ransom!" Apparently, commented Burton later, he was used to resolving issues with cash. Burton's Druze donkey driver warned the Greek that

Burton was the English consul of Damascus, but to no avail.

Isabel Burton, admiring her husband's presence of mind, reported later that had it not been for the self-possession of Burton and Tyrwhitt Drake, as well as the aid of their friends, none of them would have escaped alive.

A veteran soldier, Burton reportedly remained quiet and restrained despite the hail of stones. When Isabel ran to him to bring him his revolver he gestured for her to withdraw so as not to distract him, though she stayed nearby to carry him out should he be wounded. Meanwhile, she shoved Burton's pistol into her belt, resolving to kill at least a dozen of the attackers if anything untoward happened to her husband.

Matters worsened. Three of Burton's servants were severely wounded, leaving three against a mob of angry barbarians. Two of the Greeks jumped Burton, who pulled a gun out of the belt of one of them, shooting into the air. Isabel, understanding the signal, rushed to call nearby English and Americans to come with their

weapons. When the attackers saw a dozen armed Americans and Englishmen making their way towards them, they fled.

Burton's attempts to bring about the imprisonment of the ringleaders of the assault encountered were thwarted by perjury: before he had time to submit his report to the Turkish and British authorities, the Greek Orthodox distributed a document stating that Captain Burton had entered the Greek church with the intention of desecrating it, taken pictures off the walls, broken lamps, and shot at the priest. Mrs. Burton, it was said, wearing only a nightgown and with a sword in her hand, had also entered the church, trampled the broken fixtures, and perpetrated various other acts unbefitting a woman.

A Greek Orthodox bishop signed the document and submitted it to Istanbul and London. Since it was the first of the testimonies to arrive in the hands of the authorities, it did a great deal of damage to Burton's reputation and was among the factors that finally brought about his dismissal from the position of consul in Damascus.

Splendid Reception for Lincoln's Secretary of State in Jerusalem

1871

Former Cabinet Member Welcomed with Festive Military Ceremony

William Henry Seward (1801-1872) was an American statesman, one of the founders of the Republican party, governor of New York from 1838 to 1842, and a member of the US Senate from 1849 to 1861. He also served as secretary of state in the cabinet of Abraham Lincoln during the American Civil War. Seward, who was seriously injured during Lincoln's assassination, continued after his recovery to serve as secretary of state until 1869. In 1870, he set off on a trip around the world accompanied by his adopted daughter and several friends. His visit to the Holy Land was short—less than two weeks in June of 1871—but during what amounted to a stay of a dozen days he was able to visit Jaffa, Ramla, Jerusalem, and Bethlehem.

Worthy of special mention is the grand reception held for the American party in Jerusalem. Seward's adopted daughter describes the event in the travel book she wrote: As they descended the road leading to the city, they suddenly heard the deafening notes of Turkish military music—the Turks were paying Seward a rare honor. A large tent, above which flew a

blood-red flag bearing a crescent, had been erected in his honor. On the road leading to it, an infantry regiment and cavalry company stood in formation. To the accompaniment of military music, Seward dismounted his horse and was led along a line of saluting soldiers up to the tent where the pasha of Jerusalem and other notables awaited him.

A quantity of refreshments was served, including traditional Turkish

coffee. The diplomat's daughter relates that though Jerusalem had been witness to many grand displays, the modern age had certainly not seen such an extraordinary one as this, in which an American citizen was received with the honor, magnificence, and governmental ceremony befitting only kings and conquerors.

The parade shows were held again for Seward on his way back both to Ramla and Jaffa. From Jaffa he set

William Henry Seward.

sail for Beirut, Europe, and to his homeland. Seward died a year after his return to the United States.

The Franciscans Build Additional Hostels

1873

Following the rise in the number of pilgrims in the Holy Land, the hostel at the Monastery of Saint John the Baptist in Ein Karem (left) and the hostel and dining room at the new monastery on Mount Tabor (above) were built.

217

Catholics and Greeks Clash in Bethlehem's Church of the Nativity
Greeks Prevent Catholics from Hanging Tapestries

The Austrian Georg Gatt was a former resident of Tirol who taught at a school in Jerusalem founded by Eliezer Ratisbonne (a Jew from Alsace who had converted to Christian-

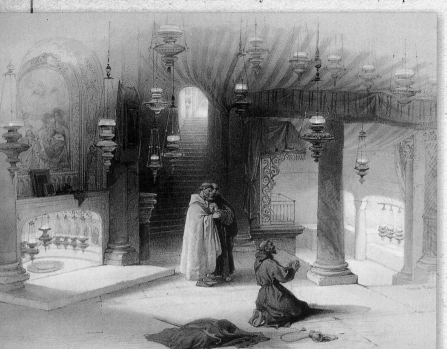

Lamps and tapestries in the Grotto of the Nativity, by D. Roberts.

had yet suffered bodily harm.

Two weeks after Easter, the Greek Orthodox mustered a large group of local thugs in the Church of the Nativity. Within a few minutes, the pace of

events in the church quickened: the Greeks, whose numerical strength was the greater, boldly began to hang their new lamps in place of the broken ones. The head Franciscan protested the action as an infringement of the status quo. When the Greeks disregarded his appeals, a few of the Franciscans attempted to forcibly prevent the installation of the lamps.

A real brawl broke out, led by the Greek Orthodox bishop. The Greeks, having armed themselves with sticks, stones, and rifles, threw themselves on the Franciscans and the other Catholics who streamed into the church.

The Franciscans, outnumbered by the Greeks and realizing that they were unable to offer any real resistance to their enemies and the soldiers who supported them, attempted to retreat from the church and return to their monastery. During their escape, four Franciscans and another Catholic were wounded. Nevertheless, the

Franciscan withdrawal failed to put an end to the battle, as the Greeks continued to shoot into the monastery through its open gates.

The moment the fight had begun the Franciscans had rung the monastery's bells in order to enlist the help of nearby compatriots, A gardener ran into town to threaten the Greek Orthodox with the intervention of his patron, the Austrian consul. The threat made an impression, and the Greeks momentarily interrupted their attack, enabling the Franciscans to close the two doors connecting their monastery to the Church of the Nativity.

By the time the hostilities finally ceased, the Greeks had already inflicted great damage on the Franciscans' fixtures in the Grotto of the Nativity.

The following day, all of the consuls in Jerusalem gathered on the spot. The Catholics among them voiced loud protestations while the Russian consul defended the Greek Orthodox position. To prevent a renewed outburst, the local garrison was reinforced.

ity and become a Catholic monk). From 1872 to 1874 Gatt served as deputy director of the Austrian hostel located near the third station of the Via Dolorosa. Afterwards he was appointed head of a mission in Gaza.

Gatt published one of the best nineteenth-century books about Jerusalem. In it he records a dispute between Catholics and Greek Orthodox that occurred in 1873 at the Church of the Nativity in Bethlehem.

The root of the disagreement was an argument that arose after a fire broke out in the Grotto of the Nativity in Bethlehem. According to the Catholic Franciscans, the Greek Orthodox had intentionally set fire to the Catholic tapestries decorating the walls of the grotto; the Greeks claimed that the blaze was simply an accident, for which they were not at fault. When the Catholics received new tapestries in place of those that had burned, the Greek Orthodox opposed their hanging them. Sensing trouble, the Ottoman authorities sent soldiers to the site to maintain order.

Nevertheless, a conflict seemed unavoidable. When the Franciscans deviated from their regular route during one of their Easter processions that year, the Greek Orthodox hastened to block their way. A few days later a second fight broke out, during which the Franciscans shattered forty-eight of the lamps of the Greek Orthodox in the church. Still, no one

Greek Orthodox Build Monastery and Church on Mount Quarantel
Forty Caves and Hermitages

By the end of the twelfth century, the Judean Desert was alive with Greek monks inhabiting caves and monasteries. Even after the defeat of the Crusaders, the monks continued to live in the Judean wilderness, though in fewer numbers and at risk of persecution at the hands of the Muslims.

In 1864, Mount Quarantel was explored by Henry Baker Tristram, who counted forty caves and hermitages on the spot. Additional caves punctuated the southern side of the mountain. Ten years later, the Greek Orthodox patriarchate began to renovate the site, erecting a monastery and church on the side of the mountain.

The monastery was constructed in the middle of the slope facing east towards Jericho, above twenty-five hermit caves. From its church, which was dedicated to the Annunciation, a staircase leads to the Chapel of the Temptation, which houses the stone seat on which, according to tradition, Jesus sat while the devil tempted him.

The monastery on Mount Quarantel. A late nineteenth-century photograph by Bonfils.

French Physician Stays in Pasha's Tent at Tiberias Hot Springs

1875

At the end of the nineteenth century, France excelled in publishing ornate editions of heavily illustrated books on the Holy Land bound in especially fancy bindings. The largest and most luxurious was the travel book of Dr. Paul Lortet, head of the department of medicine at the university of Lyons. The enormous volume was decorated with 364 amazingly lovely woodcuts based in part on photographs but attempting to conceal this with great artistry. The illustrations were copied

the cure in their salubrious waters.

Lortet relates that a small city of fabric pavilions was put up around the pasha's tent to accommodate his many companions. The Bedouin sheikhs from the area, and even those from the distant Hauran, arrived in great numbers to welcome him and assure him of their fidelity. The sight, says Lortet, was exceedingly strange. Turkish sentries in the service of the pasha, black-skinned men dressed in red robes whose hems were embroi-

Lortet's camp under the pine tree of Godfrey of Bouillon just outside Jerusalem. By P. Lortet.

Paul Lortet at the Sea of Galilee.

repeatedly, usually without acknowledgment of their source.

Near the hot springs in Tiberias Lortet met the pasha of Syria, a famous figure in those days, who had made the journey to the baths to rest from the cares of the day and to take

dered with silver and gold, were posted everywhere. At some distance from the others, the sheikhs of the desert, dressed in their somber robes, sat in a circle smoking in great solemnity, while their magnificent horses, tied to spears stuck into the ground, gazed around with their huge eyes.

This colorful and vital crowd, the

tents above which flags fluttered in the wind, the lake of frothy waves, and the steep surrounding hills all merged into a magic scene illuminated by the blinding rays of the sun.

The pasha received Lortet and his companions in a tent made of blue and white silk, with many couches and cushions. His pavilion was for the most part open to the lake, enabling a fresh wind to blow through it, carrying with it the sound of lapping waves. The opening also afforded a good view of the Sea of Galilee, laid out like a blue cloth flowing to the mountains of the Golan opposite, which soared up into the translucent skies.

After Lortet and his companions waited a few minutes, the pasha entered and seated himself on a sofa, with his guests near him. The various secretaries and assorted military

attaches, their costumes adorned with golden embroidery, sat beside the guests. The pasha wore a long Syrian robe and sported a fez on his head. He was a tall, stout man, and his tired face was made homely by a large, very red nose. His wise lively eyes, however, made up for his nose. The pasha chatted with his visitors in excellent French.

Before Lortet left him, the pasha ordered the preparation of a *firman* in which he instructed all of the sheikhs to place armed escorts at the disposal of the Frenchman's party. The secretary prepared a large sheet of paper and with his left hand swiftly drew a symbol in an ornate Arabic script. He then approached the pasha, and with a deep bow handed him the paper. The pasha drew a silver stamp out of a small leather wallet. His secretary dipped it in ink and the pasha stamped the page, the incised symbol appearing in negative on a black ink background.

1875

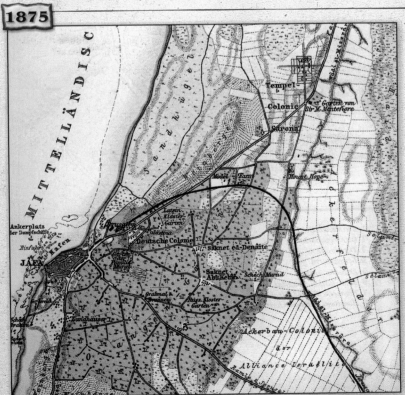

A map of Jaffa from the Baedeker guide.

Baedeker Guide to Holy Land Published

Professor Socin Composes Comprehensive Illustrated Book

Albert Socin (1844-1899) was an expert in Semitic languages, a professor at the universities of Tubingen and Leipzig, and one of the founders of the German society for the exploration of the Holy Land. Within the framework of his first journey to the East, he spent almost a year in Egypt, passed through Syria on his way to the Holy Land and eastern Palestine, and continued on to Iraq.

It was during this journey that Socin acquired the foundations of his proficiency in Eastern languages and customs. The description of the Holy Land portion of his trip was published forty years after his death, in 1937, in the yearbook of the German society for the exploration of the Holy Land. Not of high quality, his descriptions were not originally intended for publication.

In 1873 Socin was sent on a second trip to the Holy Land and Syria, this time on behalf of the Karl Baedeker publishing house in Leipzig. The Baedeker press specialized in publishing travel guides that gained an enormous following—so much so that today the name "Baedeker" is a generic term for any travel guide.

The Baedeker for the Holy Land and Syria, written mostly by Socin, was printed in German in 1875 and in English the following year. A book of more than six hundred densely printed pages, it includes maps and illustrations and is a veritable treasure trove of information on the Holy Land—not only its sites and antiquities, but its nineteenth-century hotels, stores, economy, and tourist facilities.

CHAPTER X

THE SUNSET OF THE OTTOMAN EMPIRE

1876-1917

he Tanzimat period drew to a close when Sultan Abed el-Hamid II (1876-1902) rose to power. In contrast to his predecessors, el-Hamid emphasized Islamic values, building numerous mosques and Muslim schools. During his reign, the democratic constitution of 1876 was not implemented and his government became increasingly totalitarian; ironically, the Tanzimat amendments forged the tools that made his rule more efficient.

El-Hamid's pan-Islamic policy attempted to unite the Turks and the Arabs throughout the Ottoman Empire and strengthen the ties between the government and its Muslim citizens. One of his most significant achievements was the reinforcement of Turkish government in the hinterlands. The power of the Bedouin was reduced everywhere, and they were forced to vacate some of the fertile plains and valleys of the Holy Land that they had appropriated during the period of the central government's impotence. Cities like Beersheba and Beit She'an were rebuilt and rehabilitated in order to tighten the government's hold in these outlying areas, but the trend ground to a halt when the central government changed.

The 1908 rebellion of the Young Turks resulted in the deposition of the sultan and brought Turkish nationalist ideals to the fore. As the new rulers of the Ottoman Empire began to foster the concept of Turkish nationalism, Arab nationalism was also on the rise—what had previously been the Turkish government's ally was now its enemy.

At the same time, Turkish foreign policy changed. Formerly a loyal friend of Britain, who had supported Turkey in its struggle against Russian attempts at domination, Turkey now allied itself with Germany, and eventually joined forces with the Germans in WWI. As a direct result of the subsequent defeat, the Ottoman Empire finally crumbled.

European imperialism throughout the world peaked at the end of the nineteenth century, when its tentacles reached every part of the globe. The Turkish empire, despite its attempts at reorganization, remained a relatively weak kingdom, ripe for the multiplication of European attempts to extend Continental influence throughout its territories.

Great Britain—who won the race and obtained control over the Holy Land after WWI—had not previously invested

General Allenby enters Jerusalem through Jaffa Gate, accompanied by the commanders of the French and Italian expeditionary forces. Allenby dismounted his horse at the city gate in order to enter Jerusalem on foot, as a pilgrim—a gesture of the general's respect for the holy city, which was reverting to Christian hands after nearly eight hundred years of Muslim rule.

Previous pages: The Abu Nabut Fountain in Jaffa, which served as a starting point for pilgrims heading to Jerusalem. By F.E. Paris.

much in the establishment of religious institutions in the county. Despite this fact, Britain had led the modern research on the Holy Land's history by means of its Palestine Exploration Fund, which officially started its work in 1864.

Towards the end of the nineteenth century the economic situation in Europe and the Holy Land improved and the number of European tourists arriving in the Holy Land increased. Railways were laid (the first, from Jaffa to Jerusalem, was completed in 1894) and steamships from all corners of the world began to anchor at the ports of Jaffa and Haifa. Scientific delegations operated in the Holy Land, European products were imported, first-class hotels opened, and group tours of Protestant and Catholic societies disembarked to see the sights.

The population of the Holy Land grew, reaching about three quarters of a million souls in 1914. At that time, about ten percent of the country's inhabitants were Christians, most of whom were Arabic speakers and about three quarters of whom were urban dwellers. About half of the Christians were Greek Orthodox, though at the beginning of the nineteenth century approximately ninety percent of the Christians in the Holy Land had been Greek Orthodox.

US President Grant Visits Holy Land During World Tour

Trip Funded by *New York Herald* Produces 1,250-Page Book

A street in Jaffa, 1890, by G. Bauernfeind.

US President Ulysses Simpson Grant.

US President Ulysses Simpson Grant (1822-1885), hero of the American Civil War (during which he was appointed commander in chief of the victorious army of the North), was elected president of the United

preter Rolla Floyd. Young, the book's author, relates that in Jerusalem one of the most magnificent receptions of the entire trip was held in Grant's honor—quite as if he were Alexander the Great entering an occupied city.

Also according to Young, Grant would have preferred to arrive in the holy city quietly, as an ordinary pilgrim, so that he would have had time to see more. Thus he declined the suggestion of the city's governor that fifty members of the local garrison's

The atrium of the Church of the Holy Sepulcher, by C. Werner.

States for two consecutive terms (1869-1877).

At the end of his term in office, Grant set out on a world tour that was to last two years and was funded by James Gordon Bennett, owner of the *New York Herald* newspaper. Grant was accompanied on his journey by one of the paper's top correspondents, Dr. J.R. Young, who filed dispatches about the former president's tour. From these reports, a 1,250-page book was later compiled.

Twenty-two of the pages were dedicated to Grant's experience of the Holy Land, though he only visited Jaffa, Ramla, and Jerusalem. In the holy city his guide was the American inter-

band accompany him everywhere he went. Grant actually spent almost all of his time in Jerusalem receiving visits from the governor, various consuls, and religious leaders. During the dinner held in his honor he finally had no alternative but to listen to the efforts of the military band.

Nonetheless, Grant somehow found time for a short stroll along the Via Dolorosa, where he was joined by a group of beggars. As a result of the Old City's imperfect paving, the party slid rather than walked along in the mud. Grant's main visit was to the Church of the Holy Sepulcher, of course, where he was received by the Greek Orthodox archbishop.

New Churches Built in Cana

In 1879, a new Franciscan church dedicated to the miracle of the wine was erected in the village of Cana over the remains of a Crusader church that had in turn been constructed over the ruins of a Byzantine church. The new church was designed according to the plan of a church in Salzburg, the birthplace of the head of the Franciscan Order in Cana.

In 1886 the Greek Orthodox church in the village—originally built in 1556—was also reconstructed. Today, two stone jars are displayed in the church; according to Greek Orthodox tradition, they are two of the six original jars from the wedding at which Jesus turned the water into wine.

Above: The water jar in the Church of Nathanael at Cana. **Right:** The facade of the Franciscan Church of the Miracle at Cana.

1880 Franciscans Rebuild Church of Saint Catherine

In 1880 the Franciscans rebuilt the Church of Saint Catherine in Bethlehem's Church of the Nativity. The new church was constructed over the remains of a twelfth-century Crusader church that had been dedicated to Saint Catherine in the fourteenth century. The new structure integrated within it the Crusader cloister, which survived almost in its entirety.

The Crusader cloister at the Church of Saint Catherine.

Na'in's New Church

1878

In the distant past, two ancient churches commemorating the miracle of the revival of the widow's son *(Luke 7:11-16)* stood in the village of Na'in. In 1878 the Franciscans purchased the site, which included the ruins of a mosque built over an ancient synagogue, and in 1888 built on the spot a modest church with an altar and two pictures depicting the miracle. Photograph by Bonfils.

An American Colony in Jerusalem

1881 Established After Tragedy of Spafford Family of Chicago

Horatio Spafford, a wealthy attorney from Chicago, his wife Anna, and their four daughters lived in a lovely home in the Lakeview neighborhood of Chicago.

In 1873 Anna Spafford took her daughters on a tour of Europe. While they were at sea, a violent storm arose, sinking the ship and taking the lives of all four Spafford daughters. Anna Spafford, who had been miraculously saved, returned brokenhearted to her home in Chicago. She and her husband dedicated themselves to church work, but comfort and relief from sorrow remained elusive. The couple finally decided to emigrate to Jerusalem, and convinced a few of their friends to join them in a communal life in the holy city.

Anna Spafford.

The Spaffords and their friends—fourteen adults and five children—arrived in Jerusalem in 1881 and

Left: The American Colony Hotel. **Below:** Damascus Gate in a photograph by the American Colony. **Right:** The Via Dolorosa in a photograph by the American Colony.

laid the foundations for a settlement called "The American Colony" ever since. Initially they rented a house in the Old City, near Damascus Gate, but shortly afterward moved to the building known today as the American Colony (now a famous hotel).

The Americans were soon joined by a few Swedish families (Anna Spafford was of Norwegian descent). The members of the colony established a children's hospital in the building where they had first lodged, ran an educational institution for Muslim girls, and provided much assistance to Jerusalem's poor.

The residents of the colony made their living from agriculture, trade, and light manufacturing, especially of souvenirs for tourists. A collection of their photos is housed today in the Library of Congress in Washington.

Hunting Trip of Rudolf, Heir to the Austrian Throne

Upon His Return Home, Tension between Rudolf and His Father Mounts. The Prince Commits Suicide at Mayerling in 1889.

The slow decline of Austria cast a shadow over the entire life of the Austrian heir to the throne, Rudolf (1858-1889), the only son of Kaiser Franz Joseph I. Rudolf was a talented man and an excellent writer; many of his articles were published anonymously in newspapers.

While his father the emperor believed that change would merely hasten the end of the Austrian empire, Rudolf was of the opinion that dramatic modernization and the establishment of a federation were necessary to its survival. He feared that his

father's conservative policies would bring about the ruination of the empire before he, Rudolf, would have time to assume the crown.

In order to distance himself from the poisonous atmosphere of the court, Rudolf left in 1881 on a trip to Egypt and the Holy Land. The journey had been made before him by his father, his uncle the emperor of Mexico, and his grandfather, the prince of Bavaria. Among Rudolf's interests was ornithology, the study of birds, and he made a list of the species of birds he encountered as he hunted in the Holy

Land. While not comprehensive, as was the study of the English scholar Tristram, Rudolf's record is interesting and of some importance.

The prince wrote an account of his journey and published it anonymously that same year. Since the identity of the book's author was in any case known to all, in the second edition his

name was mentioned explicitly. Many interesting illustrations—the work of the court painter Franz von Pausinger—were included in the later edition.

Prince Rudolf chronicled his entry into Jerusalem: When his party crested the top of a ridge, they saw before them the desolate heights of the holy city, relieved by nary a plant nor tree. From afar, the bluish-gray mountains of Transjordan could be seen.

Above: Prince Rudolf lands at Jaffa.
Left: The prince spent the night at the Austrian hostel in Jerusalem.
Below: Prince Rudolf's party returns from boar hunting, by F. von Pausinger.

The landscape near them was yellowish-gray in hue, and notable for the absence of vegetation of any kind.

As they drew nearer they began to recognize the first signs of their proximity to Jerusalem: the large group of Russian buildings with its five-towered church, the Valley of the Cross, and the Mount of Olives. The city itself was not yet visible.

Upon the royal party's entry into Jerusalem, a sort of triumphal arch with an inscription in Hungarian was erected in their honor. The sides of the road were lined with crowds of people waiting to catch a glimpse of the prince: Jews from all over the world, Christians from Anatolia, Greek Orthodox, European pilgrims, Christian women from the East (some veiled), Copts, English tourists in unromantic attire, Muslim peasants, and hunchbacked beggars, all stood along the road, waiting to greet Rudolf and his guests.

When the prince returned to Austria, his relationship with his father and the government became even more strained. On the night of January 30, 1889, the prince committed suicide in his little hunting lodge at Mayerling, after shooting his lover, Princess Maria Vetschera.

A New Church in Bethpage  1883

In 1883 the Franciscans built another church, this time in Bethpage. In order not to attract the attention of the Ottoman authorities, the structure was designed much like an ordinary

In 1874 C. Clermont-Ganneau discovered the stone from which Jesus mounted the donkey at Bethpage. During the Crusader period it had been decorated with drawings.

Above: Charles Clermont-Ganneau. **Left:** The Church of Bethphage.

house. The apse was built much later, in 1897, and the bell tower was erected only in 1954. In the same year, frescoes depicting the victorious entrance of Jesus into Jerusalem and the events connected with Palm Sunday were also added to the church.

British General Gordon Discovers Garden Tomb
Site Named in His Honor After His Death

1883

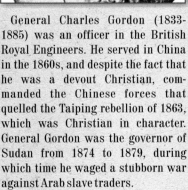

General Charles Gordon (1833-1885) was an officer in the British Royal Engineers. He served in China in the 1860s, and despite the fact that he was a devout Christian, commanded the Chinese forces that quelled the Taiping rebellion of 1863, which was Christian in character. General Gordon was the governor of Sudan from 1874 to 1879, during which time he waged a stubborn war against Arab slave traders.

In 1883, Gordon visited the Holy Land. A religious man, he was concerned by the debate over whether the Church of the Holy Sepulcher in Jerusalem was in fact located on the spot where Jesus was buried. Influenced more by mystical considerations than rational and archaeological induction, he sketched the shape of a skeleton on a map of Jerusalem and found that the skull (i.e., the location of Golgotha) lay to the northeast of Damascus Gate, in the place previously identified by various Protestant scholars as the true burial place of Jesus.

It happened that when looking at the hill at the site from a certain angle, it had a certain resemblance to a skull, and on its slope an ancient tomb was discovered. At first the place was called "The Hill of the Skull," and then, after Gordon's death, "Gordon's Calvary." The spot, which was to become a popular pilgrimage site, has been called the Garden Tomb since 1892.

The Garden Tomb in Jerusalem.

St. Peter's Church in Jaffa

1884

Saint Peter's Church in Jaffa, which commemorates the saint's visit to the city and the vision he had in his dream, was built from 1884 to 1888 on the remains of a Crusader fortress erected by Saint Louis, the French king.

At the portal of the church are heavy metal doors decorated with the Franciscan symbol and the crown of the Spanish monarchy, which contributed to its construction.

An aerial photograph of Jaffa and the Church of Saint Peter.

Czar Alexander III Builds Church on Mount of Olives

Czar Alexander III erected a church in Jerusalem to the memory of his mother, Czarina Maria Alexandrovna, and dedicated it to Mary Magdalene. The church was built with the financial assistance of the grand duchess Elizabeth Feodrovna, wife of the duke Sergei, both of whom participated in its consecration ceremony.

The duchess expressed a wish to be buried in the church, and when she died during the Russian Revolution her body was smuggled to Beijing and from there to Jerusalem in accordance with her wishes. In 1919 she was entombed in the church secretly in order not to harm the recently renewed relations between the governments of England and Russia.

Right: The Mount of Olives and the Church of Mary Magdalene in construction. A photograph by Bonfils from the late nineteenth century.
Below right: The sarcophagus of the grand duchess Elizabeth Feodrovna.
Below: The Church of Mary Magdalene.

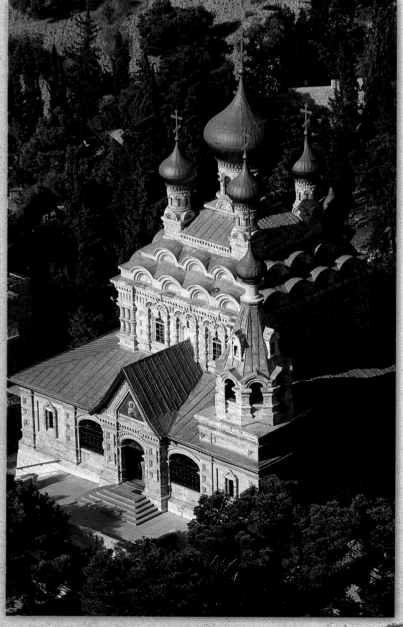

Ancient Manuscript of Gospels Discovered in Saint Catherine's Library
Scottish Twins Find Parchment

In their youth, the Scottish twins Lewis and Margaret Dunlop Gibson studied ancient as well as contemporary Greek. The former traveled to Greece, and in 1883 published a book on life in the country that was translated into modern Greek. Aside from Greek, she also studied Arabic, Hebrew, and Aramaic.

In 1889, one of Lewis' friends, Rendel Harris, discovered in the library at St. Catherine's Monastery in Sinai a second-century manuscript of the Athenian Greek philosopher Aristides' *Apology*, which had previously been known only in part. He believed the monastery library probably contained additional inter-

esting manuscripts worth examining.

When they heard Harris' news, the two sisters decided to set out for Sinai. Before their departure, Harris taught them methods of photographing documents and they received instruction in Aramaic grammar and deciphering the church alphabet, in which some of the manuscripts were written.

The sisters soon arrived in Cairo, where they arranged a caravan for the continuation of their journey and received recommendations from the archbishop of the Greek Orthodox church, who was also in charge of Saint Catherine's Monastery. At the beginning of February 1892, the twins ▶

began their work in the library of the monastery, where they (as opposed to many other travelers and scholars) were well received because of their command of spoken Greek, the language of the monks.

The sisters' thorough preparations paid off, and the two discovered among the library's texts a fourth-century manuscript with most of the four books of the Gospel of the New Testament, in their Aramaic version. The manuscript was a palimpsest, a manuscript whose earlier text has been erased and then written over (a custom that usually resulted from the high price of parchment). Often, the original text has been imprinted so deeply on the parchment that complete erasure is impossible, and those with sharp eyes can still make it out.

Some of the manuscript's 358 pages were stuck together, and an attempt to separate them threatened to damage the treasure. Nevertheless, the sisters drew the sheets apart with patient care and discovered underneath signs of the original text—of the books of the Gospel. Since an earlier manuscript of the four books of the Gospel had never been found, the discovery was of great importance.

The sisters photographed the entire manuscript, but upon their return to England realized that the photographs did not enable the original manuscript to be read properly. It was thus decided to send a second delegation comprised of the two sisters and three experts from Cambridge University (and their wives) the following year. The party of eight spent several months at Saint Catherine's deciphering the manuscript.

In 1894, the text of the four books of the Gospel discovered by the sisters was published by Cambridge University. The two returned to the Sinai Peninsula four more times in order to examine additional manuscripts from the monastery's library. Although they did not uncover any more rare finds, their research clarified what material was to be found in the library.

For their troubles, the sisters received wide recognition from the scientific world and honorary doctorates from the universities of Saint Andrews and Dublin.

Once, travelers were drawn up into the Monastery of Saint Catherine on ropes.

Travails on a Turkish Train

Riding the Rails to Jerusalem

Matilde Serao was an Italian author who wrote novels about upper-class Italian society, as well as short stories and plays. Together with her husband, she founded and edited two Italian newspapers. Though today both she and her work have been forgotten, at the beginning of the twentieth century Serao was at the pinnacle of her success. She set out on her trip to the Holy Land as a tourist, but the travel book she wrote about it was original and interesting.

Serao's book, though totally unheard of today, enjoyed great success in its time—thirty editions were published in Italy within two years. Of special interest is the Italian author's rendering of her trip to Jerusalem on the train that had begun to operate only one year previously.

Given the brief nature of the train journey, Serao reports, the ticket price of twelve shillings was relatively expensive. There were only two classes—first and second—but even in first class the seats were of unfinished wood and had neither cushions nor armrests, making them much less comfortable than even the third-class cars in Italy.

Jerusalem's train station. The journey from Jaffa was shortened to four hours.

The train left nearly an hour behind schedule, as the Turks had no idea how many people would be traveling and seemed to have lost their composure. They behaved with great arrogance toward the passengers, who were crowded into the stuffy cars protesting and shouting in all possible languages. At the last minute, when the Turks realized that no room was left to accommodate the remaining passengers, another car or two were added and the train finally set out amidst general confusion while people argued with each other in loud tones—a phenomenon Serao notes as common procedure in the region.

There was usually an unplanned stop along the way, and Serao's train was indeed held up for forty minutes, as the engine's water needed replenishing. Upon the resumption of the journey, the engineer was forced to travel at top speed in order to make up for the lost time, making for a very bumpy ride.

Serao reports that the uncomfortably narrow cars were poorly constructed and the route arduous. On one side of the track rose a steep slope, and on the other, a deep valley no less precipitous. The train negotiated a tortuously curving track, its engine and cars swinging and swaying terribly. It was therefore best not to look out of the windows, but rather to turn one's attention to the inside of the car and wait patiently for what was yet to come. Though the train apparently often skipped off the track, there had as yet been no serious incidents...

According to Serao, the rail journey to Jerusalem, which could not have been less romantic, left an impression contrary to all expectations and a deep aversion to the name Zion printed on the green train ticket. She would undoubtedly not return by train, sitting in an unbearable compartment stuffed with fat Turks, some of them half sleeping but most of them smoking in their favorite position—one shoeless foot (no Turk would wear his shoes a minute more than necessary) resting on the arm of his seat.

It was unfortunate, Serao adds, that the train passed so quickly by the lovely Sharon Plain, where the Philistines fought the Israelites, and Sorek Valley, in which Delilah overpowered Samson, where the train moved so fast that there was no chance of glimpsing anything through the trees and steam.

The arrival in Jerusalem was no better, and Serao's spirits fell even further. Imagine arriving at the city of David and Solomon at such excessive speed! To the happy but exhausted pilgrims who managed to get to Jerusalem in those days after overcoming hardship, adventure, and suffering, the city appeared as a tranquil refuge of divine peace. Even just a few years previously, people who arrived in Jerusalem slowly—by carriage, on horseback, or on foot—could kneel and fall upon the holy ground while they were approaching the city's ancient gates. Those approaching the place in Serao's day—when the updated world boasted modern industrial innovations—sped into Jerusalem inside an airless train and disembarked from it to the sounds of the curses of porters.

German Kaiser Wilhelm II on Showy Propaganda Tour of the East

Cook's Pilgrim Inaugurates Evangelical Church and Lays Cornerstone of Dormition Abbey

No other political figure contributed so much to the creation of the tense and turbid European atmosphere that brought about WWI as Wilhelm II, the German kaiser. The ruler of Germany set out on a propaganda tour of the East after the German army had threatened both France and Russia.

Wilhelm's actions dragged Europe, which since the end of the Napoleonic wars had enjoyed one hundred years of peace, into another age of war. His aggressive speeches, his lack of tact, and his adventurous foreign policy all undermined the security of the inhabitants of Europe and the serenity of the continent.

One such high-profile gesture was the kaiser's visit to the Holy Land in 1898. Unlike the quiet personal visits of other rulers and princes, Wilhelm's was a showy propaganda tour escorted by an unprecedentedly large entourage. It signaled the beginning of the kaiser's campaign to force

Above: Kaiser Wilhelm II and his wife Augusta Victoria. A painting on the ceiling of the Augusta Victoria church.
Left: Kaiser Wilhelm II arrives at the new quay at the port of Haifa, built in honor of his visit.
Below: Wilhelm II enters Jerusalem.

Above: The kaiser returns from the consecration ceremony of the Church of the Redeemer in Jerusalem.
Right: Augusta Victoria, the German Protestant hostel that Wilhelm II built on the Mount of Olives in honor of his wife, Augusta Victoria. The hostel was intended to lodge pilgrims and serve as a rest house for German settlers in the Holy Land. The complex includes a church and a campanile that rises to a height of sixty meters. Today the building functions as a hospital.

England, Russia, and France out of their positions in the Holy Land and the entire Turkish East.

Ultimately, the kaiser's plan succeeded: Turkey, whose relationship with England had survived the entire nineteenth century, became Germany's ally in the First World War—and its partner in defeat.

Upon its arrival at the coast of the Holy Land, the kaiser's fleet weighed anchor in the waters of Haifa Bay; to allow Wilhelm to disembark, a new quay had been installed. On roads paved especially for the visit, the German convoy passed through the Sharon to Jaffa and from there to

Above: Kaiser Wilhelm II and his entourage near Jerusalem.
Below: The tent camp built by Thomas Cook and Sons Ltd. for the kaiser and his entourage north of Jerusalem.

Templers Present Album to Kaiser

The Templers were members of a German Christian sect that was expelled from the Lutheran Church in 1858. Having organized themselves into a new congregation called the Tempelgesellschaft, they set about their objective of realizing the end of days as foretold by the prophets by establishing colonies in the Holy Land.

The Templers inaugurated their settlement experiments in the Holy Land in 1866. They established colonies at the foot of the Carmel within the city limits of modern-day Haifa, in Tel Aviv, Jaffa, and Jerusalem. Overcoming the many hardships inherent in the pioneering life, they became wealthy and successful farmers, and in 1875 there were 750 Templers in the Holy Land.

When Kaiser Wilhelm II arrived for his visit to the Holy Land, the Templer settlers in Jaffa presented him with a gift they had prepared especially for him—a book of paintings of the Holy Land. In 1902, when the Templers established a colony not far from Lydda, they called it Wilhelma in honor of the kaiser.

In the course of World War II, the British concentrated the Templers in quarantine camps and expelled them from the Holy Land.

Jerusalem. The kaiser, who was given to extravagant displays, felt himself a modern Crusader, though the preparations for his journey were made by the English travel agency Thomas Cook and Sons Ltd. The kaiser was thus referred to in the British satirical magazine *Punch* as "Cook's Pilgrim."

An enormous tent camp was erected in the uninhabited section of north-western Jerusalem, and Cook and Son saw to it that nothing of the magnificence and luxury the imperial entou-rage was accustomed to was lacking.

The kaiser took advantage of his stay in the Holy Land to inaugurate the Evangelical Church and to lay the cornerstones of the German Catholic church—the Church of the Dormition on Mount Zion—and a hostel on the Mount of Olives that was named after his wife Augusta Victoria.

The German's visit was one of the factors that provoked England, France, and Russia to join forces against Germany in WWI.

The Templer colony in Jerusalem. A painting from the album presented to Wilhelm II.

An Adventure Without Geese

Renowned Swedish Author Selma Lagerlöf Visits Jerusalem. Wins 1909 Nobel Prize for Her Book on Swedes in the City.

Members of the American Colony in their grand living room.

Selma Lagerlöf.

The well-known Swedish author Selma Lagerlöf, who wrote *The Wonderful Adventures of Nils*, set out for a trip to the Holy Land in 1900. Lagerlöf visited Jerusalem, staying there for some time. The American consul told her about the American-Swedish colony in the city but warned her not to make contact with its members because of their anomalous religious tendencies. The writer decided to visit them anyway at their spacious house on Nablus Road in the Husseini Quarter north of the Old City. She was deeply impressed by the unique group of ex-patriots, with whom she soon became fast friends.

Out of this visit emerged the book *Jerusalem*, which won its author the Nobel Prize—the first granted to a woman—in 1909. Changing their names, Lagerlöf used the figures of the members of the colony as the heroes of her novel. Anna Spafford, the founder of the colony, appears in the book as Mrs. Gordon, and her tempestuous life story is told with only minor changes. Lagerlöf dedicated most of her novel to the Swedes among the group, and describes at length the religious background of their immigration to Jerusalem and their difficulties in becoming accustomed to life there.

Jerusalem Attracts Eccentrics From Around the World

Mrs. A. Goodrich-Freer, who lived in Jerusalem from 1901 to 1924, wrote a book packed with stories about Jerusalem in which she tells of the customs and lives of the Muslim women in the city, the concept of the evil eye,

Daily life in Jerusalem. Arab women carry water *(above)* and bake pita bread *(below)*. Photographs by Bonfils.

December 17. That same evening, torrents of rain pelted the city.

Freer also analyzes the status of the various powers in the city, emphasizing Russia's imperialistic intentions, the organization of its widespread pilgrim network, and the contacts the Russians were attempting to establish with the local Arab population.

She reports at length on the quarrels between the Catholic and Greek Orthodox monks at the Church of the Holy Sepulcher that ended in bloodshed on Easter of 1901. Her book, which is not lacking in humor, also includes a chapter dealing with the eccentrics and the religiously delusional from throughout the world who flock to Jerusalem.

According to Freer, Seventh-Day

Adventists, Baptists, Mormons, and Christian Scientists were all to be found in Jerusalem. One born-again Englishman expressed his sorrow for his sins by beating his wife—the activity that had caused him the greatest regret in the first place.

Freer tells the tale of a female pilgrim in town who, considering herself an ascetic, attempted to enter the strictest of women's convents. Despite the opposition of its leaders, she cut off all of her hair upon entering the convent. After a few days had passed it became clear that she lacked the required call to the vocation, and ever since had wandered the city in search of a wig merchant.

In the Tishbi Colony, English and American citizens were led by none

other than Elijah the prophet. Strange figures were present at any religious celebration: godfearing people who spent their days in caves, or monks and nuns who had either been expelled from or had left their orders, living afterwards according to their own individual systems.

Freer describes how in 1858 a group of Saxons led by a coal miner who had been directly informed by Satan that the crowning of the Anti-Christ would take place in Jerusalem arrived in town. Unfortunately, the coronation was delayed, and the group did not have enough money to subsist. They were saved by the members of the American Colony, who themselves held some unusual religious views, though their worldly contributions to city life proved beneficent.

Irish penitents in Jerusalem. The woman, barefoot, distributes coins to mendicants while they crawl along the filthy cobblestones on all fours.

Muslim foods, the status of the Husseini family, and the languages in which various subjects were studied in Jerusalem's schools.

Freer reports that in 1898, a drought year, the governor of Jerusalem asked the city's Jews to go to Mount Moriah and pray for rain. The Jewish elders refused to pray on the mount, requesting permission to pray at David's Tomb instead. Permission was granted, and the prayers were held on

Mount Zion Church of Dormition Inaugurated: Cornerstone Laid in 1898

Kaiser Wilhelm II Receives Plot from Sultan During His Tour of the Holy Land

The German Church of the Dormition was built on a plot of land given by the Turkish sultan to the German kaiser Wilhelm II during the latter's 1898 visit to Jerusalem. The kaiser transferred the property to the Benedictine Order of monks, who built one of the most magnificent churches in Jerusalem on the spot.

The church was designed by the architect Heinrich Renard of Cologne, who was inspired by the Palatine Chapel in Aachen erected in the ninth century in honor of Charlemagne.

Before construction commenced in Jerusalem, excavations were carried out and the remains of the large Byzantine church of Hagia Zion (considered the "mother of all churches") as well as those of the Crusader church built on top of it were unearthed.

The church commemorates the spot where Mary, mother of Jesus, fell asleep. Over its main altar is a painting of the Holy Spirit descending to the apostles at Pentecost *(Acts 2:1-4)*. One of the six altars in the church's nave is dedicated to Saint Willibald, the first English pilgrim to visit Jerusalem (which he did in the year 724).

The Church of the Dormition.

Sultan Funds Research Trip Searching for Natural Resources in the Dead Sea

Refuses to Pay Geologist Blankenhorn Full Salary Until Sued

French and German scholars began to study the natural resources of the Holy Land during the nineteenth century. Among them was Max Blankenhorn, who visited the Holy Land many times—in 1894, 1904, 1905, and 1908. Some of his trips were funded by the Hejaz rail company, but his 1908 junket was backed by Sultan Abed el-Hamid II, to whom much of the land around the River Jordan and the Dead Sea belonged.

Blankenhorn was a new species of geologist. Unlike his predecessors, he was not concerned only with theoretical science; he was also interested in the possibility of commercial utilization and refinement of natural resources. Thus, for example, he searched in the Dead Sea area for deposits of copper and signs of oil. He saw the regional deposits of phosphates, whose extraction was to begin during the Mandatory Period, as the most commercially important natural resource.

Blankenhorn did not receive all of the 13,000 francs owed him by the sultan. Such were conditions in the

Above: Max Blankenhorn meets with the governor of Jerusalem at Blankenhorn's camp.
Left: The Dead Sea, by the Comte de Forbin.

Ottoman Empire at the end of its days that even the sultan did not see fit to pay his emissaries their entire salaries. Even the gold medal he sent to Blankenhorn was lost along the way and never reached the geologist.

After the sultan was deposed following the rebellion of the Young Turks, Blankenhorn sued him and succeeded in compelling him to pay most of his debt.

Grigory Rasputin.

1911

Rasputin, Advisor to Russian Czar, Criticizes Attitude Towards Pilgrims

Grigory Rasputin (1872-1916), a native of Siberia, was a religious mystic who became a monk in 1904. His was to be an historic role. Nicholas II, the last of the czars of the house of Romanov, and his neurotic wife finally had a son—after four daughters, at last an heir to the throne! Unfortunately, the boy was a hemophiliac; the slightest wound could have led to his death. To avoid his being hurt, a huge sailor carried him everywhere.

In 1907 the czarina was told that Rasputin would be able to cure her son with his supernatural healing powers, and he actually did succeed in improving the boy's condition. The czarina, overwhelmed with gratitude to the monk, invested Rasputin with a great deal of power within the royal court. Even the czar, having initially opposed his influence, eventually capitulated to it, and many times brought fateful decisions to Rasputin for resolution.

Rasputin visited the Holy Land in 1911, and the manuscript in which he recorded his impressions of it has been preserved to this day. Rasputin criticizes both the disorder on the ships that transported pilgrims and the hostels in the Holy Land. He complains that more attention should be paid to the pilgrims, who ought to be transported more cheaply. Further, the Russian Orthodox Holy Land society should not demand payment for hot water and rooms, and should provide one meal a day. The pilgrims, the monk claimed, were treated like a flock of sheep.

Rasputin's comments hit their mark and attempts were made to improve services for Russian pilgrims, who arrived in the Holy Land in ever greater numbers until the last days before WWI. Heavy losses in the early part of the war brought with them increasingly vehement accusations against the czarist court and against Rasputin personally, since many saw

Russian pilgrims on their way to bathe in the River Jordan.

The Sergei Hospice in the Russian Compound.

the disproportionate influence of the monk on the czar as one of the reasons for Russia's decline.

On December 16, 1916, Rasputin was assassinated by plotters from within the Russian court.

1912

British Journalist Stephen Graham Makes Pilgrimage with Russian Masses

One of the Few Who Wrote of the Thousands of Russian Peasants

The majority of nineteenth-century Holy Land pilgrims, and even those who arrived up until WWI, came not from Western Europe but from Russia. Among them were a few intellectuals who wrote books about the journey, but concerning the thousands of simple, faithful Russian peasants who greatly outnumbered them we hear almost nothing from Russian literature. The British journalist Stephen Graham, who participated in one of the last Russian pilgrimages as a rank and file pilgrim, provides us with the lacking material.

Graham, who spoke fluent Russian, joined the journey at its inception, in Russia. He sailed with the pilgrims in one of their ships and participated in all of their travels in the Holy Land as well. Less interested in the sites of the Holy Land than he was in the pilgrims

themselves, he left descriptions of several of his fellow travelers.

The first figure in Graham's cast is a peasant called "Dyadya" (uncle)—a poor man around fifty-five years of age with a delicate build. A simple man, he had the fortitude characteristic of northern peasants, as he hailed from the Tver region. The beggars, Arab peddlers, and porters usually cheated him, but he was contented with his lot.

When Dyadya set out from his hometown on his pilgrimage to Jerusalem, the other peasants mocked him, saying it was foolish to travel to Jerusalem. Even the village priest expressed doubts about whether his pilgrimage would please God. After Dyadya's encounter with the other pilgrims in his party, however, his mood, as well as his confidence, improved, and he enjoyed the trip.

Another character was a monk named Yevgeny—a man of about sixty-five years of age who loved to drink and lived his life exuberantly, remaining young even in his old age. He was prepared to give sermons on board ship as well as to preach against the presence of young women. Always willing to intervene spiritedly in other people's affairs, he fought for his prejudices with all his might.

Philip was a very different type: a tall peasant with broad shoulders and a stout body, his large dark face was dirty and unshaven, and his nose and cheeks swelled above a round chin. His physiognomy was dreamy and pleasant, but he had sly eyes. He knew everyone, and if arguments broke out at the hostel (in the Russian Compound in Jerusalem) he would settle them with an authoritarian manner that impressed his fellow peasants.

Philip was unkempt, and his room was stuffy. He courted customers on behalf of souvenir shops, and served as an agent for priests who would pray for naive peasants in return for payment. Philip also smuggled contraband to Russia and sold souvenirs—religious articles and Turkish goods.

In short, Philip was a man lacking all scruples. Blithely breaking all of

Russian pilgrims buy candles in Jerusalem.

the rules of the Russian Orthodox Holy Land society, he made clandestine arrangements with all of the petty clerks so that he did not pay a penny for his living quarters, gave no one his passport, and received his meals gratis.

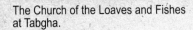

Remains of Sixth-Century Byzantine Church Discovered at Tabgha

1911

Two Decades Later, Mosaic Floor of Miracle of Loaves and Fishes Unearthed

The Church of the Loaves and Fishes at Tabgha.

The remains of a Byzantine basilica from the sixth century were discovered at Tabgha in 1911, though only two decades later did excavations expose the structure and its magnificent mosaic floor. The floor, considered to be one of the loveliest mosaics ever unearthed in the Holy Land, is decorated with wonderful illustrations of the natural world and various geometric motifs. In the apse of the church is the rock on which the miracle of the loaves and the fishes is said to have occurred. Beside it is a depiction of a pair of fish and a basket full of loaves of bread.

The mosaic of the loaves and fishes from the Byzantine floor at Tabgha.

PEF Sends Lawrence of Arabia to Survey Byzantine Cities

1914

British Intelligence Agent Operates in Holy Land Under Cover of Archaeological Research

Several years before WWI, the Palestine Exploration Fund returned to the Holy Land to renew its surveying activity, this time in the territories west of the Arava. This time, probably not just purely scientific interests motivated the expedition, since the maps that were to be prepared had military potential from the outset. Indeed, when war broke out, the maps were put to use by the British forces, giving them an advantage over the Turks, who had no maps of the desert regions in the northern Sinai Peninsula at their disposal.

At the head of the mapping operation was Captain Stewart Francis Newcombe, and under him, five separate teams, all of which operated independently. The system was designed to enable them (given the pressured circumstances) to complete the survey work at a faster pace than that of the Survey of Western Palestine carried out forty years earlier. It was clear to all that war was approaching and that time was short.

After the survey work had already commenced, another squad was added to Newcombe's delegation; it was to become more famous than the others. At its head were two young English archaeologists, Charles Leonard Wooley, who was to make a name for himself after the war by excavating Ur of the Chaldees, and Thomas Edward Lawrence, who during the war would become famous throughout the world as Lawrence of Arabia, the central figure behind the Arab rebellion of the tribes of the Hejaz and Transjordan.

Both Wooley and Lawrence had done archaeological research in the Middle East previously, and had apparently been in contact with the British military intelligence then. This time their role was to serve as scientific cover for Newcombe's work. Nevertheless, they had the full cooperation of the Turkish Kaimakam of Beersheba, Arafan Bey, who was responsible for the territories in which they intended to work. Arafan, of course, had his own motives; he was hoping that the Englishmen's research would enable him to expand Turkish rule over the outlying regions of his territory. In the final judgement, the contacts made by Newcombe, Lawrence, and Wooley with the local Bedouin tribes helped their side exclusively, aiding the British in their operations against the Turks during the war.

Wooley and Lawrence's scientific work included the listing, photographing, and identification of ruined Byzantine cities in the Negev Mountains. They also examined the roads leading eastward from Sinai, as well as places like Beersheba and Aqaba, which were to play a central role during the course of the war.

In order to camouflage the military intelligence nature of this work, ex-PEF officer Herbert Kitchener, the acting governor of Egypt (and later, when war broke out, Britain's omnipotent war minister), gave an order to delay Lawrence's enlistment in the army until his and Wooley's book of findings was completed.

The book was published with amazing speed in 1915 as the third yearbook of the Palestine Exploration Fund. It is partially written in Lawrence's brilliant personal style, well-known from his later books. The publication was Kitchener's way of camouflaging the military character of Lawrence and his colleagues' work in the areas under the influence of the Ottoman Empire and avoiding claims of infringement upon its sovereignty.

Lawrence relates that at the beginning of their work the Englishmen were assisted by Arafan Bey, who, suspecting them of nothing, was very friendly. The team's similarly excellent relations with the Arabs would be

T.E. Lawrence—Lawrence of Arabia.

sustained throughout the project. Each of the local tribes had a negative opinion of the characteristics and integrity of its neighbors, but Captain Newcombe embarked upon his work by making the acquaintance of all of the local sheikhs, obtaining a measure of tolerance for himself and the members of his group that often developed into friendship even in the absence of the usual cash lubrication.

After Lawrence completed his work he set out for Egypt, where he officially joined the British intelligence and left on its behalf for Hejaz. From there he organized the progress of the Arab tribes northward to Aqaba and Damascus. His friend Wooley also operated as a British intelligence officer in Egypt.

THE HOLY CITY SURR

white sheet from the American Colony hospital, tied it to a pole, and gave it to al-Husseini (the original flag is still in the Imperial War Museum in London).

The surrender itself was not so simple. Al-Husseini set out to meet the English forces, and first encountered two cooks—Privates Church and Andrews—who had set out to look for chickens for the officers' mess and in their search—upon which they had embarked without any arms—had

reached the outskirts of the city, where the mayor and his many escorts from among the city's inhabitants found them. The mayor wanted to surrender the city to Church and Andrews, but they declined the honor and returned to their regiment.

The mayor then ran into two British sergeants—Hurcomb and Sedgewick from the British Sixtieth Division. Though the meeting was commemorated in a photograph, they also evaded accepting the surrender. The mayor, who was beginning to get tired, made his third attempt after

Al-Husseini, the white flag, and Sergeants Hurcomb and Sedgewick at the site of the second surrender attempt, where a commemorative monument *(inset)* stands today.

On December 8, 1917, the Turkish defense collapsed for the last time. Under pressure from the German officers stationed in the Holy Land, who did not want to be blamed for the destruction of the holy city, the Turkish forces decided to abandon Jerusalem without a fight.

At seven o'clock in the morning on

December 9, the bell on the door of the American Colony in Jerusalem rang. When Anna Spafford opened it, Jerusalem's mayor, Hussein Hashem al-Husseini, told her that he intended to surrender to the British that day, and that he had wanted to inform her first. Spafford, close to tears, broke into a hymn of thanksgiving. She ripped up a

The Unfinished Church
1917 of Be'er Ya'acov

In 1860 the Greek Orthodox purchased the ruins of the Crusader church in Be'er Ya'acov from the Turks and began to build a new church, which was intended to resemble the Crusader church. Its construction ceased after the Russian Revolution, when the flow of funds from Russia dried up.

IDERS TO THE BRITISH

meeting two artillery officers—Majors Beck and Bury—from the same division who had gone out on reconnaissance near Lifta. Similarly refusing to accept the surrender, the two at least reported the matter by phone to the divisional command upon their return to their regiment.

Meanwhile, another attempt to capitulate was being made, this time before Lieutenant Colonel Bailey, the commander of one of the brigades of the Sixtieth Division, who was touring the area with several junior officers. Bailey struck up a conversation

Right: Colonel Baily *(standing)* conversing with Brigadier General Watson *(mounted)*. Next to them stands al-Husseini.
Above: The letter of surrender.

Above: General Allenby on the Temple Mount.
Left: General Allenby announces the establishment of a military government at the Citadel.

with al-Husseini and dispatched one of his officers to transmit a message to the division commander. A second officer, a Major Cook, went into town to take over the post office.

While he was there, the last of the Turkish soldiers withdrawing from Jerusalem passed by the building. Colonel Bailey was meanwhile joined by the commander of another brigade, Brigadier General Watson, and the two entered town to the sounds of the cheers of the crowd. At

the same time, the divisional commander Major General Shee's automobile entered the city.

One of the women from the American Colony stood in the middle of the road in the path of Major General Shee and vehemently demanded supplies for the hospital managed by the American Colony, since the Turks had left them without food or medications. At this point, al-Husseini, who had finally returned from the western suburbs of the city, also approached Major General Shee and handed the British commander the letter of surrender he had received from the Turkish governor. After a long morning, he had finally managed to turn the city over to the British.

The First World War

The Holy Land was a secondary and marginal arena in the First World War, but even there the warring sides experienced difficulty coping with the new opportunities that the industrial and scientific age had granted the battlefield. It is reasonable to presume that Admiral Nelson would have attacked the long and undefended coastline of the Ottoman Empire, but the conservative British navy of the early twentieth century did not do so. In the Holy Land, the cavalry was still being used as a crucial military force at a time when horses had long since vanished from European battlefields.

When war broke out, the Turks immediately canceled the capitulations and began to put pressure on religious minorities like the Armenians and national minorities like the Arabs. As a result, the English succeeded in organizing an Arab rebellion in Hejaz and Transjordan under the leadership of the Englishman since given the sobriquet "Lawrence of Arabia." Commanded by a German officer, Colonel von Kressenstein, the Turks tried twice to cross the Suez Canal to Egypt, but their supplies did not suffice for either operation, and the Turkish forces, repelled, beat a retreat.

The British conquered Sinai in 1916. They attacked Gaza twice at the beginning of 1917 but were beaten back, at which point a new British general, Sir Edmond Allenby, was brought into the arena. His forces, which included Australians and New Zealanders, numbered about ninety thousand men. Opposite them were positioned approximately sixty-five thousand Turks, reinforced by German staff officers and Austrian artillery. This time, both sides brought machine guns, artillery, numerous vehicles, and warplanes to the Holy Land for the first time.

Instead of frontally attacking Gaza during the third British offensive, as everyone anticipated, Allenby assaulted Beersheba, disabling the entire Turkish troop arrangement. Allenby advanced his troops mainly along the coast from Gaza to Jaffa, then turned them east to conquer Jerusalem on December 8, 1917. For the first time since 1244, Christians ruled the holy city.

The final stage of conquest was in the autumn of 1918, when Allenby smashed through the Turkish front, conquered Damascus and Aleppo, and accepted the surrender of all the Turkish forces in the arena. Following the victory, the entire Holy Land passed into the hands of the British, though the renewed Christian rule of the country was to last for only thirty years.

CHAPTER XI

TWENTIETH-CENTURY PILGRIMAGE

From 1917 Onward

The enormous development of transportation methods in the twentieth century completely changed the nature of pilgrimage to the Holy Land. No longer an arduous journey to a hostile nation, fraught with danger and suitable only for adventurers, pilgrimage became a tourist excursion that was rendered increasingly comfortable and convenient as modern means of transportation improved. The prolonged and perilous sail, the poor roads, the inescapable payment of bribes, the assaults by bandits, and the disgraceful lodging conditions all slowly disappeared. Modern ships, aircraft, automobiles, improved roads, and fully-equipped hotels transformed pilgrimage into an easy and affordable enterprise.

During the first half of the century, the British Empire ruled Palestine. As they did in many of their other colonial holdings, the British concentrated on developing an efficient system of roadways and did much to improve the railroad network. The British, as opposed to the Ottomans, viewed Jerusalem as a legitimate capital and a suitable hub of governmental institutions, and they took great care to preserve its historical character. They established a non-sectarian, non-sovereign body to attend to the preservation of the Old City, its holy places, and its many archaeological sites.

During this period Jerusalem's population was a true melting pot. The civil servants of the British government, the many foreign consuls who resided in the city, the various churches, the tourists and pilgrims who visited throughout the year, prominent visitors, and the journalists who passed their tours of duty in the holy city all contributed to its markedly cosmopolitan character.

Palestine passed World War II in relative tranquility. Though nearby, the war's aggressions almost did not touch the Holy Land, aside from the bombing of Haifa and Tel Aviv in 1940.

In 1947, the United Nations resolved to terminate the British Mandate in Palestine. At the end of the war that broke out immediately after the execution of that decision, the country was left divided between the Jews and the Arabs, and the former established the State of Israel. Control of the holy places was likewise divided between two nations: East Jerusalem and the Old City, with most of the Christian holy places, was under Jordanian rule; West

Jerusalem (the New City), was under Israeli rule. Bethlehem, Hebron, Nablus, and Jericho, all on the West Bank of the River Jordan, were under Jordanian control. Nazareth, Mount Tabor, Galilee, and the Sea of Galilee and its environs were in Israeli hands. As a result of the hostile relations between the two peoples, most pilgrims were forced to choose between visiting the holy places in the Hashemite Kingdom and those in Israel.

After the 1967 war, control of Jerusalem in its entirety as well as the West Bank reverted to Israeli hands together with the administration of the holy places, and pilgrims could once again freely visit all of them without worrying about divided cities. The State of Israel preserved the right of freedom of worship and granted the heads of all the religious sects within its boundaries the right to determine protocol in the places sacred to each.

Following the signing of the Oslo Accords between Israel and the Palestinians in 1993, dominion over Jericho, Bethlehem, Nablus, and the rest of the cities of the West Bank of the River Jordan was transferred to the Palestinian Authority.

During the second half of the 20th century many new Christian churches and religious institutions were constructed and there was a large increase in the number of pilgrims—most of whom now arrived by air.

The two most distinguished visitors to arrive in the Holy Land during this period were Pope Paul VI and Pope John Paul II.

Pope Paul VI arrived in the Holy Land for a very short trip in 1964; during his visit he consecrated the new Church of the Annunciation in Nazareth.

Pope John Paul II visited the Holy Land in the year 2000 to commemorate the second millennium of the birth of Jesus Christ, as well as to realize a life-long wish to visit personally the sites of the Gospel.

Previous pages: The Palm Sunday procession on the Mount of Olives, by M. Milner.
Inset: Pope John Paul II on the Mount of Beatitudes, by GPO.
Background: The public mass on the Mount of the Beatitudes, by GPO.

12 Christian Nations Build the Church of All Nations at Gethsemane

Consecrated in 1924, Garden Church Considered One of the Most Beautiful and Important in Jerusalem

At the beginning of the twentieth century a joint effort was made by several countries to build a new church at Gethsemane. Twelve nations took part in the cooperative endeavor: Argentina, Chile, Brazil, Mexico, Italy, France, Spain, England, Belgium, Canada, Germany, and the United States. Many Catholic communities from other countries also contributed to the building of the church: the Catholic community of Australia donated the fence of thorns crowning the Rock of Agony in the church.

The design work was done by the celebrated ecclesiastical architect Antonio Barluzzi, who integrated symbols of the contributing nations into the twelve domes of the church. In general terms the church resembles the ancient church uncovered in excavations on the site, though it is substantially larger. The style of the edifice is nearly classical.

In order to reflect the atmosphere of great sorrow that fell upon Jesus when he prayed at this spot, the light in the church was dimmed by partially opaque windows of purple alabaster. Part of the original stone, next to which Jesus prayed and which was already integrated into the Byzantine church, is likewise incorporated into the apse of the new church; it is surrounded by an iron balustrade fashioned as a crown of thorns. Birds perch among the thorns next to the

The facade of the Church of All Nations, one of the loveliest in Jerusalem.

cup of agony. The church also boasts a number of mosaics located in the apses on the east, in the domes, and on the gables of the facade. Stars dot a dark blue background in the domes, and olive branches grace the corners of the ceiling.

The church, consecrated in 1924, is considered one of the loveliest and most important in Jerusalem.

Church of the Transfiguration on Mount Tabor Rebuilt

Construction Faithful to Contours of Earlier Crusader Church

The latest Church of the Transfiguration was built by the Franciscans between 1919 to 1924 according to a design by the architect Antonio Barluzzi. The church is built along the contours of the Crusader church built by Tancred, prince of Galilee, on the mountain's summit.

The architect preserved the remains of the ancient church and integrated them into the new structure. The two towers of the facade were built over two medieval chapels, one of which is dedicated to Moses and the other to Elijah today. The original vault of the crypt from the Crusader period is presently covered by a mosaic commemorating events from the life of Jesus.

The Church of the Transfiguration.

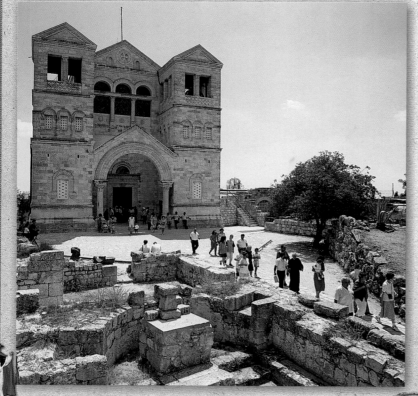

King Robert Bruce Arrives in Jerusalem

600 Years After His Death

The great Scottish king Robert Bruce, who ruled over Scotland from 1306 to 1329, requested in his will that his heart be buried in Jerusalem.

The heart, mummified in a gold box, was given to a member of the Scottish aristocracy, who undertook to bring it to the Holy Land for burial. On his way the messenger passed through Spain, where he was killed in the war between the Spanish and the Muslim Moors, and the king's heart did not reach its final resting place. (According to one of the traditions, the king's heart was found and returned to Scotland for burial.)

Six hundred years after the death of the king, the inhabitants of the Scottish cities of Dunfermline and Melrose decided to make their heroic king's wish come true and placed a memorial tablet in the floor of Saint Andrew's Church in Jerusalem that reads:

In remembrance of the pious wish of King Robert Bruce that his heart should be buried in Jerusalem. Given by the citizens of Dunfermline and Melrose in celebration of the 6th centenary of his death. 1329-7th June 1929.

The memorial tablet in Saint Andrew's.

New Church on Mount of Beatitudes

Fourth-Century Church of the Beatitudes Unearthed

In 1935, the ruins of the ancient Church of the Beatitudes were uncovered on the slope of the mountain opposite the Church of the Primacy of Peter. The church comprised a small chapel and outbuildings; its walls were hewn out of basalt. Crosses and inscriptions carved by centuries of pilgrims are still visible at the site.

The church was built at the end of the fourth century and restored at the beginning of the seventh century. Excavation data testify to the fact that at the end of its days the edifice served the Muslims for secular purposes.

In 1938, on the summit of this mountain, the Mount of Beatitudes, a new church was built and dedicated to the Sermon on the Mount. The church was designed by the Italian architect Antonio Barluzzi. The mountain soaring above Tabgha and the Sea of Galilee commands a stunning view of the places connected to the beginning of Jesus' mission in the region of the Sea of Galilee.

The church, octagonal in shape, is topped by an impressive copper dome whose blue-green color harmonizes

An aerial photograph of the Mount and the Church of Beatitudes.

well with its surroundings. The eight sides of the church symbolize the eight verses in the Sermon on the Mount. The intentional simplicity of the church was intended to emphasize a connection with the landscape viewed from it: the Sea of Galilee, the blue skies, the blooming wildflowers, and the native birds—the natural world of the area of Jesus' ministry.

Franciscans Rebuild Church of the Primacy of Peter

Saint Helena's Fourth-Century Church Refurbished

The Church of the Primacy of Peter in Tabgha.

The first Church of the Primacy of Peter was erected in Tabgha as early as the fourth century. While it was abandoned in the twelfth century, at the end of the Crusader period, it was subsequently restored in the thirteenth century. A short while later it was destroyed and left to lay in ruins for the following seven centuries.

The Franciscans built the present church in 1939. South of it are the stone platform and steps mentioned by Egeria (a fourth-century pilgrim) on which, according to tradition, Jesus appeared before his disciples after his resurrection. Near the steps, along the shoreline, stand twelve heart-shaped columns known as "The Twelve Thrones." They are dedicated to the twelve disciples who will judge the people of Israel.

VISIT PALESTINE

"Visit Palestine," a British Mandate poster encouraging tourism to the Holy Land.

Palm Sunday Procession Renewed

Jesus' triumphal entrance into Jerusalem is commemorated in the Palm Sunday procession that has set out from Bethphage since the Crusader period. The Muslim authorities forbade the procession in 1563, but it was renewed in 1933 and continues until today.

The Catholic Palm Sunday begins with the solemn entrance of the Latin patriarch into the Church of the Holy Sepulcher and a pontifical mass.

The traditional procession leaves Bethphage at noon in the direction of Jerusalem, descends the Mount of Olives, enters Jerusalem via the Lions' Gate, and comes to a conclusion in a ceremony in front of Saint Anne's Church next to the Bethesda Pool, also known as the Sheep's Pool.

Right: Palm Sunday mass in the Church of the Holy Sepulcher.
Below: At the Church of Bethphage.

The Palm Sunday procession on the Mount of Olives (*right*); the Knights of the Holy Sepulcher (*upper right*); entering Jerusalem via the Lions' Gate (*center*); the concluding ceremony at Saint Anne's Church (*above*).

Church of the Visitation in Ein Karem Completed

New Edifice Integrates Remains of Ancient Church

The ancient church site that the Franciscans bought from Muslims in Ein Karem at the end of the seventeenth century was excavated in 1937; a year later construction began on its upper portion, which was to be completed only in 1955.

The church, which is built on two levels, was designed by the architect Antonio Barluzzi. On its lower level are preserved the ancient remains identified as the house of Elizabeth.

In the lower church are also three frescoes commemorating various events connected to Ein Karem: the Visitation, Elizabeth hiding her son John, and Zachary in the temple.

The upper church is decorated with wonderful wall paintings that are the product of a cooperative effort between an Italian painter and an Is-

Above: The wall of verses.
Left: An aerial photograph of the Church of the Visitation.

raeli painter. The columns at the entrance to the nave, which is dedicated to Mary, are decorated with verses from the Magnificat; over them are portraits of female figures from the Bible. On the wall of the courtyard opposite the church are plaques in dozens of languages with verses from the Magnificat.

Cornerstone Laid for New Church of Annunciation

The Basilica of the Annunciation in Nazareth is one of the largest and most ornate churches in the Middle East. Its recent history begins in 1955, when the old Church of the Annunciation was demolished for purposes of reconstruction. The new church, which was designed by the Italian architect Giovanni Muzio, was consecrated in 1969. The planners wanted to simultaneously preserve and integrate the remains of the holy grotto and build an especially grand church that would be able to accommodate as many of the Christian faithful as possible. The architectural solution was a two-level church.

Its western facade is designed in the shape of a pyramid, at the peak of

which stands a statue of Jesus. On the upper portion of the facade are carved the figures of Mary and the angel Gabriel, with the figures of the four Evangelists below them. The three splendid doors are made of copper with bronze panels depicting various events from Jesus' life.

The upper church is impressive in size. Its high dome, which was fashioned in the shape of a white lily, is almost the sole source of light in the church. It opens out towards the rock that houses the grotto, and symbolizes the Holy Spirit's descent to Mary. The floor is decorated with a tessellated marble design in which are integrated

The Basilica of the Annunciation.

the names of popes who expressed admiration for Mary. Lovely mosaics adorn the apses and walls of the nave.

The ceremony of the Annunciation in the Basilica of the Annunciation.

Extensive Renovation of Mount Zion's Cenacle

Ex-Mosque Now Open to Christians

In 1960, extensive renovations were carried out in the Cenacle on Mount Zion. In the course of the work, layers of peeling paint covering the walls were removed and the remains of pictures and ornamentation from the Crusader period revealed.

Next to the column on the right of the entrance, symbols of Crusader knights from the twelfth century were uncovered, among them two shields whose colors were well-preserved, thanks to the layers of plaster and paint that had protected them from harm over the ages. On the upper shield is an inscription with the name of the German city of Regensburg, an important city during the time of the Crusades and the site of the famous meeting between the Byzantine delegation and Emperor Louis VII. Next to another column is an engraving of a shield bearing a cross. In other places in the hall, traces of the paintings that once covered the walls of the Crusader church were discovered.

The renovated Cenacle.

After the Franciscans were expelled from Mount Zion in the sixteenth century the place served as a mosque and entrance to it was forbidden to Christians. Since 1948 the State of Israel allows members of the various religions to pray at the site, but, in accordance with the rules of the status quo, forbids any type of religious ceremony.

THE PAPAL PILGRIMAGE

One of the most important Christian pilgrimage of the twentieth century was that of Pope Paul VI—the first pope to visit the Holy Land—from January 6 to 7, 1964. During a brief stay of only two days, Pope Paul visited all of the holy places: the River Jordan, Nazareth—where he gave an inspiring sermon—Capernaum, Tabgha, the Mount of Beatitudes, Mount Tabor, and Bethany.

In Jerusalem, at the culmination of his visit, the pope prayed at the Cenacle and the Church of the Dormition, walked the Via Dolorosa, and conducted a mass at the Church of the Holy Sepulcher. The Holy Father's tour concluded with morning prayers at the Church of the Nativity in Bethlehem, after which he returned to Rome.

Mass in the Grotto of the Annunciation

The pope set out on his route from Amman, Jordan to Nazareth in Israel, stopping on his way to pray by the River Jordan and meet with religious leaders. Once in Nazareth, Pope Paul VI celebrated mass in the Grotto of the Annunciation, where according to tradition the angel Gabriel revealed to Mary that she would give birth to the Messiah. The pope knelt on a red cushion at the entrance to the Church of the Annunciation and kissed a silver cross that was handed to him. Sprinkling holy water from a silver chalice, he blessed and dedicated the church.

The pope then proceeded to celebrate mass in the Grotto of the Annunciation and the Church of the Annunciation, after which he addressed the assembled, as well as all those witnessing the moment via media broadcasts, in a sermon.

The pope presented the church with a diamond to be affixed on the cross at its altar and an ivory crown for the head of its statue of the Virgin Mary.

Right: The pope at the Basilica of the Annunciation.

A Moment of Prayer at the Sea of Galilee

Pope Paul then drove to Tabgha via Cana, where Jesus is said to have performed his first miracle during the wedding at which he changed the water into wine. The pope entered Tabgha's Church of the Loaves and Fishes on a red carpet, knelt before the altar in prayer, and then stepped beyond it to stand at the spot where tradition has it that Jesus performed the miracle whereby the multitude was fed from five loaves of bread and two fish.

At the Church of the Primacy of Peter the Holy Father knelt at the rock where Jesus is said to have designated Peter "the rock" on which his church on earth would rest. Leaving the church, the pope then crossed the few steps to the shore of the Sea of Galilee, which shimmered in the bright sunshine. He knelt and dipped both hands in the water, remaining for a moment in prayer.

Above: The pope on the steps upon which Jesus appeared, next to the Church of the Primacy of Peter.
Above left: A mosaic commemorating the visit of the pope to the Church of the Primacy of Peter.

From Capernaum to the Mount of Beatitudes

Standing next to the four pillars of the ancient synagogue in Capernaum, the pope emotionally concluded a short prayer of thanksgiving with the words "Hallelujah, Hallelujah." Afterwards, his convoy set out on its journey to the Mount of Beatitudes. At the church of the Mount of Beatitudes on the summit of the mountain overlooking the Sea of Galilee, the distinguished visitor gave the Sermon on the Mount.

Right: At the ancient synagogue in Capernaum.
Below: The pope at Capernaum.

On Mount Tabor

On Mount Tabor the Franciscan monks scattered roses along the path leading from the courtyard to the entrance of the Church of the Transfiguration at the mountain's peak. The church bells tolled and the monks knelt as the pope walked along the path of flowers. He then stood on the balcony overlooking the Jezreel Valley for several long minutes, unable to tear himself away from the sight of the landscape stretching out below him.

The pope strides along the rose-petal-strewn path leading to the Church of the Transfiguration (*below*), then leaves the Church of the Transfiguration (*left*).

In Jerusalem: Pope Welcomed with Chiming Bells

The pope arrived at Mount Zion around eight o'clock in the evening and was welcomed by the ringing of the bells of the Church of the Dormition. He first entered the Cenacle, where he knelt and prayed, and then he and his entourage continued on to the Church of the Dormition, where the Holy Father prayed at the central altar and descended to the crypt—the location of the statue of Mary sunk in eternal slumber. After a few minutes the pope returned to the church's nave to give a sermon emphasizing the necessity for friendship and love among all Christian sects as well as between Christianity and other religions.

From Mount Zion the pope drove into Jerusalem's Old City, which at the time lay in the Hashemite Kingdom of Jordan. He paused outside Jerusalem at the hillside village of Bethany and changed his cassock in the rectory of the Church of Saint Lazarus, which commemorates the raising of Lazarus and Martha and Mary's meeting with Jesus.

In the Old City Pope Paul made his way up the Via Dolorosa, following the route along which Christ carried his cross to the place of his crucifixion. Bending over to pass through a low doorway, the Holy Father arrived at the little square before the Church of the Holy Sepulcher.

The doorway to the church was dark with clergy. The pope entered the massive edifice and made for the small marble structure in the center of the rotunda—the Holy Tomb. He stooped once again to enter its inner chamber, knelt, and kissed the cracked and crooked slab of marble that covers Jesus' burial place. He then visited the Latin Chapel, where mass was said.

A moment of prayer at the Cenacle.

Morning Prayers in Bethlehem

Pope Pleads for Christian Unity

The last public event of Pope Paul's busy tour of the holy places took place in Bethlehem, where the pontiff knelt at a crimson prie-dieu set before the altar at the Church of the Nativity while the organ sounded and neon lights flashed *Gloria in Excelcis*. Following the mass, the pontiff delivered in French a discourse whose central theme was church unity.

"This is the historic hour in which the church must live her profound and visible unity," he said. "It is the hour in which we must realize the wish of Jesus Christ that they be perfectly one...This calls for a concerted effort in which every section of the church must play its part. May each one give ear to the invitation that Christ is issuing through our voice...

"We declare once again that we are ready to consider every reasonable possibility by which mutual understanding, respect, and charity may be fostered so as to smooth the way to a future—and please God not too distant—meeting with our Christian brothers still separated from us.

"The door of the fold is open. We

Right: The Holy Father prays at the Grotto of the Nativity
Below: In the atrium of the Church of the Nativity..

wait, all of us, with sincere hearts. For the present, we ask of our separated brothers only that which we set before ourselves as our objective—namely, that every step towards reunion and interchange of views should be inspired by love of Christ and the church...

"Our sole interest is to proclaim this faith of ours," the pope concluded. "We ask for nothing except the freedom to profess it and to offer to anyone who will freely accept it this religion which is the relationship between God and men instituted by Christ, our Lord."

First Satellite Broadcast from Saint Catherine's Church in Bethlehem

Millions Glued to Television Screens for Mass at Church of the Nativity

The Christmas midnight mass of 1967 was broadcast live and transmitted via satellite to millions of faithful throughout the world. Millions of Christians around the globe were glued to their television screens, witnessing the mass conducted at Jesus' distant birth place.

Midnight mass in the Church of the Nativity in Bethlehem.

Shipping News: Boat from the Time of Jesus Discovered

1986

On May 11, 1986, after a tractor sank off the beach of the Sea of Galilee about three hundred meters south of Kibbutz Ginosar, ancient coins that had long lay hidden beneath the water's edge were expelled onto the beach. Two brothers, members of the kibbutz, came across the coins and began to search for other finds along the water's edge. They shortly found some

"Jesus' Boat," as it is called, in the process of preservation.

nails and pieces of wood that looked like they belonged to the remains of a boat submerged in the water nearby.

Archaeologists called to the spot found a boat 8.2 meters long and 2.3 meters wide, made of at least seven different types of wood. In an examination of the wood seams and beams of the boat, there appeared to be many similarities to boats that sailed the Mediterranean Sea up to and during the Roman period. In further excavations, a cooking pot and a ceramic oil lamp from the

early Roman period were also found, testifying that the boat dates from the first century AD.

The vessel is the most ancient ever discovered in the Sea of Galilee. It can apparently be dated to the time of Jesus, raising the possibility that it is connected to one of the nautical events that occurred on the Sea of Galilee during the Roman period—perhaps the big naval battle of 67 AD.

According to Josephus Flavius' records of that year, the warriors of Migdal boarded numerous boats after Vespasian surrounded the city. The Roman general accordingly ordered the construction of boats or barges; after they were completed, Roman soldiers boarded them and overcame the Jews after an intense naval battle.

The ancient boat after it was removed from the Sea of Galilee.

Josephus relates that in the wake of the battle the coast was littered with splinters of shattered boats.

Since its discovery, the boat has undergone a process of preservation in a special wax material that was intended to replace the water that had penetrated the wood. The boat is on display to the public in a pavilion built especially for it at Kibbutz Ginosar on the bank of the Sea of Galilee.

New Baptismal Site

The traditional baptismal site on the River Jordan near Jericho is closed to visits by pilgrims most days of the year. For the convenience of pilgrims who wish to dip in the Jordan, a new baptismal site was built at the outlet of the river from the Sea of Galilee, not far from the city of Tiberias.

1980

Robbery in Church of Holy Sepulcher!

Sword and Jewels Stolen from Madonna

In March of 1992, a valuable sword and several jeweled items that adorned a statue of the Madonna at Station XIII in the Church of the Holy Sepulcher were stolen. The statue of the Madonna was brought from Lisbon to Jerusalem in 1778, and until its theft had been decorated with a gold sword, a gold crown, and various jeweled and gold accessories donated by the devout.

The thief broke into the glass cabinet containing the statue with a screwdriver and removed the sword and the jeweled objects. He then went over to the church's collection box (which was empty), where he was surprised by an Orthodox monk. The robber threatened the monk with a gun, forced him into a bathroom, and fled.

The incident was the fourth time the statue has been robbed. In the previ-

The statue of the Madonna at Station XIII.

The renovations of the dome of the Church of the Holy Sepulcher are completed.

ous theft, in 1973, the Madonna's crown had been taken, though until now the missing objects have always been retrieved and returned to the church. The church officials believe that this time too the valuables will eventually be returned to their proper place.

Jesus Weeps at Bethlehem's Church of the Nativity

Tears Stream from Picture of Jesus: Miracle or Optical Illusion?

A fourth-century picture of Jesus located in the Church of the Nativity is shedding tears, or at least so they claim in Bethlehem. The eyes of the painted Jesus seem to be filled with tears and winking at believers. A resident of Bethlehem who visited the church relates that when he looked at the portrait of Jesus hanging high on one of the columns of the church, he suddenly saw the Savior wink at him and then begin to weep.

A priest serving in the church scoffs that the story was fabricated by over-eager tour guides in their zeal to draw tourists to Bethlehem. Contrary to his statements, the Bethlehem representative of the Greek Orthodox archbishop of Jerusalem claims that the incident was miraculous and represents a sign sent by Jesus to strengthen the faith of the devout. Others explain the phenomenon by saying that the weeping Jesus is merely an illusion created by the play of light and shade. There are also those in Bethlehem who fear that the wink is a bad omen: "Perhaps an earthquake, or maybe a war," according to one local resident.

US President Clinton, First Lady Hillary, and their daughter Chelsea light candles on the Christmas tree at the Church of the Nativity in Bethlehem.

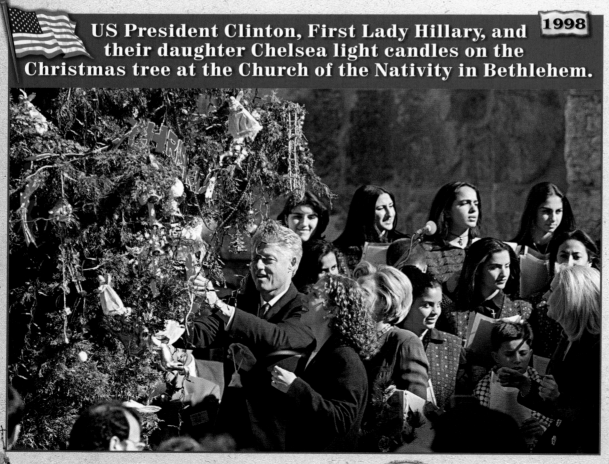

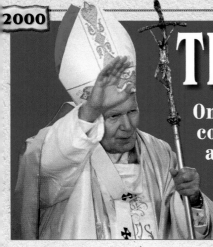

THE JUBILEE PILGRIMAGE

On 21 March 2000, Pope John Paul II arrived in the Holy Land, to commemorate the second millennium of the birth of Jesus Christ, as well as to realize a life-long wish to visit personally the sites of the Gospel—in his words: "To come here and to pray in the most important places which, from ancient times, have seen God's interventions, the wonders he has done."

The Land Where God Pitched His Tent

The Pope's journey through the Holy Land lasted five days, in the course of which he met with regional political leaders as well as with the heads of the various religious denominations in the Holy Land. Nonetheless, the main emphasis lay on a personal and private pilgrimage to the various Christian Holy Sites.

Following his visit at the site of Jesus's baptism on the River Jordan, the Pope continued to Bethlehem, the birthplace of Jesus. The next day he prayed at the Cenacle, the room of the Last Supper on Mount Zion in Jerusalem. On the third day the Pope conducted a public mass at the Mount of the Beatitudes, high above the Sea of Galilee. Following this he visited the ruins of the house of Peter the Fisherman at Capernaum, as well as the Church of the Primacy of Peter at Tabgha, concluding with prayers at the Tabgha Church of the Loaves and Fishes adjoining the lakeside. On 25 March, the Feast Day of the Annunciation, the Pope celebrated a festive mass at the Basilica of the Annunciation in Nazareth, followed on the evening of the same day by a private mass at the Basilica of the Agony at Gethsemane.

The final day of the papal visit was devoted to Jerusalem. His first destination was the Temple Mount and the Western Wall, from where the Pope continued through the Old City to ceremonies at the Church of the Holy Sepulcher. Later that day the Pope returned to the Holy Sepulcher for a private visit, before bidding farewell to Jerusalem and the Holy Land, and emplaned for his return journey to Rome.

When he arrived in the Holy Land,

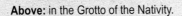

Above: in the Grotto of the Nativity.

Above right: at the Church of the Holy Sepulcher.

Right: prayers at the Tabgha Church of the Loaves and Fishes.

Left: a private mass at the Basilica of the Agony at Gethsemane.

the Pope said:

"Yesterday, from the heights of Mount Nebo I looked across the Jordan Valley to this blessed land. Today, it is with profound emotion that I set foot in the Land where God chose to 'pitch his tent' (Jn 1:14; c£ Ex 40:34-35; 1 Kgs 8: 10-13), and made it possible for man to encounter him more directly.

"In this year of the two thousandth anniversary of the Birth of Jesus Christ, it has been my strong personal desire to come here and to pray in the most important places which, from ancient times, have seen God's interventions, the wonders he has done. 'You are the God who works wonders. You showed your power among these peoples.' (Ps.77:15).

"My visit is both a personal pilgrimage and the spiritual journey of the Bishop of Rome to the origins of our faith in 'the God of Abraham, of Isaac and of Jacob (Ex 3;15).' It is part of a larger pilgrimage of prayer and thanksgiving which led me first to Sinai, the Mountain of the Covenant, the place of the decisive revelation which shaped the subsequent history of salvation. Now I shall have the

privilege of visiting some of the places more closely connected with the Life, Death and Resurrection of Jesus Christ. Along every step of the way I am moved by a vivid sense of God who has gone before us and leads us on, who wants us to honor him in spirit and in truth, to acknowledge the differences between us, but also to recognize in every human being the image and likeness of the One Creator of heaven and earth."

On the Mount of the Beatitudes

The central event during the Pope's visit to the Holy Land was the mass he celebrated on the Mount of the Beatitudes, opposite tens of thousands of pilgrims who gathered around the Sea of Galilee

"How many generations before us have been deeply moved by the Sermon on the Mount!" the Pope exclaimed. "How many young people down the centuries have gathered around Jesus to learn the words of eternal life, as you are gathered here today! How many young hearts have been inspired by the power of his personality and the compelling truth of his message! It is wonderful that you are here!

"Jesus does not merely speak the Beatitudes. He lives the Beatitudes. He is the Beatitudes. Looking at him you will see what it means to be poor in spirit, gentle and merciful, to mourn, to care for what is right, to be pure in heart, to make peace, to be persecuted. This is why he has the right to say, 'Come, follow me!' He does not say simply, 'Do what I say'. He says, 'Come, follow me!'"

Annunciation in Nazareth

"25th March in the year 2000," said Pope John Paul II at the Grotto of the Annunciation, "the Solemnity of the Annunciation in the Year of the Great Jubilee: on this day the eyes of the whole Church turn to Nazareth. I have longed to come back to the town of Jesus, to feel once again, in contact with this place, the presence of the woman of whom Saint Augustine wrote: 'He chose the mother he had created; he created the mother he had chosen.' (Sermon 69, 3, 4.) Here it is especially easy to understand why all generations call Mary blessed (cf. Lk 2:48.) - - -

"We are gathered to celebrate the great mystery accomplished here two thousand years ago. The Evangelist Luke situates the event clearly in time and place; 'In the sixth month, the angel Gabriel was sent by God to a town in Galilee called Nazareth, to a virgin betrothed to a man named Joseph ... The virgin's name was Mary' (I:26-27.) But in order to understand what took place in Nazareth two thousand years ago, we must return to the Reading from the Letter to the Hebrews. That text enables us, as it were, to listen to a conversation between the Father and the Son concerning God's purpose from all eternity.

"You who wanted no sacrifice or oblation prepared a body for me. You took no pleasure in holocausts or sacrifices for sin. Then I said... 'God here I am! I am coming to obey your will' (10:5-7.) The Letter to the Hebrews is telling us that, in obedience to the Father's will, the Eternal Word

Above: the public mass on the Mount of the Beatitudes.
Left: Pope John Paul II at the Grotto of the Annunciation.
Right: festive mass at the Basilica of the Annunciation.

comes among us to offer the sacrifice which surpasses all the sacrifices offered under the former Covenant. His is the eternal and perfect sacrifice which redeems the world. - - -

"Our Jubilee Pilgrimage has been a journey in spirit, which began in the footsteps of Abraham, 'our father in faith' (Roman Canon; cf. Rom 4;1 1-12.) That journey has brought us today to Nazareth, where we meet Mary, the truest daughter of Abraham. It is Mary above all others who can teach us what it means to live the faith of 'our father'. In many ways, Mary is clearly different from Abraham; but in deeper ways 'the friend of God' (cf. Is 41:8) and the young woman of Nazareth are very alike.

"Both receive a wonderful promise from God. Abraham was to be the father of a son, from whom there

Eucharist in the Upper Room

During a private service at the Cenacle on Mount Zion, Pope John Paul II said: "Celebrating this Eucharist in the Upper Room in Jerusalem, we are united with the Church of every time and place. United with the Head, we are in communion with Peter and the Apostles and their Successors down the ages. In union with Mary, the Saints and Martyrs, and all the baptized who have lived in the grace of the Holy Spirit, we cry out: Marana tha! 'Come, Lord Jesus' (Cf. Rev 22:17). Bring us and all your chosen ones, to the fullness of grace in your eternal Kingdom. Amen."

would come a great nation. Mary is to be the Mother of a Son who would be the Messiah, the Anointed One. 'Listen!' Gabriel says, 'You are to conceive and bear a son... The Lord God will give him the throne of his ancestor David... and his reign will have no end.' (Lk 1:31-33.)

"For both Abraham and Mary, the divine promise comes as something completely unexpected. God disrupts the daily course of their lives, overturning its settled rhythms and conventional expectations. For both Abraham and Mary, the promise seems impossible. Abraham's wife Sarah was barren, and Mary is not yet married: 'How can this come about,' she asks, 'since I am a virgin?' (Lk 1:34.)

"Like Abraham, Mary is asked to say yes to something that has never happened before. Sarah is the first in the line of barren wives in the Bible who conceive by God's power, just as Elizabeth will be the last. Gabriel speaks of Elizabeth to reassure Mary: know this too: your kinswoman Elizabeth has, in her old age, herself conceived a son." (Lk 1:36.)

"Like Abraham, Mary must walk through darkness, in which she must simply trust the One who called her. Yet even her question, "How can this come about?", suggests that Mary is

ready to say yes, despite her fears and uncertainties. Mary asks not whether the promise is possible, but only how it will be fulfilled. It comes as no surprise, therefore, when she finally utters her faith: 'I am the handmaid of the Lord. Let what you have said be done to me.' (Lk 1:38.) With these words, Mary shows herself the true daughter of Abraham, and she becomes the Mother of Christ and Mother of all believers.

"But we have also come to plead with her. What do we, pilgrims on our way into the Third Christian Millennium, ask of the Mother of God? Here in the town which Pope Paul VI, when he visited Nazareth, called 'the school of the Gospel', where 'we learn to look at and to listen to, to ponder and to penetrate the deep and mysterious meaning of the very simple, very humble and very beautiful appearing of the Son of God' (Address in Nazareth, 5 January 1964), I pray, first, for a great renewal of faith in all the children of the Church. A deep renewal of faith: not just as a general attitude of life, but as a conscious and courageous profession of the Creed: 'Et incarnatus est de Spiritu Sancto ex Maria Virgine, et homo factus est.'

"In Nazareth, where Jesus "grew in wisdom and in age and grace before

God and men' (Lk 2:52), I ask the Holy Family to inspire all Christians to defend the family against so many present-day threats to its nature, its stability and its mission. To the Holy Family I entrust the efforts of Christians and of all people of good will to defend life and to promote respect for the dignity of every human being.

"To Mary, the Theotokos, the great Mother of God, I consecrate the families of the Holy Land, the families of the world.

"In Nazareth where Jesus began his public ministry, I ask Mary to help the Church everywhere to preach 'the 'good news' to the poor, as he did (cf. Lk 4:18.) In this 'year of the Lord's fervor', I ask her to teach us the way of humble and joyful obedience to the Gospel in the service of our brothers and sisters, without preferences and without prejudices."

At the Empty Tomb

The Pope dedicated his last day in the Holy Land to Jerusalem and the Church of the Holy Sepulcher. Standing by the Holy Tomb, the Pope said:

"The tomb is empty. It is a silent witness to the central event of human history: the Resurrection of our Lord Jesus Christ. For almost two thousand years the empty tomb has borne witness to the victory of life over death. With the Apostles and Evangelists, with the Church of every time and place, we too bear witness and proclaim: 'Christ is risen! Raised from the dead he will never die again; death no longer has power over him.'"

John the Baptist's Cave Discovered

In excavations carried out near Ein Karem, the town in which he was born, a cave was discovered containing drawings of John the Baptist alongside a network of pools and a basin carved in the rock for anointing feet with oil.

Has the spot where John the Baptist secluded himself been discovered?

Shimon Gibson, the archeologist who discovered the cave, is convinced that it served as a place of seclusion for John the Baptist and after his death became a gathering place and pilgrimage site for Christians. It appears that the cave was selected for its function for three reasons: first, because of its secluded location; second, due to its size; and third because it already contained an ancient network of pools, which could be used for baptisms. The cave is part of a large water system, which was carved into the mountain rock to a depth of twenty meters. A ten meter long corridor leads into a perpendicular shaft opening up into the ceiling of the cave. At the end of the corridor there is a stairway leading into one of three

Above: Gibson points to the figure of John the Baptist carved into the wall of the cave.
Left: an indentation carved into the rock for anointing of feet with oil was discovered in the cave.

external, plaster pools located on the mountain slope above the underground reservoir inside the cave.

From shards of utensils found on the spot, and from an examination of the plaster it appears likely that the system was built in the eighth century BCE. According to the findings at the site, the water system was not in use from the seventh or sixth century BCE but the subterranean reservoir continued to serve the residents of Zuba, the nearby town, until the second century BCE.

The findings show that in the period in which John the Baptist was alive, a group of people again began to use it and they held religious ceremonies in it which included baptism in water in the innermost portion of the cave and anointing of feet with oil in the special indentation carved in the rock so that it would fit the right foot. These ceremonies took place in the cave until the second century CE.

At a later period Byzantine monks, who apparently came from the monastery in Ein Karem, adopted the cave. The theory is that it was they who chiseled the pictures that were discovered on the ancient plaster on the walls of the cave. Appearing in these is the figure of John the Baptist and a drawing of his severed head as well as crucifixes and other images connected to his life and death. This is the most ancient drawing in the Middle East in which the figure of John the Baptist appears. The cave was abandoned in the Crusader period, when the local inhabitants fled from the battles in fear, and it was forgotten for hundreds of years, until it was discovered accidentally in 1999.

Prisoners Uncover Oldest Church in the World at Armageddon

Two fish—ancient symbol of Christianity.

In excavations carried out at the prison located in Megiddo—also known as Armageddon and referred to as the place where the kings of the whole world will gather for the battle on the great day of God Almighty (Revelations 16, 14-16)—the most ancient church in the world has been discovered.

In the excavations, which were carried out with the assistance of the prisoners, the remains of a building were discovered which belonged to an officer in the Sixth Roman legion, and they included a mosaic floor with three Greek inscriptions, geometric decorations and a medallion decorated with two fish, the ancient symbol of Christianity. The northern inscription is dedicated to the Roman officer, who donated money for the building of the mosaic floor. The eastern inscription is dedicated to the memory of four women. The western inscription reads: "The God-loving Aketous has offered this table to the God Jesus Christ, as a memorial."

In the center of the structure remains of a table or altar were found. This apparently is the most ancient church ever discovered - not only in the Holy Land, but in the entire world. Experts date it to the end of the third century or beginning of the fourth century. The table, also mentioned in one of the inscriptions, is one of the most sensational discoveries in the excavation. It is possible that its discovery points to the fact that in those days the faithful were not accustomed to gathering around an altar but would sit around a simple refectory table as Jesus and his disciples did at the Last Supper.

The Madonna Lily (*Lilium candidum*) is a flower that grows wild in the Galilee region. The lily flowers in nature at the end of May. A group of Israeli scholars, led by Dr. Michele Zaccai, found a way to move up its flowering to Annunciation Day. In the picture: Dr. Zaccai presents a bouquet of lilies to the bishop of Nazareth on Annunciation Day.

THE WAY OF THE CROSS

During the week, the Via Dolorosa, which leads from the Praetorium to the Church of the Holy Sepulcher, is a street like any other, but once a week, on Friday afternoons, when the Procession of the Cross passes along its entire length, it travels back in time two thousand years. Of the fourteen stations that comprise the Way of Sorrow, nine are along the way to the Church of the Holy Sepulcher and five are inside it. Eight of the outside stations are commemorated with churches or small chapels, and additional chapels and holy sites connected with Jesus' final path dot the route.

Station I—Jesus is Condemned to Death: Station I is located in the courtyard of Omariye College, whose current building was erected in the Mameluke period on the foundations of the Antonia fortress from the time of Herod. Today there is no church or chapel on the spot to commemorate the events of Jesus' trial; a Crusader-period chapel commemorating the crowning of Jesus with thorns that stood in the southern portion of the courtyard was destroyed by an earthquake in 1927.

Station II—Jesus Takes Up the Cross: Station II is in the Chapel of the Condemnation next to the Church of the Flagellation. The chapel, which was renovated by the Franciscans in 1903, was built over the remains of a Byzantine church, of whose form it is reminiscent.

Station III—Jesus Falls for the First Time: For many years Station III was marked by two broken columns. In 1947 a new chapel was built on the spot with the help of donations from Polish soldiers who were in the Holy Land at the time. Today a museum with an archaeological collection is located at the site.

Station IV—Jesus is Met by His Mother: Station IV is located in a chapel marked by a lintel depicting Jesus and his mother. A few steps away is the Armenian Catholic church, built in 1881 and dedicated to Mary. In a crypt constructed on the level of the ancient road is a mosaic floor: at its center is the image of a pair of sandals. The floor may belong to a church from the fifth and sixth centuries. The sandals were mentioned in texts from the fourteenth century as marking the place where Mary stood while her son passed by carrying the cross.

Station V—Simon the Cyrene Helps Jesus Carry the Cross: This station is located at the corner of the street. The current chapel, dedicated to Simon the Cyrene, was built by the Franciscans in 1895. Until then the spot was marked by a grooved stone mounted on the wall.

Station VI—Veronica Wipes Jesus' Face: This station is marked by a column recessed in the wall. According to tradition, this was the home of Veronica, who approached Jesus with a damp handkerchief and wiped the sweat from his face. The spot was purchased by the Greek Catholics in 1883, and two years later the Church of Saint Veronica was built there, apparently on top of the remains of a sixth-century church.

Station VII—Jesus Falls for the Second Time: This station is known as the Judgement Gate. Legend has it that the city gate upon whose threshold Jesus fell under the burden of the cross was located here. Inside the chapel, which belongs to the Copts, is a tall column that has survived from

The Processsoion of the Cross passes along thet Via Dolorosa.

the double row of columns that once lined the length of the Cardo Maximus —the main street of the Roman city.

Station VIII—Jesus Speaks to the Women of Jerusalem: This station is marked by a stone bearing a cross and a Latin inscription with the message "Jesus Christ is Triumphant" mounted in the wall. The place is near Golgotha, but access is blocked by a Greek Orthodox church.

Station IX—Jesus Falls for the Third Time: Further along the road in the direction of the Church of the Holy Sepulcher is a staircase on the right ascending to the roof of the Church of the Holy Sepulcher. A column that has survived from the Roman Cardo marks the station.

Station X—Jesus is Stripped of His Garments: This station, the first one within the Church of the Holy Sepulcher, is in the Chapel of the Sorrows, though the portal to the chapel is closed and you can only see into it from the window at Station XI. During the Crusader period this room served as the entrance to Golgotha. The room, along with its unusual dome and rich decorations, has been preserved in its entirety. Today the chapel is in the hands of the Latin patriarch and is dedicated to Jesus' mother Mary and John the Baptist.

Station XI, XII, and XIII are on Golgotha, where Jesus' suffering came to an end. Golgotha is divided into two main chapels: the right-hand one (Station XI) belongs to the Latin patriarchate, the one on the left (Station XII) belongs to the Greek Orthodox, and between them is Station XIII, which is under Franciscan control.

Station XI—Jesus is Nailed to the Cross: The silver altar in Station XI is from the period of the Renaissance, and was donated to the church by the Tuscan Duke de Medici in 1588.

Station XII—Jesus Dies on the Cross: Below the altar in this chapel is a silver disk, in the middle of which is a hole signifying where the cross was placed. Two additional black disks on either side of the altar mark the crucifixion sites of the two thieves.

Station XIII—Jesus is Taken Down from the Cross: This station is located between Station XI and Station XII. The altar at the station, called the Altar of Our Lady of Sorrows (Mater Dolorosa), is dedicated to Mary. On it is a sixteenth-century gold-plated statue of the Madonna, with precious stones and a gold crown. The statue was brought to the church from Lisbon in 1788, and is kept in a glass cabinet, around which hang gold gifts offered by pilgrims.

According to tradition, after Jesus was brought down off the cross, Joseph of Arimathea and Nicodemus laid his body on this slab of stone, anointed it with fragrant oils, and wrapped it in shrouds. The Stone of the Anointing is located just inside the entrance to the Church of the Holy Sepulcher. Three pairs of candelabra flank the stone, representing the Franciscans, the Greek Orthodox, and the Armenians.

Station XIV—The Holy Tomb: Jesus was buried close to the site of the crucifixion in a tomb cut in a rock belonging to Joseph of Arimathea. When the Church of the Holy Sepulcher was built, the tomb was separated from the rock surrounding it and a magnificent rotunda was built around it. During the Crusader period the building was renovated and the tomb overlaid with marble.

The tomb is divided into two parts: an anteroom known as the Chapel of the Angel and the Chapel of the Holy Tomb. In 1808 the dome of the rotunda collapsed in a fire that caused damage to the tomb as well. The structure that presently surrounds the tomb was built by the Greek Orthodox after the nineteenth-century fire. The empty tomb, covered with a cracked marble slab, is located on the right of the inner chamber. The chamber is small, and only three to four people can enter it at one time, which is why there is always a long line of believers at the entrance of the tomb.

BIBLIOGRAPHY

Bahat, Dan. *The Illustrated Atlas of Jerusalem*, Jerusalem, 1989.

Bartlett, William Henry, and Allom, Thomas. *Syria, The Holy Land, Asia Minor, &c.*, London, 1838, 3 vols.

Ben-Arieh, Yehoshua. *Painting Palestine in the Nineteenth Century*, Jerusalem, 1993.

Forbin, Louis Nicolas de. *Voyage dans le Levant en 1817-1818*, Paris, 1819.

Hallam, Elizabeth. *Chronicles of the Crusades*, London, 1989.

Horne, Thomas Hartwell. *Biblical Keepsake*, London, 1835.

Irby, Charles Leonard, and Mangles, James. *Travels in Egypt and Nubia, Syria, and Asia Minor During the Years 1817 & 1818*, London, 1823.

Lortet, Paul. *Syrie d'aujourd'hui*, Paris, 1884.

Lynch, William Francis: *Narrative of the United States' Expedition to the River Jordan and the Dead Sea*, London, 1849.

MacGregor, John. *The Rob Roy on the Jordan*, New York, 1869.

Mayer, Luigi. *Views in Egypt*, London, 1801.

Nir, Yeshayahu. *The Bible and the Image*, Philadelphia, 1985.

Paris, Francois Edmond. *Souvenirs de Jerusalem*, Paris, 1862.

Perez, Nissan N. *Focus East*, New York, 1988.

Pierotti, Ermete. *Jerusalem Explored*, London, 1864.

Prawer, Joshua. *The World of the Crusaders*, Jerusalem, 1984.

Prawer, Joshua. *A History of the Latin Kingdom of Jerusalem*, Jerusalem, 1984, 2 vols.

Raboisson, l'Abbé. *En Orient en Palestine et en Syrie*, Paris, 1887.

Roberts, David. *The Holy Land*, London, 1842-1849, 3 vols.

Rogers, Mary Eliza. *Domestic Life in Palestine*, London, 1862.

Salomon, Yehuda, and Milner, Moshe. *Jesus 2000*, Tel Aviv, 1998.

Saulcy, Felician de. *Jerusalem*, Paris, 1882.

Schiller, Ely. *Jerusalem and the Holy Land in Old Engravings and Illustrations (1483-1900)*, Jerusalem, 1981.

Schiller, Ely. *Jerusalem in Rare Lithographs and Engravings*, Jerusalem, 1981.

Schur, Nathan. *History of Jerusalem*, Tel Aviv, 1987, 3 vols.

Schur, Nathan. *Twenty Centuries of Christian Pilgrimage to the Holy Land*, Tel Aviv, 1992.

Thomson, William McLure. *The Land and The Book*, London, 1859.

Tristram, Henry Baker. *Scenes in the East*, London, 1870.

Twain, Mark. *The Innocents Abroad, or the New Pilgrim's Progress, Excursion to Europe and Holy Land*, Hartford Conn., 1870.

Warren, Charles. *Underground Jerusalem*, London, 1876.

Wilkinson, Jhon. *Egeria's Travels to the Holy Land*, Warminster, 1981.

Wilkinson, Jhon: *Jerusalem Pilgrims*, Jerusalem, 1977.

Wilson, Charles William, and Warren, Charles. *Recovery of Jerusalem*, London, 1871.

Wilson, Charles William: *Picturesque Palestine*, London 1880-1882, 4 Vols.

Acknowledgments

The Jewish National & University Library, Jerusalem, Israel

Rechavam Zeevy